W9-CEI-293

My Life in Progressive Politics

My Life in Progressive Politics

Against the Grain

Joseph D. Tydings with John W. Frece

With a foreword by Joe Biden

TEXAS A&M UNIVERSITY PRESS | *College Station*

This paper meets the requirements
of ANSI/NISO Z39.48-1992
(Permanence of Paper).
Binding materials have been chosen for durability.
Manufactured in the United States of America

Library of Congress Cataloging-in-Publication Data

Names: Tydings, Joseph D. (Joseph Davies), 1928– author. | Frece, John W.,
    author.
Title: My life in progressive politics: against the grain / Joseph D.
    Tydings; with John W. Frece.
Description: College Station: Texas A&M University Press, [2018] | Includes
    bibliographical references and index.
Identifiers: LCCN 2017039901 (print) | LCCN 2017041866 (ebook) | ISBN
    9781623496289 (ebook) | ISBN 9781623496272 | ISBN 9781623496272
    cloth: alk. paper)
Subjects: LCSH: Tydings, Joseph D. (Joseph Davies), 1928– |
    Legislators—United States—Biography. | United States. Congress.
    Senate—Biography. | United States—Politics and government—1945–1989. |
    Maryland—Politics and government—1951–
Classification: LCC E840.8.T93 (ebook) | LCC E840.8.T93 A3 2018 (print) | DDC
    328.73/092 [B]—dc23
LC record available at https://lccn.loc.gov/2017039901

To my adoptive father,
Millard E. Tydings,
who courageously served
in the US Senate
for twenty-four years,
and to my grandfather,
Ambassador Joseph E. Davies,
adviser to three US presidents

Contents

A gallery of images follows page 106.

Foreword

Joe Tydings and I never got to work together in the Senate. He served a few years ahead of me. But his six years in office showed him to be a man I would have been proud to fight alongside—a man of principle who, to this day, cares deeply about the direction of our country.

Joe and I come from different backgrounds. We took different paths to the Senate. Despite those differences, however, our politics ended up in the same place. The values that drive Joe, and that are on display throughout these pages, are the same values that have always animated my passions.

When I think back to my early years in the Senate, I was building on groundwork that Joe had helped to lay—from opposing the senseless carnage of the war in Vietnam to expanding civil rights protections for all Americans.

We both believe in standing up against the abuse of power to ensure that every American gets a fair shot. We are both committed to the basic principle that every single person is entitled to be treated with dignity. We both understand that the point of public service is to make a difference in people's lives.

Joe also embodies a code that I've lived by my entire political life—it's the advice that I give to everyone thinking about running for office—decide what's worth losing over. Joe brought a progressive foresight to a range of difficult issues of the 1960s, and he demonstrated genuine courage to stand up for what he knew to be right, even when he knew it might hurt him politically. So while the Senate lost Joe Tydings after only one term, the American people continued to benefit from the leadership he demonstrated in office for decades afterwards.

In reading this memoir, you can't miss the salient parallels to challenges facing our nation today. The issues on which Joe staked his Senate career a half-century ago are the same ones that still require our advocacy and attention. Protecting voting rights. Safeguarding our environment. Pushing back against the forces of inequality that are hollowing out the middle class. Standing up for common-sense gun safety laws.

These are also the challenges that our broken politics are making it harder to address constructively. Joe remembers, as I do, a time when the other party was merely the opposition, not the enemy. When members of Congress could disagree and debate and still share a meal together. When we talked to one another and even counted among our friends those whom we opposed on policy. We could question the other's judgment without questioning their motive.

Joe tells a story of our American past that is both engaging and thought provoking. But perhaps the most striking piece of this book is the poignant letter Joe pens to our future—to his grandchildren and, by extension, an entire generation of new leaders.

Like me, Joe was inspired by the example of John and Bobby Kennedy and their call to service. As young men, we sought the chance to get involved and translate our ideals into reality. Today, however, as Joe notes, we are seeing our shared calling "slandered and dishonored" and young people increasingly turning away from public service.

Today's young people are the most tolerant, capable, and engaged generation our country has ever produced, and we desperately need more of them to make the choice to get involved in the political process. There's no other profession in the world that allows you to do so much good for so many people. And I hope, as Joe does, that this book inspires more young people to get involved.

Run for office. Ruffle feathers. Go against the grain.

Whatever challenges we face, Americans never give in to hopelessness or helplessness. We are a nation of possibilities. And I believe today, as I always have, that we hold in our hands the power to shape the course of history. That's another thing Joe and I share—a deeply rooted faith in this country and the fact that there's nothing we can't overcome if we remember who we are as a nation and what we've always striven to be.

Joe Biden
47th Vice President of the United States

Acknowledgments

I have a pretty good memory, but I also have lived a pretty long and active life, and the details of long-ago events, precisely when things happened, who was involved, and what was said, are frequently hard to recall with any precision.

To help me and John pin down these details, we did a fair amount of research, but we also relied heavily on my friends and former colleagues who were there with me and who were able to refresh my memory by recalling stories or the specifics of stories that I had forgotten. Whenever possible, we have used verbatim quotes from participants in my story, but in some cases we had to rely on quotes as best as I or my colleagues could recall them.

Three people in particular gave hours of their time discussing my early years as US attorney and my later years in the US Senate: Steve Sachs, Hardin Marion, and John McEvoy. Beyond spending hours recounting the stories of our times together, all three read draft chapters, offered comments and edits, filled in the blanks, and suggested deletions, changes in tone or emphasis, or provided other advice that helped us throughout this book.

Sachs and Marion were helpful in recalling our years together as young prosecutors, and Marion and McEvoy remembered stories from our years together in the Senate in ways that staff can often see and recall but a senator cannot. I also wish to thank Alan Wurtzel, my first legislative assistant, who gave of his time to discuss my early Senate years.

I also want to thank the author Priscilla Cummings, who happens to be John Frece's wife and his first and most trusted reader, for her insights and suggestions throughout this process. It was Priscilla's idea, for example, that my epilogue be written in the form of an open letter to my grandchildren.

Mark Wasserman, senior vice president for the University of Maryland Medical System, also contributed his insight into the workings of the system board, on which I still actively serve.

Much of the research for this book was done at the Hornbake Library of the University of Maryland, where we were lucky to have the expert assistance of Anne S. K. Turkos, the university archivist, and Elizabeth A. Novara, curator for historical manuscripts and special collections, including the Joseph D. Tydings Papers, which are on deposit there.

Other research was done through the treasure trove of old newspaper clips—*Baltimore Sun, Washington Post, New York Times*, and more—that are now fully digitized and easily accessible by computer from the Baltimore County Public Library.

Thanks also to Suzanne Wooton, a former *Baltimore Sun* and *Washington Post* editor, who volunteered her time to read through and edit the manuscript.

Over the years that we v orked on this book, I also consulted Jo-Ann Orlinsky, Al Figinski, and .uman Semans and appreciate their help.

Finally, our thanks ⸜ Jay Dew, our editor at Texas A&M University Press, who agreed to t ⸜e on this project and has been a pleasure to work with in every conve ,ation we have had.

Joseph D. T ⸜ings
Harford C unty, Maryland

John ⸜. Frece
Ar apolis, Maryland

PART I

A Political Life

It is not the critic who counts; not the man who points out how the strong man
  stumbles, or where the doer of deeds could have done them better.
The credit belongs to the man who is actually in the arena,
whose face is marred by dust and sweat and blood;
who strives valiantly;
who errs, and comes short again and again, because there is no effort without
  error and shortcoming;
but who does actually strive to do the deeds:
who knows the great enthusiasms, the great devotions, who spends himself in
  a worthy cause;
who at the best knows in the end the triumph of high achievement,
and who at the worse, if he fails, at least fails while daring greatly,
so that his place shall never be with those cold and timid souls who know neither
  victory nor defeat.

—THEODORE ROOSEVELT, AT THE SORBONNE, PARIS, APRIL 23, 1910

CHAPTER 1

Against the Grain

We could hear the *wop wop wop* of the rotors before we ever saw the two helicopters descend over the trees. Excited by the sound, nearly two dozen of us rushed from the historic old stone manor house and across the front lawn of Oakington, our family home on the Chesapeake Bay.

We all wanted to watch as the president of the United States stepped off his helicopter.

Little did I realize, however, that the president's second visit to Oakington that summer evening in 1963 would dramatically change my life and have a profound impact on the direction of the Democratic Party in Maryland for decades to come.

I had first met John F. Kennedy nine years earlier when I, as president of the Young Democrats of Maryland, had invited the US senator from Massachusetts to speak at our Jackson Day dinner at the Emerson Hotel in Baltimore. I was two years out of law school and in my first year as president of the Young Democrats. I drove to Washington in my blue Chevrolet to pick him up. He was only in his second year in the Senate, but I was tremendously impressed by the young senator, who seemed to me far older than his years.

By that August night in 1963 at Oakington, Kennedy was president of the United States and already revving up for a reelection campaign in 1964. His brother Robert, with whom I had become close friends, was now attorney general of the United States and, thanks to the Kennedys, I was the US attorney—the chief federal lawyer and prosecutor for the US government—in Maryland.

Our discussion that night would launch me into a seat in the US Senate. That I would run for the Senate was not totally unexpected; my adoptive father, Millard E. Tydings, had represented Maryland in the Senate with distinction for twenty-four years.[1] And I had been active in

---

1. Millard E. Tydings served in the US Senate from March 5, 1927, until January 3, 1951.

Maryland politics since I was a freshman at the University of Maryland. But the president's visit unexpectedly accelerated my timetable by about two decades.

The president and his brother, Bobby, had both been to Oakington, the 550-acre farm and estate near Havre de Grace that my father had bought in a 1935 bankruptcy sale for his new bride, my mother, Eleanor.

For nearly three decades, a steady stream of the political elite of the nation—vice presidents and future presidents, Supreme Court justices, senators and members of Congress, Cabinet secretaries, and foreign diplomats—had traveled to Oakington. On successive weekends each spring, my father and mother hosted a pair of gala lunches on the lawn for members of the Senate, half one Saturday and the other half the next. Senator Kennedy had spent the night at Oakington while campaigning with me in the Maryland presidential primary in 1960. So to have a president visit was, at least to the members of my family, not as extraordinary as it might sound, but that night there was a palpable buzz of excitement.

The president's return to Oakington was purely a social affair. There were no elected officials on the guest list, no planned press coverage. I had invited a group of young Maryland friends who were attractive, bright, and leaders in their communities—the kind of people I knew the president liked to be with. The group included young Maryland doctors, a prominent investment banker, the young heir to a major family business empire, the legal counsel to the Catholic Archdiocese of Baltimore, and their wives.

Paul B. "Red" Fay Jr., the president's close personal friend from their days together as PT boat commanders, and JFK's youngest brother, Edward "Teddy" Kennedy, drove up from Washington. By then, Fay was under secretary of the navy, and Teddy was serving his first year in the Senate. First Lady Jacqueline Kennedy did not accompany her husband because she was nearly eight months pregnant.[2] My lovely wife, Ginny, was there, and of course my elegant and dynamic mother, Eleanor Davies Tydings. (My father had passed away two and a half years earlier. Sad, because he would have savored the president's visit.)

---

2. Unfortunately, one week later Jacqueline would give premature birth to their son, Patrick Bouvier Kennedy, by emergency Caesarean section at a US Air Force hospital in Massachusetts. Born five and a half weeks early, Patrick would die two days later, on August 9.

To make his trip to Oakington feasible, White House schedulers arranged for the president to fly to the US Naval Academy in Annapolis, where he addressed the incoming class. With twelve hundred plebes standing stiffly at attention in front of Bancroft Hall, the president said, "Why don't you all stand at ease?" The plebes had never heard such an informal order. Nobody moved. The president turned to the superintendent, Rear Admiral Charles C. Kirkpatrick, and said, "I guess, Admiral, that comes later in the course." The plebes burst out laughing, prompting the admiral to step to the microphone and command, "Stand at ease."[3] The president also received a series of three ear-splitting cheers when he granted the plebes the customary presidential amnesty, erasing demerits accumulated for minor offenses.[4]

It was around 7:30 p.m. when the two olive green Marine Corps helicopters finally set down on the lawn at Oakington. The president, still dressed in a blue suit with blue striped tie, stepped out of the second chopper, his thick hair whipped by the breeze from the still swirling rotors. Out of the first helicopter, his aides carried a rocking chair that the president could use to ease his chronically crippled back.

White House staff had been at Oakington for most of the previous week, setting up security as well as installing white telephones and other communications equipment in case the president needed it. We knew he couldn't stay long, so after quick introductions we all moved into the beautiful dining room of the "big house," where my mother still lived. It was always called the "big house" to distinguish it from the many other houses at Oakington, including the smaller stone home Ginny and I had built along the bay a short walk to the south, just past a lovely ravine called Boat House Hollow.

We seated President Kennedy between Ginny and my mother at the mahogany table. The president loved attractive women. He had met Ginny several times, including just three weeks earlier when we, as the president's guests, were among a party of thirty celebrating Fay's birthday aboard the presidential yacht *Sequoia* on an evening cruise down

3. Paul B. Fay Jr., recorded interview by James A. Oesterle, February 5, 1971, sec. 316, JFK #4, John F. Kennedy Oral History Collection, John F. Kennedy Presidential Library and Museum, Boston, MA.

4. Thomas T. Fenton, "President Is Cheered at Academy; Pays Impromptu Visit, Sees Museum, Addresses Plebes," *Baltimore Sun*, August 2, 1963.

the Potomac.[5] She and Anita Fay, Red's wife, were among his favorites.

My mother was at her best in this setting. She had spent most of the previous three decades married to a US senator, and she was the daughter of Ambassador Joseph E. Davies, friend and adviser to Woodrow Wilson, Franklin Delano Roosevelt, and Harry S. Truman and a former ambassador to both Russia and Belgium. Her stepmother, with whom she was very close, was Marjorie Merriweather Post, founder and principal shareholder of the General Foods Corporation and perhaps the wealthiest woman in the country for a generation. My mother had rubbed shoulders with dignitaries and the wealthy throughout most of her life and was well past the point of being overawed or intimidated.

During dinner, as was my custom, I slowly circled the table, standing behind each of the guests, introducing them one by one to the president, telling him a little about who they were and what they did.

Among the twenty-two at the table were Jerold Hoffberger and his wife, Alice. Jerry was then president of National Brewing Company, the Baltimore brewery that made National Bohemian beer—or "Natty Boh," as it was known locally. He also owned a controlling interest in the Orioles, the major league baseball franchise in Baltimore. The Hoffberger family had always been friends and supporters of the Tydings family. My closest friend at the table was Francis X. Gallagher, legal counsel to Archbishop (and later Cardinal) Lawrence Shehan. Frank, there with his wife, Mary, had a wonderful Irish personality and was a great lawyer and a superb political operative.[6] Jerry and Frank were soon to play critically important roles in my political career.

When I finished with the introductions, my mother welcomed the president to Oakington and gave a bit of the long, interesting, and mildly ribald history of our home. Then, with a wry smile, the president said, "Well, now I'm going to have Red Fay stand up and tell you about

5 Fay interview by Oesterle, February 5, 1971, sec. 306.

6. Also there, along with their wives, were two successful young doctors from the Johns Hopkins Hospital: Earl and Martha Galleher and the cancer surgeon R. Robinson "Bricks" Baker and his wife, Jean, a professor at Goucher College. Also there were my sister, Eleanor; Raymond Mason, a friend and business associate from Jacksonville, Florida; and Truman and Nellie Semans. Truman at that time was president and chair of Robert Garrett & Sons, an investment banking firm that first opened in Baltimore back in 1819. Information on Robert Garrett & Sons from http://en.wikipedia.org/wiki/The_Garrett_Building; on Truman Semans from http://www.brownadvisory.com/AboutUs/UserProfile/tabid/171/ID/24/Default.aspx.

the Kennedys!" Everyone laughed, but of course Red couldn't resist the bait.

After dinner came the singing. It was our custom at important parties at Oakington to have some music. To get us going that night, we had brought in a great singer, Charles "Buster" Brown, the leader of Rivers Chambers, a Baltimore jazz orchestra that frequently played at parties. Pretty soon, Fay and an enthusiastic Teddy Kennedy grabbed the lead as we launched into "The Wearing of the Green" and other Irish ballads.

We all had a grand time, but I knew the president couldn't stay long. After several songs, the president, Hoffberger, Gallagher, and I stepped into the library to talk politics before the president boarded his helicopter for the hop back to Washington.

I had been an early Kennedy supporter in 1960 even as others in Maryland backed Lyndon Johnson or other candidates. At age thirty-one, I had become the attorney for the Kennedy primary campaign in Maryland, then the "political agent," campaign secretary, and finally manager for his state campaign. After the early Maryland primary, I became the campaign coordinator for Delaware and Florida before, during, and after the Democratic National Convention that summer in Los Angeles. When Kennedy beat Richard M. Nixon that November, Robert Kennedy said they wanted to give me a job in the administration. I asked for and was nominated to the post of US attorney for Maryland.

Now, suddenly, President Kennedy was standing in our family home and beginning to talk to me about my political future.

Democrats held solid control of the Eighty-Eighth Congress, but those hefty majorities did not necessarily translate into support for the president's initiatives, especially on the hugely contentious issue of civil rights.[7]

In 1963, the United States was still a country segregated by race, especially in the South and in border states, including Maryland. In the US Senate, segregationist Democrats from the South controlled most key committees. President Kennedy needed more people in the Senate who thought like him. His election had already signaled a generational

---

7. Democrats had a 65-to-35 advantage in the Senate and a 255-to-177 advantage in the House of Representatives.

change in American politics that had attracted an influx of bright young people into federal and state governments. As he plotted his second term, he knew he needed more Senate votes behind him.

He suggested that I run for the US Senate from Maryland in the 1964 election, taking on the Republican incumbent, J. Glenn Beall Sr. My privately held, long-range political plan had been to move through the Maryland General Assembly, then to the House of Representatives, and then—maybe by the time I was in my mid-fifties—run for the US Senate. I had not planned to run at the age of thirty-five.

Then again, in 1963 I felt like I had already gone against the grain most of my political life.

Given the prominence of my family, many had expected me to go to Princeton or Yale or some other Ivy League university, but I chose the University of Maryland instead. As a freshman state legislator, I had bucked the governor and the legislative leadership on a number of fronts, including on savings and loan reform, civil rights, insurance reform, and the end of slot machine gambling in Maryland—all issues where I was opposed by powerful vested interests.

I was appointed US attorney over the strenuous objections of leaders of my own political party in Maryland and intense opposition from almost the entire Maryland congressional delegation. I suspect when I later successfully prosecuted two sitting members of Congress and the Speaker of the Maryland House of Delegates for savings and loan fraud—all three of them members of my own political party—the old guard who had opposed my appointment must have realized their worst fears.

In the years to come, and against the odds, I would beat out Maryland comptroller Louis L. Goldstein, the candidate recruited and endorsed by the state party organization and the powerful AFL-CIO, to become the Democratic nominee for the US Senate in 1964. It was the only election Goldstein would lose in a storied Maryland political career that spanned four decades.

Despite my father's fiscal conservatism, I was firmly in the reform or progressive wing of the Democratic Party. I supported civil rights when restaurants, hotels, movie houses, and even whole neighborhoods were segregated by race. As a senator, I made powerful enemies of the National Rifle Association, gun manufacturers, gun store owners, and hunters (who believed the blatantly false but politically effective NRA propaganda) by pushing for strong national gun control laws. I later attracted the enmity of the Nixon administration by opposing not one but two presidential nominees for the Supreme Court because I thought they were unqualified. I even antagonized my benefactors, the Kennedy family, by challenging the appointment (pushed behind the scenes by family patriarch Joseph P. Kennedy) to the bench of Francis X. Morrissey, a nominee clearly unqualified and unfit for a federal judgeship.

I pushed for family planning services at home and abroad when too few were willing to talk about the need for population control or to make the link between family size and poverty. And when it became obvious to me that our incursion into Vietnam was a serious mistake, I stood up and said so, even if it meant a serious break with the president, the leader of my party.

As a freshman senator ranked last in seniority, I was fortunate to serve during an extraordinary six years in which the US Senate confronted one momentous issue after another—voting rights, fair housing, school prayer, environmental protection, "one man, one vote," the rights of defendants to have an attorney, and reform of federal juries and the federal judiciary. My 1970 campaign bumper sticker proclaimed, "Joe Never Ducks the Tough Ones," and to me that was more than just a slogan.

In March 1970, I received one of the great honors of my life, the annual National Brotherhood Citation from the National Conference of Christian and Jews, one of the leading civil rights organizations in the nation. Previous recipients had included Presidents Truman, Eisenhower, Kennedy, and Johnson, and Patrick Cardinal O'Boyle. I was just a freshman US senator. The organization indicated the award was for "the depth and strength of [my] convictions that the principle of equal justice under law must be extended to all persons," and for "foresight, courage, personal example and leadership."[8]

8. The full citation, awarded at a dinner in Washington on March 5, 1970, reads, "The National Conference of Christians and Jews, dedicated to the promotion of intergroup understanding and cooperation, justice and equality of opportunity for all, cites the Honorable Joseph D. Tydings, United States Senator from Maryland: For the depth and strength of his conviction that the principle of equal justice under the law must be extended to all persons; For his effective leadership in helping secure the enactment of significant civil rights legislation, particularly the Voting Rights Act of 1965, and the Civil Rights Act of 1968; For his ceaseless

Over those years, I was always aware that my stand on guns, or civil rights, or Vietnam, or any of those other thorny issues might cost me my seat when I was up for reelection. But, like my father, I had faith that if I explained the positions I took to voters, they would then understand and still support me.

But these and many other fights would not unfold until I had served some five years in the Senate. That August night in 1963 at Oakington, the president and I did not discuss any issues. He simply encouraged me to run for the Senate and said he would back me. How could I—why would I—do otherwise?

Beall, a traditional Republican, had held the seat for two terms, but at sixty-nine he seemed vulnerable and the antithesis of the youthful trend sweeping the nation. The president suggested I talk with Bobby about the details of what I should do next, and, with that, he was off for the short flight back to Washington.

Of course neither the president nor I had any way of knowing what was in store for us. Less than four months later, John F. Kennedy would make his fateful campaign trip to Dallas. I never imagined that night that I would have to run for the Senate without his help or that when I ran for reelection six years later, in 1970, I would have to do so without the help of his brother Bobby.

The turbulent sixties were upon us. Youthful rebellion. Long hair, sex, drugs, and rock 'n' roll. Carnage in Vietnam. Police dogs and fire hoses unleashed on black citizens in the South. Sit-ins, urban riots, and landmark civil rights laws. The Beatles, the "British invasion," and Woodstock. Dr. Martin Luther King Jr. and the marches on Washington. Black Panthers, Yippies, and the Chicago Seven. Lyndon Johnson's Great Society. Richard Nixon's dirty tricks.

And, tragically, political assassinations that crippled many Americans' best hopes for the future.

efforts to restructure and reform our administration of justice system; For his leadership in securing Congressional support for District of Columbia government programs designed to overcome problems occasioned by race and poverty; [and] For his foresight, courage, personal example and leadership, the National Conference of Christians and Jews presents the National Brotherhood Citation to the Honorable Joseph D. Tydings."

CHAPTER 2

Oakington

The guest room where Jack Kennedy slept when he stayed at Oakington, the one with the ceiling that featured a raised ornamental plaster image of Cupid pursuing a half-naked nymph, was at the southern end of the house in what our family loved to call the Wicked Wing.

Two beautiful wings to the old stone manor house were designed in the early 1900s by the renowned New York architect Stanford White.[1] He was commissioned to design them by his friend, James L. "Jimmy" Breese, a millionaire investment banker from New York who purchased the central portion of the Chesapeake Bay estate in 1905.[2]

How much of the rest of this little story is true, and how much is simply Tydings family legend, is hard to sort out. But I have substantiated the general gist of this tale from a number of sources, and, in any event, this is how that part of the house became known to us as the Wicked Wing.

During the fall and winter each year, Breese would come down to Oakington, ostensibly to shoot canvasback ducks that, in those days, were so plentiful they would almost blacken the sky over the Susquehanna Flats at the northernmost end of the Chesapeake Bay. [3] Breese—as the story goes—would bring with him not only a number of his wilder gentleman friends but also a bevy of young New York chorus girls. I have on reliable sources that he would leave standing orders at the Aberdeen livery stables that if Mrs. Breese were to show up unexpectedly, they were

---

1. White was admired for his design of structures such as the triumphal arch at Washington Square in New York City, the Lovely Lane Methodist Church in Baltimore, Fifth Avenue mansions for the Astors and the Vanderbilts, and the "cottage" known as Rosecliff in Newport, Rhode Island.

2. Caroline H. Keith, *"For Hell and a Brown Mule": The Biography of Senator Millard E. Tydings* (Lanham, MD: Madison Books, 1991), 283–85.

3. Just north of Oakington is the mouth of the Susquehanna River, which accounts for about half of the fresh water that enters the Chesapeake Bay.

to take her by mule the slow way around to Oakington while simultane-ously sending word directly to the estate by a shorter route across the bridge at Swan Creek to move their female guests back to New York.

Among those who allegedly came down was the beautiful model and chorus girl Evelyn Nesbit. For a time, Nesbit was reputedly White's mistress, and it was their alleged fling in the room where Kennedy would sleep more than half a century later that prompted us to label that section of the house the Wicked Wing. The White-Nesbit relationship became immortalized in a 1955 movie, *The Girl in the Red Velvet Swing*, a refer-ence to a swing that hung from ivy-twined ropes in the Manhattan apart-ment where White was reputed to take his young female conquests.[4]

Buying Oakington

Growing up at Oakington was one of the great influences in my life.

There has been a farm named Oakington on that site where the Susquehanna River empties into the Chesapeake Bay since an origi-nal land grant recorded in 1659, although a series of different families have owned it. At the time my adoptive father, Millard Tydings, became interested in buying the property, he was forty-five, halfway through his second term in the US Senate, and considered one of the most eli-gible bachelors in Washington. He had been a decorated hero in tough fighting in France during World War I and later became Speaker of the Maryland House of Delegates, a member of the Maryland Senate, a member of Congress, and, beginning in 1926 at the age of thirty-six, a US senator.

My mother, Eleanor, came from a prominent and financially and politically successful Wisconsin family. Her father and my namesake, Joseph E. Davies, was a brilliant and successful lawyer who had come to Washington with President Woodrow Wilson. He became a friend and adviser to three presidents and served as American ambassador to Russia and Belgium. My mother attended Vassar and was a Washington

4. White met a spectacular end when in June 1906, at a high-society event at the rooftop theater of Madison Square Garden, he was shot three times at point-blank range by Nesbit's jealous and enraged husband, the millionaire Pittsburgh coal and railroad heir Harry Kendall Thaw. In the lurid "trial of the century" that followed, Thaw was found not guilty by reason of insanity.

debutante in 1921. On a trip with her parents to Asheville, North Carolina, a year after her debut, while attending a Christmas party, she met Tom Cheesborough, the tall, handsome son of a prominent North Carolina family. They fell in love and married in 1926. I was born two years later and my sister Eleanor—"Little El"—followed in 1932.

By 1935, however, events would begin to unfold that would transform my family and catapult my life in a completely new direction. By the end of the year I would have a new stepfather who was a respected national political leader, a new step-grandmother who was one of the wealthiest women in the country, and a different and suddenly brighter future for my sister and me.

The bigger world in 1935 was coming apart. Spain was edging toward civil war; Benito Mussolini had turned Italy into a fascist police state; the military had taken over the government in Japan; Adolf Hitler and the Nazi Party had seized dictatorial control of Germany; and the United States was still mired in the Great Depression despite efforts by its new president, Franklin Delano Roosevelt, to put Americans back to work.

My mother's marriage to Tom Cheesborough also had fallen apart. After my parents left Biltmore Forest, North Carolina, for New York City, my biological father's behavior was no longer restrained by his prominent family. He became a regular participant in New York night life, drinking excessively and womanizing. He had trouble keeping the jobs my grandfather found for him. By early summer 1935, the situation had become so intolerable that my mother told him she planned to seek a divorce. I was six and my sister, two.

My mother moved us into my grandparents' beautiful home in Washington.[5] That fall I started second grade at a private school, Beauvoir. Earlier that spring, my mother had met Millard Tydings at a luncheon in the Capitol given by the Democratic leader of the Senate. Here is how she described seeing him for the first time in her autobiography, *My Golden Spoon:*

> We sat in the Ladies' Gallery before lunch. I looked down upon the elderly lions on the floor below. They were almost all stout

---

5. The house was located at 2941 Massachusetts Avenue and as of 2017 was the residence of the ambassador from Saudi Arabia.

and balding and I was beginning to be sorry I had come. . . . I was becoming more and more bored and depressed when the door from the Democratic cloakroom flew open and so did the door into my future. A tall, slender, good-looking man strode in and up the Democratic side aisle. I had never seen a man with such magnificent carriage. His shoulders were as wide as the rest of him was slim and he carried his handsome head high.

It was not an electric shock that I experienced when I saw him, but something almost as stunning. I had never seen him before, but I recognized him! This was the man I had always hoped for.[6]

Over the next several months, as my mother prepared for a divorce, she began to date and fall in love with Millard Tydings and he with her. Upon learning that she planned a several-month trip to Europe, Tydings proposed that they be wed as soon as her divorce was final. She agreed.

On June 18, my mother and her father, Joe Davies, boarded the ocean liner *Europa* and sailed to Europe. Among the passengers was Marjorie Merriweather Post, who at the time was in the process of divorcing her husband of fifteen years, the financier E. F. Hutton. She had met my grandfather at a dinner in Palm Beach earlier in the spring and the two had secretly fallen in love.[7] After the ship docked in Europe, my grandfather informed Emlen Davies, his wife of thirty years, that he too wanted a divorce. He planned to marry the beautiful heiress, Marjorie Post, as soon as both of their divorces were final. My grandmother was devastated and my mother shocked by the news, which caught them both by surprise.[8]

When my mother returned to the States two months later, Millard Tydings was waiting for her. Almost immediately, he took her by car to see Oakington. The property was not far from the Tydings family home in Havre de Grace. As a youth, Millard Tydings had often walked the Oakington shoreline and admired the waterfront farm but never thought it possible he could afford to buy it. Now he had an opportunity to acquire it at the Depression-era bankruptcy price of $50,000, but the option

6. Eleanor Davies Tydings Ditzen, *My Golden Spoon* (Lanham, MD: Madison Books, 1997), 46.

7. Nancy Rubin, *American Empress: The Life and Times of Marjorie Merriweather Post* (New York: Villard Books, 1995), 208.

8. Ditzen, *My Golden Spoon*, 66.

to buy was about to expire. He told my mother that he would not buy Oakington unless she wanted to live there. In a rush, they drove in his black Packard roadster through the Maryland back roads and forded a stream before coming to the brick pillars that marked the beginning of the long, curving driveway lined with white pine and leading to the old mansion.[9]

Pausing at the pillars, the senior senator from Maryland leaned over and kissed my mother, starting a romantic custom they repeated for decades whenever they entered the lane to Oakington.

Although Oakington had fallen into complete disrepair during the bankruptcy years, with peeling paint and wildly overgrown rhododendron, azaleas, and weeds, my mother fell in love with the place. With financial help from Davies, his soon-to-be father-in-law, Tydings and my mother purchased Oakington that fall and began renovations. It became the family home for nearly the next half century.[10]

By the end of 1935, my mother had divorced Tom Cheesborough and her father had divorced Emlen Davies. On December 15, Joe Davies married Marjorie Merriweather Post in her beautiful three-floor apartment at Fifth Avenue and West Ninety-Second Street in Manhattan. Twelve days later, my mother married Senator Millard E. Tydings at the handsome Massachusetts Avenue home of her mother, Emlen Davies, in Washington, DC. My mother was thirty-one years old, fourteen years younger than her new husband.

The following year I started third grade at the Aberdeen public school. By fifth grade, with my parents spending the winter months in Washington while Congress was in session, I entered the McDonogh School, built on eight hundred rolling acres in Owings Mills, Maryland, about twenty minutes northwest of Baltimore. At the time, McDonogh was a military school and I was one of some three hundred boarders, almost a third of whom were poor inner-city boys from Baltimore on full scholarship. Another three hundred students commuted to school each day.

My eight years at McDonogh were a wonderful and formative educational experience. McDonogh had a dynamic and inspirational headmaster, Louis E. Lamborn. I had an opportunity to be a senior cadet

9 . Keith, "*For Hell and a Brown Mule,*" 283–85.

10. Ditzen, *My Golden Spoon*, 68–74.

officer, captain of the varsity football team, and an all-star lacrosse player my senior year.

All my life I have remained grateful for my McDonogh years and the friendships that began there. Today, McDonogh is considered one of the finest college preparatory schools in the Mid-Atlantic region.[11]

My life suddenly had three new influences: living the country life at Oakington, experiencing the splendor afforded by my new step-grand-mother's fortune, and my constant exposure to the work of two master politicians—my grandfather and my new adoptive father.

Country Life

In the years between Jimmy Breese's ownership and that of my parents, the proprietor of Oakington was Commodore Leonard Richards, who consolidated several farms into the single 550-acre tract.[12] Richards spent an enormous amount on improvements at Oakington—investments that I think would easily cost $20 million to $30 million today.[13]

11. The origin of the McDonogh School is worth recounting. It was initially funded through a grant from John McDonogh, a wealthy bachelor and merchant banker who, when he died in 1850, left about $2 million to be divided between New Orleans and Baltimore, two cities where he had worked and lived. Although a slave owner and notorious miser, McDonogh stipulated that the money be used to teach poor children from the inner city—both white and freed black—to read and write. His heirs contested this unprecedented bequest, and it took years before his will was ultimately upheld by the Supreme Court of the United States. Despite John McDonogh's intent, the first African American students were not admitted until 1959. New Orleans used the money it was bequeathed to create a series of thirty public schools named after their benefactor. Baltimore, which already had a public school system, used the money to create McDonogh, a residential farm school outside the city, in 1873. The first headmaster was Colonel William Allan, an 1860 honors graduate in mathematics from the University of Virginia who served on the staffs of Confederate Generals Stonewall Jackson and Jubal Early. Afterward, at the invitation of Robert E. Lee, Allan joined the faculty at Washington University in Lexington, Virginia (which became Washington and Lee University in 1871). He agreed to become McDonogh's headmaster on the condition it become a military school.

12. Richards had made a fortune from the Atlas Gunpowder Company, which had been part of E. I. du Pont de Nemours and Company until the monopoly it had in the black powder and dynamite business was broken up in 1912.

13. Richards bought two adjoining farms, remodeled and essentially modernized the "big house," built a beautiful stone pier, and constructed a series of magnificent farm buildings, barns and stables, a concrete hog house, tenant homes for resident farmers, a multicar garage with apartments above it, a greenhouse, a tennis court, and extensive landscaping. It was Richards who tore down the Stanford White wing at the north end of the main house and replaced it with a wing built of local Port Deposit granite. He also added a beautiful solarium on the Chesapeake side of the house. It was a comfortable semicircular room with a white

When he died before the stock market crash of 1929, his estate consisted almost entirely of stocks. Afterward, the value of his holdings fell so low that his estate was declared insolvent. That's why Oakington was available for purchase at a bankruptcy price. It also was the middle of the Depression, and most people were not looking to invest in large, run-down waterfront estates, no matter the price.[14]

Oakington was always a working farm, with wheat, corn, and other crops, as well as poultry and cattle. Farming in the early 1930s was not mechanized, and we used large gray and black Percheron draft horses to pull wagons and farm implements. Once a summer we would bring in a threshing machine, but otherwise it was hard manual labor.

Three families worked the farm for my father and lived on the property: the Clarks, the Shirleys, and the Cains. George Clark, the chief farmer, had four sons, the youngest of whom, Tommy, was about three years older than I. The Shirley family sons, Jim and Kenneth, and the Cain family son, Robert "Sugar," and I were almost inseparable. We worked the farm, crabbed and fished and swam, hunted ducks, and went to the Aberdeen public school together in what I still consider idyllic years before I went off to McDonogh.

To run the place on a day-to-day basis, Dad brought from Washington a marvelous married couple named Bob and Nadine Livingstone. Dad had met Bob during the Depression when Bob worked at the Anchorage, an apartment building in Washington where Dad had shared an apartment with Representative Sam Rayburn of Texas, the future Speaker of the US House of Representatives.

Bob had emigrated from a poor mining district in Scotland. Nadine was from South Carolina and was a fabulous cook. Bob also filled just about every other position at Oakington—butler, footman, chauffeur, and manager of the house. He had a fabulous sense of humor. I can recall him looking at me at breakfast and saying, "Where'd you go after you combed your hair, Joe?" The Livingstones were a major part of my

lattice interior and windows all around providing lots of light and broad panoramic views of the bay and, on clear days, of the Eastern Shore.

14. On the grounds at Oakington was a gorgeous two-hundred-year-old boxwood hedge, probably originally planted to shield the outdoor privy. There was a beautiful formal garden, as well as a wisteria arbor, a grape arbor, peonies, iris, and rhododendron. The house was surrounded by grand shade trees—oak, elm, walnut, and pecan. My father planted chestnuts, and I helped plant more than fifty fruit trees.

growing up at Oakington. I ate every meal with them when my parents were away. They were loving surrogate parents and a large part of my early years.

We always had horses at Oakington. Mother rode when she was younger, and I started riding when I was about six. I had a Chincoteague pony named Comanche from the time I was eleven.

Horses and riding, in fact, have been an integral part of my entire life. At McDonogh, I was major of the cavalry troop and on the horse and pony show team from the seventh grade on. For two summers, I was the senior stable boy and responsible for helping to take thirty-seven horses from McDonogh to Major Lamborn's great summer camps, Red Cloud and Red Wing, on Lake Champlain. Major Lamborn directed me to teach riding to the girls who were my age, but he had more in mind than just equestrian instruction. He told me he wanted me to get more experience being around young women. At the farm, I was surrounded by boys, and McDonogh was all male, too. At first, teaching the girls to ride was a challenge, but it later developed into a great summer!

In August 1946, as part of the US occupation of war-ravaged Germany after World War II, I served in the Horse Platoon of the 6th Constabulary Regiment, Third Army, one of the last horse cavalry units in the US Army.

Later on, my wife, Ginny, also loved horses and was a fine rider. My sister, Eleanor—whom I have always simply called Sister—was and still is a great rider and fox hunter. She served for twenty-five years as the joint master of the Elkridge Harford Hunt, one of the oldest and most celebrated hunts in the nation. I hunted with them until I reached the age of seventy-six.[15]

In 1970, Congress passed a bill of mine that became the Horse Protection Act, drafted to try to protect the beautiful Tennessee Walking Horses from the vicious, despicable, and crippling soring practices that to this day are still cruelly employed simply to help their riders win

15. Even today, Sister and I share ownership (with Gerry Brewster, son of my former Senate colleague Daniel Brewster) of a promising steeplechase horse, and my home is in the middle of Harford County horse country, surrounded by pastures filled with grazing horses. Inside, I keep my old English saddle and trophies from various races on display, and my tall riding boots are still lined up in the boot room just off the kitchen with other fox hunting paraphernalia. My nephew, Joe Davies, and his wife, Blythe, are two of the most celebrated steeplechase riders in the nation.

trophies. I am still working with members of Congress to strengthen and fund my original legislation. More than two-thirds of the US Senate and more than two-thirds of the House of Representatives have co-sponsored the new legislation, but opposition from the Republican leader in the Senate, Mitch McConnell of Kentucky, has kept the measure from coming up for a vote.

In honor of my work, the Humane Society of the United States, the largest animal protection organization in the nation, presented me with the 2016 Humane Horseman of the Year award at a ceremony at the National Press Club in Washington, DC.[16]

My other passion growing up at Oakington was duck hunting. The Chesapeake Bay and Swan Creek, on which Oakington fronted, provided great hunting for the thousands of canvasback, redhead, and blackhead ducks attracted to feed on the wild celery, tea leaf, and other grasses that grew in the Susquehanna Flats. It was part of the great Eastern Flyway. From the 1930s through the 1950s, millionaires would come down from New York to hunt. Canvasback ducks were the king of the ducks: the biggest, the fastest, and the best eating.

I sometimes feel like I grew up in a duck blind. In fact, I spent more time in a duck blind with my father than any other time I would see him. Every fall we built at least two offshore duck blinds along the Oakington shoreline and another four or five onshore.

Commodore Richards had built a massive stone pier that jutted into the bay; it is so solid, Chesapeake storms may never wash it away. As soon as boats with outboards became available, we used them to make the long trips to and from the blinds. My father bought a large Hacker-Craft speedboat, and, after I became a university student, I had a Chesapeake 20 sailboat. Each summer we would build a swimming raft and anchor it off the end of the stone pier so we could swim in the deep, cool channel that paralleled the Oakington shoreline.[17]

16. For more than sixty years, the Humane Society of the United States has celebrated the protection of all animals and confronted all forms of cruelty. It is the largest provider of hands-on services for animals in the nation, caring for more than one hundred thousand animals each year and helping to prevent cruelty to millions more through the advocacy campaigns it undertakes. The ceremony at which I received my award was held on January 18, 2017.

17. We had many parties on the bayside lawn at Oakington, including weddings and dress balls. My sister, Eleanor, was married there, as was my youngest aunt, Emlen. My parents

In 1982, twenty-one years after my father's death, no one in the family was still living at Oakington. My mother, sister, and I decided to sell the "big house" and the main part of the farm. After turning down impressive offers from New Jersey gambling interests, we sold the main house and about 147 adjoining acres to Father Martin's Ashley, a private, nondenominational, nonprofit drug and alcohol addiction treatment center. It opened as an eighty-five-bed, in-patient treatment facility on January 17, 1983. Over the years, the treatment center has acquired about half of the original 550-acre estate.

My sister and I refused to sell to developers the southern half of the property, which runs along the Chesapeake Bay and abuts Swan Creek. Instead, for less than half of what the developers had offered, we sold the property jointly to the State of Maryland and Harford County for use as a beautiful park. Much of the parkland is still leased to local farmers to grow crops. The little stone house that Ginny and I had built a short walk from the big house was sold to a private homebuyer.

Marjorie Post—"Mummy Da"

There was no more beautiful home in Maryland than Oakington. But the homes owned by my step-grandmother, Marjorie Post, in New York City, Long Island, the Adirondacks, and Palm Beach—plus the four-masted sailing yacht *Sea Cloud*—opened up a style of life for me that was unsurpassed.

In 1914, when Marjorie Post was only twenty-seven, her father, C. W. Post, died, and she ultimately inherited the Postum Cereal Company and with it a tremendous fortune.[18] Mummy Da—the affectionate name I gave my grandfather's new wife—was a brilliant, hardworking, and incredibly organized businesswoman in an era before women had even gained the right to vote. When Marjorie was a young girl, her father would take her with him on business trips to educate her in the ways of machines and male-dominated corporate management.[19]

Assisted by Hutton, her second husband, she transformed her father's successful but one-dimensional breakfast cereal company into one of the

would invite local volunteer firefighters and their families for annual picnics on the lawn, and we had countless Democratic political gatherings there.

18. Kenneth Lisenbee, *Marjorie Merriweather Post: A Biography*, 2009, www.paulbowles. org/marjoriemerriweatherpost.html

19. Rubin, *American Empress*, 39.

first diversified conglomerates in the nation, the General Foods Corporation. By the summer of 1929, General Foods had purchased Jell-O, Swans Down Cake Flour, Hellman's Mayonnaise, Maxwell House Coffee, Kool-Aid, Sanka, Log Cabin Syrup, and other well-known brands. They capped this rapid expansion by buying Birdseye, a small company in Gloucester, Massachusetts, that was experimenting with the new concept of fast-freezing food to seal in the flavor and texture.[20] The year after she married my grandfather, she joined the board of directors of General Foods, becoming the first woman to serve on the board of a major American corporation.[21]

To me, her wealth was never ostentatious—it was just there. She owned a fifty-four-room, three-story luxury apartment atop a twelve-story high-rise on Manhattan's Upper East Side that featured a dining room capable of seating 125; she also had a mansion named Hillwood on 176 hilly and wooded acres on what was known as the Gold Coast of Long Island. She personally planned and oversaw the building of Mar-a-Lago, still the most beautiful home in Palm Beach, Florida.[22] She also personally helped design and participated in the building of *Sea Cloud*, then the largest sailing yacht in the world, as well as the design of Camp Topridge on Upper St. Regis Lake in the Adirondacks in upstate New York. She loved family visits, and as the only grandson on either side, I got to visit them all regularly.

Camp Topridge was at the time primarily reachable only by boat. Upper St. Regis Lake was the summer home of many multimillionaires. Their beautiful residences were all called camps. But to call Topridge a "camp" does it a disservice. The beautiful log-built main lodge, with huge stone fireplaces, was built on a rocky and forested spit of land separating two small lakes. There were more than sixty other buildings spread across more than two hundred acres of Adirondack woods, including eighteen cabins for guests, each with a sitting room, fireplace, and maid. It took a staff of about eighty-five to run the place.[23]

20. Ibid., 138–44.

21. Ibid.

22. The name Mar-a-Lago is Latin for "from sea to lake," referring to the location of the estate on a Florida barrier island between Lake Worth and the Atlantic Ocean.

23. Mummy Da bought the camp, located about twelve miles northwest of Saranac Lake, in 1921, twice changed the name, and later built a Russian dacha on the property to be my grandfather's office when he was there. There was a putting green, a tennis court, a web of

If Camp Topridge could be considered "rustic," then Mar-a-Lago was the other extreme—the embodiment of wealth.[24] Built on eighteen prime acres fronting on the Atlantic Ocean, it took six hundred construction workers and artisans six years to build Mar-a-Lago, at a final cost of $8 million in 1927. That was, of course, just two years before the stock market crash that ignited the Great Depression.[25]

To build Mar-a-Lago, Dorian stone was brought in by boat from Italy. The mansion had thirty-six thousand fifteenth-century Spanish decorative tiles, marble floors, antique Cuban roof tiles, gold leaf on the ceiling, and a two-ton dining room table fabricated in Florence, Italy. There was a nine-hole golf course, a swimming pool, citrus groves, and an underground tunnel to a private ocean beach and cabana. Within the cavernous reception halls of the crescent-shaped Mar-a-Lago, Mummy Da was the undisputed queen of the Palm Beach social season each winter.

In 1969, Mar-a-Lago was designated a National Historic Site, and Richard M. Nixon accepted it in 1972 as a winter White House, although neither he nor his immediate successors ever stayed there. That, however, has changed. After the property was returned to the Marjorie Merriweather Post Foundation, it was bought in 1985 by the New York real estate developer Donald J. Trump, restored, and eventually converted to a luxurious membership club, the Mar-a-Lago Club.[26] During the 2015–16 presidential campaign and since his election as president in November 2016, Trump has frequently retreated to Mar-a-Lago.

hiking trails, and a magnificent boathouse for launching canoes, fishing, or swimming. The private Spectacle Pond was stocked with rainbow trout. Mummy Da collected fine art and historical memorabilia all her life, and she maintained at Camp Topridge a marvelous collection of American Indian artifacts, including Apache playing cards, Sitting Bull's tomahawk, and Geronimo's warbonnet. Rubin, *American Empress*, xii.

24. In 1974, the Marjorie Merriweather Post Foundation donated Camp Topridge to the State of New York, which in 1985 sold the property and 105 acres to Harlan Crow, a Dallas real estate investor, who uses it as a private retreat. It is not open to the public. Lisenbee, *Marjorie Merriweather Post*.

25. Because of the ever-present threat of hurricanes in Florida, Mummy Da insisted that geologists identify the strongest bed of coral on the barrier reef to which the structure for Mar-a-Lago could be securely attached. The property they identified between Lake Worth and the Atlantic Ocean was, at the time, nothing more than thick Florida jungle. Rubin, *American Empress*, 153.

26. Lisenbee, *Marjorie Merriweather Post*.

There is a certain irony that Mummy Da wanted Mar-a-Lago to become a winter White House; now, at least for the current president, it has become one. In her will, Marjorie Post left Mar-a-Lago to the federal government for use as a wintertime retreat for presidents, but the federal government returned the property to her foundation. Federal officials feared high maintenance costs and political concerns that the estate might be viewed as too ostentatious for a president to use—worries that President Trump seemed not to share.

By the time Trump purchased Mar-a-Lago, it had fallen into disrepair, and, to his credit, he did an excellent job restoring it. But one change he made still irritates me and members of my family. Without asking permission, Trump altered the official coat of arms that in 1939 had been granted by the British government to my grandfather, Ambassador Joseph Davies, and had been incorporated into the décor of Mar-a-Lago. Typical of Trump, he removed the word "Integritas," Latin for integrity, from the bottom of the coat of arms and substituted his own name, "Trump." My grandfather would be rolling over in his grave if he knew Trump was using his crest. I am sorry to say that banishing the concept of "integrity" is a sad metaphor for the Trump presidency.[27]

And then there was the *Sea Cloud*. Originally named *Hussar V* when it was launched in 1931, Mummy Da renamed it after she divorced Hutton. The four-masted barque was, at 322 feet, longer than a football field.[28]

The *Sea Cloud* was, in a way, as elegant as Mar-a-Lago. It featured matching his-and-her cabins for the owners, each with a working charcoal-burning fireplace. The vessel was outfitted with marble bathrooms and bathtubs, walk-in closets, expensive paintings, Louis XVI furniture, and intricate wood paneling. It had a barbershop, a bar, a smoking room, a laundry, a movie theater, and an oceangoing crew of seventy-two.[29] In addition to between twenty-seven and thirty sails, it was powered by four diesel engines that gave it a cruising range of twenty thousand nautical miles without the need to refuel.[30]

27. Danny Hakim, "The Coat of Arms Said 'Integrity': Now It Says 'Trump,'" *New York Times*, May 28, 2017.

28. While the ship was still on the drawing boards, Mummy Da rented a warehouse in Brooklyn and laid out the three decks and all the interior rooms. She had taken courses in nautical engineering and actually went to the Krupp Germaniawerft shipyard in Kiel, Germany, to monitor construction of the vessel in 1930 and 1931.

29. Rubin, *American Empress*, 185–86.

30. *Sea Cloud* was fast and sturdy. In World War II, it was leased to the government for

Before she married my grandfather, Marjorie Post and Hutton had sailed on several long trips aboard the ship, often with a tutor aboard for their daughter, Nedenia. "Deenie," as we called her, would grow up to become the TV, film, and Broadway actress Dina Merrill.[31]

After Mummy Da and my grandfather married in 1935, they boarded the *Sea Cloud* in Bermuda and enjoyed a honeymoon cruise in the Caribbean, where my mother and my new stepfather joined them.

In May 1938, my grandfather was transferred from the Soviet Union to become ambassador-at-large in Europe and ambassador to Belgium. The family spent that Christmas together at Mar-a-Lago, and the following summer, in June 1939, I boarded the fabulous ocean liner *Normandy* for my first trip to Europe to visit him. This trip came about three months before Hitler invaded Poland and only a year before the Nazi blitzkrieg swept across Belgium, the Netherlands, Luxembourg, and France. But what a trip! It was first class in every way. I was only eleven and accompanied several of my grandfather's old friends, including Richard Smith Whaley, chief justice of the US Court of Claims; Sidney Weinberg, who was about to take over as senior partner of Goldman Sachs (and would later be nicknamed "Mr. Wall Street" by the *New York Times*); Dr. Bill Morgan, a famous eye, ear, and nose physician; and my granddad's law partner, Ray Beebe; plus David Dugan, a young doctor sent along primarily to look out for me. Our first stop was London, where we stayed at Claridge's, and then on to Paris, where we stayed at the Ritz, before going on to Brussels.

Our return trip was aboard the *Sea Cloud*, which my grandfather and Mummy Da had brought to Europe to have available for vacation trips or to entertain important officials and friends. While in the Soviet

one dollar a year, the masts removed, and the hull painted gray. It was refitted for use as a weather observation ship, first for the US Coast Guard and later for the US Navy. While it had brushes with German submarines and participated in rescue operations, it perhaps distinguished itself the most by becoming the first racially integrated ship in the armed forces since the Civil War. For services rendered, the *Sea Cloud* was awarded the American Campaign Medal and the World War II Victory Medal. *Sea Cloud*, Wikipedia, http://en.wikipedia.org/wiki/Sea_Cloud.

31. As a child, Deenie had her own specially built children's suite at Mar-a-Lago where, decades later, another daughter of wealth, Ivanka Trump, stayed while visiting her father, Donald Trump. During her acting career, Dina Merrill appeared with numerous stars, including in films with Tony Curtis, Elizabeth Taylor, Glenn Ford, and Burt Lancaster, among others. Aljean Harmetz, "Dina Merrill, Actress and Philanthropist, Dies at 93," *New York Times*, May 22, 2017.

Union, he and Mummy Da lived in Spaso House, the home for American ambassadors in Moscow, but entertained aboard the *Sea Cloud*, which was docked at Leningrad.[32] Among the *Sea Cloud* guests in Belgium was Elisabeth, queen consort of the reigning monarch, King Albert.

Marjorie Merriweather Post was a remarkable woman and wonderful to me, always treating me as her own grandson. My sister and I were always welcome wherever she was. We used to ride in the same guide boats up in the Adirondacks when we would portage in, and I sometimes vacationed with her there when my grandfather was elsewhere. She stayed fit, had a great figure, and was quite beautiful, although I always thought she was modest about her appearance.

She was straightforward with everyone, and she and I grew to be close. We would have long, serious talks about how I was getting along in life. I recall a time when we were having lunch together and I mentioned a young woman I was dating. She immediately wanted to know whether I thought the young woman would "pitch in and work"; she wanted me to size her up before the relationship got serious. She always looked out for me and was a very influential person in my life.

Throughout her long life, Marjorie Merriweather Post exemplified propriety, punctuality, organization, and positive thinking. She was kind, gentle, and both publicly philanthropic and privately charitable. Shocked by the unemployment and bread lines created by the Great Depression, she financed the Marjorie Post Hutton Canteen, which fed destitute men, women, and children at a church facility on Thirty-Fifth Street and Fifth Avenue in New York City from 1930 to 1935. She also raised thousands of dollars for the Salvation Army Women's Emergency Aid Committee and for homes for the elderly, health care centers, and other charities. [33] Her political outlook was egalitarian, and she was a strong supporter of Franklin Roosevelt.[34]

---

32. In 1953, Marjorie Merriweather Post sold the *Sea Cloud* to the first of a series of different owners, among them the Dominican Republic dictator Rafael Trujillo. In the 1970s, the vessel was bought and restored by the German-based Hansa Treuhand group and the affiliated Sea Cloud Cruises fleet. Lisenbee, *Marjorie Merriweather Post*.

33. Rubin, *American Empress*, 178–81.

34. By contrast, E. F. Hutton was such a vocal critic of FDR that it resulted in his being pushed off the board of General Foods. Rubin, *American Empress*, 197–98.

Political Influence

It would have been impossible to be around Joseph E. Davies and Millard E. Tydings without developing a tremendous interest in politics and world and national affairs.

Joe Davies's political career started with his work as a young prosecutor in Wisconsin, but it skyrocketed under Woodrow Wilson, who in 1915 made him the first chair of the Federal Trade Commission. During the Wilson years, he and Franklin Roosevelt, then assistant secretary of the navy, became fast friends, and my grandfather helped raise money for FDR's 1932 presidential campaign.

By the mid-1930s, President Roosevelt believed another war was coming in Europe and wanted someone to go to the Soviet Union to assess the strength of the Soviet army and industrial capacity and to get a read on Soviet leader Joseph Stalin. The Ivy Leaguers in the State Department opposed recognition of the communist government there, but the president wanted to establish communications with Stalin and the Soviet leaders. He asked my grandfather to give up his successful law practice and serve as the United States' second ambassador to the Soviet Union. His primary responsibility was to improve US relations with the new communist government.[35] After he returned to the United States, he became a confidential adviser to President Roosevelt on Soviet affairs and a conduit for sensitive issues between Soviet officialdom and the president. He was told to bypass the State Department and the embassy personnel in Moscow and communicate directly with the president.

Nine weeks after the Nazis surrendered, Ambassador Davies became one of four US conferees—along with President Truman, Secretary of State James F. Byrnes, and Admiral William D. Leahy, head of the Joint Chiefs of Staff—to the summer 1945 conference in Potsdam, Germany, where the map of postwar Europe was sorted out. Behind the scenes, the United States wanted the Soviets' support for creation of the United Nations, then being debated in San Francisco, and a promise to invade Japan if use of the not-yet-perfected atomic bomb failed to end World

35. In 1941, Simon and Schuster published a popular book by Davies, *Mission to Moscow*, which sold approximately seven hundred thousand copies and was translated into several languages. In 1943, the book was adapted for a movie starring Walter Huston as Davies and Ann Harding as Marjorie Post Davies.

War II. President Truman's counterparts were Joseph Stalin of the Soviet Union and, at first, Winston Churchill and, later, Clement Attlee of Great Britain.

Joe Davies was the real deal.

So was Millard Tydings, who formally adopted my sister and me shortly after his election to a third term in the US Senate in 1938. Like me, my adoptive father was raised in a troubled home. I inherited from him his profound anger over the injustices of life. Just as I went to the University of Maryland, he had attended the predecessor institution, the Maryland Agricultural Technical College in College Park. Just as I was in the Reserve Officer Training Corps (ROTC) there, so Millard Tydings had attended the Maryland Agricultural College when it was a military school prior to his service in World War I. Just as he went into the army, into the Maryland legislature, and into the US Senate, so did I.

But whereas he was a hard-nosed southern conservative, I was known throughout my political career as a progressive or liberal. My father believed that the least government was the best government, and he was always concerned about keeping the cost of government down. He repeatedly introduced legislation to require the federal government to have a balanced budget. He supported states' rights. While his critics complained he opposed too many New Deal programs and was too comfortable with the segregation policies of the South, he nevertheless earned a reputation for integrity, accomplishment, and courage.

It was Millard Tydings who, as speaker of the Maryland House of Delegates in 1920, pushed through the legislation that created the modern University of Maryland. In the US Senate, he was the principal sponsor of legislation that granted the Philippines formal independence from American control. The beautiful carved wooden desk I used when I was US attorney and a member of the US Senate and that I still use to this day was a gift of appreciation to my father from the newly independent government of the Philippines.[36]

In 1933, Millard Tydings was the sole member of the Senate to introduce a resolution directing the president to send a formal protest to the chancellor of Nazi Germany over the treatment of German Jewish

---

36. By the time my father received the desk, he was out of office and he never used it. My plan is to bequeath it to the University of Maryland.

citizens. Although the resolution was killed in a Senate committee, he nevertheless participated that year in a major rally held in New York City protesting Hitler's unconscionable treatment of German Jews.

In the early days of FDR's first term and the depths of the Great Depression, he supported a number of early New Deal measures, such as the Emergency Banking Act and formation of the Civilian Conservation Corps. But, true to his conservative roots, he soon felt Roosevelt's New Deal legislation was going too far, so he tried to put on the brakes.[37] Their split reached a nadir in 1937, when he led the opposition to FDR's bill to "pack" the Supreme Court. Roosevelt retaliated by trying to purge him and three other conservative Democrats in their state primaries in 1938. FDR came to Maryland to campaign personally against my father. It didn't work. My father was reelected overwhelmingly.

The two leaders might never have reconciled had it not been for my father's desire to support Great Britain as it prepared for war against Hitler. Dad was a strong supporter of military preparedness, understood the danger posed by Hitler, and worried the security of the United States was in jeopardy. Congress had passed the Neutrality Act, which restricted what the country could do to help Great Britain in the war against Germany, and the president's opponents were threatening to impeach him for secretly circumventing those restrictions. Dad defended Roosevelt's flank, becoming one of the foremost senators in backing the president's preparedness efforts, and he later introduced and managed many of the major naval appropriations for the war.

McCarthy's Attack on My Father

After the war, my father engaged in a valiant but ultimately unsuccessful effort to expose and stop the wild and unsubstantiated claims being made by Wisconsin Senator Joseph McCarthy about communists infiltrating the federal government. McCarthy specifically claimed there were fifty-seven card-carrying communists in the State Department. He went so far as to call General George C. Marshall, the great military leader and statesman, a "traitor." His faction blamed the State Department for the communists' success in China after it pointed out that the Chinese military

37. When the Senate was asked to approve Roosevelt's proposal to set up the Social Security program, Millard Tydings, rather than vote yea or nay, voted a noncommittal "present."

and political leader Chiang Kai-shek was, in reality, an incompetent warlord who never would be able to defeat the Chinese communists.

When no other Democratic senator would step up, my father agreed to head a special Senate committee to investigate McCarthy's accusations, which concluded that his charges were a fraud and a hoax. Unrepentant, McCarthy and his allies—including California Senator Richard M. Nixon—accused my father of whitewashing a treasonable conspiracy by protecting communists.

The McCarthy camp then took full control of the campaign of Republican John Marshall Butler, a Baltimore lawyer who ran a despicable, false, and corrupt political campaign against my father in 1950.

The worst falsehood, disseminated as part of a four-page tabloid sent to a half million Maryland households on the last day of the campaign, was a phony composite picture that purported to show my father engaged in close conversation with Communist Party USA leader Earl Browder. McCarthy's aides, in cahoots with the conservative management of the *Washington Times-Herald* newspaper, doctored a photograph of my parents with my father's arm around my mother; they removed my mother from the picture and inserted a picture of Browder, a man my father had never met or spoken to.

The smear, at least in part, enabled Butler to defeat my father.

The following year, a bipartisan Senate subcommittee investigated the election and issued a unanimous report that called Butler's tactics "a despicable, back-street type of campaign" and said it was "destructive of fundamental American principles." It specifically said the tabloid mailer, cynically entitled *From the Record*, contained "misleading half truths, misrepresentation and false innuendos" that had impugned my father's patriotism.[38] And it said McCarthy and at least three of his aides were directly, but secretly, involved in the preparation and distribution of the mailer.[39]

38. Gerald Griffin, "Senate Unit Assails Butler Campaign, Sees Candidate Negligent," *Baltimore Sun*, August 4, 1951, 1. Newspapers noted that my father had won the Distinguished Service Cross for his battlefield heroism in France during World War I.

39. In addition to the fake photograph, the investigation revealed that the Butler campaign had engaged in a series of political lies. It identified numerous instances of failure by the campaign to report contributions or expenditures as required by state or federal laws, among them a sweetheart deal to print the damaging tabloid the *Washington Times-Herald* had offered to the Butler campaign. Clayton Knowles, "McCarthy Linked to Tydings Tabloid," *New York Times*, March 14, 1951, 34. Another example of free but unreported political support came

Despite this evidence, the Senate subcommittee said it was insufficient to remove Butler from office. Instead, it recommended that the Senate adopt stronger laws against the use of such tactics in the future.[40]

The only person punished for all of this was Butler's campaign manager, Jon M. Jonkel, a twenty-five-year-old public relations man from Chicago who pleaded guilty to six charges of violating the state Corrupt Practices Act and was fined $5,000 but spared jail time.[41]

As for McCarthy, it took the full Senate four long years after that 1950 election—until December 1954—before it finally passed a resolution censuring McCarthy and effectively putting an end to his demagoguery. Butler was among the twenty-two senators who voted against the censure resolution.

My father returned home to Oakington after his defeat, resumed the practice of law, and in 1956 launched a short-lived campaign to reclaim his Senate seat. After he had won the nomination, however, he was forced to drop out due to a severe illness, thus ending his political career.

Over the years, living at Oakington was far more than just an upbringing. It was a continuous lesson in government, power, and politics and a venue where national and state leaders regularly convened for political powwows and social gatherings.[42]

Through it all, the most influential people in my early life were my father and grandfather, my mother, and Major Lamborn, the

in the form of commentaries attacking my father aired by the broadcaster Fulton Lewis Jr. on the Mutual Broadcasting Corp. Both the *Times-Herald* and Mutual Broadcasting were owned or largely controlled by the *Chicago Tribune*, then under the direction of arch-conservative Robert Rutherford "Colonel" McCormick. Gerald Griffin, "Tydings Urges Criminal Libel Action in Butler Case," *Baltimore Sun*, February 21, 1951, 1.

40. Griffin, "Senate Unit Assails Butler Campaign, Sees Candidate Negligent,"

41. It was revealed during Jonkel's trial that he was introduced to Butler by Ruth McCormick Miller, the *Chicago Tribune* publisher's niece, who was then editor of the *Times-Herald*. After the election, Ruth McCormick Miller divorced her husband and married Garvin E. Tankersley, the assistant managing editor of the *Times-Herald* and the man who actually doctored the photograph. Edward F. Ryan, "Jonkel Fined $5000 after Guilty Plea," *Washington Post*, June 5, 1951, 1.

42. Among those who visited Oakington were Vice President Alben W. Barkley; Chief Justice Earl Warren; Senator (and future President) Harry S. Truman; future President George H. W. Bush; and Senator (and future Vice President) Walter "Fritz" Mondale. Senator Birch Bayh and his son, Evan, used to come up, as did Representative Morris K. "Mo" Udall, and Republican Senators Chuck Percy and Mark Hatfield and their wives. My father's great friend, the Ohio Republican Senator Robert Taft, was a frequent visitor. Sam Ervin of North Carolina—later of Watergate fame—also visited, as did Fritz Hollings of South Carolina, and others.

headmaster at McDonogh. These were the people who made me who I am. But it was my father's example that became the model for my own political career.

My father's political approach was aligned with the great philosophy espoused by Edmund Burke in his 1774 speech to the Electors of Bristol. Like Burke, my father believed his responsibility was to do what was best for his constituents, the people he represented, even if it was unpopular, rather than to follow the herd. Here's how my father's biographer, Caroline H. Keith, described it in her book, *For Hell and a Brown Mule*: "He listened to others, but made up his mind based on his own judgment. Constituents could yelp all they liked if they disagreed, he said, but he would be guided by his own sense of what was right."[43]

My father's decades of distinguished service were ultimately terminated by campaign lies. In time, my political career, like that of my father, would also be cut short, at least in part, because of the dirty tricks of the Nixon White House.

43. Keith, *"For Hell and a Brown Mule,"* 193.

CHAPTER 3

A Plan for Life

I never planned to enlist in the army. I did it almost on the spur of the moment.

I had just graduated from the McDonogh School in June 1946 and was working on the farm at Oakington that summer. I had not decided which Ivy League college to attend, although my mother favored Princeton because of my academic standing and athletic record.

I was in Havre de Grace early one Saturday evening when I noticed an army recruiter's bus parked there. On an impulse, I decided to see what the recruiter had to say.

World War II combat had ended, but we still had more than a million troops overseas waiting to come home and armies of occupation to staff and organize in Germany and Japan. Germany had been devastated—cities leveled by bombs, hundreds of thousands of homeless refugees, no food or medicine, and, in some cases, little in the way of government. Our country, however, was weary from war and having trouble finding enough soldiers to go over and help with the occupation.

The recruiting sergeant told me they were offering a unique, one-time deal. You could enlist in whichever branch of the army you wanted, pick where you'd like to be stationed, and serve only eighteen months instead of three years. If you enlisted before the end of the year, you automatically would be eligible for the benefits of the GI Bill when you got out.

Frankly, I was tired of school and was not looking forward to college. The idea of military life appealed to me. After all, I had been wearing a uniform and doing military drills as a student at McDonogh since I was in the fifth grade, and by the time I graduated I had become the cadet major of the cavalry. To me, the thought of enlisting seemed like a pretty good deal: I'd get to see a bit of the world, serve my country, and line up tuition for college.

I went home and told my family what I was thinking of doing. My mother was not enthusiastic, but both my father and grandfather thought it was a good idea, so I enlisted. I knew that service in the army overseas would allow me to see what the real world was like on my own and away from my protected environment.

Germany

After basic training at Fort McClellan in Alabama, I boarded a Victory troopship that crossed the Atlantic and arrived at the German port of Bremerhaven in December 1946. Along with other infantry replacements, I was sent by troop train across Germany to US Constabulary headquarters in Bamberg. In 1945 the Allied victors, while meeting at Yalta and Potsdam, had divided postwar Germany into four parts—a British sector to the north, a small French sector to the west, an American sector to the south and southeast, and a big Russian sector to the east.

General George S. Patton, commander of the Third Army, had been given major responsibilities in 1945 to organize the postwar occupation. As part of his response, he established an elite mobile unit called the US Constabulary. It consisted of mechanized cavalry regiments, at least six of which had been horse cavalry prior to 1938. At peak power, the constabulary consisted of three brigades, ten historic regiments, and about thirty-five thousand soldiers. Each regiment had spotter planes, Jeeps and armored cars, a motorcycle platoon, and a horse platoon for patrolling the roughest terrain.[1]

Horse platoons like that of the 6th Constabulary were among the last active horse cavalry units in the US Army.

I was initially assigned to constabulary headquarters in Bamberg, but because of my experience in the McDonogh cavalry and with ponies and horses, I was transferred to the Horse Platoon, 6th Constabulary Regiment. Our platoon was sent to a crossroads about fifty miles from the beautiful, historic city of Coburg, north of Bamberg. We were billeted in a little town called Neuendorf, where we were directed to patrol the border along a forty-mile section between the US and Soviet zones.

1. "The U.S. Constabulary in Post-War Germany (1946–52)," prepared by DAMH-FPO, US Army Center of Military History, last updated May 20, 2011, http://www.history.army.mil/html/forcestruc/constab-ip.html.

The Cold War had just started and the Allies were concerned that the Soviets would be running agents across the boundary line into the US zone. There were not many roads where we were patrolling, so we would ride in two-man teams twenty miles north and back or twenty miles south and back. Each patrol took about six hours. We would periodically pick up someone, sometimes former German officers with their uniforms still in their knapsacks.

In the closing days of the war, General Patton—himself a well-known horseman—sent troops to a remount station in German-controlled Czechoslovakia to save some of the best horses in Europe before the advancing Soviets could get there. Among the horses saved—possibly from the dinner tables of the famished Red Army—were some 250 Lipizzaners, 100 of the best Arabs in Europe, and some of the German cavalry's finest horses. The Lipizzaners had been moved there by the Germans from a Yugoslavian royal stud farm, as well as from the Piber stud farm in Austria, which to this day supplies horses for the famous Spanish Riding School in Vienna.[2]

As a result, the US Constabulary horse platoons had the finest mounts. Each trooper had two horses. Most were magnificent warmbloods (that is to say, part thoroughbred). Our platoon leader had a beautiful Lipizzaner. One of my two horses, Wahoo, was an outstanding show jumper. I wish I could have brought him home.

A Cold Winter

That first winter I was overseas, 1946–47, was one of the coldest of the twentieth century. Many German civilians were destitute and needed food. The Soviets had counterfeited the German mark, so it was worthless. US troops were paid in scrip, which we could exchange for dollars only after we were sent home. But GIs could get some basic items at the PX, like chocolate bars, soap, and two cartons of cigarettes a week. Cigarettes soon became a major medium of exchange all over Germany.

I did not smoke or drink, so I became the safe choice for platoon "cigarette treasurer." Each week, I'd collect two packs of cigarettes from each

2. Karen Jensen, "How General Patton and Some Unlikely Allies Saved the Prized Lipizzaner Stallions," originally published in *World War II* magazine and published online on *History.net*, September 18, 2009, at http://www.historynet.com/patton-rescues-the-lipizzaner-stallions.htm.

trooper and our lieutenant—about sixty-six packs a week—and then use the cigarettes to hire the Germans who lived nearby to work for us. They, in turn, would use the cigarettes they earned to barter for whatever they needed to survive. Germans in the farm areas were very poor, but they were not as hungry as people in the bigger cities.

We took over a small former brewery in Neuendorf and turned it into our platoon command post. We used the brewery office as our headquarters and converted the showroom into a mess hall for recreation and parties. As platoon treasurer, I was able to dole out cigarettes to hire people to cook and clean, to muck out our stables, to fix our saddles and shoe our horses, and even to hire a five-piece German band. The band played every night, usually until midnight on weekends. Our place became so well known that top officers from the squadron in Coburg would drive out to hear our German band play American songs, including some country and bluegrass ballads we had taught them.

Dad's Visit

I was just a corporal, and nobody—including my commanding officers—had any idea I was the son of a US senator, one who happened to chair the Senate Armed Services Committee. When asked, "Are you related to Senator Tydings?" I always said, "I know the family—they're very well respected."

In November 1947, after I had been in Germany almost a year, Dad told me he was coming over for a weeklong inspection to see how the occupation was going. I was to quietly obtain a weekend pass, he would leave his tour, and we would meet in Heidelberg for the weekend. Typically, he stayed with the commanding generals. The wife of one of the generals could not understand why he wanted to slip off to Heidelberg. I suspect she probably thought he had a sweetheart there—or what was known in Germany in those days as "a schatzi"—until my father finally admitted, "Well, I've got a son over here."

"Oh? Is he in school in Heidelberg?" she asked.

"No, as a matter of fact, he's in the army."

"He's in the army? The US Army?" she replied with surprise. "Is he an officer?"

"No, no, no," my father said. "He's a corporal. He's in a horse platoon at the 6th Constabulary."

After that, things began to change for me. The commanding general called the colonel commanding the 6th Constabulary Regiment to announce, "You've got the son of the chairman of the Senate Armed Services Committee in your horse platoon. Do you know that?" He did not.

Soon the regimental plane landed in a cow pasture near Neuendorf with orders to pick up Trooper Joe Tydings and fly him to Frankfurt to meet his father, Senator Millard Tydings of Maryland. Can you imagine what my platoon leader must have said? When we were together in Frankfurt, where we met before moving on to Heidelberg, my father was invited to a luncheon at which none of the military officers in attendance was below the rank of general or "bird" colonel. He asked me to join him, but as I headed to my place at the table, a captain pulled me aside and said, "Corporal, what are you doing in the dining room?"

"Well, I'm going to lunch," I replied.

And he said, "That's the generals having a lunch for Senator Tydings."

"I know," I said. "I'm supposed to be there, Captain." So he went in and checked and in a minute came back and somewhat sheepishly said, "Okay!"

But my cover was completely blown. By the time word got around, they were writing about me in *Stars and Stripes*.

During the eleven months I was stationed in Neuendorf with my thirty trooper "brothers," we had no radio, no television, and no newspapers, except for *Stars and Stripes*. Riding for miles on horse patrol so far from home, I began thinking about what I would do once I got back to Maryland. I was alone and completely on my own. The army was my home. Instead of spending Christmas Eve at Oakington or in the warmth and luxury of Mar-a-Lago in Palm Beach or Hillwood on Long Island, I spent it pulling guard duty in the snow. I began to focus seriously on what I wanted to do in my life, what sort of future I should seek.

It was during this period that I decided I would try to follow my father's path: a career as a lawyer to support a family, but with a goal of public service just like his. I would attend the University of Maryland as an undergrad and law student, practice law in Baltimore and Harford County, run for the state legislature from Harford County, then Congress, and then the Senate—just as my father had done, although he had been elected to the Senate at age thirty-six and I knew my timetable would be much longer and slower.

I mapped all of that out while I was overseas. By the time I had returned from Germany and was discharged from the army in January 1948, I knew what I wanted to do in life. And I was in a hurry to do it.

The University of Maryland

It is not an exaggeration to call Millard Tydings one of the fathers of the modern University of Maryland. He graduated in 1910, when it was known as the Maryland Agricultural Technical College. It was originally created in 1857 to teach Maryland farmers how to save their farms from the soil depletion caused by too many years of planting tobacco. After southern states seceded at the outbreak of the Civil War and southerners left Congress, Lincoln was able to push through the Morrill Act in 1862, which created the system of land-grant colleges.[3] The Maryland Agricultural Technical College became the land-grant college of Maryland.

When Millard Tydings returned from World War I, he became, at age thirty, the youngest Speaker of the Maryland House of Delegates. He introduced the "Speaker's bill" to combine the Maryland Agricultural Technical College in College Park with the four professional schools in Baltimore—law, medicine, pharmacy, and dentistry—into a single state-wide university called the University of Maryland. Before that, the various schools in Baltimore were privately owned businesses that had been given the name "University of Maryland" by legislative fiat. The newly combined university would be governed and controlled by a board of regents and the president of the University of Maryland in College Park.[4]

As a result of Dad's connections with the university, he was friends

3. The Morrill Act, sponsored by Representative Justin Morrill (R-VT), provided each state with thirty thousand acres of federal land for each member of the congressional delegation from that state. The land was then sold by the states and the proceeds used to fund public colleges that focused on agriculture and the mechanical arts. It was signed into law by President Abraham Lincoln on July 2, 1862. Sixty-nine colleges were funded by these land grants, including Cornell University, the Massachusetts Institute of Technology, and the University of Maryland. Library of Congress Virtual Services, Digital Reference Section, http://www.loc. gov/rr/program/bib/ourdocs/Morrill.html.

4. The statutory merger took place to prevent the bankruptcy of the medical school. The College Park campus assumed all of the debts and liabilities of the Baltimore schools, and the University of Maryland Board of Regents assumed complete control.

with the university president, H. C. "Curley" Byrd. While I was in Germany, he had Byrd send me a set of freshman textbooks so I could get a head start. Jim Tatum, then the Maryland football coach, must have known I had been captain of the football team at McDonogh, because he sent me news clippings about the university team. The people I got to know at the University of Maryland provided me with links to people all over the state, and they were invaluable when I later ran for public office. They remain an important part of my life to this day.[5]

The University of Maryland at College Park has had only two graduates elected to the US Senate—my father and I.

When I enrolled in February 1948, I was all business. My focus was to get on the dean's list and stay on it. I wanted to play football and lacrosse, as I had done at McDonogh. In those first two college years, I rarely dated—I just didn't have the time. I was always working, partly because I was trying to complete three years' worth of classes in two and a half years and was carrying about twenty-one credits a semester. My grandfather, who had a huge influence on me, always advised, "He travels fastest and farthest who travels alone."

I roomed at the university with Harley Williams, a close friend who had been my roommate at McDonogh from the fifth through eighth grade. Harley was just out of the US Marine Corps and I was just out of the US Army. They put us in a third-floor room in what was called Dorm M with two young high school graduates. That first night, radios were blaring and everyone on our floor was partying.

The following morning, Harley, a big, strong athlete who had once played semipro football, and I convened a meeting of everybody on the hall. We said, "Gentlemen, the third floor of Dorm M is going to have the following rules: at seven o'clock, hall radios go off, no loud talking. At nine o'clock, you can turn radios on and do all the talking you want until 9:30. At 9:30, lights are going to go off in the hall; all radios go off; you're in your own room, and we don't want to hear any noise. Now, if there is a problem, just speak up and step outside and we'll take care of it." We didn't have any problems after that.

5. I graduated from the University of Maryland with a bachelor's degree and from the law school there as well. I was student body president, president of the college Young Democrats, leader of the prize-winning platoon in the ROTC program, and—decades later—a three-time gubernatorial appointee to the governing board of regents, including one term as chair. I still serve on the board of the University of Maryland Medical System.

I had done well in sports at McDonogh, and in my freshman spring at Maryland I made the varsity lacrosse team and became a starter on defense. We lost to Johns Hopkins in our final game that year and again the next, ending a chance of becoming national champions.

In fall 1948, I played freshman football and got to know several of the varsity team's star players, including fullback Ed Modzelewski, who later played in the National Football League. I also became friends with Elmer Wingate, a six-foot, three-inch receiver who became an All-American and later played professionally for the Baltimore Colts. During the summer of 1948, Elmer joined me for two weeks at Camp Topridge. While there, my grandfather sent us to Montreal to meet the Bronfman family, founders of the Seagrams liquor empire. My grandfather had been the company attorney. We stayed with Alan Bronfman, who had cofounded Seagrams with his brother, Sam. The Bronfmans were small in size and, by comparison, Elmer and I looked so large that people in Montreal thought we were their bodyguards brought in from the States.

In May 1949, a group of us got dates and went to the movies in Washington to relax. After the movies, I suggested we stop for a bite to eat at Tregaron, the beautiful estate near Rock Creek Park that my grandfather had purchased in 1940. All we wanted to do was raid the icebox. We didn't realize my grandfather was holding a poker game there that night with President Truman, Chief Justice Fred M. Vinson of the Supreme Court, Truman aide Clark Clifford, and other dignitaries in his office in the separate Russian-style "dacha" that Mummy Da had built for him there. As we approached the house, one of the two regular Tregaron night watchmen alerted me about the president's presence. We were immediately questioned by two Secret Service agents. They accepted our credentials and we proceeded to the kitchen to make sandwiches. I have always regretted that I did not send a note in to my grandfather and ask that we all be introduced to his guests.

In the early postwar years, enrollment at the University of Maryland was exploding as thousands of returning veterans tapped into the GI Bill. The aviation pioneer Glenn L. Martin, who had a huge manufacturing plant east of Baltimore during the war, had donated $1 million to endow the engineering school at the university. Campus enrollment soared from 4,000 in 1945 to 10,000 just one year later. When I arrived on campus in February 1948, it was so crowded that some returning vets were sleeping in army bunk beds in the armory next to the main administration building. By 1985, enrollment had peaked at 38,679.[6]

In spring 1949, my third semester at Maryland, Harry Gamble, a fraternity brother and fellow McDonogh graduate, said he and other McDonogh grads wanted to put me up for student government president. It didn't take me long to agree.

There were two political parties on campus, each generally backed by different groups of fraternities and sororities. My fraternity was associated with the Old Line Liberals, which had lost the previous election. Our strategy was to hold onto the fraternities and sororities we had before, line up new ones, and then try to get votes from independent students who commuted. I did not tell my father I was running because I did not want to embarrass him if I lost, but my grandfather encouraged me and reviewed my campaign materials, including letters sent to every student. I organized and recruited a full ticket of candidates for every class and student government office. We not only won but captured almost every elective position.

My yearlong tenure as the student body president ran from June 1949 through May 1950. That first summer, I joined other student government presidents at a National Student Association meeting at the University of Illinois, where I saw for the first time a magnificent college student union building. When I returned to College Park, I initiated a student government petition drive seeking money in the capital budget of the state for a student union at College Park. The petition proposed that students pay a fee to help defray the cost. It would take four or five years before the General Assembly finally appropriated the money, but it was the Maryland student government when I was president that first spearheaded the project.[7]

6. University of Maryland Timeline, www.umd.edu/timeline. Today, enrollment has been slimmed down to around twenty-six thousand, and the school has ten separate colleges, offers more than ninety majors, and is attended by students from more than 120 countries. *Just the Facts*, University of Maryland, www.admissions.umd.edu/about/JustTheFacts.php.

7. In 1983, when I was serving as chair of the University of Maryland Board of Regents, I insisted that the student union building be named after Adele H. Stamp, who had been the first dean of women there in 1922, a position she held for thirty-eight years, until her retirement in 1960. When I was an undergraduate and student body president, Dean Stamp had been particularly helpful to me. Years later, she later supported my bid for the US Senate.

Construction of a student union obviously is not the only thing that has changed since my college days in the mid-twentieth century. McKeldin Library, the huge building that stands at one end of the central lawn of the campus and has the big, bronze terrapin statue in front, had not been built. There were only two dorms for women—all the rest were for men. Every women's dorm had a house mother, and young men were not allowed above the ground floor and had to be out of the main level by 9:00 p.m. Even fraternity houses had house mothers, and some houses were only then beginning to get televisions. Most parties revolved around a piano or guitar, a keg of beer, and singing. There was drinking, of course, but not like there is today. Only a few students had automobiles. I had saved enough money in the army to buy a car, but my grandfather gave me a small Ford coupe the summer after my first semester.

Young Democrats

By fall 1950, I had studied for five semesters at College Park, taken two additional summer courses at George Washington University, and worked at my grandfather's Washington law firm, Davis Richberg. I had earned the three years of college credits that were necessary in those days to enroll at the law school in Baltimore and had moved into an apartment on Bolton Street. I roomed with Gus Sasscer, son and namesake of a legendary congressional representative and Maryland political power broker from Prince George's County, Lansdale G. Sasscer. Gus and I became lifelong friends. We were ushers in each other's weddings. We walked to class together every day and dined at a boardinghouse in the evenings. Each afternoon, I worked at my father's law firm, which had offices in Baltimore.

The fall I entered law school, Dad was up for reelection to a fifth term. I spent my free time driving him around the state, and he appeared to be certain of winning—until the McCarthy crowd began to sabotage his campaign and Republicans started painting him as "soft on communism." It was despicable.

The big defeat for Democrats came in November 1950. It was the midterm election during Truman's second term, a point in the election cycle when the party out of power typically makes significant gains. My father was defeated, 53 percent to 46 percent, by John Marshall Butler.

Theodore Roosevelt McKeldin, a former Republican mayor of Baltimore, was easily elected governor of Maryland, beating incumbent Democrat William Preston Lane Jr.[8]

While I was at College Park, I helped organize the University of Maryland Young Democrats. It was not until after the 1950 election debacle, however, that I realized that if the Democratic Party was to have any chance to rebound in the next election, it desperately needed a revitalized network of Young Democrats.

First, in my freshman year in law school, I focused on a Young Democrats club for law students. I met two energetic law students, Edgar Silver (later a state legislator and judge) and Joe Casky. Edgar was entering the University of Baltimore School of Law and Joe was entering Mount Vernon School of Law.[9] We joined ranks and organized the Young Democrat Students of Law, drawing members from all three schools.

Before leaving office, Governor Lane had persuaded a popular young state senator from Baltimore, Leroy Preston, to be statewide president of the Young Democrats. There were only a handful of Young Democrats clubs around the state at that time. In February 1951, the statewide executive committee of the Young Democrats, such as it was, met in Baltimore to discuss the sweeping political losses. The meeting got off to a bad start when Senator Preston unexpectedly announced his resignation. Fortunately, Ed Storm, a state senator from Frederick, agreed to serve in his place. They decided to hold a state Young Democrats convention that September to spark interest and create enthusiasm. Nobody, however, wanted to organize the convention. Suddenly, the existing senior leadership spotted me, a freshman law student with the name Tydings, and said I should undertake the job. I was somewhat taken aback, but I agreed to do it. I immediately talked about it with my father, who said, "If you're going to run a convention, it is going to cost money. And, you're going to have to raise it, locate a site, and recruit a keynote speaker. You'd better go

8. Lane had become unpopular for raising the sales tax to pay for projects that had been deferred during the war, such as new schools, new roads, and a new bridge across the Chesapeake Bay. In the second congressional district, Republican James Devereaux ousted incumbent Democrat William P. Bolton, which evened the Maryland congressional delegation at three Democrats and three Republicans. Nationally, Democrats suffered losses across the board, though retaining slim majorities in the both houses of Congress and in the Maryland General Assembly.

9. Founded in 1935 as part of Eastern College, the Mount Vernon School of Law merged with the University of Baltimore School of Law in September 1970.

see my friend, Mr. Sam Hoffberger." And that is how I was introduced to the Hoffberger family, including Roy and Jerry Hoffberger.

I went to see Mr. Sam, who readily agreed to help and asked his nephew, Leroy Hoffberger, to assist me. Roy, then a young lawyer in the family firm, would one day become godfather to my eldest daughter, Mary. Together, we started to raise money, booked a convention hotel in Annapolis, drafted a convention brochure, and prepared an invitation list. I went to Washington and, with the help of the Tydings name, convinced Senator Estes Kefauver of Tennessee to be our keynote speaker.

At that time, since there were few Young Democrats clubs in Maryland, I started organizing Young Democrats clubs in each of the twenty-three counties throughout the state. That is really where I first built my statewide political base. I realized I had to organize chapters if I wanted delegates to come to our convention.

We decided Wicomico County was a key county on the Eastern Shore. I identified Hamilton Fox, the state's attorney, as the most prominent young Democratic officeholder there, so I drove down, went into his office cold, and asked him if he would join us. Ham Fox, thirty-seven (I was just twenty-three), had a fine war record and was a popular local prosecutor. He agreed to organize a club in Wicomico County. We became lifelong friends. He was always a key political supporter.

That's what I did all over the state. I was told I had to meet the conservative state senator from Dorchester County, Frederick C. Malkus Jr., but was warned he would be hard to get along with. But we hit it off, especially after I offered to make him permanent chair of the convention. He agreed to organize his county.

In Queen Anne's County, I lined up Linwood Yates, a friend from the University of Maryland, and from Cecil County I got Bill Burkley and Tucker Mackie. I just kept moving, county by county—Jimmy Lynch in Caroline County; Walter Baker at Washington College, in Chestertown; Jamie Byron and Victor Cushwa, Washington County; Richard E. "Dick" Lankford and Jim Morton in Anne Arundel. I got Lloyd L. "Hot Dog" Simpkins to organize down in Somerset County; Ray Coates, my law school classmate, in Worcester County; John Thomas Parran in Charles County; and J. Frank Raley and John Hanson Briscoe in St. Mary's.

As I recruited Democrats around the state, I often arranged to stay the night at their homes. This was a great way to get to know people and their families and what made them tick. It sort of sealed a bond between us and enabled me to thoroughly understand the political and public concerns of the county.

As the convention drew near, we learned that Baltimore Mayor Tommy D'Alesandro had suddenly realized the growing importance of the Young Democrats. He wanted his own candidate, Frank Valle, to be elected president. D'Alesandro wanted to use our new network as his own stepping board to the governorship. I did not think it was right for us to do all the work and for him to come in and dictate who the president was going to be. We decided to put together our own slate of officers, with Anne Arundel County State's Attorney Jimmy Morton as our candidate for president. When the votes were counted, we had won every officer slot except for vice president; we controlled the Young Democrats of Maryland.

This may have been the first time—but certainly would not be the last time—I would go up against the top party leaders and political bosses in Maryland.

We adopted a constitution to govern the activities of the Young Democrats and set up an executive committee, with one representative from every club, to meet every two months. I was elected national committee representative, which was the second senior elected position. I would serve for two years until the next state convention, when I planned to run for president myself.

My first big project was to organize a Jackson Day dinner in Baltimore in January 1952. This was an ambitious undertaking, but my father's old and great friend, Alben W. Barkley, the former US senator from Kentucky who had become Truman's vice president, agreed to be our speaker. His acceptance gave us momentum. Our next problem was to sell tickets, set at $100 a person, which was maybe the equivalent of nearly $1,000 for a ticket today. In the end, we broke even financially. After the event, the vice president drove up to Oakington to spend the weekend.

The following year our speaker was Senator Henry M. "Scoop" Jackson, newly elected from Washington State, and the year after that, 1954, our speaker was John F. Kennedy. I invited them personally and always drove to Washington to pick them up for the dinners.

The people we recruited over the years for the Young Democrats would become a Who's Who of Maryland politics—state legislators, members of Congress, governors, judges, mayors, and party leaders. For me, organizing the Young Democrats was a lesson in how you begin to put together a statewide political campaign: finding supporters throughout the state, some with big names already and others who were simply loyal and willing to do the hard, nitty-gritty work.

I had a plan and a network. And I began to understand how to generate publicity and raise money.

PART II

Reform and Independence

It ought to be the happiness and glory of a representative to live in the strictest union, the closest correspondence, and the most unreserved communication with his constituents. Their wishes ought to have great weight with him; their opinion, high respect; their business, unremitted attention. It is his duty to sacrifice his repose, his pleasures, his satisfactions, to theirs; and above all, ever, and in all cases, to prefer their interest to his own.

But his unbiased opinion, his mature judgment, his enlightened conscience, he ought not to sacrifice to you, to any man, or to any set of men living. These he does not derive from your pleasure; no, nor from the law and the constitution. They are a trust from Providence, for the abuse of which he is deeply answerable. Your representative owes you, not his industry only, but his judgment; and he betrays, instead of serving you, if he sacrifices it to your opinion.

—EDMUND BURKE, SPEECH TO THE ELECTORS OF BRISTOL, 1774

CHAPTER 4

Against the Legislative Tide

By 1954, I was ready to make my first run for a seat in the Maryland General Assembly, but I was stopped from doing so—at least temporarily—by an unlikely obstacle: my father.

I was just twenty-six. I had graduated from law school the previous year, was practicing law with the firm of Tydings, Sauerwein, Benson and Boyd, and had been elected president of the Young Democrats of Maryland. Everything seemed to be clicking along right on schedule.

But 1954 was also a gubernatorial election year, and my father was backing the candidacy of H. C. "Curley" Byrd, who for nineteen years had been president of the University of Maryland. Dad and most of the Democratic leaders in Maryland could not stand Byrd's opponent in the Democratic primary, George P. Mahoney, who by 1954 had already run for statewide office twice (for governor in 1950 and for the US Senate in 1952) and had lost both times. Before Mahoney's long, divisive career was finally over, he would run for either governor or the Senate nine times over twenty years, including once against my father, once very briefly against my mother, and once against me. He never won a general election, but his presence on the ballot was almost always disruptive and more often than not more helpful to Republicans than Democrats.

In 1950, Mahoney had taken on the incumbent governor, William Preston Lane Jr., in the Democratic primary. Lane barely won but had been so damaged by Mahoney that he lost the general election to Republican Theodore McKeldin.

McKeldin was up for reelection, and Dad wanted to organize Democrats in Harford County and throughout the state for Byrd. He just wasn't quite sure where I fit into that plan. He knew I wanted to run for the House of Delegates but asked me to hold off announcing my candidacy.

I wanted to run on a ticket with an old friend, Thomas J. Hatem, who had been a couple of years ahead of me at both College Park and law school. Tommy's family owned a store in Havre de Grace, and Tommy often visited me at Oakington. He was from a big Catholic family, and because Mahoney was Catholic, Tommy—like many other Catholics in Maryland—supported him. I think Dad was concerned that if I joined with Hatem, I might be seen as aligned with Mahoney.

The other issue that summer—and for many years to come—was civil rights. In May 1954, the Supreme Court under Chief Justice Earl Warren handed down the unanimous *Brown v. Board of Education* ruling that ordered desegregation of public schools. Mahoney was a staunch segregationist. Byrd favored what he called "home rule," the squishy concept of letting each jurisdiction decide how it should respond to the Supreme Court ruling. But McKeldin took the honorable position, saying he would support the Supreme Court decision—that is, he would follow the law.

In those days, Harford County was represented by one senator and four delegates. We all ran countywide, not by districts. In addition to Hatem, the other Democrats who were running for the House that year were W. Dale Hess, from near Fallston in the upper end of the county, and Charlie Moore, whose father had owned the *Democratic Ledger* newspaper in Havre de Grace. I had helped Hess get his start in politics by encouraging his election as president of the Young Democrats of Harford County. Dale and Tommy both backed me when I was elected state president of the Young Democrats in 1953. They wanted me to declare early in 1954 as part of a Young Democrats ticket for the House of Delegates. Incumbent delegate William S. James was running for the state Senate seat in the district. I strongly supported Billy, but the others did not.

By the time I finally got into the race, Hatem, Hess, and Moore were already running as a team. I joined them at campaign events, but—almost as an early indicator of how my entire political career would unfold—I ran independently. We got along well enough, so they were not going to push me out. But I was more aligned with James than I was with them. All four of us won in the June 28 primary.[1]

Campaigning was much different in those days than it is today. My big campaign piece was a four-by-seven-and-a-half-inch postcard with a black-and-white picture of me in a suit and tie staring straight into

---

1. My friend Tommy Hatem actually received a few more votes than I did, despite my well-known last name.

the camera, stern expression, hair neatly combed, and a dapper white handkerchief sprouting from my jacket pocket. Below was my biography in brief—from birthdate to McDonogh, University of Maryland, law school, army, and practice of law. A separate accounting in my election files from that year shows that I spent $601.88 on the primary campaign, mostly for advertising in five newspapers in the district, and another $180 for the general election.[2]

Wets versus Drys

The most controversial local issue in that campaign—and for the next several years—was whether Harford County, which was a "dry" county, would become a "wet" county by permitting clubs, restaurants, and bars to have liquor licenses. The sale of alcohol in Harford County restaurants, clubs, or private stores was prohibited. You could buy alcohol only in state-run stores. Clubs, particularly veterans' clubs, Moose, Elks, and other fraternal organizations, all wanted liquor licenses, as did many restaurants and entrepreneurs who wanted to open bars.

In the primary, the dispute divided the county—and local politicians—into the wets versus the drys. Some of the wets claimed Harford was losing revenue because residents were driving to Baltimore city to drink. Aberdeen women circulated a report that linked drinking and traffic accidents and that pushed tests to determine if drivers had been drinking.

I was labeled a dry, which I was not. I always opposed the idea of prohibition, but I was just unwilling to tell the clubs that I would go for anything they wanted. The issue would take years to resolve. My father had warned me to be wary of committing too early and finding myself on the wrong side.

2. By comparison, in 2010, when Mary Dulany James was elected for her fourth term in the House of Delegates from the Havre de Grace district, she raised $191,459 from 810 contributors, according to state election records. Much of it was donated by special interests: unions, pharmacies, real estate agents, nursing homes, emergency physicians, banks, energy companies, law firms, state troopers, homebuilders, drugstores, soft drink manufacturers, grocers, and so on. I personally donated $1,550 to her for that campaign, but I was among the smaller group of individual—as opposed to corporate—donors. This example is not meant to pick on former delegate James but rather to demonstrate the vast change over the past half century in both the magnitude and source of campaign spending for most candidates for the Maryland General Assembly.

"Looking ahead to future elections, I would not be maneuvered too far from base because the 'wet' vote is much more active and cohesive and vociferous than is the 'dry' vote," my father wrote me shortly after I was elected. "So, I would be pretty careful not to get maneuvered into a 'dry' position. . . . I would talk this over frankly with Billy James, but I would use my own judgment after listening to him." Dad suggested that some Harford residents thought I was only in favor of the big establishments and did not care about the working man. My father said he did not want me to get started off on the wrong foot. It was signed simply, "Daddy."[3]

That September, something else happened that would change my life. I went up to Cecil County to watch the steeplechase races that are held each year at the big duPont estate, Fair Hill, and met a beautiful young woman from Delaware named Virginia Campbell. We started dating, and within a year we were married.

First, however, I had to get through the November general election. Hatem, Hess, Moore, and I ran together as a ticket and we all won. This time, I was the leading vote-getter with 7,595 votes to Hatem's 6,989, Moore's 6,472, and Hess's 6,410.[4] Billy James became our new state senator.[5] But Curley Byrd was swamped by McKeldin, who became the first Republican governor ever to win a second term in Maryland.

The General Assembly

In December, I invited a group of the newly elected legislators from around the state to Oakington. I had recruited many of them into the Young Democrats. I thought it would be a good idea for us to get together to renew our ties and discuss the new legislature and what we might do together. I thought that if we could stick together on some issues, we might be able to make a stronger impact in the legislature and not always have to follow the dictates of the assembly leadership.

3. Millard Tydings to Joseph D. Tydings, February 7, 1955, Joseph D. Tydings Collection, Hornbake Library, University of Maryland, College Park.

4. *Maryland Manual*, 1955–56, election results, Maryland State Archives, Annapolis.

5. After I was elected, I received a lovely congratulatory note from Senator Kefauver of Tennessee, who had been the keynote speaker at our first Maryland Young Democrats convention. "We are all so proud of you Joe," he wrote, "and are looking forward to seeing you over here soon . . . Estes." Senator Estes Kefauver of Tennessee to Joseph D. Tydings, January 13, 1955, Tydings Collections, Hornbake Library.

When we arrived in Annapolis, the four of us from Harford County rented side-by-side rooms in the Maryland Inn, the venerable old hotel at the top of Main Street, a block from the State House.[6] I roomed with Hess, but almost immediately I was at odds with my three colleagues.

John C. Luber of Baltimore was up for reelection as Speaker of the House. Hatem, Hess, and Moore were supporting him and aligning themselves with the House leadership. But, not for the last time, I pushed against the legislative tide and instead backed Luber's opponent, Delegate Perry O. Wilkinson of Prince George's County. I did not know Luber, but I did know Perry—he had supported me when I ran for president of the Young Democrats. It did not matter to me that Wilkinson had no chance of winning. I just felt he had earned my vote. Across the hall, the Senate elected Louis L. Goldstein of Calvert County as Senate president.

One way I separated myself from my county colleagues was to follow my grandfather's advice and begin writing a weekly report for the local newspapers in our district. The "Legislative Report to the People of Harford County" was simply about what was going on in the General Assembly. My three colleagues got upset when I started doing that because it forced them to put together a newsletter of their own. During that first term, Billy James and I also grew closer, even as my relationship with the other Harford County delegates, particularly with Hess, began to fray. The three of them would sometimes team up against me on a Harford County issue, but because of my close friendship with Billy, I knew he could stop anything that we really opposed if it got out of the House and over to the Senate.

I was a reformer in the legislature from the beginning. I wanted to end slot machine gambling in the four southern Maryland counties where it was then legal. I was for civil rights when few other Maryland lawmakers were. I supported the right of workers to organize and opposed antiunion right-to-work legislation. I was a leader in the effort to require mandatory automobile inspections, and I chaired a committee that wrote a reform of the insurance code for the state. And I was the

6. The 170-year-old inn had just been refurbished in 1953, and other legislators, including the Baltimore County delegation, also obtained lodging there. In prior years, the majority of delegates, as well as news reporters, had rented rooms in Carvel Hall, the hotel (since demolished) that had been built over the formal backyard garden (since restored) of the historic colonial-era brick home of William Paca, signer of the Declaration of Independence and three-time governor of Maryland.

primary champion of bills to regulate state-chartered savings and loan associations.

For taking some of these positions, I became persona non grata with key members of the leadership.

The Judiciary Committee

As a lawyer, I was assigned to the thirty-two-member House Judiciary Committee, and what an all-star committee that turned out to be!

Two of us, Daniel B. Brewster and I, later became US senators. Four became state circuit court judges: Ridgely P. Melvin Jr., Lloyd L. "Hot Dog" Simpkins, Edgar P. Silver, and John N. Maguire. Melvin later became a judge on the intermediate appellate court for the state, the Court of Special Appeals. Republican George R. Hughes Jr., from western Maryland, became minority leader and the father-in-law of Governor Parris N. Glendening. Carlton R. Sickles became the at-large congressional representative for Maryland and nearly became the Democratic nominee for governor in 1966. Another committee member, Harry R. Hughes, would later become the first transportation secretary for the state and then be elected in 1978 to the first of two terms as governor.[7] Of this group, seven of us (all but Brewster and Simpkins) were elected for the first time in 1954, part of a big incoming class of sixty-one freshman delegates.[8] In 1958, Republican Charles McC. Mathias Jr. was elected a delegate and also appointed to the Judiciary Committee, on which I still served. He, too, would later become a US senator.

The battle between wets and drys in Harford County lingered on through almost my entire time in the General Assembly. Most Maryland counties in those days were dry. Just a few weeks before I resigned from the legislature in 1961, I discovered that Wicomico County had enacted a sensible local liquor law that allowed licenses for legitimate restaurants with a certain minimum number of tables or for long-established clubs or fraternal organizations. I asked Billy James if he would support such a bill for Harford County, and he said he would. Local bills of this kind

7. Governor Harry Roe Hughes with John W. Frece, *My Unexpected Journey: The Autobiography of Governor Harry Roe Hughes* (Charleston, SC: History Press, 2006), 40.

8. Associated Press, "Legislative Orientation Meet Called," *Frederick (MD) News*, November 5, 1954, 9.

are rarely if ever enacted without the support of the local delegation.

I circulated a copy of the bill to Hatem, Hess, and Moore, who were with the wets; their goal was to let the county offer a liquor license to any restaurant or club regardless of size or how long it had been in operation. I told them I was about to introduce it and that Senator James would support it. They could either join us or suffer the wrath of the restaurants and clubs in Harford County. As you might expect, they joined us and the bill was passed.

The assortment of issues legislators faced then and now is staggering. In 1955, the state budget was $30 million in the red, and Governor McKeldin proposed raising both the state income tax and the sales tax. Both ideas were defeated, but a separate measure to begin collecting state income taxes through automatic payday withholding (as the federal government was already doing) was approved.

Senator James introduced a bill to build as a toll road the new Northeast Expressway from Baltimore through Cecil County to the Delaware state line. Approval of this legislation also sped up the timetable for building a new bridge spanning the Susquehanna as part of that road. That bridge was named in honor of my father. The forty-nine-mile Northeast Expressway was dedicated by President Kennedy on November 15, 1963, just a week before his assassination, and shortly thereafter it was renamed the John F. Kennedy Memorial Highway.[9]

Civil Rights

Against the backdrop of countless mundane issues that always arise in a General Assembly session came the most divisive issue of our time: extending civil rights to African Americans, who, nearly a century after the Civil War, were still treated as second-class citizens or worse. It was an issue I would champion throughout my General Assembly and US Senate career, often against great odds.

African Americans had begun to make modest gains in claiming their

---

9. Other bills that first session called for licensing of chiropractors; limits on the catching of rockfish north of the Bay Bridge; a ban on highway billboards; a proposal to let the Harford County commissioners float a loan to build a new library; a measure to appropriate money to transfer the USS Constellation, a relic of the War of 1812, from the Boston Navy Yard to Baltimore; proposed taxes on cigarettes and gasoline; and the design of a proposed new state government office building in Baltimore.

constitutional rights through action in the federal courts, but they were stymied in state legislatures. Maryland, a southern state in both attitude and practice, was no different. The races were segregated in schools, in movie theaters, in hotels and restaurants, in almost all phases of life. It was not until 1954, the same year I was elected, that black Marylanders for the first time were elected to the General Assembly: Truly Hatchett to the House of Delegates and Harry A. Cole to the Senate.[10]

Governor McKeldin was sympathetic to the call for greater civil rights for the African American residents of the state, but a majority of legislators opposed any change. I did not. I am sure I was influenced in my thinking by both my mother and my grandfather. There were two incidents that stick with me today that helped shape my views because they demonstrated how egregious and hurtful these policies were.

The first happened right after I started practicing law. Charlie Wenzel, a lacrosse teammate from the University of Maryland, became lacrosse coach at Loyola College in Baltimore and asked me to help out. I spent three hours every spring afternoon in 1953 and 1954 coaching the Loyola defense. My annual compensation was one Loyola College sweat suit.

The second year, the team had a very fine African American player. We had a game with Swarthmore College in Pennsylvania and were driving home when we stopped for dinner at a restaurant in Glasgow, Delaware, just short of the Maryland line. As the team started to walk into the restaurant, the owner told us we could not bring the African American player in. The team was outraged, and Charlie and I were quite upset. The poor kid told us he wanted to stay in the bus to avoid embarrassing us and said we could bring him some food, but when his teammates refused to stay there, he started crying. We were not about to eat there, so we all got back on the bus and headed into Maryland without supper.

The second incident involved the Young Democrats. When I started setting up clubs around the state, I organized clubs in two primarily African American districts in Baltimore. In 1954, we planned a September meeting and banquet in Ocean City that was to include delegates from across the state. When I told the hotel manager that some of our delegates were African American, he said they could eat at the banquet

10. "Truly Hatchett, Negro from Baltimore's 4th District, set a precedent by becoming the first member of his race ever elected to the Maryland General Assembly." Associated Press, "Fewer GOP in Next Md. Legislature," *Frederick (MD) News*, November 3, 1954, 1.

but would not be allowed to sleep in the hotel. I said, "Well, that's too bad, because we are going to have to take the banquet elsewhere." After some argument, the manager backed down and let all of our meeting attendees stay at the hotel.

Those two incidents taught me anew what people of color were up against. They made me more determined than ever to change our laws to protect the civil rights of minorities in every way I could.

But we made little progress that first legislative session, or for years to come. Harry Cole introduced a public accommodations bill, but it was such an impossible task that he called it a "moral victory" when the measure received a meager nine votes against the nineteen that sent it back to committee to die.[11]

A statement from a 520-member civic group, the Glen Burnie Improvement Association, was typical of the "separate but equal" theory of that time: "We do not feel that forced association of the races is a solution to the problems of segregation faced by both races. Proper facilities on a comparable basis as those offered to the white race is in order, but this attempt to legislate complete desegregation is an effort to force the desires of a minority group upon the will of the majority of white citizens of this state."[12]

The demand for civil rights for African Americans was an issue that would come back again and again in future years, and I would provide leadership every time. Sadly, it is still a big issue today.

Ginny

In August 1955, following my first year in the House of Delegates, I married Virginia Reynolds Campbell at her family's summer home on Herring Creek near Lewes, Delaware.

---

11. A Republican who was first elected by narrowly beating the incumbent candidate backed by the northwest Baltimore political machine of James H. Pollack, Harry A. Cole went on to have a distinguished career in public service. He was appointed in 1977 as the first African American on the Maryland Court of Appeals, the highest court in the state, where he served for fourteen years. Among his notable opinions was one that upheld the right of the state to fund abortions for poor women. He also wrote many dissenting opinions, including the lone dissent in a decision that upheld the method the state used for funding local schools. Judge Cole died in 1999 at age seventy-eight.

12. Statement from the Glen Burnie Improvement Association, 1955, Tydings Collection, Hornbake Library.

Ginny was attending school at Marjorie Webster Junior College in Washington, so she was close enough that we could see each other regularly, especially when I was in Annapolis. Often when we would go out, her twin sister Mary would come along, sometimes with her own date and sometimes just by herself.

Ginny and I had been dating for less than a year when, in May 1955, we announced our engagement. I was twenty-six; she was eighteen. I actually proposed to her in the front parlor of a lovely home overlooking the Severn River where she stayed when she visited me in Annapolis. She said yes but told me I first had to meet her parents and ask her father for permission. I greatly admired her father, Captain Frederick MacGregor Campbell, who was president of the Delaware Bay Pilots and the son of Captain Harold Campbell, an old-time sea captain who had once sailed big square riggers. I also got along really well with her mother, who had various talents, golf being among them. She was a Delaware state golf champion.

My mother provided the engagement ring, which she had been given by my biological father, Tom Cheesborough. It was made up of diamonds from his two great-grandmothers, one the wife of a Confederate colonel in the Civil War and the other the wife of a Union army colonel.[13]

It was a big wedding on the lawn of the Campbells' summer place, which was named Camelot. Mary Campbell was her twin sister's maid of honor, and my father was my best man. We had ten ushers, among them Ginny's brother, Frederick; my football teammate Elmer Wingate; my law school roommate, Gus Sasscer; and my political ally Roy Hoffberger.

A number of politicians were at the wedding. I remember that a week before the ceremony my father told me, "You've got to invite Mayor D'Alesandro from Baltimore—he's in Ocean City and he feels offended." So we invited Mayor D'Alesandro.

It was a blistering hot day, and after the ceremony was over I got tossed into Herring Creek still wearing my grandfather's formal cutaway jacket and striped trousers.[14] For years my mother liked to tell the story of how they had to suppress their laughter when they spotted the hole in the sole of my shoe when I knelt at the altar.

13. Eleanor Davies Tydings Ditzen, *My Golden Spoon* (Lanham, MD: Madison Books, 1997), 346.

14. Ibid.

A huge photograph of Ginny in her ivory silk wedding gown and bridal veil and clutching her bouquet of white butterfly orchids and fragrant stephanotis appeared on the front page of the *Baltimore Sun* society section the next day.[15] We moved into an apartment in Baltimore, and that fall Ginny began teaching kindergarten at a school in the Pimlico area of the city. I split my time between practicing law and my duties as a legislator.

Dad's Final Campaign

I am not sure it is possible to describe the extent of the pain and disillusionment my father felt after he was smeared by Joseph McCarthy and then beaten by Butler in 1950, although he never complained one word about it. He was a Washington stoic. I could never understand why the public didn't see McCarthy for what he was: a mean-spirited, self-aggrandizing demagogue. Yes, my father had his detractors—for his support for segregation, or for his general disdain for unions and the labor movement. But I believe my father was a great and courageous state legislator and US senator.

Dad stubbornly kept after McCarthy, even after his 1950 defeat. The following year, he offered McCarthy and Senator William E. Jenner, an Indiana Republican and one of the most conservative members of the Senate, $5,000 in cash if they would show a grand jury evidence that there were communists in the State Department, as McCarthy had publicly and repeatedly claimed.

"Both you and McCarthy say you have the evidence," Dad wrote in a letter that was widely reported in the newspapers. "Well, Bill, what are you waiting for? I can't believe you and McCarthy are going to let these traitors continue to work for our Government when you and Joe have the evidence to prove that 57 card carrying communists are in the State Department."[16]

When Dad got no response, he doubled the reward to $10,000 and wrote a sarcastic letter offering to help McCarthy "get all these rascals in jail."[17]

15. "Wed to Mr. Joseph D. Tydings," *Baltimore Sun*, August 21, 1955.

16. William Knighton Jr., "Tydings Puts $5,000 Taunt Up to Jenner," *Baltimore Sun*, November 5, 1951, 1.

17. Dad wrote that he had concluded that McCarthy had not responded either because

In 1956, after declaring he was not going to run for his old US Senate seat again, my father changed his mind at the eleventh hour. By then, Millard Tawes, the state comptroller, had joined with the big labor unions to organize most of the state in support of George Mahoney for the Senate. Tawes did that to extract a promise from Mahoney that he would not run against Tawes for governor in 1958.

When my father asked my advice, I said that to win he would have to compress a full year of campaigning into two months and that would endanger his health. Tragically, I was correct.

By early that year, however, a number of longtime Democratic leaders in Maryland, led by Mayor D'Alesandro, had begun urging Dad to run again. Then newspapers around the state began a drumbeat of support, with letters signed by various elected officials, urging him to run. My mother and I discussed all the pros and cons with him and the strain a campaign would place on him at his age (he was sixty-six). He took a train to New York on business, and when he returned a couple of days later, he announced he had changed his mind and was going to run. My mother and I objected, but he had made up his mind.[18]

He officially filed for office two weeks before the deadline. I was in the middle of my second legislative session, I was trying to pick up what legal cases I could, and Ginny and I were starting to build a house on two acres of land at Oakington that my parents had given us. Once he filed, I left the legislature to begin full-time organizing and campaigning for him. When I could, I drove Dad to campaign events and heard him speak. He was a tremendous speaker.

In the primary, Dad was once again up against the seemingly omnipresent Mahoney. One hot campaign issue was how Maryland should respond to the 1954 Supreme Court school desegregation ruling. This was a time when a number of US senators—men with whom my father had worked closely for years—had signed the so-called "Southern Manifesto" calling for resistance to court-ordered segregation. Dad's

the initial reward was too small or because McCarthy was "physically unable to make the journey to the grand jury room." Then he said he had abandoned the physical disability theory after he recalled that McCarthy "had resigned from the war and had gone back to Wisconsin just before the heavy fighting really began." "Tydings' Offer to McCarthy Is Doubled; Now Says He'll Pay $10,000 for Proof of Reds in State Dept.," *Washington Post*, November 12, 1951.

18. Ditzen, *My Golden Spoon*, 348–49.

conservative instinct was to side with those who were arguing for a
"separate but equal" solution to the race question, but I said, "Dad, you
can't say 'Separate but equal.' You've got to say you'll follow the law of
the land."

Dad listened to me. In fact, toward the end of that election he told
my mother he wanted me to come to Washington as his chief of staff
once he won reelection. As one who really admired Millard Tydings, not
only as a father but as a statesman, that offer was a real honor. I don't
think I would have done it had he won; I probably would have continued to practice law. But it was very flattering. That was the greatest vote
of confidence I ever received from him.

In the final week of the campaign, Dad's health began to desert him
and he was almost hospitalized. He and my mother divided up his final
speaking engagements between the two of them, and Dad won the May
7 primary with 142,238 votes to Mahoney's 134,246.

They then went to the Homestead in Hot Springs, Virginia, for a
week of rest and recuperation. My father vowed to slow down his campaigning in the general election. It did not help that he smoked three
or four packs of cigarettes a day. Within a few weeks, he had a relapse
and complained of an awful pain in his head. He was taken to the Johns
Hopkins Hospital in Baltimore, where he remained for forty-six days. A
team of doctors diagnosed him as suffering from encephalitis, an acute
inflammation of the brain. "The best you can hope for," one doctor told
my mother, "is that the senator will get worse slowly."[19]

When we got back to Oakington, my mother summoned the Democratic Party brain trust of the state: Mayor D'Alesandro; Lane, the former governor; E. Brooke Lee of Montgomery County; Lansdale Sasscer
of Prince George's County; and several others, to figure out what to do.
They urged my mother to run in my father's place, but she refused, saying she had to care for him. They considered me as a possible replacement, but I was too young to qualify.

Eventually my mother relented, but her candidacy only lasted about
forty-eight hours, when she narrowly lost her bid to be the nominee in
a Maryland Democratic Party convention vote to—who else?—George

19. Ibid., 351–52.

P. Mahoney. We had been certain Dad would have beaten Butler in a rematch, but we will never know.

The final tally in that November 1956 election was 473,059 votes for Butler and 420,108 for Mahoney.

CHAPTER 5

Regulating Savings and Loan Associations

Sometimes a simple, almost innocuous act can have ramifications throughout a lifetime.

G. Kessler "Kess" Livezey owned the Livezey Lumber Company in Aberdeen. He was a local business leader and friend of our family, and, after my election to the General Assembly in 1954, he was one of my constituents.

Kess Livezey and I didn't always see eye to eye politically. In my first year in the House of Delegates, for example, he wrote me a letter urging me to support antiunion right-to-work legislation, which I had no intention of doing.

Livezey's son went to McDonogh. When I heard the young man had won some sort of sporting event, I dashed off a quick note of congratulation. His father wrote me back, asking if I would be willing to meet with him and another man, Frank Simik, to discuss a possible business opportunity. We met at Simik's office in Belcamp, where the Bata Shoe Company complex was located.

Livezey told me he had heard that it was possible to organize a federal savings and loan (S&L) association in which deposits would be insured by the federal government. He asked me if I would be interested in helping them organize a new federal S&L in our county. In addition to his lumber company, Livezey owned a lot of land and knew that ready access to low-cost home mortgages would be good for his business. I was just starting out as a lawyer, so I jumped at the chance, even though I knew practically nothing about S&Ls, federal or otherwise.

That early 1954 meeting, sparked by a simple congratulatory letter to a McDonogh cadet, led me onto a path none of us could have foreseen. My involvement with—and growing knowledge of—savings and loan associations would lead me into a sharp confrontation with the governor of Maryland and legislative leaders over the failure to regulate state-chartered S&Ls. In time, my knowledge of S&Ls would help me successfully prosecute two members of Congress and one of the highest-ranking members of the General Assembly, all of whom were engaged in S&L fraud. My work with S&Ls would lead to my lifelong friendship with Raymond Mason, who had founded a federal S&L in Jacksonville, Florida; that relationship would later complicate my bid for reelection to the US Senate.

But in 1954, what I needed to do was to learn about the savings and loan industry.

State and Federal S&Ls

When savings and loan associations were first created in Maryland, they were simply small, local mutual associations, often centered in a community or ethnic enclave; the Polish-American Savings and Loan Association was a typical example. Local residents would pool their savings and then be able to borrow money to build homes. Residents themselves would manage these "thrifts." Prior to World War II, they were generally unregulated, but at that time there really was no need for regulation. They were usually solid as a rock.

Federal S&Ls were substantially different. They were created in 1934 in response to the massive bank failures during the Great Depression. Because deposits were insured by the Federal Savings and Loan Insurance Corporation, federal S&Ls were closely regulated and regularly audited by bank examiners from the Federal Home Loan Bank. Borrowers were required to have a substantial down payment as a condition for each mortgage. In a word, they were safe.

After my meeting with Livezey, I drove to Washington to learn everything I could about federal S&Ls. I met with some of the top people on the Federal Home Loan Bank board, who were very helpful in telling me what we had to do to organize a federal S&L in Maryland.

I began by recruiting a number of our leading citizens to be on the board of directors of our S&L. On March 29, 1956, the First Harford Federal Savings and Loan Association opened in Aberdeen, and it was immediately successful. Even today, I can drive around Aberdeen and see the homes that our S&L financed. During the years I was involved, we never had a home foreclosure.[1]

It was so successful, in fact, that the following year I "crossed the Susquehanna" into neighboring Cecil County and organized the Cecil Federal Savings and Loan Association, where I also became secretary and attorney. Soon my knowledge in the savings and loan field began to spread, and I was hired by a Baltimore attorney to help organize a federal savings and loan association there.

Around the same time, the absence of regulation of state-chartered S&Ls in Maryland began to be noticed nationally, and not in a good way. Maryland was one of the only states that did not regulate S&Ls. As a result, outside wheeler-dealers flocked to Maryland. All you needed were to get three signatures on a piece of paper and to pay a fee of about twenty-five bucks and you could start a savings and loan association and then do and advertise almost anything you wanted. There was no check on who these people were, what sort of capital was backing up the association, or what insurance—if any—they had on their customers' deposits. Many advertised absurdly high rates of interest that they promised to pay depositors, and some offered prizes to lure customers and their money. There were no standards, no examinations, no oversight. The operators made bad loans, often insider loans designed to enrich themselves. Suddenly, Maryland S&Ls began to declare bankruptcy with shocking frequency, and depositors began losing their life savings. The fraudulent and corrupt practices that began to flourish in Maryland in the late 1950s would have been illegal in every other state that regulated state-chartered S&Ls.

Savings and Loan Regulation

In November 1958, I was reelected to a second term in the House of Delegates. As I became more aware of what was happening in many

1. In April 1979, long after my affiliation with the S&L had ended, the First Harford Federal Savings and Loan Association failed, a precursor to a national savings and loan crisis in the 1980s. In 1986, it became Atlantic Federal Savings Bank and moved to Baltimore. In 1997, it shifted to become a commercial bank named Susquehanna Bank with headquarters in Hagerstown. Federal Deposit Insurance Corporation, http://research.fdic.gov/bankfind/detail.html?bank=30860.

state-chartered S&Ls in Maryland, I was appalled no one was doing anything about it.

One major reason things were allowed to go on unchecked, I later discovered, was that some top politicians in Maryland—including influential members of the General Assembly—were involved with and profiting from these fly-by-night operations. In time these individuals would include, among others, A. Gordon Boone of Baltimore County, soon to become Speaker of the House. But I didn't know all of that for another couple of years.

In 1959, I decided to use my position on the House of Delegates Judiciary Committee to begin looking into this issue in more depth. By the time the 1960 session approached, I had decided to introduce legislation that would, for the first time, regulate, restrict, and require regular inspections of all savings and loan associations chartered in Maryland.

By now I had a trusted colleague to help me. My best friend from law school, Frank Gallagher, had been elected to the House of Delegates in 1958, and he too was appointed to the Judiciary Committee. Frank had been a year ahead of me in law school. While there, he had simultaneously taught ethics at Johns Hopkins University, worked as a *Sunpapers* political reporter, and was a law clerk in the city solicitor's office in Baltimore. In addition to S&L issues, Frank and I worked together on civil rights and measures to protect organized labor.[2] He was a fine lawyer, had a razor-sharp intellect, and an innate understanding of politics. His wise counsel and close friendship were always vital components in any political successes I achieved in the legislature and beyond.

Gallagher was a good complement to me: his great Irish personality was much less abrasive than mine. I tended to mix it up quicker than perhaps I should have. By contrast, Frank didn't make strong enemies. The powers that be in the state respected Frank and liked him. The powers that be did not always like me, largely because I asked too many questions and did not fall in line. The animosity that I generated from the Democratic leadership over my efforts to regulate S&Ls is a prime

2. After Gallagher left the legislature to become counsel to the Catholic Archdiocese in Baltimore, Archbishop (and later Cardinal) Lawrence Shehan became one of the first bishops in the southern states to come out publicly in favor of civil rights by banning segregation in all of the Catholic institutions in Baltimore. I attribute that position to the behind-the-scenes influence of Frank Gallagher.

example of how I got under their skin. I wasn't trying to make enemies, but neither was I willing to go along just to get along.

I introduced my S&L legislation in the thirty-day session of 1960. It was bitterly fought and resisted by powerful legislative leaders. But I garnered influential editorial support from the *Baltimore Sun* and the *Washington Post*, whose investigative reporters also wrote stories that provided me with background information and facts I could not have discovered on my own and that helped solidify public support.

In an effort to curb some of the most flagrant abuses, my bill would have required those who incorporate savings and loan associations in Maryland to have been residents of the state for a minimum number of years, prohibited S&Ls from using the word "insured" as part of their name, and required all S&L officers to sign an affidavit stating that they were representing their own interests and not fronting for others.[3] Those who violated the provisions would be subject to up to three years in jail and a fine of up to $10,000.[4]

We had a heck of a fight, but on the final day of the session, with the entire legislature snowbound in Annapolis, my S&L bill passed. An alliance of large, federally insured S&Ls supported my legislation because they realized that bankruptcies and corruption in state-chartered S&Ls would reflect badly on the well-run and well-regulated federal S&Ls. Many of the smaller, uninsured firms predictably fought against the bill. Over my objections, the provision that would have prohibited S&L officers from borrowing from their own association was stripped from the bill. I considered what was left as a stop-gap measure, but it was clearly better than nothing.[5]

Immediately upon passage of the bill, officers of state-chartered S&L proclaimed it "unconstitutional" and urged Governor Tawes to

3. My bill was House Bill 93, "Building, Homestead and/or Savings and Loan Associations," introduced in the 1960 session of the Maryland General Assembly.

4. The bill also would have required each S&L association to prepare a publicly available statement of financial condition within thirty days of the annual audit of the business. Importantly, the bill would specify that officers and employees of an association could borrow money from that association only on their own home or from their personal savings account with the association. No business in which someone connected with the association had an interest of more than 15 percent would be eligible for a loan from the institution. "Savings Bill Is Due; Tydings Says It Is Designed to Correct Some 'Abuses,'" *Baltimore Sun*, February 10, 1960.

5. Laurence Stern, "Maryland Assembly Quits; Enacts Loans Curb," *Washington Post*, March 4, 1960.

veto it. They accused me of having a financial interest in promoting the bill because of my ties to the federally insured S&Ls in Harford and Cecil Counties.[6] At the end of March, Governor Tawes held a veto hearing to hear from both sides. Opponents called my bill "unthinkable, unconstitutional and abominable" and labeled it a "rich man's bill [designed] just to put the small associations out of business."[7] But it was backed by the Better Business Bureau of Baltimore, among others, and was judged to be "constitutional" by the state attorney general.

A week later, Governor Tawes vetoed it, saying in a publicly released letter that he had been torn between his "acute awareness" of the criticism leveled against Maryland for not regulating S&Ls and "my considered conviction that this legislation represents neither an adequate answer to this criticism nor a proper approach to the problem with which we are faced." He said he was particularly concerned about the potentially adverse effect the bill might have on small neighborhood associations, most of them located in Baltimore, which he said were run "by responsible citizens of our state who, in many instances, give of their time and talents for nominal remuneration and, by so doing, perform a much-needed service to the communities in which they live." The governor conceded that S&Ls had engaged in much false advertising that implied that deposits were insured by the federal or state government when, in fact, that was not the case. But he said that while the bill the General Assembly had passed "sanctioned criminal processes," it did not create a true system of regulation.[8]

The Case Commission

Governor Tawes also knew his veto would create so much criticism and political furor that he had to do something about the issue.

To his credit, he said he was sympathetic to the goal of the bill and

6. Ejner Johnson, "Savings, Loan Agencies Map Fight on State Regulation; 2 Groups Blast Bill as Unconstitutional," *Baltimore News-Post*, March 25, 1960.

7. Henry L. Trewhitt, "Savings, Loan Data Are Aired; Tawes Weighs Legislation at Spirited Hearing," *Baltimore Sun*, March 30, 1960.

8. Governor Millard Tawes to Speaker Perry O. Wilkinson, Maryland House of Delegates, letter explaining the governor's veto of HB 93, "Building, Homestead and/or Savings and Loan Associations," April 6, 1960, Joseph D. Tydings Collection, Hornbake Library, University of Maryland, College Park..

announced in his veto letter his intention to create a special commission to study the issue and recommend a new version of the legislation to the 1961 General Assembly session. To head the commission, he appointed Richard W. Case of Baltimore, an outstanding lawyer and fiscal adviser to the governor. At the request of my close friend, Lloyd "Hot Dog" Simpkins, who chaired the Judiciary Committee and was a delegate from the governor's home county of Somerset, Tawes added me to the commission. The Case Commission was to report findings to a special legislative subcommittee on savings and loan associations chaired by Delegate Marvin Mandel, then head of the thirty-six-member House delegation from Baltimore.[9] Working over the summer, we rewrote the legislation and presented the revised version to the governor for introduction in 1961.

That turned out to be one of the most intense, politically volatile sessions in years. The political shenanigans exposed during that session in connection with the Case Commission bill were the subject of a continuous stream of news articles throughout the region.

Our Case Commission proposal was fairly straightforward. It would establish a nine-member commission with regulatory power over all state-chartered savings and loan associations and would create a new state agency headed by a director with considerable supervisory control over S&Ls. Importantly, it would require every S&L to fully disclose to the public the financial structure it had, would limit giveaway programs designed to attract investors, and would forbid S&Ls from offering a guaranteed minimum rate of return to investors. The two commission recommendations that generated the most opposition were ones that would forbid multistock corporations from operating S&Ls and would prohibit S&Ls from investing in second mortgages unless they already held the first mortgage on a property.[10]

The relative merits of the legislation, however, were soon overshadowed and almost obscured by a bigger political problem that began to surface at the beginning of the 1961 session: the disclosure that a number of key legislative leaders—men who were going to be asked to vote on the bill to regulate S&Ls—were officers and stockholders of Security

9. In later years, Mandel would become Speaker of the House of Delegates and then governor.

10. "2nd Mortgage, Stock Curbs in Loan Bill Opposed," *Baltimore Evening Sun*, February 8, 1961.

Financial Insurance Corporation (known simply as Security), a firm ostensibly created to insure S&L deposits. Apart from the obvious conflict of interest raised by their involvement was the more fundamental question about whether Security was a legitimate insurance company with adequate financial resources necessary to insure customer deposits. The answer, we were to learn, was that it was not and did not.

Newspaper stories identified the officers in Security as a group of Baltimore County politicians, led by Boone, then the House majority leader. Others included Michael J. Birmingham, who was the first elected county executive of Baltimore County and who was by then a member of the Democratic National Committee representing Maryland; Roy N. Staten, chair of the Baltimore County delegation; and Charles F. Culver, vice-chair of the House Committee on Banking, Insurance, and Social Security. Other shareholders included John Grason Turnbull, a judge on the Baltimore County Circuit Court, and James A. Pine, a state senator, also of Baltimore County.[11]

Adding to the politically explosive atmosphere, Maryland US Attorney Leon Pierson was making headlines that winter by prosecuting for fraud the officers of a Maryland S&L and the Chicago financiers behind it. Federal prosecutors claimed that officers of Commercial Savings and Loan of Baltimore knew that Security, the company that was allegedly insuring the deposits, did not have sufficient assets to do so. Moreover, it was revealed that a Chicago lawyer, Henry McGurren, had provided the $450,000 that was used to capitalize Security during a face-to-face meeting with Boone in Towson.[12]

Culver, who had been installed as president of Security, was vice-chair of the committee that had killed a bill designed to limit the amount of insurance Security could write. He loudly defended his position at a legislative hearing.

"There may be a conflict of interest," Culver publicly conceded in testimony before his own committee, but he added, "I don't see why I

11. David Culhane, "House to Get Insurance Bill," *Baltimore Evening Sun*, February 8, 1961. Michael J. Birmingham served a single two-year term, from 1956 to 1958, before losing his reelection bid to Christian H. Kahl..

12. McGurren had once identified himself as counsel for International Guaranty and Insurance Company of Tangier, Morocco, another bogus deposit insurance company that we later exposed after I became US attorney for Maryland. Charles Whiteford, "Insurance Firm Backer Is Revealed," *Baltimore Sun*, February 13, 1961.

should be prevented from defending myself and my family from financial ruin just because I'm a member of the legislature."[13] Boone and Staten looked on from seats in the hearing room.[14]

In 1960 alone, the year my first S&L bill was introduced, 174 new building and loan enterprises were chartered in Maryland, bringing the total to more than 650. Many of those seeking charters were undoubtedly doing so before my legislation, or any similar legislation, went into effect and required them to successfully pass an examination prior to receiving a charter. At least 27 of those seeking charters that year were insured by Security, which meant, in reality, that there was no valid insurance to protect customers' deposits.

"It is unmistakably clear that no member of the legislature or the executive branch of the state government should be in this kind of business," the *Washington Post* declared in a February 1961 editorial. "No officials anywhere can be trusted to regulate their own businesses or to make legislative judgments affecting their own pocketbooks." It went on to note that the House of Delegates had rules that forbade members from voting on "any question in the results of which he has immediate personal or financial interests."[15]

In early March, with the bill to regulate S&Ls still moving through the legislative process, the *Washington Post* disclosed in a front-page story that Boone and his law associate, J. Thomas Ellicott, had received more than $51,000 in legal fees from Security during the first seventeen months the company was in existence.[16]

Against this unseemly backdrop, the House of Delegates seemed resigned to do the job it faced, passing the S&L regulation bill on a vote of 116–0, but only after a subcommittee chaired by Mandel had added fifty amendments to the original Case Commission draft. When the revised bill landed in the Senate, members of the House urged Mandel's

13. Culver quoted in Laurence Stern, "Del. Culver Will Defend His Loan Firm at Hearing," *Washington Post*, February 1, 1961.

14. After I became US attorney for Maryland, I prosecuted Culver, along with others, for savings and loan fraud. He pleaded "no contest" to the charges.

15. "Maryland's Time of Trial" (editorial), *Washington Post*, February 14, 1961.

16. Laurence Stern, "Boone Got $51,275 in Legal Fees; Loan Firm Lists Payments to Md. House Chief, Aide," *Washington Post*, March 3, 1961. Ellicott, it troubles me to admit, was a former president of the Young Democrats of Maryland.

counterpart, Senator John C. North, to bring it up quickly for a vote and pass it as it stood. Instead, North—at the request of Dick Case and me—closely examined the bill. What he discovered was a secret amendment that would have rendered the bill almost meaningless. Without the knowledge of the sponsors of the legislation, Mandel had quietly inserted language that would have had the effect of exempting existing multistock S&Ls from the law—exactly the opposite of what was intended. Case was outraged, as were North and I.[17]

In legislative parlance, the Mandel amendment was a "snake"— a mischievous and secretive effort to change the effect of legislation without anyone realizing it until it was too late. Snakes regularly slither into bills when they can easily be missed as the end-of-session workload increases in the rush to adjournment. Even if discovered, snakes can be deadly to legislation because any change that would strip the snake amendment from the bill would mean that the entire piece of legislation would have to be returned to the house of origin for concurrence. Anyone motivated enough to add a snake amendment to a bill in the first place might be in no hurry to consider the legislation a second time, knowing that if the General Assembly were to adjourn without final action on the bill, the bill would die and nothing would change.

In this case, however, a little sunshine on the problem forced Mandel to back down. Although he protested that there was nothing sneaky about what he had done, he agreed to take the bill back to the House before the Senate acted on it, delete the offending amendment, pass it again, and send it back to the Senate for final approval, all of which he did.[18] The minute that bill was enacted into law, state auditors began to audit the records of state-chartered S&Ls.

In addition to the Case Commission bill, I introduced a second bill that would require companies that insure deposits to buy reinsurance— a new way of laying off risk—if they have any single risk greater than 10 percent of their assets. Documents from Security showed that it was insuring $38 million worth of deposits but had only a little more than $1 million in assets. The House amended the bill to give Security two

17. Henry L. Trewhitt, "Case Charges 'Tampering' on Loan Bill; Protests Amendments in House; Future of Plan Jeopardized," *Baltimore Sun*, March 9, 1961.

18. Ibid.

years to comply. Boone, Culver, and Staten all worked behind the scenes to try to kill the bill but in the end excused themselves from voting as the House passed it, 110–1.

Boone was particularly angry, rising to speak "on personal privilege."[19]

"The time has come to talk of many things, of shoes and ships and cabbages and kings," he said, borrowing from Lewis Carroll. "What has occurred is a direct insult to the House of Delegates and more particularly to the chairman of the subcommittee [Mandel]." Boone went on to say that Case had "overstepped his bounds" and warned that he "had better watch his step in the future. Commissions are appointed, not anointed." At Boone's suggestion, almost the entire House of Delegates stood and applauded Mandel.[20]

But those of us who had been working so hard on this issue not only had the last word but got the satisfaction of victory. I defended Case on the floor of the House and said I resented anyone attacking him, adding that he had done a "masterful job" with the bill. I was quoted in the newspapers as saying that the Case Commission bill, combined with my bill limiting the risk that insurers could take, "serves notice that Maryland is no longer the happy hunting ground of financial speculators and operators determined to make a quick killing at public expense."[21]

In the process, however, I had made some powerful enemies who would go out of their way to try to stop me from making my next career move.

19. Boone quoted in Laurence Stern, "Enactment Today Seen on Loan Bill," *Washington Post*, March 10, 1961.

20. Ibid.

21. Tydings quoted in Trewhitt, "Case Charges 'Tampering' on Loan Bill; Protests Amendments in House; Future of Plan Jeopardized.".

CHAPTER 6

Kennedy Man

I first became tagged as a "Kennedy man" shortly after two other long-time Kennedy men from Massachusetts, Larry O'Brien and Torby Mac-donald, showed up in Annapolis in February 1960. It was the middle of the thirty-day General Assembly session, and I was in my sixth year in the House of Delegates.

Torbert H. "Torby" Macdonald, a Massachusetts congressional representative since 1954, had been John F. Kennedy's roommate at Harvard, usher at his wedding, fellow PT boat commander in the South Pacific, and close personal friend. Lawrence F. "Larry" O'Brien Jr., who with Kennedy aides Dave Powers and Kenneth O'Donnell would become known as JFK's "Irish Mafia," had directed Kennedy's successful Senate campaigns in Massachusetts in 1952 and 1958 and would begin to organize and direct his national presidential campaign later that year.

In the cold winter of 1960, O'Brien and Macdonald were trolling the political streams of the Maryland General Assembly hoping to catch some supporters for their progressive young candidate from New England. They knew this effort might be a challenge. Maryland was south of the Mason-Dixon line and conservative in political outlook and tradition. Yet, I knew that within the state there were a number of politically active constituencies, especially Catholics, who would find Kennedy an attractive candidate.

Gov. J. Millard Tawes, from the rural oyster and crabbing community of Crisfield on the lower Eastern Shore of Maryland, was quietly backing the candidacy of Lyndon B. Johnson of Texas, the Senate majority leader. In a face-to-face meeting with JFK, Tawes did what he could to dissuade Kennedy from running in the presidential primary in Maryland.[1]

---

1. Maryland was one of only thirteen states holding presidential primaries that year.

Kennedy, more challenged than dissuaded, dispatched Macdonald and O'Brien to Maryland. They passed word that they would like to meet with any state legislators who would be willing to support Kennedy. Six or eight of us younger, more progressive members volunteered.

I talked to my father about it first, as I always valued his political advice. Senator Kennedy was far more liberal than my father, and I didn't want to upset him. My father said, "That's fine. I won't embarrass you. You go ahead and do what you can do, and I will not get involved with another candidate."[2] Dad had chaired the Senate Armed Services Committee when Lyndon Johnson was a junior committee member, and he was not a Johnson fan.

Nominating Rules

Presidential primaries in 1960 were neither as widespread nor as important as they are today. The Democratic National Convention, which was to be held in Los Angeles later that summer, was to become one of the last "brokered" conventions. Since only about a dozen states held presidential primaries that year, the selection of delegates would be fought over and the nomination secured through deal-making in "smoke-filled rooms" prior to and at the convention.

Four years later, Lyndon Johnson would run unopposed at the 1964 Democratic convention, but four years after that the 1968 party convention imploded in ugly battles over Vietnam, civil rights, and other contentious issues. Johnson's vice president, Hubert Humphrey, who had not participated in any party primaries, won the nomination. Opponents of the war, African Americans, and those who backed other candidates felt their voices had been shut out and demanded that nominating rules be reformed. They set up a commission that recommended sweeping changes in how presidential nominees would be selected, beginning

2. Quote recalled in Joseph D. Tydings, transcript of interview by Doug Washburn, June 30, 2013, 13–15, Harford Living Treasures Oral History Project, Harford County Public Library, Belcamp, MD.

with the 1972 election.[3] Those changes resulted in a proliferation of party primaries and caucuses in the states.

These days, the identity of party nominees—Democratic and Republican alike—is known well before convention delegates take their seats. Conventions now are almost devoid of drama or uncertainty. They are more like coronations or political "infomercials."

Elections have drastically changed in other ways since 1960. Unlike modern campaign staffs that plan electoral strategies a year or more before voting gets under way, the Kennedy team did not begin organizing in Maryland until just three months before the May presidential primary. Kennedy's name was on the primary ballot in only ten states that year, and he campaigned in only a handful of them.

The follow-up came about a week after the legislative session ended. I was working at our small family law firm, Tydings & Rosenberg, when I got a call from Eddie Morris, my friend Frank Gallagher's uncle and a prominent Catholic layperson and businessman. Eddie asked me to come down to the Emerson Hotel in Baltimore to meet Joseph A. Curnane, a Kennedy political lieutenant who had been sent down from Boston to oversee the Maryland primary campaign.[4] Kennedy was campaigning against Humphrey in Wisconsin, and then both candidates were headed to West Virginia, which was going to be a key test of whether a Catholic

3. The Commission on Party Structure and Delegate Selection was chaired by Senator George McGovern of South Dakota and Representative Donald M. Fraser of Minnesota. It produced rules that broadened participation in the candidate selection process. Among the changes: state party organizations were required to develop written rules to govern delegate selection as a way of keeping party leaders from manipulating the delegate selection process; the number of ex-officio delegates was limited, again designed to lessen the power of party leaders; delegates could not be chosen before the election year, to protect them from being controlled by party leaders; and the so-called "unit rule," which allowed the top vote getters in a state primary or caucus to win all of the delegates in that state, was changed to give minority groups more of a chance to become delegates and have their voices heard. Many of these rules were modified in later years, but they began the sharp and steady increase in the number of states holding presidential primaries or party caucuses. Steven S. Smith and Melanie J. Spring, "Choosing Presidential Candidates," in *Reforming the Presidential Nomination Process*, ed. Steven S. Smith and Melanie J. Spring (Washington, DC: Brookings Institution, 2009), https://www.brookings.edu/wp-content/uploads/2016/07/reformingthepresidentialnominationprocess_chapter.pdf.

4. Joe Curnane and I got along very well once he got over the fact that my family did not have the resources to make major campaign contributions. The best Ginny and I could afford was $250 from each of us. No member of the Kennedy family ever questioned me or mentioned a campaign contribution.

candidate could win in an overwhelmingly Protestant state. The Maryland primary was to be held a week after the one in West Virginia.

Curnane said he needed an attorney to file the official papers so Kennedy could be a candidate in Maryland. I said, "Certainly, I'll be the attorney. I'll get everything filed. Get it done tomorrow and make certain everything is clean and spic and span."[5]

Two days later, they called me again. "Well," they said, "we need a political agent now." The political agent is the person who signs all required campaign filings and whose name appears on all campaign advertisements, pamphlets, and other materials. I said, "Sure, I'll be the political agent." That meant that on every piece of campaign literature would be the words, "John F. Kennedy for President by authority of Joseph D. Tydings, Political Agent."[6] Three weeks later, I was managing the Kennedy campaign in Maryland.

While I advised on the rest of the state, Curnane concentrated on Baltimore.[7] With only three months to go, I discovered that the Kennedy organization in Maryland was almost nonexistent. We were starting from scratch. We did not have a single political or organizational endorsement. There were no congressional district chairs, no county chairs, no district chairs for Baltimore city, no women's chair, no veterans' committee, not even an organization of Catholic groups. They had not decided if or when JFK or his family would come to Maryland to campaign.

Our first task was to organize the state, but for that I had a head start. Beginning in 1950, I had helped activate Young Democrats clubs

5. Tydings interview transcript by Washburn, 16–17.

6. Ibid., 16.

7. Curnane summoned the bosses of the various political fiefdoms in the city—what he later described as "the worst bucket of political tripe anybody could inherit . . . all these people running their own little strongholds." Included were James H. Pollack, Irvin Kovens, Patrick F. O'Malley, Joseph M. Wyatt, William L. Hodges, Thomas D'Alesandro, Philip Goodman, and Harold Grady. Years later Curnane recalled addressing the group, many of whom were political enemies of each other: "Look, gentlemen," he said. "My name is Joe Curnane and I'm down from Boston. Now do you think it is possible for you bunch of bastards to put down your guns and your knives at least long enough for us to proceed?" There was silence, until Tommy D'Alesandro started to laugh, and they all joined in. "D'Alesandro put his arm around me and he said, 'I like you, Joe. We'll work with you.'" Joseph A. Curnane, transcript of recorded interview by John F. Stewart, November 29, 1966, 62–63, John F. Kennedy Oral History Collection, John F. Kennedy Presidential Library and Museum, Boston, MA.

all over Maryland. I also had assisted in my father's final, illness-shortened Senate campaign in 1956, so I knew the players and the political landscape in Maryland. By 1960, I had built a strong statewide network.

But our lack of preparedness entering that campaign was pretty disconcerting because it seemed to me that Maryland could be a really important place for Kennedy to rebound following his probable loss in West Virginia. I was certain—as were almost all informed, active Democratic officeholders nationwide—that he was going to lose in West Virginia, a state where only 5 percent of the population was Catholic.

But Kennedy shocked us—and most of the country—by winning big in West Virginia with 61 percent of the vote to Humphrey's 39 percent. He had managed to turn the West Virginia primary into a referendum on religious tolerance, and the strategy paid off.[8] He suddenly became not only a viable Democratic candidate for the presidency but possibly the front-runner.

I arranged for him to kick off his Maryland campaign the night of May 12 with a speech at Washington College in Chestertown because I was worried about his chances on the conservative Eastern Shore. I felt we'd do well in Baltimore and the Washington suburbs and possibly elsewhere, but the Eastern Shore would be tough.

The West Virginia victory changed everything. To my surprise, it suddenly seemed like every politician in the state wanted to be seen with Kennedy, including many who had resisted his candidacy. Everybody wanted their picture with him. That night I realized just how sharp and knowledgeable JFK really was. For the previous ten weeks, I had regularly traveled to Washington to meet with his brother Bobby, as well as with O'Brien and others. I was always seeking campaign resources and dates for family members and the candidate himself to be in Maryland, as well as generally reporting on the organizational progress in our state. I was surprised and flattered that on almost every trip, Senator Kennedy met with me alone to better understand what was going on in Maryland. He already knew many top state leaders personally, but by the time my briefings were concluded he knew precisely who was helping and who was sitting on the fence.

---

8. Theodore H. White, *The Making of the President, 1960* (New York: Atheneum, 1961), 109.

That night in Chestertown, all of the fence-sitters lined up to ask for a photo with Kennedy. I was just a few feet away as they paraded by for their minute with the candidate, and often Kennedy would catch my eye, smile, and wink. He knew exactly what was happening.

Could a Catholic Be Elected?

In Maryland and across the country, the burning question always just beneath the surface was if a Catholic could be elected president. In 1928, former New York Governor Al Smith became the first—and, until Kennedy, the last—Catholic to be a major party nominee for president. He lost by a landslide to Herbert Hoover, who won forty of the forty-eight states. Smith's defeat was attributed in large part to anti-Catholic prejudice.

In the intervening decades, the Catholic population in the United States had grown from about 16 percent when Smith ran to between 20 and 26 percent by the time JFK was a candidate.[9] No one knew in the spring of 1960 if those numbers could change the outcome, or if religious views or prejudices had changed. There were conspiratorial questions about whether a Catholic president would threaten the constitutional separation of church and state. Would a Catholic president be more beholden to the pope in Rome than to the American people? There were concerns about birth control, government financial aid to parochial schools, and other issues with religious overtones. In time, Jack Kennedy would forcefully address the Catholic question head on. But at this early stage, such issues were an ever-present shadow over the campaign.

After the Chestertown speech, Kennedy flew to DC for the night. He was up early Friday morning to hit the campaign trail in Hagerstown, despite suffering great pain in his back. Rather than accompany him, Bobby joined me, and the two of us campaigned for JFK in my home county of Harford. I later caught up with Senator Kennedy for about seven more hours of nonstop campaigning in Baltimore, Baltimore County, and Anne Arundel County. We planned to finish that long day at Oakington before campaigning Saturday on the Eastern Shore and

9. Ibid., 238.

in southern Maryland, but by that Friday night we were famished and Torby Macdonald suggested we stop to get a bite to eat in Baltimore.

I picked a restaurant, which at that late hour was pretty empty. It was Friday and Kennedy was Catholic, so he ordered fish, but the restaurant was out of good fish dishes. Torby, impatient, said, "Come on, Jack, for Chrissake," and Kennedy relented and ordered a steak. No sooner had we ordered than a big family—grandmother, parents, kids—whom we had not noticed, stood up to leave. They spotted Kennedy and began waving and cheering. I was almost certain they were Irish-Catholic Democrats. Without missing a beat, Kennedy leaned over to Macdonald and said, "Torby, get out in that kitchen and tell them don't bring those steaks back until the coast is clear!"[10]

It was late when we finally got home to Oakington. Torby and Kennedy slept in the "big house," where my mother still lived. We were all up at daybreak to set out again, beginning in Havre de Grace and then driving across the Susquehanna to Cecil County, where Kennedy spoke to a crowd in front of the courthouse in Elkton. From there, we repeated the act on county courthouse lawns all the way down the Eastern Shore.

We had to make two thirty-minute layovers in Easton and Salisbury so Kennedy could stretch out on a bed and relieve the omnipresent pain in his back. He used that time to call Democratic political leaders, particularly Catholic leaders, asking for their support at the Democratic National Convention in Los Angeles in July.

Around 3:00 p.m., we boarded the *Caroline*, the Kennedy family plane, at Salisbury and flew across the bay to spend the afternoon and early evening in southern Maryland before driving our candidate back to Baltimore for two final speeches, a television appearance, and an 11:30 p.m. flight to Oregon, his last primary. As we were riding through the Washington suburb of Prince George's County, Kennedy asked, "How bad is this Catholic thing going to hurt me here?" To put his mind at ease, I quickly replied, "Senator Kennedy, every Marylander in this car is a member of the Ancient, Free and Accepted Masons," a fraternal organization viewed as anti-Catholic by the Catholic Church and many rank-and-file Catholics. "That ought to tell you something."[11]

10. Tydings interview transcript by Washburn, 20–21.

11. Ibid., 22–23.

Kennedy received 200,454 votes, more than any other candidate in the history of Maryland presidential primaries up to that point. Oregon Senator Wayne Morse finished second, with 49,323 votes.[12]

The Delaware and Florida Primaries

Bobby Kennedy called me about a week after the Maryland primary to say the campaign wanted me to go to Delaware to help line up a slate of Kennedy delegates at the Democratic Party convention in that state on May 26. I was somewhat familiar with Delaware, which is just a short drive from Oakington. My wife's family, the Campbells, lived in Delaware, and I had a law school classmate who was a delegate to that convention. The mayor of Wilmington and various Catholic groups were backing Kennedy, so I felt our chances there were at least 50–50.

Each of the three counties in Delaware was supporting a different candidate. Southernmost Sussex County, the most rural and conservative, backed Missouri Senator Stuart Symington, whose campaign was almost solely focused on national defense. Kent, the middle county, was backing Johnson.[13] The more urban and liberal New Castle County and the biggest city in the state, Wilmington, were for Kennedy.

I spent most of my time meeting with delegates to the convention and assessing who was for whom and whose vote could be shifted to the Kennedy column. On a weekly and sometimes daily basis, I communicated this intelligence to Bobby Kennedy, Kennedy aides Ted Sorenson and Steve Smith, Kennedy secretary Evelyn Lincoln, and even to Senator Kennedy himself. As they headed to the national convention in California in July, the Delaware count was this: one delegate vote committed to Johnson, one to Symington, three still on the fence, and seven for Kennedy. But that would change.

In late May, the campaign needed help in Florida.

The situation in Florida was much more difficult than in Delaware. Delegates had already decided that on the first ballot at the convention they were going to support their "favorite son" candidate, US Senator

12. Charles G. Whiteford, "State Camp of Kennedy Is Jubilant; Latest Totals Give Senator 200,454 Votes in Primary," *Baltimore Sun*, May 19, 1960.

13. Lyndon Johnson, personally conflicted about whether to jump into the race, did not formally announce his candidacy until July 5, five days before the Democrats would convene in Los Angeles to nominate their candidate.

George Smathers. They thought that would give them greater bargaining leverage in the second or any subsequent ballots. If they didn't like a candidate's position on an issue—say, civil rights—they might be in a position to influence a change or wrangle a promise or concession from a future president.

This was not my first national party convention nor my first exposure to a "favorite son" candidate. In 1940, at age twelve, I had joined my father, mother, and grandfather aboard a special Tydings for President train to the Democratic convention in Chicago. Like Smathers in Florida in 1960, my father was the favorite son candidate from Maryland in 1940. The train was bedecked with banners and loaded with Marylanders, singing and shouting "Tydings for President."[14] Franklin D. Roosevelt, of course, would be nominated for an unprecedented third term at that convention, but my father and the president were on the outs after my father opposed FDR's court-packing plan in 1937.

We have a great family photo of us all in Chicago for that convention, with my mother and me flanked by my grandfather and father, each of them wearing a three-piece suit and a stylish straw boater. I was attired in a smart double-breasted suit and tie, my blond hair neatly combed, a Maryland armband high around my left bicep, and a huge Tydings pin with ribbons on my lapel.

On June 11 and 12, a month before the 1960 convention, Florida Democrats convened in Orlando. Senator Kennedy couldn't go, so Bobby went, and he took me along.

It seemed likely that at least two-thirds of the Florida delegates would ultimately back Johnson, a fellow southerner with a long congressional record in support of the segregationist policies of the South. As if to underscore the position of the delegation on what in those days was often called the "Negro question," one of the first acts of the Florida convention was to nominate C. Farris Bryant for governor, a conservative who would not threaten the status quo.

Bobby, however, charmed the conventioneers in Orlando and used his quick wit to make friends. One of JFK's biggest supporters in Florida, a two-time gubernatorial aspirant and reformer named J. Brailey

14. Eleanor Davies Tydings Ditzen, *My Golden Spoon* (Lanham, MD: Madison Books, 1997), 202–3.

Odham, paid out of his pocket for a breakfast and a dinner for the delegates so Bobby could get his message across before they arrived in Los Angeles. Thirty-one of the forty-two came. Bobby and I worked until 1:30 in the morning buttonholing delegates and pressing for votes for Jack. We went to a local eatery in the wee hours of Sunday morning, but Bobby was up early several hours later to attend mass.[15]

Bobby wowed them when he spoke that day, recounting Jack's primary election victories and how he had beaten the "redoubtable" Republican Henry Cabot Lodge for senator back in 1952. Afterward many conceded that Kennedy would get some share of the Florida vote after the first ballot went to Smathers. Said one local newspaper columnist the day after Bobby's talk, "His smile and his logical brain were hitting on all eight cylinders and I don't know of anything a brother could have done, in addition to what he did, to help a brother."[16]

The National Convention in Los Angeles

The outcome of the 1960 convention was by no means certain.

The various campaigns—Kennedy, Johnson, Humphrey, Symington, and even two-time presidential candidate Adlai Stevenson of Illinois—arrived in Los Angeles still vying for every delegate vote and half-vote they could get.[17] Multiple ballots were a real possibility.

Stevenson was the opponent we worried most about because he and Kennedy were vying for the same liberal base. As long as Stevenson was an active candidate, he kept his delegates away from Kennedy. We knew if Kennedy were to win, he needed to do it on the first ballot. After that it would be dicey.

As I look back a half century later at the list of forty-eight delegates and twenty-three alternates (I was one of the alternates) from Maryland to the 1960 Democratic National Convention in Los Angeles, it is

15. Henry Balch, "Hush Puppies," *Orlando Sentinel,* June 13, 1960, clipping from the file Florida: Delegates, May 27–July 9, 1960, and undated, in Presidential Campaign Files, 1960, Pre-Presidential Papers of John F. Kennedy, Kennedy Presidential Library and Museum, Boston, MA.

16. Ibid.

17. I knew Adlai Stevenson because he was a personal friend of our family. He spent about five days with us at Oakington over Thanksgiving following his 1952 defeat by Dwight Eisenhower. He loved to shoot, and we took him hunting.

an astonishing collection of men and women—but mostly men—who would make names for themselves, both good and bad, in Maryland in the years to come.

In addition to Governor Tawes, among the delegates were at least four future candidates for governor (Thomas B. Finan, George P. Mahoney, Blair Lee III, and David Hume), none of whom would be successful; three mayors of Baltimore (J. Harold Grady, Philip H. Goodman, and Thomas D'Alesandro); Democratic National Committee member Michael J. Birmingham, who would try to prevent me from becoming US attorney; at least two future Speakers of the Maryland House of Delegates, one of whom (A. Gordon Boone) I would later prosecute for savings and loan fraud; the state comptroller, Louis L. Goldstein, who would become my opponent in the 1964 Democratic primary for the US Senate; an array of Baltimore political bosses—Irvin Kovens, James Pollack, Patrick O'Malley, and Joseph Wyatt; George Hocker, the beer lobbyist who became Governor Tawes's principal political adviser; Rep. Daniel Brewster, with whom I would later serve in the US Senate; Edward S. Northrop, a state senator who would become a federal judge before whom I would later argue cases; Sam Hoffberger, father of my political patron Jerry Hoffberger; and even Ernest Cory, a young lawyer who would later unfortunately get mixed up in an unseemly racetrack deal that would send Maryland Governor Marvin Mandel, Kovens, and four others to prison. (Cory's eighteen-month sentence was suspended.) It was quite a group.

In Los Angeles, I was named coordinator for Delaware and Florida and was expected to keep track of delegate votes. Maryland was bound by law to support Kennedy, at least on the first ballot, and we didn't want to let the voting go beyond one ballot.[18]

All of the Kennedy coordinators paid their own way for transportation, hotel rooms, and meals. We were spread across the city because the delegations were assigned to various hotels around Los Angeles.[19] I was lucky: both the Delaware and Florida delegations were lodged at the eleven-story Biltmore Hotel, which also was home to the Kennedy

18. The last time that had happened had been 1952, when Stevenson finally nailed down the nomination on the third ballot.

19. Tydings interview transcript by Washburn, 25.

headquarters, the headquarters of all the other major candidates except Stevenson, the Democratic National Committee, and all of the television networks.[20]

The coordinators were an integral part of the organization, helping to round up and count votes. We met every morning at 7:30 a.m. in Bobby's hotel suite, where each coordinator would report on the vote count in their delegation, what Senator Kennedy could do to line up more votes, who could speak to individual delegates, and so on. I remember one morning one of the coordinators got to our meeting about half an hour late and Bobby chewed him out. "If you can't be here on time, then we don't need you. We'll get somebody else," he said. That's how serious things were.[21]

Here is how the veteran journalist Theodore H. White described the Kennedy campaign coordinator operation in Suite 8315 in his book *The Making of the President, 1960:*

> Control as exercised from 8315 was precise, taut, disciplined—
> yet as casual as that of a veteran combat army, bloodied in bat-
> tle, which has learned to know all its own component parts and
> recognizes the full reach of its skills and courage. The combat-
> proved Kennedy area commanders of the spring primary wars
> had all arrived in Los Angeles on the Saturday before the con-
> vention. To their forces had been added almost a score of young
> men from the Massachusetts delegation, handpicked the previ-
> ous spring by the Kennedy organization for style, poise, political
> savvy, and for the precise purpose of operating on the Conven-
> tion floor, as now they were supposed to do. In all, some 40 del-
> egate-shepherds were assigned each to a particular state delega-
> tion that was theirs to cultivate; each was given packets of name
> cards listing the assigned state delegates by name, profession,
> hobby, children, wife, peculiarity, religion, and sent out to oper-
> ate. They were instructed, as they found shifts in any delegation,

20. Joseph D. Tydings, memo to John F. Kennedy and Robert F. Kennedy regarding recent (June 11–12, 1960) Florida Democratic Convention, June 14, 1960, from the file Florida: Delegates, May 27–July 9, 1960, and undated, in Presidential Campaign Files, 1960, Pre-Presidential Papers of John F. Kennedy.

21. Tydings interview transcript by Washburn, 25–26.

to report such changes to a private tabulating headquarters in Room 3308 at the Biltmore; and there, every hour on the hour from Friday through balloting day, a new fresh total, accurate to the hour, was to be prepared. For five days, the shepherds were told, they were not to sleep, see their wives, relax, frolic or be out of touch with 8315. Each morning, for the five Convention days from Saturday to the Wednesday balloting, they were to gather in room 8315 for a staff survey [at 7:30 a.m.], then disperse to their tasks.[22]

The night before the actual voting started, I went to a meeting of the twenty-two delegates from Delaware, each of whom held a half vote.[23] At the time, the eleven total convention votes of Delaware were evenly split, with five and a half aligned with Kennedy and the other five and a half with Johnson. But the Kennedy delegates were confident that a majority of the delegation was actually in the Kennedy camp. With that in mind, I persuaded the full delegation to hold a secret ballot and then cast all eleven of the votes it had for whichever of the two candidates won. My thinking was that the eleven votes of tiny Delaware would be more meaningful to the overall vote in a close convention ballot if they were all cast for a single candidate rather than split up in single digits for Kennedy and Johnson, or perhaps Symington and Stevenson.

I happened to know that one of the delegates being counted as a Johnson man was really strongly for Kennedy. Robert D. "Buzz" Thompson Jr., a young attorney from Georgetown, Delaware, was a friend and former classmate at the University of Maryland.[24] He quietly told me that when it went to a secret ballot, he would switch his vote to Kennedy, who would then win the entire delegation. That sounded good to me, and, without checking with anybody, I told him to go ahead.

Well, when the secret ballot was over, somehow Johnson ended up with six votes and Kennedy only had four and a half (the other half-vote was cast for Symington by a delegate who later confessed she meant for

22. White, *Making of the President*, 157.

23. "State Democrats Select Delegates to Convention," *Wilmington (DE) Journal*, May 26, 1960.

24. In later life, Thompson would become a circuit court judge in Sussex County, Delaware.

it to go to Stevenson).[25] I am sure Buzz's half-vote was among the four and a half for Kennedy, which meant that two of our other Kennedy half-votes had unexpectedly switched to Johnson. This was considered an upset victory for the conservative delegates from the middle and southern parts of the state. "My God," I exclaimed in horror.

I grabbed a telephone and immediately called Bobby and said, "I have really screwed up." I explained what I had done and how terribly I felt. Bobby listened and then calmly said, "Well, learn by it in the future." He said the one thing I had done right was to call him immediately because he felt the Kennedy camp could adjust to the situation. But I was mortified.

"The vote was a shocker," exclaimed the *Wilmington Morning News* political columnist Bill Frank.[26] If there was ever a time when I deserved to have someone climb all over me, that was it, but Bobby just told me to learn to be more cautious the next time.[27]

Of course, the next night John F. Kennedy won the Democratic presidential nomination on the first ballot despite the fact that the eleven Delaware votes went to Johnson and the twenty-nine Florida votes went to Smathers (JFK won all twenty-four of the Maryland votes).[28]

In a surprise move, the day after that Kennedy picked the Texan Lyndon Johnson to be his running mate.

The General Election

After the convention, Bobby called to tell me he wanted me to be responsible for Delaware and Florida in the general election and to report back to him. It is a good thing I'm a self-starter because the direction I got from the Kennedy camp, at least at first, was pretty general. What they wanted was information and advice from a trusted, objective observer not involved in the politics of that state. They told me to go to Florida and

25. Cy Liberman, "State's 11 Votes Go to Johnson under Unit Rule," *Wilmington (DE) Morning News*, July 14, 1960, 1.

26. Bill Frank, "Lesson in Politics," *Wilmington (DE) Morning News*, July 14, 1960, 22.

27. Tydings interview transcript by Washburn, 26–28.

28. John F. Kennedy Fast Facts: First Ballot for Presidential Nominees, Kennedy Presidential Library and Museum, http://www.jfklibrary.org/Research/Research-Aids/Ready-Reference/JFK-Fast-Facts/Tabulation-of-Ballot-1960.aspx?view=print.

Delaware and tell them how they were doing, how the Democrats were organized, and what I thought of the operation and what should be done.

That the Kennedy campaign would place a Marylander in the middle of political campaigns in Delaware and Florida was no accident. All over the country, O'Brien systematically sent outside coordinators into states because he felt they could better referee disputes.[29]

In Florida, I just started meeting everyone I could. Doors seemed to open easily for me, perhaps because my name was Tydings and—at least in Jacksonville—because I got help from my close personal friend and business colleague Raymond Mason. The first thing I did was to meet with Governor LeRoy Collins, who by Florida standards was generally considered a liberal. I spent a couple days with him getting briefed on Florida politics.

Then, to get the conservative view, I met with Farris Bryant, who had been nominated to succeed Collins. I met with Representative Dante Fascell of Florida and the mayor of Miami, as well as state party leaders and just about anybody else who could help me understand the state and the relevant issues there.

As with any state, there were, of course, politically explosive local issues, but the big issues in Florida—and in Delaware and, to a lesser extent, in Maryland—were race and religion.

We couldn't have been as successful as we were in that 1960 campaign had it not been for the various volunteer Citizens for Kennedy groups that we helped form in each state. This important element of the Kennedy-Johnson campaign was headed by Byron "Whizzer" White.[30] These groups were usually made up of liberals who worked for JFK and were independent of the state party organization. In addition to the main Citizens for Kennedy groups, there were Youth for Kennedy, Senior Citizens for Kennedy, Farmers for Kennedy, and similar groups. Of course there were also various Catholic groups for Kennedy.[31]

29. White, *Making of the President*, 249.

30. White had been an All-American football star at the University of Colorado, served as an intelligence officer during World War II, graduated magna cum laude from Yale Law School, became deputy attorney general in the Kennedy administration, and, in 1962, was appointed by JFK to the Supreme Court, where he served until 1993.

31. In Delaware, Citizens for Kennedy was led by Alexis duPont Bayard, a member of the prominent duPont family in that state. Joseph D. Tydings, undated post-1960 general election confidential memo to John F. Kennedy, Robert F. Kennedy, and Larry O'Brien regarding

Richard Nixon, meanwhile, was up to his old (that is to say, dirty) tricks. Reprising a tactic he had used to great effect in his 1946 congressional campaign in California against Helen Gahagen Douglas, the Republican camp in Florida tried to link Kennedy to the Communist Party. At a time when Soviet Premier Nikita Khrushchev was frequently referred to in newspaper headlines as "Mr. K," the Nixon camp began distributing cards—intentionally and provocatively colored red—to Florida voters that said, "One Mr. K. Is Enough—Vote Republican."[32]

At the end of August, Bobby sent a memo to all state coordinators requiring a weekly written report, "submitted in duplicate," with one copy going to him and the other to O'Brien. We were to alert headquarters of our whereabouts at all times. Another memo a day later said the campaign was facing "severe financial limitations" and would therefore be charging for campaign materials: $7.55 for a box of one-inch Kennedy or Kennedy-Johnson buttons, $35 for a box of three-color Kennedy bumper stickers, and so on. If the state needed them, then we had to raise the money locally and send a check to the national headquarters for the materials.

Kennedy's first televised debate with Nixon that fall gave us a tremendous boost.[33] It made viewers realize that Senator Kennedy was clearly qualified to be president. As Theodore White points out, only 11 percent of Americans had televisions in 1950, but by 1960 that number had climbed to 88 percent. Plus, compared with Nixon, the photogenic Kennedy seemed a master of this suddenly indispensable political medium.[34]

personnel in Delaware, Joseph D. Tydings Collection, Hornbake Library, University of Maryland, College Park.

32. Nathan Miller, "Questionable GOP Tactics in Florida Charted Here," *Baltimore Sun*, undated clipping, Tydings Collection, Hornbake Library. Republicans like Nixon typically expressed concerns about the Soviet Union because, among other things, the founding principle of the state was communism. The hawkish GOP stance toward the Soviet Union continued for decades during the Cold War and for years afterward, right up until Donald Trump became president. That is why it is so peculiar, mystifying, and worrisome that President Trump has consistently voiced his high regard for Russia and the dictatorial leader of Russia, Vladimir Putin. It doesn't make any sense. Does Trump simply admire Putin because he is a strongman? Or, do Russians have something on Trump they could use to blackmail him? Or, is Trump merely trying to protect his private business dealings in Russia? Or, did Russia interfere with the 2016 US presidential election to help Trump win? None of these possible explanations is reassuring.

33. There were four debates, held September 26 and October 7, 13, and 21, 1960.

34. White, *Making of the President*, 279.

Still, we were getting little help from black voters, who should have been on our side.[35] I begged the campaign to send more "colored organizers."[36]

We knew we needed a big win in Dade County around Miami to offset certain losses in the Republican center of the state. As presidential elections are tight in Florida even today, we thought the vote would be close.[37] In an October 25 memo to campaign headquarters, I boldly (and wildly optimistically, as it turned out) predicted that "with TV and radio, we should carry Florida by a margin of around 20,000 to 30,000 votes."[38]

I thought the vote in Delaware also looked good for Kennedy, but close. Crowds of thirty thousand to thirty-five thousand turned out for JFK's visit, compared to crowds of eight thousand to nine thousand for Nixon's. "My own estimate is that we will carry Delaware by under 5,000 votes," I predicted.[39]

John F. Kennedy, of course, was elected president in 1960, but it was the closest national election since 1916. Kennedy received 34,220,984 votes to Nixon's 34,108,157, an 112,827-vote margin of victory out of more than 68 million votes cast.

The votes of African Americans and Catholics proved pivotal to

35. The Democratic National Committee had circulated a tabloid entitled *A Leader Like Roosevelt—Kennedy for President*, which contained ten pictures of JFK with various prominent African Americans and which set out his civil rights positions. Kennedy, it said, supports "the right of every American to live in a decent home in a neighborhood of his choice [and] the right of every American to have equal access to the voting booth." *A Leader Like Roosevelt—Kennedy for President*, undated Democratic National Committee campaign newspaper on Kennedy and civil rights issues, Tydings Collection, Hornbake Library.

36. The other issue that was hurting us was a pro-union plank in the Democratic Party platform that called for repeal of right-to-work laws. Right-to-work laws are designed to make it difficult, if not impossible, for labor unions to successfully organize in most states. Martin Anderson, the owner-publisher of two Orlando newspapers, was "crucifying us with cartoons and editorials everyday" on the issue, and I suggested that they get Lyndon Johnson to call his "old friend" and ask him to ease up on us. Joseph D. Tydings to John F. Kennedy, Robert F. Kennedy, and Larry O'Brien, memo dated October 5, 1960, regarding the status of the Kennedy campaign in Florida, Tydings Collection, Hornbake Library.

37. By the end of October, both LBJ and JFK had campaigned in the state. Most of the Florida congressional delegation was now in our camp. Ethel Kennedy and Jean Kennedy Smith held successful Teas for Kennedy over the course of two days in six cities across the state. (In Jacksonville, they stayed with my friend Raymond Mason.)

38. Joseph D. Tydings to Robert F. Kennedy and Larry O'Brien, memo regarding the general election in Florida, October 25, 1960, Tydings Collection, Hornbake Library.

39. Ibid.

Kennedy's victory. African Americans, who had been skeptical of Kennedy when the campaign began, shifted strongly in his favor after he and Bobby intervened on behalf of the civil rights leader, the Reverend Martin Luther King Jr., following his arrest in Georgia. In the end, as many as 70 percent of black voters went for Kennedy, tipping the outcome in his favor in at least eleven states.[40]

Although Catholics had voted consistently with the Democrats since the big wave of Irish immigration began in the 1850s, an estimated 78 percent voted for Kennedy in 1960.[41]

In Maryland, Kennedy rolled up 559,746 votes, slightly more than the Republican Dwight D. Eisenhower had won in Maryland just four years earlier. Kennedy also won in Delaware but, alas, lost in Florida despite a 48,000-vote margin in Dade County. As we feared, we were routed in Republican central Florida.

I spent the next couple of weeks sending confidential wrap-up memos to JFK, Bobby, and O'Brien that told them who had worked the hardest for them in the Florida and Delaware campaigns and who I felt should be rewarded with positions in the administration. I'm sure other state coordinators were doing the same thing.

Almost immediately I was asked to be one of only six marshals at the Kennedy inaugural parade, meaning I was assigned a car and chauffeur and a military aide with instructions to "lead Division No. II in the parade."[42]

"The attire for the affair is formal morning attire, this being cutaway coat, stripe pants, silk high top hat, turn down collar (white), four-in-hand tie (black and white stripe), black leather shoes, black overcoat, grey double breast vest and grey gloves," I was directed in a letter from the co-chair of the parade committee.[43]

Everybody was riding high when we won. There was no doubt I had truly become a "Kennedy man."

40. White, *Making of the President*, 354. The eleven states were, Illinois, New Jersey, Michigan, South Carolina, Texas, Delaware, Maryland, Missouri, North Carolina, Pennsylvania, and Nevada.

41. White, *Making of the President*, 355.

42. F. Joseph Donohue, co-chair, Inaugural Parade Committee 1961, to Joseph Tydings, January 11, 1961, letter in possession of Senator Tydings.

43. Ibid.

CHAPTER 7

A Prosecutor the Organization Didn't Want

By early 1961, I had worn out my welcome with the Democratic leadership in the Maryland General Assembly. The prevailing culture in Annapolis, as in most legislatures, is for junior members to be seen and not heard, to avoid making waves, and to obediently follow the lead of their elders. I respected legislative tradition, but I was determined to be my own man, just as my father had been.

Over my seven-year tenure in the House, the positions I took on civil rights, reapportionment, slot machine gambling, and other issues were often at odds with the legislative bosses. And my efforts to regulate the savings and loan industry, of course, did not help because S&L operators were padding the pocketbooks of the majority leader of the House of Delegates and other top Democratic politicians.

I may have been a Democrat with an inherited pedigree in state party politics, but by my second term in the House of Delegates I was persona non grata with the majority of Democrats who controlled the legislature and the state. I knew they would be delighted to see the last of me.

Yet, while they wanted me gone, they wanted me to go anywhere but to the one job that I had my eye on: US attorney for Maryland. The thought that I would become a federal prosecutor simply scared the hell out of some powerful leaders of the entrenched Democratic organization in Maryland.

After JFK's election, I knew that as "one of Kennedy's young men" I was in line for a federal post, if I wanted one. But I wasn't sure at first which one I wanted. For advice, I turned to a politically savvy friend, the relatively new US senator from Washington State, Henry M. "Scoop" Jackson. I had met Scoop back in 1953, when he was the Young Democrats' Jackson Day speaker.

Scoop and I had become fast friends. He frequently came up to Oak-ington on weekends and even once dated Ginny's attractive twin sister, Mary. Scoop was crazy about "Twinny" (as I called her), although he was then in his mid-forties and about twice her age.

Scoop knew my long-range ambition was to follow in my father's footsteps and one day be elected to the US Senate, but as an intermedi-ate step I wanted to make my name as a trial lawyer. Before being elected to Congress, Scoop had been a county prosecutor in Washington State, and he suggested I ask the Kennedys to make me the US attorney for Maryland. He said there was no better way to get broad trial experience, and, if I did a top-rate job, it could improve my qualifications for higher office.

So when Bobby Kennedy asked me if I wanted to come to Wash-ington in a sub-Cabinet post or to take a position overseas, I declined and told him I wanted to be US attorney. He was surprised. I asked if he needed me to send him letters of recommendation, which at the time I thought would have been easy to obtain, but he said, "No, no, no, that's not necessary." But later, as opposition to my appointment built during the increasingly tense 1961 legislative session, I regretted not having done so.

News of my possible move first surfaced publicly within a week of JFK's inauguration.[1] From my perspective, the timing could not have been much worse. I was then in the heat of the bitter legislative battle over my efforts to regulate S&Ls. I feared the spotlight on my personal career could undermine that effort and shift attention away from the political corruption scandal that was steadily being revealed in the newspapers.

Opposition to my appointment began surreptitiously at the national level. All six Democrats in the Maryland congressional delegation, accompanied by Michael J. Birmingham, the Democratic National Com-mittee (DNC) member for Maryland, secretly traveled to Connecticut to meet with John Bailey, the new chair of the DNC. They delivered a definitive message: the president could appoint Joe Tydings to any posi-tion in Washington or overseas with their support, but he was person-ally unacceptable to be named US attorney for Maryland. They further

---

1. John F. Kennedy was inaugurated as the thirty-fifth president on January 20, 1961.

agreed that all Kennedy administration appointments in Maryland should first be cleared by a group that was to include Governor Tawes; Tom Finan, then chair of the state Democratic Party; Birmingham; and the six Democratic congressional representatives from Maryland. Birmingham, who was known as "Iron Mike," was, of course, one of the officers of the Security Financial Insurance Corporation. The others in this group were part of the Maryland governing cabal, some of them close to Boone, Mandel, Staten, or others whose hands were deep in the S&L mess. Security was at the center of the corruption scandal I was exposing in the legislature.[2]

The legislature was in about the third week of the ninety-day session when suddenly, on a Sunday evening, Bobby Kennedy telephoned me to say he had been getting blowback from the Democratic National Committee, the Maryland congressional representatives, and others.

"Jesus Christ, Joe, don't you have a single friend in Maryland?" was the way the exasperated Kennedy opened the conversation.

I explained to Bobby the situation in Annapolis and why the opposition to my appointment was so intense. He said he understood, but told me, "You've got to get at least one congressman to say you are not 'personally objectionable.'"

Five days after JFK's inauguration, Bailey, the national Democratic Party chair, came to the governor's mansion in Annapolis to meet with the entire anti-Tydings group plus George Hocker, the governor's political adviser. Almost to a man, they agreed that the next US attorney for Maryland should be someone from Baltimore, which, of course, would rule me out. Even Thomas F. Johnson, who represented the rural Eastern Shore in Congress, said he thought the next prosecutor should be from Baltimore. Each proposed his own Baltimore candidate, but the favorite appeared to be Herbert R. O'Conor Jr., son and namesake of the late senator and governor.[3]

Within days, I got wind of this meeting and went to see Governor Tawes, Birmingham, and Finan to ask them to tell Bobby Kennedy that I was qualified for the job. Tawes picked up the phone to call the

2. Drew Pearson, "Patronage Test over Tydings Hints Party Feud in Maryland," *Washington Post*, February 14, 1961.

3. Ibid.

president's brother, but Birmingham stopped him and reminded him of their agreement on how the organization was going to handle Kennedy administration patronage jobs.

After Birmingham and Finan left, however, Tawes called Bobby and put in a plug for me. Tawes and I had always gotten along, and I suspect that my Judiciary Committee chair, Lloyd Simpkins, who was friends with us both, may have put in a good word for me.

When Bailey heard what Tawes had done, he knew that stopping me would be more difficult "because all along Bobby has wanted Tydings." Birmingham and the Maryland congressional representatives were all incensed, saying they felt Tawes had double-crossed them.[4]

Others jumped in against me. Baltimore Mayor J. Harold Grady, who had come to office with the backing of the Irv Kovens political machine, which included Mandel, pushed for the federal prosecutor to be from Baltimore. My family's longtime antagonist, George Mahoney, joined with Grady to call Kennedy aide Larry O'Brien to lobby on O'Conor's behalf.[5]

Worried, I called Joe Curnane, the Kennedy lieutenant from Boston who had supervised the Kennedy primary campaign in Maryland, and asked what I should do. "There is only one person who can save you," he said, "and that is Robert Kennedy."

Maryland had seven congressional representatives in those days. Daniel B. Brewster was Gordon Boone's law partner, so he was not going to help. George H. Fallon, Edward Garmatz, and Richard Lankford were likely to go along with the state organization, as was Johnson. Charles McC. Mathias Jr., from western Maryland, was a friend, but he was a Republican and had no say in the matter.

My only possibility was Representative Samuel Friedel, whose largely Jewish district in Baltimore was also the home territory of Morris "Moose" Rosenberg, my partner in the new Tydings & Rosenberg law firm.[6] Through Moose, we got Friedel to say I was not "personally

4 Ibid.

5. James MacNees, "Tydings Seen Due as U.S. Attorney," *Baltimore Sun*, February 16, 1961.

6. When my stepfather, Lieutenant Colonel Millard Tydings, returned from fighting in World War I, he and a fellow officer from the 29th Division who lived in Bel Air, Maj. Bob Archer, formed the law firm of Tydings & Archer. Soon they were joined by Baltimore lawyer

objectionable." It was that close. I could get only one of the six Demo-crats to support me. We didn't even try the others because we would not have had a chance.

The vehement opposition to my appointment bothered the presi-dent. I've been told that he and his brother were discussing my possible appointment and JFK said something to the effect of "Bobby, we love Joe. He's just about a family member. We all like him. He's been with us. But you can't ask me to appoint him United States attorney when all the leading politicians in Maryland are against him."

To which Robert Francis Kennedy, by then the attorney general of the United States, is said to have replied to his brother, "Mr. President, that's why he's going to be our US attorney in Maryland." There is prob-ably no other attorney general who could have made such a statement to a president. It was my privilege to work for Robert Kennedy as US attorney, and there is simply no way I would have gotten that position if he hadn't stood up for me.

I formally resigned from the General Assembly on March 24, 1961.[7] I was sworn in as the US attorney for the District of Maryland on April 5 in an impressive ceremony in the principal courtroom of the federal courthouse in Baltimore. Federal Judges Roszel C. Thomsen, W. Calvin Chesnut, and R. Dorsey Watkins were all there. Leon Pierson, the man I was replacing, presented me with my presidential commission and used the moment to praise me for having "courage in advocating certain leg-islation" that he said had done credit to the state. He was referring to my efforts to bring about savings and loan reform.[8]

Herbert Levy and the firm became Tydings, Levy & Archer. When Dad publicly split with Presi-dent Roosevelt in 1938, Levy left to start his own firm, which eventually became known as Gordon Feinblatt. Dad and Archer brought in Alan Sauerwein, and the firm became Tydings, Sauerwein & Archer. It later expanded by adding partners Murray Benson and Cookman Boyd and became Tydings, Sauerwein, Benson and Boyd. Moose Rosenberg was the first associate and later a young partner in the firm, originally recruited by Levy. I began working at the firm while in law school in 1950 and continued up until 1958, when I asked to become a partner. Others in the firm agreed, but they said if they did so they were going to stop paying my father his annual salary, even though he was one of the founders of the firm. By then, Dad was seri-ously ill and unable to come into the office. When I heard that, Moose Rosenberg and I decided to leave and form our own firm, Tydings & Rosenberg. Dad's name remained at the top of our letterhead and his annual salary was paid without interruption until he died in 1961.

7. Associated Press, "Tydings Quits as Delegate," *Washington Post, Times Herald,* March 25, 1961, D3. W. Lester Davis, who had been chairing the Harford County State Democratic Central Committee, was appointed to fill the remainder of my term until the 1962 elec-tion.

8. "Oath Given to Tydings; Federal Bench Welcomes New U.S. Attorney," *Baltimore Sun,* April 6, 1961.

The only cloud in this otherwise bright picture was that my father died on February 9, 1961, the night before I learned for certain that President Kennedy was going to appoint me as US attorney. Dad had been gravely ill since he had come down with shingles and other health problems four weeks after winning renomination to the Senate in 1956. He finally passed away at Oakington at age seventy.[9]

Otherwise, I was pretty happy to be the new US attorney. I had a great young family and a wonderful home. I felt I had a solid record in the House of Delegates. I had overcome the opposition of the dominant political organization in the state to claim a job that not only was important but that would improve my legal credentials and surely raise my visibility statewide.

This was the next step, and I was only thirty-two.

9. Millard Tydings died of pneumonia and complications from encephalitis.

CHAPTER 8

A Thirty-Two-Month Learning Experience

When I became US attorney, one of the first people I went to for advice was eighty-eight-year-old Federal Court of Appeals Judge Morris A. Soper.[1] It was a wise move.

Judge Soper had held my job a half century earlier, from 1900 to 1909. He was a man with incredible experience and a brilliant career of public service.

"I'll tell you, the most important thing you'll ever do as US attorney," he forcefully told me in that first meeting, "is to pick the best possible assistants—really qualified, great assistants." To be successful, he insisted, I needed to surround myself with lawyers who were at least as qualified as I.

Of the young lawyers I recruited or retained, one later became attorney general for the United States; one became US attorney for Maryland, attorney general for Maryland, and a candidate for governor of Maryland; one became a US district judge in Maryland; another became a special assistant attorney general for Maryland; and two became state circuit court judges (or their equivalent) in Maryland. One became a nationally recognized trial lawyer, another chaired the Legislative Black Caucus in the Maryland House of Delegates, and others became prominent state trial attorneys and partners in major law firms.

One of the carryover assistants I persuaded to stay was John R. Hargrove Sr., who in 1957 had become the first African American assistant

1. Soper, first appointed to the federal bench by President Warren G. Harding in 1923, was by 1961 serving on senior status with the Fourth US Circuit Court of Appeals. Although the Fourth Circuit was based in Richmond, Virginia, Judge Soper maintained chambers in the old Post Office Building on the northwest corner of Calvert and Fayette in Baltimore, which also housed the federal courts, the FBI, the postal inspectors, and the US attorney's offices.

in the office. He was what you would call a Lincoln Republican. I elevated him to chief assistant with the responsibility to train us all—including myself—to be federal prosecutors. I also wanted John to run the office, because I intended to try major cases myself. John was a fine lawyer but no firebrand. He was a "go slow," "go carefully," "do your job" pro who loved to try cases. He was a perfect mentor for my young, brilliant, exuberant—but inexperienced—staff and a tremendous resource for me, a neophyte US attorney.[2]

Even though John was the second-ranking US Justice Department official in Maryland, that did not shield him from the indignities of racial segregation in Baltimore and across the South in 1961. About the only places near our office where African Americans would be served meals were Read's Drug Store or the staff cafeteria at the nearby Internal Revenue Service (IRS) office. A number of my assistants would go with John to lunch at one of those places or they would bring in brown bag lunches and eat with him in the office to save him from the embarrassment of having to confront that awful reality.

I was also lucky to inherit Beatrice "Bea" Hudson, an outstanding office manager and personal secretary. Bea was a solid "right hand"— the equivalent of another Hargrove. In fact, when I went to the Senate in Washington, I offered to double Bea's salary if she would work for me there, but she did not want to leave her job in Baltimore.

We furnished my office with a hide-a-bed couch that I used whenever I worked too late to drive home. Bea would wake me up when she arrived around 7:30 a.m. and I would shower downstairs in the chambers of Judge Edward S. Northrop, an old friend from the General Assembly who had just been appointed a federal judge. This schedule enabled me to work an extra three hours a day, which became important when trying major cases. I can still remember using my office to change into my tuxedo before departing for formal events at the White House.

Another excellent carryover assistant was Arnold M. Weiner, whom my predecessor, Leon Pierson, had first appointed in 1958. At the end of my first year, Arnold returned to private practice, but within a year I

---

2. Beginning in 1974, Hargrove served as a judge on two different courts in the city of Baltimore. He was appointed as judge of the US District Court for the District of Maryland by President Ronald Reagan in 1984, a position he held until his death in 1997.

lured him back as a special assistant to help us try a politically explosive savings and loan bribery case involving two sitting members of Congress.[3]

The first new assistant I hired was Daniel F. McMullen Jr., from Cumberland in western Maryland. I had not known Dan before, but I knew members of his well-respected family and he had a reputation as a bright, responsible young attorney.

I had never met any of the first seven assistants I hired before our initial interviews.[4] And none of us had much trial experience. Although I had been trying cases in the circuit courts of Harford, Cecil, and Baltimore Counties and the city of Baltimore for six years by the time I became US attorney, I had tried only one major jury case by myself in a US district court. Fortunately for me, that case was before Chief Judge Roszel Thomsen, who was to become a mentor to me not only while I was US attorney but also later when I became a US senator. None of my young assistants even had the limited trial experience that I had.

The day I was sworn in, Moose Rosenberg, my partner at Tydings & Rosenberg, gave me a tip on another young lawyer he thought I should consider. Stephen H. Sachs, son of one of Moose's friends, had graduated from Haverford College and Yale Law School and had been a Fulbright Scholar. He had been a law clerk for Henry W. Edgerton, a federal judge who was a liberal Roosevelt appointee and who became chief judge of the US Court of Appeals for the District of Columbia Circuit. I was so new to the job that the day I interviewed Steve, I somehow locked us both in my office and we had to bang on the door to have Bea Hudson let us out.[5]

3. After being the law clerk for Simon E. Sobeloff, chief judge of the US Court of Appeals for the Fourth Circuit, Weiner served as assistant US attorney, special assistant US attorney, and special assistant to the Maryland US attorney general. He has become a nationally prominent defense attorney whose clients have included former Maryland Governor Marvin Mandel, former Maryland Representative Edward Garmatz, and former Baltimore Mayor Sheila A. Dixon.

4. Whenever a new US attorney takes office, it is customary to hire new staff assistants. In my case, I kept two carryovers, John Hargrove and Arnold Weiner. The inherited assistants who briefly worked for me until they were able to find positions elsewhere were Robert E. Cahill Sr., Russell Smouse, Carl Lorenz, Dan Honneman, and John Underwood. In all, as many as eighteen different assistant US attorneys worked for me during my nearly three years as federal prosecutor in Maryland. When I started, I was authorized only five assistants, a number that grew to seven my second year and had grown to nine by my final year. By comparison, the US attorney's office as of March 2015 had eighty-one assistant US attorneys.

5. After Steve departed from his post as an assistant US attorney in 1964, he, too, went to work for Tydings & Rosenberg and helped me in my 1964 Senate campaign. I was

I told Steve I would hire him, but with one condition: out of political courtesy, he needed to get his local congressional representative, Sam Friedel, to bless his appointment. Friedel was hesitant to do so because his own political patron, Baltimore boss Jack Pollack, disliked Steve's father. I had a little heart-to-heart chat with Friedel in which I said, "Sam, I advise you to approve Steve Sachs because I am going to name him tomorrow regardless of what you do and you really don't want to alienate an important family in your district." Representative Friedel promptly endorsed Sachs. It was a lesson in political independence that seemed to impress my newly hired young assistant, because Steve still repeats the story after all these years.[6]

My third appointment proved not only to be a great assistant US attorney but someone who would become critically important to my election to the US Senate and my career there. I discovered J. Hardin Marion by thumbing through the listings of Maryland lawyers in the Martindale-Hubbell directory, the Bible of who was who in the legal world. Marion was the first lawyer who caught my eye.

His résumé from Washington and Lee University in Lexington, Virginia, was a bit like mine at the University of Maryland, but he was stronger in law school: he was a member of the honor societies Phi Beta Kappa and Omicron Delta Kappa, as well as the law student honors society, Order of the Coif. He had been editor of the *Washington and Lee Law Review*, was a candidate for student body president during his first year in law school, and was a young attorney at Piper & Marbury, one of the premier Baltimore firms.

Marion had helped put together a group of lawyers for the Kennedy/Johnson campaign in 1960, but he and I had never met until I called him out of the blue and asked him to join me for dinner to discuss

instrumental in getting him appointed as US attorney in 1967, a post he held until 1970. Among the high-profile cases Sachs prosecuted were those of the anti–Vietnam War group known as the Catonsville 9 in 1968; the labor racketeer Guido J. Iozzi Jr., head of the Baltimore building and construction trades council who was convicted of extortion under the Hobbs Act and sentenced to fifteen years; and Representative John Dowdy of Texas, who was convicted of corruption and perjury. In 1978, Steve was elected attorney general of Maryland and reelected in 1982. In 1986, he was an unsuccessful candidate for the Democratic Party nomination for governor of Maryland. Among his many cases as a private attorney, he represented FBI Director L. Patrick Gray during the Watergate investigation and, later, Dr. Elizabeth Morgan in a high-profile child custody case.

6. Stephen H. Sachs, "Times with Tydings," a reminiscence written for the fortieth anniversary of the 1964 Tydings Senate victory, September 12, 2004, in possession of Senator Tydings.

a possible job in the US Attorney's Office. He said he'd think about the offer, but I had to call him back two or three times before I finally persuaded him to join our staff. His decision would reshape both of our lives.[7]

As our staff expanded in my second year, I brought in Daniel W. Moylan and Robert J. Carson, both University of Maryland Law School graduates.[8] Then, toward the end of 1962, I recruited Benjamin R. Civiletti, who was clerking for Judge Calvin Chesnut.[9] In October 1962, Judge Chesnut died at age eighty-nine, and Civiletti was suddenly available. My staff and I thought he would be a good fit for our office. We were right. In later years, he so distinguished himself in the US Department of Justice that, in 1979, President Jimmy Carter appointed him attorney general of the United States.

When Hargrove departed in 1962 to become a Baltimore city judge, I hired Robert Kernan, a Justice Department attorney, to manage our office. Finally, just before I resigned as US attorney, I hired Paul Kramer and Joseph H. H. Kaplan, although I had left the office by the time they were cleared to start work.[10]

7. Hardin Marion left the US Attorney's Office with me in 1963 to help run my 1964 campaign for the US Senate. He then became my chief administrative assistant in the Senate. He served in 1967–68 as an elected delegate to the Maryland constitutional convention. He returned to the Tydings & Rosenberg law firm in Baltimore, where he rose to become the managing partner from 1968 to 1998. Hardin was an active trial and appellate attorney, representing many national corporations, such as IBM and the Stroh Brewery Company, in business and commercial lawsuits.

8. Carson, who was from a fine Havre de Grace family, had been Phi Beta Kappa, Order of the Coif, and editor of the *Maryland Law Review*. Moylan, who was from a distinguished western Maryland family, had clerked for William L. Henderson, the chief judge of the Court of Appeals, the highest court in Maryland. From 1982 until his retirement in 1997, Moylan served as an associate judge on the Circuit Court of Maryland for Washington County.

9. Benjamin R. Civiletti graduated from Johns Hopkins University in 1957 and the University of Maryland School of Law in 1961. Before joining us in the US Attorney's Office in 1962, he clerked for Judge W. Calvin Chesnut of the US District Court. He moved to the US Justice Department, where he headed the Criminal Division and then became deputy attorney general under Attorney General Griffin B. Bell. When Bell resigned in 1979, he became the first Italian American attorney general of the United States. In that post, Civiletti argued several high-profile cases, including those involving American hostages held in Iran and Nazi war criminals residing in the United States. Opinions written by Civiletti interpreted the Constitution and federal law to say that government cannot operate until Congress agrees on a spending bill, setting the stage for partial government shutdowns in later years. In 2008, he chaired a Maryland commission on capital punishment and voted with the majority to abolish the death penalty in the state. Civiletti was born in Peekskill, New York, in 1935, and is a retired partner and past chair of Venable LLP. A newspaper article in 2005 named Civiletti as the first US lawyer to charge $1,000 an hour for his legal services.

10. In my third year, I recruited Arthur Murphy Sr., who years later was elected to the

In retrospect, I realize that issues involving savings and loan associations have been a thread in my life and the lives of some of my former assistants. I made a name for myself in the General Assembly through my efforts to regulate S&Ls. The highest-profile cases I prosecuted as US attorney involved savings and loan fraud, and to a lesser extent the same would be true for Sachs when he became US attorney.

Two decades later, after Kaplan had become the circuit administrative judge for the Baltimore City Circuit Court, he had judicial oversight on yet another savings and loan scandal that erupted in Maryland in the mid-1980s. Among the public officials with whom he would work on those S&L issues was Sachs, by then the state attorney general. Among the private attorneys brought in was Marion.

Life as a US Attorney

When you become a federal prosecutor, there is no obvious road map for which cases you will pursue. You inherit some ongoing cases. Occasionally, you are tipped off to a potential case simply by reading the newspapers or by talking with investigative reporters. But most cases are brought to your attention by an IRS or FBI agent or by another federal investigative agency, such as a US Post Office Department inspector or an agent from the Bureau of Alcohol, Tobacco and Firearms.

Sometimes the validity of a case is unclear and you order additional investigative work. When everything is in order and the case is solid, you and the investigating agent lay out the case for the grand jury and ask for an indictment. If an indictment is returned or you file a "criminal information" or charge, you then try the case in court. Some cases brought to our office did not warrant prosecution, and we had the right to decline to prosecute any case, except for those involving IRS tax

Maryland House of Delegates, where he chaired the Legislative Black Caucus. I also hired J. Edward Davis, who later represented union and industry groups before the Maryland General Assembly. I brought in Kramer, who was then a public defender in Washington, to take Marion's place and also to help pick up some of Sachs's workload while he and Civiletti were in Richmond, Virginia, trying part of a savings and loan case involving the Security Financial Insurance Corporation. Kramer spent twenty years as a federal prosecutor, rising to the position of deputy US attorney for the District of Maryland. Educated at the Washington College of Law at American University in Washington, DC, Kramer moved into private practice in 1983 and has practiced criminal law in state and federal courts for more than forty years. Kaplan had graduated from the University of Chicago Law School and had clerked for Chief Judge Frederick W. Brune of the Maryland Court of Appeals. From 1998 to 2006, Kaplan would serve as chief judge of the Baltimore City Circuit Court. He retired from the bench in October 2006.

fraud. Our young office staff cautiously felt our way step by step, often heeding advice from investigative agents with more experience.

I was thirty-two when appointed US attorney, making me the second youngest in the nation. In the early going, the veteran John Hargrove would coach and counsel my assistants, who all were in their mid-twenties, as they ventured into federal court for the first time or two.

John was a superb teacher. His technique was a mixture of careful mentoring and tough love. In step one, the fresh, eager young assistant would be a helper, sitting in the "second chair" in one of John's short trials, interviewing and preparing witnesses, and performing duties as assigned. In step two, John would occupy the second chair, advising and coaching while the young assistant, knees undoubtedly wobbly, tried the case. In step three, the kid prosecutor flew solo.

John's frequent advice to the often nervous assistant was to "take it in there and lose it." It was his way of saying that you will never be a winner if you are afraid of losing. That's how the assistants learned—and how they became among the most effective trial lawyers in the state. We seldom lost.[11]

Sometimes we would be coached by our top postal inspector, Alton J. "Al" Murray, or by a veteran IRS agent, Nathan Zeldin. They were veterans with experience in the right and wrong way to present a case in federal court, as well as invaluable coaches for me and our "freshman" prosecutors. Zeldin, for example, coached Steve Sachs and me as we tried and convicted a man named Grant Foster, who lived in Venezuela and became the first nonresident US citizen ever to be successfully prosecuted for tax evasion.[12] Al Murray and some of the FBI agents were specialists not only in locating witnesses but in how to work through comprehensive grand jury investigations and the steps we had to go through in a trial.

We also learned by our mistakes. Sachs had been on the staff only a matter of hours when Weiner—a veteran by comparison—asked him

11. Edward Bennett Williams, the renowned trial lawyer, once told me after we faced each other in the bribery trial of two former congressional representatives that I had the best group of assistant US attorneys he had ever seen in a single office, and he complimented us on how well we worked together.

12. At my request, President Kennedy wrote Zeldin a personal letter congratulating him on his work on the case.

to present one of Weiner's cases to the grand jury. Weiner assured the neophyte assistant that there was nothing to it because, he said, the grand jury always indicts. The joke in the office was that a grand jury would indict a ham sandwich if a prosecutor asked it to do so.

Usually that was right. A grand jury only hears the prosecutor's side of the case and simply has to decide if there is probable cause to bring the case to trial. Usually a government investigator accompanies the assistant into the grand jury room, lays out the details of the case, and then the jurors close the door and vote on whether to indict.

Before Steve and his agent could present the facts of the forgery case that Weiner had handed him, however, there were some preliminaries that had to be completed because this was a new grand jury. After Chief Judge Thomsen delivered some welcoming remarks, I, as the brand-new US attorney, instructed the grand jury on how cases would be presented. I decided it was an opportunity to demonstrate my historical expertise and oratorical skills. Then, as now, I loved history and particularly stories about how our own country inherited the fundamental tenets of the rule of law, which is the basis of any true democracy. I led the grand jurors back through the evolution of the jury system, beginning with the struggles between the nobles and King John of England that led to the drafting of the Magna Carta in 1215. I gave them the whole history of the Star Chamber proceedings of British monarchs (particularly Henry VIII) and how that led to a grand jury of peers—local citizens empowered to issue a charge or indictment rather than a king simply "pointing his finger." I emphasized how important it was for them to perform their solemn duty to protect the innocent as well as to indict the guilty.

The grand jury took my lesson to heart. At the end of that day, it reported "true bills" for every case except for Steve's. To add to his mortification, the next day I used the incident as a teaching moment for our entire staff. As Steve himself recounted in a letter to me years later, "it did hurt when you shared with the staff the obvious truth that if a prosecutor can't win in a secret, one-sided proceeding, his prospects for a successful career as a trial lawyer before juries that actually heard both sides of a case were decidedly limited!"[13]

13. Sachs, "Times with Tydings," 2.

Dealing with the Judges

Even the federal judges before whom we pleaded our cases recognized that we lacked the age and trial experience of our predecessors and sometimes prodded us in ways that were often embarrassing or humiliating in court but that were always indelibly instructive about how good lawyers are expected to act in a US district court.

During one of my first forays into federal court, a witness in a criminal case was testifying when suddenly I noticed Chief Judge Thomsen glaring at me at the prosecution table. As the witness continued to testify, it suddenly dawned on me that what the witness was saying was hearsay, not helpful to our case, and probably inadmissible. But it took me so long to object that when I finally spoke up, an agitated Judge Thomsen responded, "Mr. Tydings, if you had objected at any time in the last ten minutes, I would have sustained the objection. Overruled!"

Each of the judges on the federal bench in those years, of course, brought their own personalities, experience, and outlook to the cases they handled. Getting to know and understand each of them, and what they expected in court, was an important part of our job as trial attorneys.

The senior judge when we arrived in 1961 was Judge Chesnut, then eighty-seven, an appointee of President Herbert Hoover.[14] Judge Chesnut's reputation as a distinguished jurist was sealed in 1939, when the chief justice of the United States appointed him to preside over the trial of Martin Thomas Manton, chief judge for the US Court of Appeals for the Second Circuit (based in New York), who had been indicted on corruption charges.[15] A genuine conservative, Judge Chesnut was said to be so concerned about what belonged to the government and what was his own personal property that he had on his desk two containers of paper clips; one was his and the other belonged to the government.

By the time we got to know him, Judge Chesnut was beginning to experience both hearing and vision failure. In an attempt to make sure

14. However, it was Judge Soper who was the oldest judge on the US Court of Appeals for the Fourth Circuit (Maryland, Virginia, West Virginia, North Carolina, and South Carolina). He was Judge Chesnut's friend, colleague, and contemporary. The chief judge of the Fourth Circuit, Simon E. Sobeloff, had actually clerked for Judge Soper. Chesnut and Soper died within five months of each other in late 1962 and early 1963, respectively.

15. Manton was convicted of accepting bribes, sentenced to two years in the federal penitentiary in Lewisburg, Pennsylvania, and served seventeen months.

the old judge could hear testimony the first time he appeared before him, Weiner told a witness to speak up because, he claimed disingenuously, the acoustics in the courtroom were not good. An outraged Judge Chesnut blasted Weiner, declaring there was nothing wrong with the acoustics in his courtroom. Lawyers learned, instead, to tell witnesses to speak up so the jury could hear them.

The last time Weiner was before Judge Chesnut was in a case involving the transportation of stolen goods across state lines. The judge asked the clerk to hand him one piece of evidence, a pair of binoculars. Taking the field glasses in his hands and panning around his courtroom, Judge Chesnut suddenly burst out, "Ah, Mr. Weiner, there you are!" By that point, Weiner had been presenting cases before Judge Chesnut for two years, but that may have been the first time the old judge got a good look at him.

To me, the greatest of the US district court judges we worked with was Chief Judge Roszel Thomsen. He was canny and sharp and understood human nature. As Sachs said of him on the anniversary of Thomsen's fifteenth year on the bench, "he is a most contemporary man. He likes young people, young lawyers in particular. He talks to them as parents are supposed to talk to children—with respect, as if they were grown. And best of all, he listens."[16] Judge Thomsen and Judge Soper both took me under their wing, but Thomsen, in particular, looked out for me.[17]

When Judge Thomsen got angry, you knew it. He would grab a bundle of pencils from his desk and begin squeezing and rattling them. Thomsen had a temper, but it was always controlled. When he released it, it seemed to be carefully timed and calculated to make a point.

Thomsen was always approachable. I could talk to him informally about an investigation, trial schedules, or other matters that did not involve the substance of pending cases. Years later, when I was in the US Senate, I would rely on Judge Thomsen's expertise and wise advice to help me craft legislation that improved the federal judiciary nationwide,

16. From a 1969 address by Stephen H. Sachs at a Federal Bar Association dinner in Baltimore marking the anniversary of Judge Thomsen's fifteenth year on the federal bench.

17. When I was in law school, Judge Thomsen was an adjunct professor. I was not a world beater in law school, and my grades were nothing to write home about, although I did pass the bar after only two years. The only A I got in law school was in Thomsen's trial practice class.

including measures to create the federal magistrate judge system and the multidistrict litigation system for federal district courts.

Judge Dorsey Watkins was a bit different. He was sharp and brilliant with issues involving evidence. But he was not a hard-charger like Judge Thomsen.

My first year as federal prosecutor, in 1961, President Kennedy appointed two other judges to the federal bench in Maryland. One was my old legislative friend, Eddie Northrop, whose appointment I endorsed. The other was Harrison L. Winter, who had been the deputy attorney general for Maryland and whom I favored over former Baltimore Mayor J. Harold Grady, who was being considered for the seat. I had worked with Winter when he was city solicitor for Baltimore, and I liked and respected him.

The federal courtrooms where we plied our trade as prosecutors were always full of colorful witnesses, zany defendants, celebrity lawyers, unrepentant gamblers, politicians under stress (and sometimes their angry or weeping wives), clear-eyed federal investigators, tax cheaters, bank robbers and car thieves, experts in such arcane topics as handwriting, wise and thoughtful judges, and even pitiful kidnappers and murderers.

In those courtrooms, we were witnesses to a carnival of life. All of us learned a lot in a short period of time and together developed a reputation for prosecutorial independence that has carried through in that office to this day.

This portrait of me when I was a US senator from Maryland was painted by Marshal Bouldin, of Clarksdale, Mississippi, and currently hangs in Tydings Hall on the campus of the University of Maryland in College Park. Tydings family photo.

108

My adoptive father, Millard Tydings (far right), as a senior engineering student at the Maryland Agricultural Technical College (predecessor of the University of Maryland) in 1910. Tydings family photo.

Millard Tydings was a World War I hero. Tydings family photo.

Weekend at Chequers with Prime Minister Churchill.
~ May 1945 ~

Granddad (Ambassador Joseph Davies, left) visited with Prime Minister Winston Churchill at Chequers in May 1945 after serving as one of four US representatives to the Potsdam Conference. Between them is the US ambassador to the United Kingdom, John Gilbert Winant. Tydings family photo.

My mother, Eleanor Tydings. Tydings family photo.

Oakington, the Tydings family home in Harford County, Maryland. Tydings family photo.

Family Christmas in 1936 at Mar-a-Lago, the estate my step-grandmother, Marjorie Post Davies, built in Palm Beach, Florida. In 1985, the property was purchased by the New York real estate developer, and now US President, Donald J. Trump. Left to right: my mother, Eleanor Tydings; my step-cousin, Marjorie (Mahwe) Durant; my step-grandmother, Marjorie Post Davies; my grandfather, Ambassador Joseph Davies; my sister, Eleanor; and myself, age eight. Folder 5, Box 1, Series 6, Eleanor Tydings Ditzen Papers, Special Collections, University of Maryland Libraries.

Christmas Day in 1938 at Oakington with my adoptive father, Senator Millard Tydings, my new 20-gauge shotgun, and my new canoe. Folder 1, Box 1, Series 6, Eleanor Tydings Ditzen Papers, Special Collections, University of Maryland Libraries.

In my McDonogh uniform in fifth grade, dancing with my sister, Eleanor, at our Aunt Emlen Grosjean's wedding at Oakington. Tydings family photo.

Here is another picture of me in my fifth grade McDonogh uniform taken at a Christmas holiday performance in New York in 1938. With me to my left is my granddad (Joseph E. Davies) and to the right is "Mummy Da," my wonderful step-grandmother, Marjorie Post Davies. Tydings family photo.

Here I am as a senior cadet cavalry officer at the Mc-Donogh School in Baltimore County, Maryland, during the 1945–46 school year. Tydings family photo.

With twenty-eight sails flying, I returned to the United States from Europe in 1939 aboard the beautiful sailing yacht Sea Cloud, owned by my step-grandmother, Marjorie Post Davies. Tydings family photo.

My grandfather, Joseph Davies (right), and his friend Ned Tinker (second from left) see us off from Ostend, Belgium, for our return trip from Europe in 1939 aboard Marjorie Post Davies's fabulous yacht, Sea Cloud. *Also aboard for the trip home were Judge Richard Smith Whaley (center) and my grandfather's law partner, Ray Beebe (second from right). Folder 5, Box 1, Series 6, Eleanor Tydings Ditzen Papers, Special Collections, University of Maryland Libraries.*

Whenever my grandfather (Joseph E. Davies) was aboard the beautiful Sea Cloud, *he always wore this boating hat, which featured the New York Yacht Club insignia. Tydings family photo.*

At the 1940 Democratic National Convention in Chicago: (left to right) my grandfather, Ambassador Joseph Davies; me; my mother, Eleanor Tydings; and the Maryland "favorite son" candidate for president, my father, Senator Millard Tydings. Tydings family photo.

My mother and father (left) and my sister (now Eleanor Tydings Russell) and I dressed for a costume ball held at Oakington, our Harford County home. Tydings family photo.

My grandfather, Ambassador Joseph Davies; my father and mother, Senator Millard Tydings and Eleanor Tydings; and my step-grandmother, Marjorie Post Davies, at the January 1949 inaugural ball for President Harry S. Truman. Tydings family photo.

Dad chaired the powerful Senate Armed Services Committee 1949–1951. Seated (left to right): Democratic senators Lester C. Hunt of Wyoming; Estes Kefauver of Tennessee; Lyndon B. Johnson of Texas; Harry Flood Byrd of Virginia; Richard B. Russell of Georgia; Millard Tydings of Maryland, committee chair; and Republican senators Styles Bridges of New Hampshire; John "Chan" Gurney of South Dakota; Leverett Saltonstall of Massachusetts; Wayne Morse of Oregon; Raymond E. Baldwin of Connecticut; and William F. Knowland of California. (Not pictured is Democrat Virgil Chapman of Kentucky.) Tydings family photo.

116

As chair of the Senate Armed Services Committee and author of the Philippine Independence Act, my father met with General Douglas MacArthur in the Philippines as part of the celebration of the independence of the country. Tydings family photo.

My father chaired a special Senate committee that investigated and exposed the malicious lies about communists in the State Department promoted by Wisconsin senator Joseph McCarthy, but the McCarthy forces retaliated in Dad's 1950 campaign for reelection. Tydings family photo.

Part of Senator McCarthy's sordid campaign against my father in 1950 was an attempt to make him appear to be a communist sympathizer by distributing this faked composite photo that allegedly showed Dad talking with Communist Party USA leader Earl Browder, a man he had never met. It was originally a picture of my father with his arm around my mother, but they cut out my mother and inserted the picture of Browder. Tydings family photo.

Corporal Joseph D. Tydings, Horse Platoon, 6th Constabulary Regiment, Army of Occupation in Germany, 1946–47. Tydings family photo.

I was a starter on the University of Maryland lacrosse team. I'm in the center right of this picture during a Maryland game against the US Naval Academy. Tydings family photo.

JOSEPH D. TYDINGS
CANDIDATE FOR HOUSE OF DELEGATES

Born - May 4th, 1928; Graduated - McDonogh School, University of Maryland 1951; University of Maryland Law School 1953; Enlisted in the U. S. Army; served in Germany with the Third Army. Member of Veterans of Foreign Wars. Practicing Law in Harford County and Maryland Courts.

This is the campaign card I used in my first run for the Maryland House of Delegates, in 1954. Tydings family photo.

Campaigning in the Maryland presidential primary with Senator John F. Kennedy in Havre de Grace, Maryland, on Saturday, May 14, 1960 (I am on the left, with a document rolled in my hand.). Tydings family photo.

Ginny and I join my friend and mentor, the US District Court judge Roszel C. Thomsen, in a conversation with Maryland governor J. Millard Tawes (back to the camera) in April 1961 after I was sworn in as US attorney for the District of Maryland. Baltimore News American Collection, Folder 12, Box 1307, Special Collections, University of Maryland Libraries. Photo by Charles W. Hart.

As the US attorney for Maryland, I was seated at the desk my father was given by the Philippine people in recognition of his work for Philippine independence—a desk I still use to this day. I am surrounded by my assistant US attorneys: (left to right) Stephen Sachs, Edward Davis, Daniel Moylan, Benjamin Civiletti, Robert Kernan, Daniel McMullen, Hardin Marion, Arthur Murphy, and Robert Carson. (Not pictured is my first chief assistant, John Hargrove.) Tydings family photo.

I was one of the six official marshals at John F. Kennedy's inaugural parade. Here I am (far left) with President Kennedy in the parade viewing box. Also pictured (second from right) is Vice President Lyndon Johnson. Tydings family photo.

This photo was taken the day I officially filed to run for the US Senate in 1964. With me (from left) are my daughter, Mary; my son Millard; my daughter, Emlen, on my lap, and Ginny behind me. With us is my friend, Maryland secretary of state Lloyd "Hot Dog" Simpkins. Folder 32, Box 1307, Baltimore News American Collection, Special Collections, University of Maryland Libraries.

This is one of the napkins handed out at our successful Teas for Tydings campaign events during my US Senate campaign in 1964. Tydings family photo.

I am on the phone accepting congratulations from Republican J. Glenn Beall Sr., whom I defeated in the November 1964 race for the US Senate. Behind me just to my right is Jerry Hoffberger, a key supporter of my campaign. Folder 12, Box 1307, Baltimore News American Collection, Special Collections, University of Maryland Libraries. Photo by Dick Tomlinson.

122

My freshman class in the US Senate. I am flanked on the left by Minority Leader Everett Dirksen of Illinois, on the right by Majority Leader Mike Mansfield of Montana, and President Pro Tempore Carl Hayden of Arizona (fifth from left). Left to right: Dirksen, Ross Bass of Tennessee, Joe Montoya of New Mexico, Fred Harris of Oklahoma, Hayden, Paul Fannin of Arizona, me, Walter Mondale of Minnesota, George Murphy of California, Robert F. Kennedy of New York; and Mansfield. Tydings family photo.

I worked closely with Bobby Kennedy on consumer fraud issues in 1965 as part of the Senate Committee on the District of Columbia. Tydings family photo.

Bobby, Jackie, and Ethel Kennedy (behind me on the right) and I attended a fundraiser in New York City to benefit the John F. Kennedy Presidential Library following the president's assassination. Tydings family photo.

Working on the Voting Rights Act in 1965 were the Democratic whips: the chair, Phil Hart of Michigan; Edward Kennedy of Massachusetts; Birch Bayh of Indiana; and me. Tydings family photo.

As a freshman senator, initially ranked one-hundredth in seniority, I have no idea how I got a front-row position as President Johnson handed Carl Hayden, president pro tem of the Senate, a pen at a 1965 bill signing. Vice President Humphrey is just behind Johnson and me. Tydings family photo.

Senator Walter Mondale of Minnesota and I listen as President Johnson answers our questions about the Vietnam War. Tydings family photo.

Robert F. Kennedy and I are joined by Lawrence Cardinal Shehan, archbishop of Maryland, just after Bobby announced his candidacy for president in 1968. Tydings family photo.

Republican Roman Hruska of Nebraska (left); Mike Mansfield, the Democratic majority leader (right); and I review the voting roll call after the Senate passed the District of Columbia crime control bill. AP Photo.

126

President Johnson and I split over the war in Vietnam, but we were aligned on almost every other issue, particularly in our fight for civil rights and stronger gun control. Tydings family photo.

During my Senate years, my colleagues and I often played tennis competitively. Here I am with the Democratic senatorial tennis team (left to right): Bill Spong of Virginia, me, Joe Clark of Pennsylvania, Fritz Hollings of South Carolina, and Claiborne Pell of Rhode Island. We had just played and beaten a Republican team headed by Vice President Spiro Agnew. Tydings family photo.

Congratulating Paul Sarbanes after his election to the US Senate in 1976. Folder 12, Box 1307, Baltimore News American Collection, Special Collections, University of Maryland Libraries. Photo by Gene Boyars.

In 1968, I conferred with New York mayor John Lindsay, a prominent Republican who helped me in my efforts to add registration of firearms to a bill that would prohibit interstate mail-order sales of guns and ammunition. AP Photo/Bob Daugherty.

Editorial cartoonists loved to depict my fights with the gun lobby, but unfortunately, in my 1970 reelection bid, the gun lobby prevailed. Tydings family photo.

The gun lobby plastered cars throughout Maryland with bumper stickers against me because of my stance in favor of stronger regulation of firearms. Folder 1, Series 9, Joseph D. Tydings Papers, Special Collections, University of Maryland Libraries.

I was appointed by three different governors to the University of Maryland Board of Regents in three different decades. This is a picture of the regents in 1983, when I served as chair: (left to right, seated) Mary H. Broadwater; David K. Fram; Paul Moss; John S. Toll, president of the university; me; Allen L. Schwait; Connie Stuart; and (standing) Wayne A. Cawley Jr.; A. James Clark; Ralph W. Frey; Frank A. Gunther Jr.; Blair Lee III; Clarence M. Mitchell Jr.; Peter F. O'Malley; Larry McCullough, student regent; and John W. T. Webb. Tydings family photo.

Here are four former US attorneys for Maryland—two Republicans and two Democrats—gathered at my eighty-fifth birthday party. From left, Republican Richard D. "Dick" Bennett, now a federal judge; me; Stephen H. Sachs, my former assistant and later successor; and Republican Rod Rosenstein, now deputy attorney general of the United States. Tydings family photo.

To Senator Joseph D. Tydings
in great appreciation for S. 2543.
The Horse Protection Act

Papa Charcoal was a Tennessee Walking Horse that had been crippled by the vicious practice known as soring. We brought Papa Charcoal to Washington for a Life magazine story that helped pass my Horse Protection Act in 1970. I have worked for a half century to try to end the despicable practice of soring. Tydings family photo.

In honor of my work on the Horse Protection Act and other efforts to protect the beautiful Tennessee Walking Horses from the cruel practice of soring, I was named the 2016 Humane Horseman of the Year by the Humane Society of the United States, the largest animal protection organization in the nation. Tydings family photo.

Here is a great picture of my sister and best friend for life, Eleanor Tydings Russell, with me at my eighty-fifth birthday party. Tydings family photo.

With four of my five children at my eighty-fifth birthday party in 2011. From left: Alexandra, Eleanor, me, Mary, and Millard. Missing is my daughter Emlen, who was living in Australia. Tydings family photo.

My youngest daughter, Alexandra Luzzoto, with her three children, Maeve, Emma, and Ruby, in 2015. Tydings family photo.

At Bethany Beach, Delaware, with some of my family. Back row, from left: my daughter, Eleanor Gollob; nephew Joe Davies; me; daughter-in-law Susan Tydings; son Millard Tydings II. Middle row, from left: grandson Jay Gollob, granddaughter Jill Gollob, grandson Sam Gollob, granddaughter Maggie Tydings. Front row, from left: niece Blythe Davies; great-nephew Teddy Davies; his sister, Scarlet Davies; and grandson Will Tydings. Tydings family photo.

The crest, right, that President Trump displays at his American properties is a coat of arms, left, that British authorities granted to my grandfather, Joseph Davies. Left, Tydings family collection; right, Chang W. Lee/The New York Times/Redux.

CHAPTER 9

A Tangle of Savings and Loan Scams

In the years before I became US attorney, the seeds had already been sown in Maryland that would grow into a messy tangle of savings and loan corruption scandals that would occupy a good portion of our time and attention as federal prosecutors.

In nearly three years in office, we prosecuted three major savings and loan cases and a number of minor ones. We convicted a wealthy insurance executive from California for setting up a phony deposit insurance firm and fraudulently trying to use it to insure deposits in Maryland. We convicted two men from Illinois and Utah who owned—and plundered—several S&Ls in Maryland and elsewhere. We convicted a conniving financier from Florida, as well as the two former Democratic members of Congress he bought off. And we indicted the Speaker of the Maryland House of Delegates and several of his Baltimore County political associates for savings and loan fraud.

Common threads ran through all these cases. Almost all involved bogus claims, false advertising, insider dealing, and appalling misuse of depositors' funds, or they involved fraudulent assertions about the financial condition of the S&Ls or about the companies that insured S&L deposits.

Some of the same names popped up in more than one case: Stewart B. Hopps of San Francisco, C. Oran Mensik of Chicago, and J. Kenneth Edlin of Miami.[1] Hopps's shell company in Tangier, Morocco, provided

---

1. Hopps and his son, Robert, had been indicted in Maryland on mail fraud charges on July 13, 1960. Mensik, shortly before I became US attorney, had been tried in US District Court in Maryland on charges that he had set up the Commercial Savings and Loan Association in Maryland, lured customers with gimmicks for new deposits, and then illegally milked the firm by taking dividends, making speculative loans, and falsely claiming that deposits in the S&L were adequately insured. On March 24, 1961—the same day I resigned my seat in the Maryland House of Delegates to accept appointment as US attorney—a jury told Judge R.

worthless insurance for depositors at S&Ls owned or run by Mensik and Edlin. It was Edlin who secretly bribed two members of Congress in a futile attempt to have them convince Robert F. Kennedy and the Justice Department to drop an indictment against him. And it was Mensik who dispatched a Chicago lawyer with a pocketful of money to Maryland to persuade the soon-to-be Speaker of the House, A. Gordon Boone, to set up a deposit insurance firm that never had the assets it claimed.

All of this was happening in Maryland, of course, because state-chartered S&Ls were virtually unregulated, as I had warned in the General Assembly for more than two years. S&L operators could do almost anything they wanted without fear of oversight.

Stewart Hopps, the "Brilliant Ventriloquist"

Advertising sent through the US mail was what did in Stewart Hopps.

In 1958, International Guaranty and Insurance Company, the Moroccan firm for which Hopps was said to be the American manager, dropped into the mail a statement intended to drum up national interest in the deposit insurance it offered by demonstrating the company was financially sound. The problem was that the mailing contained completely false statements about the financial condition of the company.[2] Two of the many recipients of the brochure were Charles F. Jackson, the Maryland insurance commissioner, and the Baltimore Better Business Bureau, and those two mailings provided the basis for the two-count mail fraud indictment against Hopps.

Al Murray, our postal inspector, liked to say, "If I can find the fraud, I can always find the use of the mails."

In 1960, my predecessor convened a Maryland grand jury that indicted Hopps, who lived in Belvedere, a wealthy island community in San Francisco Bay near Sausalito. His indictment said that among the assets International claimed in the mailing were "worthless stocks and bonds of [four] paper corporations incorporated in Panama."[3] In my

Dorsey Watkins that it was deadlocked and unable to reach a verdict. Edlin had been indicted on November 17, 1959, for his illegal activity in two Maryland S&Ls.

2. The mailing was entitled "International Guaranty and Insurance Co., Statement of Condition, 1958."

3. Associated Press, "Insurance Fraud Seen: Hopps Indicted on Charges by Grand Jury Here," *Baltimore Sun*, July 14, 1960, 15.

opening statement at his trial, I characterized the millionaire Hopps as a "brilliant ventriloquist" who spoke through puppets around the world who operated "a web of insurance companies."[4]

"Mr. Hopps devised a scheme to defraud," I told the jury. "He wanted people, responsible people in charge of savings and loan associations and mortgage companies, to purchase insurance of International Guaranty and Insurance Company, which he controlled and dominated and from which he would profit. And, in order to effectuate this scheme he caused to be prepared a financial statement and later a brochure which were replete with false and fraudulent representations as to assets and holdings in this company."[5]

The Hopps trial was extraordinary because Hopps attributed many of the actions his company took to his associate, Eric Van Galder. Hardin Marion, my assistant US attorney, and I decided that initially we would not reveal to the judge or the jury that we knew that "Eric Van Galder" did not exist. Instead, we introduced sequential testimony and evidence that showed that Hopps controlled the actions of the mysterious Van Galder.[6]

Nadine Snyder, a typist from Hopps's San Francisco office, testified that she had seen Van Galder's signature on company statements, checks, and letters but had never seen him in person and had never received any calls for him or from him. She said Hopps or his son often dictated letters for Van Galder's signature.[7]

Another employee of Hopps recalled how the senior Hopps dictated a letter to the Tangier home office of International, then directed that the original be torn up and a carbon copy be placed in the file. Then he drafted an answer to the letter he had just written and filed, purportedly from the head of the Tangier office, and had that put in the file as well.

4. Theodore W. Hendricks, "Hopps Trial Is Under Way: U.S. Outlines Its Position in Mail Fraud Case," *Baltimore Sun*, January 22, 1963, 32.

5. United States v. Stewart Hopps, Docket No. 25360, opening statement by US Attorney Joseph D. Tydings, transcript pages 30–31.

6. Hopps's portrayal of Van Galder was initially so effective that on the third day of the trial our office received a telephone call from a Washington, DC, woman who had apparently been following the newspaper accounts of the trial. She breathlessly reported that she had just spotted Van Galder in the Miami airport getting off a flight from Panama!

7. "Letters Cited in Hopps Case: Typist Says She Never Saw Man Who Signed Them," *Baltimore Sun*, January 23, 1963, 8.

The charade fell apart when we called to the witness stand a Post Office Department handwriting expert to examine the Van Galder signature. Soon one of Hopps's attorneys interrupted to say he was willing to stipulate that the person who signed as "Eric S. Van Galder" was actually Robert Hopps, Stewart Hopps's son and co-defendant.[8]

When Van Galder turned out to be fictitious, defense attorneys tried to convince the jury that the younger Hopps (who, due to illness, was to be tried separately) had conjured up the Van Galder character to protect his father. They claimed the elder Hopps had been treated unfairly by other insurance executives ever since he advised the federal government on antitrust actions against national insurance cartels, so they had no choice but to keep his name hidden.

When that argument failed, Hopps's attorneys tried to hang responsibility on a flamboyant San Francisco lawyer named J. W. "Jake" Ehrlich, who was a stockholder in and legal counsel for International. Ehrlich's fame was built on a career of successfully defending movie stars, musicians, industrialists, and other celebrities, among them the actor Errol Flynn and the fan dancer Sally Rand.[9] Ehrlich was well aware that he was tiptoeing through the Hopps trial and could well be held responsible for the transgressions of the insurance firm. Marion and I talked about the possibility of indicting Ehrlich but concluded the insurance scam at the heart of the case was not his doing. Ehrlich's motto—and the name of the biography written about his life—was *Never Plead Guilty.*[10]

Hopps had avoided successful state prosecution for alleged insurance scams in a number of other states, but on February 13, 1963, the federal jury in Maryland convicted him of mail fraud. Judge Thomsen fined him $1,000 and sentenced him to eighteen months in prison.

8. Theodore W. Hendricks, "Mystery Man Is Identified: Hopps Agrees to Reveal Signer of Documents," *Baltimore Sun,* January 31, 1963, 33.

9. Ehrlich was the author of more than a dozen books, including a philosophical treatise on the law called *Ehrlich's Blackstone,* as well as *Criminal Evidence, Trial of the Contested Divorce Case, What Is Wrong with the Jury System,* and *The Holy Bible and the Law.*

10. After the trial, Ehrlich sent Hardin Marion an autographed copy of *Ehrlich's Blackstone* and he sent me a packet of clippings from the San Francisco newspapers about Hopps's conviction. He included a personal note that said, "When you next think you are coming to the Coast, please let me know so that I may roll out the red carpet for you. With every good wish, please believe me. Your friend. Jake." J. W. "Jake" Ehrlich to US Attorney Joseph D. Tydings, February 15, 1963, in possession of Senator Tydings.

Two Democratic Members of Congress

During his trial, Hopps testified that when his Moroccan insurance firm got into trouble, he turned to Miami money man J. Kenneth Edlin for financial help.

But Edlin had his own problems.

In a case presented to a federal grand jury in Maryland in 1959 by then Assistant US Attorney Arnold Weiner, Edlin was indicted for criminal activity in regard to the First Colony Savings and Loan Association of Prince Frederick and a company linked to it, the First Continental Mortgage Corporation of Montgomery County. He and others were accused of fraudulent advertising about First Colony, a thrift that had no investments, earned almost no income, and had never paid a dividend. One of the ads alleged the company had had "an excellent third quarter," when in fact the earnings totaled $74.30 while expenses were $100,000.[11]

Edlin ultimately pleaded no contest to the First Colony charges, served six months in federal prison, and was fined $8,000. But he still had the First Continental indictment hanging over his head when I became US attorney. So Edlin apparently decided to buy himself immunity from prosecution by befriending—and handsomely rewarding—a pair of Democratic congressional representatives, Thomas F. Johnson of Maryland and Frank W. Boykin of Alabama. In return, their job was to persuade the Justice Department to drop the First Continental indictment brought by my predecessor.

Johnson, a lawyer from the lower Eastern Shore, bore the name of the first elected governor of Maryland. In 1934, at age twenty-four, he had been appointed state's attorney, and, at age twenty-eight, he was elected to the Maryland Senate. In January 1959, he began serving the first of two terms in Congress representing the First District. By 1960, Johnson had become acquainted with Edlin. It was Johnson who introduced Edlin to Boykin, then a fourteen-term member of Congress and dean of the Alabama delegation.

Boykin was sharp but unscrupulous. The son of sharecroppers, he had left school after fourth grade. He was first elected to Congress in

11. "Save-by-Mail Firm Indicted: First Colony Accused of Scheme to Defraud," *Baltimore Sun*, November 18, 1959, 15.

1934, where he developed a reputation for being pro-business, anti-union, and isolationist on foreign affairs. His somewhat odd political slogan was, "Everything is made for love." He was an opponent of civil rights and among 101 House and Senate members from the Deep South who signed the "Southern Manifesto" in 1956 protesting the *Brown v. Board of Education* ruling.[12]

Boykin also had a reputation as a big entertainer and was known for inviting members of Congress, governors, and other important political figures to the Frank and Ocllo (his wife's name) Boykin Hunting Lodge in Double Gates, Alabama. Much of his financial success was attributed to his ability to use political power to make money. He was said to have built his substantial fortune, in part, by buying up land after getting inside information about where future highways were to be built. His primary interests were in lumber and turpentine, and his company, the Tensaw Land & Timber Company, has a website that still features a picture of Boykin's three-story white frame hunting lodge with wraparound porch and rocking chairs.[13]

But Boykin also held for many years troubled land development projects in Brooke, Virginia, and Charles County, Maryland, and he saw Edlin as the man with the money that could bail out those investments.

After our savings and loan regulation bill was signed into law in 1961, state auditors began looking at the books of First Maryland Savings and Loan, which Edlin controlled, as well as other S&Ls where they suspected financial trouble. When they ran across suspicious checks at First Maryland, they turned them over to Al Murray, our postal inspector, who called me.

The auditors discovered two separate checks, each for $250,000, made payable to the Tensaw Land & Timber Company. Each had been endorsed by Boykin and cashed by the sergeant of arms of the US House of Representatives. Those two checks were the original "smoking gun" in what became known as the Johnson/Boykin case.

12. *The Encyclopedia of Alabama*, Alabama Humanities Foundation, a service of Auburn University, the University of Alabama, and the Alabama State Department of Education, 2014, http://www.encyclopediaofalabama.org/article/h-3320.

13. Among the dignitaries who visited the Boykin Lodge over the years were Alabama governors George C. Wallace, Big Jim Folsom, and Don Siegelman; the famous University of Alabama football coach Bear Bryant; the chair of the Joint Chiefs of Staff under President Eisenhower; the evangelist Billy Graham; and General Douglas MacArthur. Evan Carden, "Where Everything Is Made for Love," *Thomasville (AL) Times*, August 3, 2006.

Maryland inspectors also found that checks were sent circuitously from Edlin's S&L to Johnson. That was when we first began to understand why we had received so many requests from the Office of the Attorney General to review and recheck the original Edlin indictment.

I first received copies of the Boykin and Johnson checks a few days before Christmas. I immediately called Attorney General Kennedy. Two days later, I presented my evidence in a two-and-one-half hour meeting with him, Deputy Attorney General Byron "Whizzer" White, and Herbert J. "Jack" Miller, the assistant attorney general for the Criminal Division. I asked for permission to bring in the FBI to interview Representatives Boykin and Johnson and subpoena and copy all relevant documents.

White was reluctant. He felt an investigation was risky and politically sensitive. At the end of the meeting, however, the attorney general gave his approval. The week after Christmas, the FBI suddenly appeared at Johnson's Eastern Shore law office to interview him and photocopy all of his documents on the spot. At the same time, agents visited Boykin in Alabama. No warnings were given, so they had no time to destroy or doctor documents.

It was a rare act of courage for the attorney general to initiate an investigation of two incumbent members of Congress of his own political party. In doing so, Robert Kennedy established a reputation within the Department of Justice—as well as within the office of the US Attorney in Maryland—that party affiliation was no longer a factor in federal law enforcement.[14]

With approval from the court, we convened a special federal grand jury to investigate the case. In my years as US attorney, we often used grand juries as an important investigative tool. We steadily presented evidence, and, as summer approached, we were prepared to indict.

The Justice Department was predictably and justifiably cautious about indicting two members of Congress, not only because both were Democrats but because the reputations of the two men, the office of the US attorney in Maryland, and the Justice Department were all at stake. Jack Miller, who was to oversee the prosecution for the Justice

14. George Beall, the US attorney for Maryland from 1970 to 1975, and the son and brother of Republican members of the US Senate, led the investigation that eventually drove a number of public officials from office, including Republican Vice President Spiro T. Agnew.

Department, wanted to be absolutely sure.[15] He repeatedly insisted we interview just one more witness, or produce one more piece of evidence, before allowing us to seek an indictment.

Against the advice of their lawyers, Johnson and Boykin demanded to testify before the grand jury. At first I suggested they not appear, but they appealed to Kennedy, who told me to let them testify. I have always believed that lawyers do their clients a disservice by letting them answer questions before a grand jury, where the prosecutor is present and the clients' legal counsel is not. Representative Tom Johnson was so driven by ego that he thought he could spin a believable tale and charm the grand jurors. But most defendants ultimately convict themselves with their own words. Indeed, both Boykin's and Johnson's testimony helped convince the grand jury it should indict, and, ultimately, their own words helped convict them.[16]

We surreptitiously escorted the two members of Congress into and out of the courthouse separately without the press ever knowing. But the delay caused by waiting on their testimony pushed the possible announcement of their indictment until almost the eve of the November 1962 election.

By mid-October, Boykin, then seventy-seven, had already lost his House seat in a statewide Alabama primary, but Johnson was up for election for a third term. To indict him before the election would obviously harm his reelection chances; to wait until afterward would lead to accusations that we sat on the indictment in an effort to retain a Democratic seat in Congress. Either way, we were sure to be accused of playing politics. We decided to play it straight and let the grand jury indict when ready. On October 16, 1962, just three weeks before the election, the grand jury indicted them both. Edlin was indicted anew, as was his Miami associate, William L. Robinson.[17]

15. Miller, a Republican, was a superb lawyer who later represented President Richard M. Nixon.

16. Johnson attorney George Cochran Doub tried to have Johnson's grand jury testimony suppressed on the grounds he had been coerced to appear. But we brought to court Nicholas Katzenbach, by then the deputy attorney general, to describe to Judge Thomsen how he had told Johnson the grand jury was about to conclude work on the case and that if he wanted to testify, he needed to do so. Thomsen ruled against Doub's motion, saying Johnson's grand jury testimony had been given voluntarily.

17. Boykin had lost his seat in May 1962. With his departure imminent, Boykin was

The principal count against the four was conspiracy—that they had conspired to defraud the public of the fair and impartial services of House members, who were public officials. The remaining seven counts described specific acts Johnson and Boykin were alleged to have committed as part of the conspiracy. They included a speech by Johnson on the House floor defending Maryland S&Ls; Johnson and Boykin's intense, months-long lobbying of Attorney General Kennedy and other Department of Justice officials on Edlin's behalf; and various payments made to Johnson and Boykin by Edlin and his alleged accomplice, Robinson.

Within forty-eight hours after the indictment was announced, Judge Thomsen called down to our office and asked Marion, the principal assistant handling the case, to come upstairs to his chambers. When he arrived, he found Johnson's lawyers already there, angrily complaining about the timing of the indictment and demanding an immediate trial before the election.

"Mr. Marion," Judge Thomsen asked, "how soon can the government be ready?"

"Your honor," Marion replied, "we can go to trial on Monday, if the defense is ready."

Despite their demand, Johnson's lawyers were not prepared to go to trial that fast. It was a bluff, and we had just called it. They likely had hoped to prove Johnson's innocence before the election or to be able to claim they could have done so if the government had not delayed the trial. But even if they could have been ready, the trial was sure to last longer than three weeks.

Instead, the trial was set for the following April. By then, Johnson had lost his congressional seat to the Republican challenger, Rogers C. B. Morton, by nearly four thousand votes out of almost sixty-three thousand cast.

"He's on Our Payroll!"

The issue was not whether a member of Congress had the right—or even the duty—to represent constituents before the Justice Department.

extolled on the House floor by colleagues, including by Johnson, who said, "He has stood out as one of the nation's leading business men." Associated Press, "Boykin Praised before Charge," *Baltimore Sun*, October 18, 1962, 56.

We sought to prove that these men were being bribed to do so, illegally using the prestige and power of their positions to influence the government for their own private gain.

Sadie Goldman, a former private secretary to Edlin, testified how "a very excited, very happy" Edlin had returned to his Miami office one day in May 1960 after meeting with Johnson and announced, "'Well, I've made a new contact. There's no stopping us now. The sky's the limit! We're going to have a chain of banks, Sadie; we're all going to be rich. Seriously, Sadie, it's a congressman!'"[18]

Goldman said she then asked Robinson, Edlin's law associate, what Edlin was talking about. "'Ever hear of Congressman Johnson?'" she testified that Robinson replied. "'Well, he's on our payroll!'"[19]

To prove the conspiracy count against the four defendants required us to show there had been at least one overt act done in support of that conspiracy. One such act was Johnson's speech on June 30, 1960, on the floor of the House defending the operation of Maryland's beleaguered state-chartered S&Ls and the reliability of their deposit insurance. Testimony later showed that Edlin and his associates helped draft Johnson's remarks and then distributed fifty thousand copies of the speech to the public to promote their businesses. Evidence also showed that Johnson was secretly paid for his services—another overt act under the conspiracy indictment.

The trial demonstrated that the two Congress members worked relentlessly to get the Justice Department to drop the indictment against Edlin. Boykin was the first to reach out to Robert Kennedy, telling him that he and Johnson wanted to discuss the pending indictment against Edlin. Boykin acknowledged to Kennedy that Edlin had become a partner in his land transactions, and he admitted the proposed developments were being held up because of the indictment. The old Congress member tried to convince the young attorney general that the developments were more important to the economic health of Maryland and Virginia than Edlin's indictment was to the Justice Department and the rule of law.

18. Theodore W. Hendricks, "Johnson Case Witness Cites Edlin Elation: Says She Learned Congressman Had Been Put on 'Payroll,'" *Baltimore Sun*, April 4, 1963, 56.

19. Ibid.

The meeting was one of at least four that Johnson or Boykin, or both together, had with Kennedy. They also had eight additional meetings with Assistant Attorney General Miller, and they telephoned the Justice Department at least sixty-three other times in a concerted effort to kill the Edlin indictment. Kennedy agreed to have Miller and his staff review the Edlin case again but afterward concluded the case should move forward.[20]

The Edlin indictment, obviously, was the heart of our case, but Edward L. Genn, Edlin's lawyer, repeatedly tried to get Judge Thomsen to instruct us not to mention it before the jury, claiming such references were prejudicial to his client. He made numerous motions for a mistrial. Finally, Judge Thomsen had heard enough. Standing up and swirling his black robes, the exasperated judge said, "Mr. Genn, you are asking me to put on the play of Hamlet with no mention of the ghost! Motion denied. Court adjourned."[21] And with that, he walked off the bench.

Tracking the Paper Trail

Often the primary tool of our trade in the office of the US attorney was to track the paper trail that criminal defendants unwittingly and inevitably left behind. The paper trail often is the key in complex white-collar crime cases. That is how we exposed the fictitious Eric Van Galder, which helped us convict Stewart Hopps. We had cases where the paper trail involved laundry tickets on which the dates had been smudged and changed. We uncovered receipt books that tracked the ill-gotten gains of bookies. We investigated dummy corporations in Canada and Panama that were set up to hide illegal activities.

In the Johnson/Boykin case, we proved that a minor change in punctuation can become proof of criminal intent. As we studied the files the FBI had seized from Johnson, Marion discovered two letters from the Congress members that purported to acknowledge receipt of payment for legal services. We suspected the payments were, in fact, bribes. On closer examination, Marion noticed that the two letters were the only ones in Johnson's entire file where the salutation was followed

20. "Boykin, Johnson Convicted," regarding Miller testimony on April 22, 1963, *CQ Almanac 1963*, 19th ed., 1106–7 (Washington, DC: Congressional Quarterly, 1964), http://library.cqpress.com/cqalmanac/cqa163–1315443.

21. Quote recalled by J. Hardin Marion in interview by the author, February 24, 2015.

by a comma rather than a colon, which was the punctuation style commonly used by Johnson's secretaries. Moreover, they were the only two letters in his file that purported to show he was paid for legal work.

We called Johnson's secretary to the stand to ask if she had typed the letters (her initials were at the bottom), but she said she could not recall. The truth almost certainly was that she was protecting her boss and the jury realized that. Our conclusion was that the two letters were phony and that Johnson had probably typed them himself but was oblivious to the customary office style. And that was what we told the jury.

Johnson insisted the nearly $25,000 sum he received from Edlin and his associates was for legitimate legal fees, real estate commissions, finder's fees, campaign contributions, and money to rent his Snow Hill law office as a branch of First Continental (even though no such branch was ever opened). Boykin received two $250,000 checks to finance his Maryland and Virginia real estate developments but maintained he had made no secret of his partnership with Edlin on the land deals.

The two Congress members got themselves into even more serious trouble when they tried to reconcile the various stories they had given to explain these payments in their first interview with the FBI, in sworn testimony before a Maryland state grand jury, and before a separate federal grand jury. By the time they got into court, they had a fourth story!

Among the files Johnson produced when initially interrogated by the FBI were legal documents related to Edlin's S&L activities. By the time he got into court, however, his attorneys had introduced the same documents, this time with newly penciled or penned notes in the margins making it appear that he had performed bona fide legal services that justified the payments from Edlin. Johnson clearly had forgotten that the FBI had photocopied the original documents months before.

On cross-examination, Marion began showing Johnson the unedited documents seized by the FBI and comparing them with Johnson's annotated versions. Marion says he can still recall watching as the sweat ran down the former Congress member's neck and into his collar.

Surprise Witness

To impress the jury about the level of pressure placed on the Justice Department by Boykin and Johnson, I called a surprise witness to the stand on the morning of April 17, 1963: Attorney General Robert F. Kennedy.

It was unlikely the attorney general would testify in a case like ours. Calling the attorney general was almost unprecedented. To keep the defense off guard, we had called Kennedy's personal secretary, then Assistant Attorney General Miller's secretary, and then Miller himself, all to discuss the number of telephone calls, personal visits, and extraordinary pressure brought to bear by Johnson and Boykin. We had done what we could to make it appear we were not planning to call the attorney general himself.

The night before, I had driven down to Hickory Hill, Bobby and Ethel Kennedy's home in McLean, Virginia, had dinner with the family, and briefed Bobby on the case. The following morning, when the attorney general's name was called, he entered the nearly empty courtroom from a door in the back.

The court clerk was so unnerved that her hands shook as she held the Bible for Bobby to take the oath. With lightning speed, word spread through the courthouse that the attorney general was on the witness stand and within minutes it was standing room only.

This was a moment of first-class legal theater. As Bobby settled into his seat on the witness stand, I asked if Johnson had indicated to him that he had been retained by Edlin.

"He did not," Bobby replied, adding later in his testimony, "Neither Congressman Johnson or Congressman Boykin ever said to me that they appeared other than in their capacity as congressmen."[22]

Bobby related the many meetings and calls the two Congress members had made to the Justice Department, saying that he was told that the Edlin indictment could have an adverse effect on the Maryland economy and that dropping it would be good for the S&L industry.[23]

22. Quotes from Theodore W. Hendricks, "R. F. Kennedy Says Johnson Chided Probe: Boykin Also 'Expressed Concern,' Attorney General Testifies," *Baltimore Sun*, April 18, 1963, 54.

23. To ingratiate himself with the attorney general, the Alabama House member told Kennedy that his plans for his property included "a development for Negroes [that would] be helpful in the problem of segregation." United States vs. Johnson, Boykin, et al., Docket No. 26067, transcript page 1675. Johnson and Boykin also repeatedly suggested to Kennedy that Edlin might be helpful to the Justice Department in a completely unrelated case involving Teamsters boss Jimmy Hoffa, Bobby Kennedy's bête noire, because of knowledge Edlin allegedly had about a stolen $100,000 bond.

The defense lawyers were so startled by Kennedy's unexpected appearance that Johnson—rashly, stupidly, and egotistically, in my opinion—decided that he, not his attorney, George Cochran Doub, would personally cross-examine the attorney general. I strongly objected, saying Johnson was represented by competent counsel and that it was improper for the defendant to cross-examine Kennedy.[24]

Johnson protested, telling Judge Thomsen, "My own counsel is not familiar with the transactions that took place with the Attorney General. I can enlighten the Attorney General on many matters he has not stated on the stand." I again objected.[25]

"I feel I have a right to cross-examine this witness," Johnson told the judge. "I have everything at stake in this case and I do not want to be deprived of that right. I am a lawyer." Thomsen permitted it, but after the trial one of the jurors told us that that was the moment when he knew for certain that Johnson was guilty.[26]

In his cross-examination, Johnson called Kennedy "General" and Kennedy politely referred to Johnson as "Congressman," even though by then Johnson had lost his reelection bid. Kennedy's responses were crisp, low-key, and firm. When Johnson asserted that the attorney general had said the economic advantages of Boykin's land development deals outweighed the indictment against Edlin, Kennedy barked back, "Certainly not. That would be completely out of character."[27]

Through his questioning, Johnson tried to get Kennedy to concede there was nothing unusual about a member of Congress or senator discussing issues or cases with the Justice Department.

24. George Cochran Doub, born in Cumberland, Maryland, was one of my predecessors as US attorney for the District of Maryland (1953–56) and became an assistant attorney general in charge of the Civil Division of the Justice Department during President Eisenhower's second term. He flew navy dive bombers against Japanese-held islands during World War II, but as assistant attorney general he was widely credited for his sensitive handling of property claims by Japanese Americans who had been removed from the West Coast and interned during the war. He studied at Princeton and graduated from the Johns Hopkins University and the University of Maryland School of Law. After leaving government, he worked for the Baltimore firm of Weinberg & Green. He died in 1981 at age seventy-nine.

25. United States v. Johnson, Boykin, et al., Docket No. 26067, transcript page 1692.

26. Ibid., 1691–92.

27. Hendricks, "R. F. Kennedy Says Johnson Chided Probe: Boykin Also 'Expressed Concern,' Attorney General Testifies," 54.

"That is true, Congressman, [but] I do not think that, since I have been Attorney General, I have had the number of visits and the amount of effort that was displayed in this case," Kennedy responded.[28]

Johnson pressed on: "Would it be correct in saying that after the institution of this suit, you have had a lot fewer visits on the part of Congressmen and Senators?"[29]

"I would think that is probably true," Kennedy replied as the courtroom audience broke into laughter.[30]

Through his questioning, Johnson insisted that the meetings with the Justice Department were merely to seek a "review" of the Edlin case, not dismissal.

"Well, Congressman," Kennedy retorted, "can you tell me why you were so anxious to come in there and have us review it if you did not want us to dismiss it?"[31]

Later in the trial, Johnson's defense claimed that my office had indicted him as revenge for Johnson's opposition to my appointment as US attorney. In fact, to minimize any appearance that I was somehow out to get Johnson, I had Marion cross-examine Johnson rather than doing so myself.[32]

The famous defense lawyer Edward Bennett Williams defended Boykin. Williams was generally recognized as one of the finest trial lawyers of the twentieth century. He was such a star in the legal firmament that the University of Maryland and University of Baltimore law schools released their students for the day so they could watch the flamboyant and brilliant attorney deliver his closing arguments.

Williams called the charges against his client "a hoax." He even took a shot at newspaper reporters, whom he called "morbid cynics who believe the worst about everybody."[33]

28. United States v. Johnson, Boykin, et al., Docket No. 26067, transcript page 1702.

29. Ibid.

30. Ibid.

31. Ibid., 1727.

32. Johnson's lawyer called to the stand a state delegate from Worcester County named Russell O. Hickman, who testified that I "resented" Johnson's opposition to my appointment. But after we showed that Hickman was actually employed by Johnson and had been a close associate of his for twenty-three years, not much more was said on the issue.

33. Edward Bennett Williams was considered a "superlawyer," the founder of the

To summarize his case, Doub, Johnson's lawyer, set up a large chart on an easel that he said would help the jurors more clearly see the linkage between the bona fide legal work Johnson had performed and the payments the House member had received. Williams also referred to the chart in his closing argument on Boykin's behalf.

That evening after adjournment, Marion, Weiner, Sachs, and I stayed up until about two or three o'clock in the morning working on my final rebuttal. Moylan and Civiletti also helped. To help prove our case, we hit on a strategy of using the same chart the defense had used.

The next day I used a thick marker to alter the defense lawyers' chart to show that the payments listed were not linked to legal services performed, as they had claimed, but to specific acts designed to quash Edlin's indictment. For each date, I methodically and slowly overwrote the chart, noting visits and calls to the Department of Justice that coincided with the payments. The result was a chart that showed the huge pressure placed on the Justice Department.

Finally, I asked the jurors to look closely at what Representative Boykin had at stake if only Edlin could remain free. Edlin would protect Boykin from foreclosure by taking over his failing land deal in Maryland and then pumping $125,000 into the project; committing $2.5 million from the two S&Ls he controlled to spend on Boykin's Maryland tract and another $500,000 on his Virginia land, thereby increasing the value of both; and making another $125,000 payment toward the Virginia project, plus purchasing the mortgage on the property for nearly $2.9 million.[34]

renowned law firm Williams & Connolly, and attorney for a long list of nationally and even internationally known defendants, ranging from Hugh Hefner, the publisher of *Playboy* magazine, to John Hinckley Jr., Ronald Reagan's would-be assassin. Williams also represented the mobsters Sam Giancana and Frank Costello, labor leader Jimmy Hoffa, fugitive financier Robert Vesco, singer Frank Sinatra, Representative Adam Clayton Powell, commodity trader Marc Rich, and Senator Joseph McCarthy, among many others. He was known for his almost total recall, often giving closing arguments (without notes) that lasted as long as two hours. He also was said to have a special way with jurors that benefited his clients. A sports fan, Williams at one time co-owned the Washington Redskins football team with Jack Kent Cooke and later owned the Baltimore Orioles baseball team. He was born in Hartford, Connecticut, and educated at the College of the Holy Cross and Georgetown University. He died in 1988 at the age of sixty-eight after an eleven-year battle with cancer. Albin Krebs, "Edward Bennett Williams, Trial Lawyer, Dead at 68; A Brilliant 'Superlawyer,'" *New York Times*, August 15, 1988; "Edward Bennett Williams," Wikipedia, http://en.wikipedia.org/wiki/Edward_Bennett_Williams.

34. United States v. Johnson, Boykin, et al., Docket No. 26067, transcript page 6193.

"That is an awful lot riding, ladies and gentlemen, on the liberty of a man . . . who can put money into the property, of a man who controls absolutely two savings and loan associations and the depositors' money therein," I said.[35]

"Public Office Is a Public Trust"

As I closed the case, I asked the jury the commonsense question of why Edlin did not go to his own congressional representative from Miami or even to the one who represented the district in Maryland where his savings and loan association was located. Instead, he had sought out Johnson and Boykin.

"Is it just coincidence that he went to two congressmen who had a personal financial stake in his freedom and the success for his business enterprises?"[36]

"I ask you," I said, "when you retire to the jury room, that you find that integrity is not for sale in this country; and that public office is a public trust; and that equal justice for all people regardless of their position is not an empty phrase; that you do justice in this case, not only to the defendants, but to all of the people of the United States."[37]

It took only three and a half hours of deliberation before the jury returned a verdict. Judge Thomsen listened as the word "guilty" was repeated thirty-two times, once for each charge against the four defendants.

Johnson was sentenced to six months in prison and fined $5,000. Boykin was fined $40,000, but due to his age and poor health (and arguments that Williams and I privately made to the judge on Boykin's behalf), he was given six months' probation. Edlin was sentenced to one year in prison and fined $16,000. Robinson was sentenced to six months.[38]

35. Ibid., 6194.

36. Ibid., 6230.

37. Ibid., 6232–33.

38. "We were all extremely proud of your efforts in connection with the Johnson-Boykin case and being well aware of all the time and hard work involved, I wanted to send my congratulations," Bobby Kennedy wrote me on his attorney general stationery following the

All except Boykin appealed, but only Johnson was successful. He argued that under the Constitution members of Congress were immune from prosecution for anything they said on the floor of House or Senate. The Fourth US Circuit Court of Appeals agreed, saying only the House of Representatives could punish Johnson for his conduct on the floor.[39] On February 24, 1966, the Supreme Court of the United States, in a 7–0 decision, concurred and overturned Johnson's conviction.[40] The high court said he could be tried again as long as all references to the speech were eliminated.[41]

His victory would be short-lived. By 1968, Sachs had become US attorney, and he tried and convicted Johnson a second time on all the charges except for the one related to his speech on the House floor. This time, the former Maryland Congress member went to prison.

The Speaker of the House Is Not above the Law

While Marion, Weiner, and I were working on the Johnson and Boykin case, Sachs and Civiletti began investigating A. Gordon Boone, who was about to become Speaker of the Maryland House of Delegates. They focused on the Security Financial Insurance Corporation, the deposit insurance firm set up in Maryland by Boone and his Baltimore County political cohorts with money from the Chicago financier Oran Mensik.

Boone, then fifty-three, was an important Democratic leader in Maryland. He lived in the upscale Ruxton neighborhood of Baltimore County, came from a socially prominent family, had a summer place in Maine, and had served with distinction in both Europe and the Pacific in World War II. He practiced law with the firm of Brewster, Boone,

verdict. "All of us here followed the case with great interest and were particularly pleased with the outcome," he stated. "Your fine handling of the matter from the beginning made a major difference—many thanks." US Attorney General Robert F. Kennedy to US Attorney Joseph D. Tydings, July 2, 1963, in possession of Senator Tydings.

39. The opinion was written by Chief Judge Simon E. Sobeloff of Baltimore. Bynum Shaw, "T. F. Johnson Case before High Court," *Baltimore Sun*, January 26, 1965, 40.

40. Adam Clymer, "Conviction of Johnson Overruled: Supreme Court Cites Use of House Speech by Prosecution," *Baltimore Sun*, February 25, 1966, C26.

41. The basis for immunity is a constitutional provision stipulating that, except for cases of treason, felony, or breach of peace, "for any Speech or Debate in either House they [i.e., senators and representatives] shall not be questioned in any other Place." US Constitution, Article I, section 6.1.

Maguire, Brennan and Cook and later with Boone and Cook. He was first elected to the Maryland House of Delegates in 1946 and, after losing a primary election for Congress in 1950, concentrated on climbing the ranks of leadership within the state assembly until he was elevated to Speaker of the House in January 1963.

When the grand jury indicted him, Mensik, and four others for falsely representing that Security was financially sound, Boone immediately stepped down as Speaker, but not until after his colleagues had given him a standing ovation.[42]

I still remember Bobby Kennedy calling me after we had alerted the Justice Department of our intention to indict Boone and his Democratic Party colleagues. "My God, Joe, can't you ever find a Republican to indict?" Bobby asked.

For months, the court heard various motions by Boone and the other defendants to dismiss the indictments, to change the trial venue, to try the defendants separately, or to disqualify Judge Watkins from the case because he had presided over Mensik's original trial back in 1961. By the time Boone finally went on trial in January 1964, I had resigned as US attorney to run for the US Senate, and Sachs and Civiletti carried on without me. Boone waived a jury trial in favor of letting Judge Watkins decide his fate.[43]

His defense largely boiled down to the claim that he left the details of running Security to others. In one humiliating exchange, a Baltimore County judge, testifying as a character witness for Boone, stated that Boone was good at politics and had an "excellent reputation for truth and veracity" but had "neither the aptitude nor the information

42. Boone was replaced on an acting basis by the chair of the House Ways and Means Committee, Delegate Marvin Mandel of Baltimore. Stephen E. Nordlinger, "Delegates Give Boone an Ovation," *Baltimore Sun*, February 21, 1963, 50. The others indicted besides Boone were Charles F. Culver, by then a former member of the House of Delegates from Baltimore County and president of Security; J. Thomas Ellicott, a Baltimore County attorney; C. Oran Mensik of Chicago, whose earlier trial in Maryland on charges related to S&Ls had ended in a hung jury; Henry McGurren, the Chicago lawyer who had delivered the $450,000 to Boone to capitalize Security; and D. Spencer Grow of Provo, Utah, a savings and loan operator in Utah and Idaho.

43. Culver, meanwhile, had pleaded no contest and been sentenced to a year in prison. Mensik and Grow were tried separately in Richmond, Virginia, in front of Judge Thomsen, and both were found guilty. Mensik was sentenced to five years and Grow, to four. Charges against McGurren were dismissed.

to practice law" and therefore left legal issues to other attorneys in his firm.[44]

Judge Watkins convicted Boone on six counts. In summarizing the case, he noted that one S&L was under criminal indictment, but Security had insured it anyway; another had records missing and was making illegal loans; and all of the S&Ls in the Security portfolio were losing money, yet Security continued to grant them insurance.[45]

Boone was sentenced to three years, fined $1,000, and stripped of his license to practice law. Hundreds of people lined the sidewalks outside the Post Office Building in downtown Baltimore to see the former Speaker of the Maryland House of Delegates, his handcuffed hands covered with an overcoat, walk to a car to be driven to federal prison.[46]

• • •

One postscript to the Boone saga—a story that Sachs likes to tell on himself:

In 1986, some twenty-two years after Boone was convicted, Sachs ran into Boone at a Baltimore County Bar Association dinner. By then, Sachs was finishing his second term as the state attorney general and was vying for the Democratic nomination for governor against Baltimore Mayor William Donald Schaefer. Boone, as Steve retells the story, was with some old cronies having drinks when he spotted Sachs and summoned him to his table.

As Sachs approached, Boone stood, hugged him, and turned to his friends to say that he had the honor of having been prosecuted by "two kids," Sachs and Civiletti, one of whom was then the attorney general of Maryland and the other the attorney general of the United States. Boone went on to assure Sachs that he knew that neither he nor Ben

44. Another state judge called to testify was asked, "What services did [Boone] perform for clients?" He replied, "Practically nothing." Theodore W. Hendricks, "Boone Seen Depending on Others: Judges Raine and Turnbull Testify at Mail Fraud Trial," *Baltimore Sun*, February 28, 1964, 42.

45. Theodore W. Hendricks, "Boone Is Convicted in Mail Fraud Scheme; No Appeal Is Planned," *Baltimore Sun*, March 6, 1964, 40.

46. After serving thirteen months at the prison camp in Allenwood, Pennsylvania, Boone was paroled. In 1969, seven judges of the Baltimore County Circuit Court voted to readmit him to the practice of law, but that decision caused such a furor that the highest court in the state, the Court of Appeals, ordered a rehearing, and Boone ultimately dropped his request for reinstatement. DeWitt Bliss, "Judges Act to Let Boone Practice Law," *Baltimore Sun*, June 25, 1969, C28; C. Mason White, "High Court Upsets Boone Bar Return," *Baltimore Sun*, November 6, 1969, C20.

were to blame for his unjust prosecution. It was all the fault of "that no good son-of-a-bitch, Tydings," he said.

Boone looked to Sachs for confirmation. Torn between his loyalty to me and his prospects as a candidate for governor before a group that could be influential with Baltimore County voters, Steve hesitated momentarily and then firmly replied, "You're right, Gordon, it really was that son-of-a-bitch, Tydings!"

Steve has dutifully apologized many times over, but he says he cannot help retelling the story because it casts such clear light on the "casual deceptions endemic to politics."[47]

I love Steve's story. Remember, I'm a politician, too.

47. Stephen H. Sachs, letter to Joseph D. Tydings commemorating the fortieth anniversary of Tydings's 1964 campaign for the US Senate, September 12, 2004, 5, in possession of Senator Tydings.

CHAPTER 10

Kidnapping, Murder, and Assassination

My almost three years as US attorney began with one of the most disturbing and heart-wrenching cases I have ever handled. It ended on one of the darkest days our nation has ever endured.

In mid-November 1960, the nude body of Michael Condetti, a seven-year-old boy, was discovered in a wooded area of Ardmore, a Maryland suburb of Washington, DC. The second grader had been sexually assaulted and strangled.

Finding and convicting his murderer was among those cases awaiting me when I arrived as the federal prosecutor for Maryland the following spring.

Ever since aviator Charles Lindbergh's infant son was kidnapped and killed in 1932, the transportation of a kidnap victim across a state line had become a federal crime, potentially punishable by death. Condetti, who lived in Washington, was lured away from a shopping center near his home where he had gone to buy a book bag. His body was found in Maryland three days later.

The FBI launched a massive investigation to find the boy's killer, interviewing thousands of people over six months, but they were stumped. The break came when FBI agents were referred to Ralph P. Oropollo, chief psychiatrist of Clifton T. Perkins Hospital, the maximum security psychiatric prison for Maryland. Oropollo helped the FBI develop a personality profile of the killer, and that profile turned out to be so accurate that one newspaper said it "proved a better match than many an artist's sketch."[1]

---

1. John P. MacKenzie, "Psychiatric Clues Linked Alvey to Boy Slaying," *Washington Post*, February 18, 1962.

Oropollo told the FBI agents that the killer probably did not drive a car since that would have been considered too masculine; probably lived alone, or perhaps with his mother; was likely a heavy drinker with a criminal record, including prior sex offenses; and probably was not the killer type but rather someone who panicked when his victim resisted.[2]

In November 1961, Miami authorities arrested a forty-one-year-old Washington area auto body worker named Joseph H. Alvey and charged him with the boy's kidnapping and murder. At his trial, which opened in late January 1962, testimony revealed that Alvey did not drive a car; lived with his mother; had a long police record, including serving five years for molesting a little boy; and was an excessive drinker.

Even though Alvey pleaded not guilty, we were convinced he was because he had given the FBI a statement that essentially retraced all of the kidnapper's movements in ways that only the real killer would have known. His confession, however, was inadmissible as evidence because the FBI had failed to warn Alvey that he had the right to remain silent.

Dan McMullen, who was an assistant US attorney, and I tried the case together. Because we had access to Alvey's inadmissible statement, we knew we could find witnesses to reconstruct and verify almost every step of the crime—from the store clerks who observed Alvey buying candy for the boy, to the two bus routes they took into Maryland, to the gruesome details of the murder.

Forensic evidence showed the boy had been strangled with a small chain he wore around his neck, a chain that held, of all things, a crucifix. I came to believe that Alvey never intended to murder the boy. I think the boy struggled, Alvey grabbed the chain, perhaps to keep him from escaping, and the boy died. Scared, he left the scene and boarded a train for Florida.

Alvey was slightly built, with graying hair and tattoos on his arms. He was described in newspaper accounts as "the black sheep of his well-regarded family."[3] He was examined by Dr. Manfred Guttmacher, one of the leading forensic psychiatrists in the country and the chief medical adviser to the state court in Baltimore. Guttmacher's conclusion was

2. Ibid.

3. Jerry O'Leary Jr., "Alvey Goes before Court Tomorrow in '60 Kidnap-Death of Condetti Boy," *Washington Star*, June 28, 1962.

that Alvey was a pedophile and extremely dangerous, yet not the type
to commit murder. His opinion was that Alvey should not be executed,
but imprisoned and never released.[4]

That decision, however, rested with the jury of ten men and two
women, which was instructed that it had three options: find Alvey not
guilty; find him guilty, but let Judge Thomsen decide his sentence; or
find him guilty and sentence him to death. When the jury was selected,
I tried to strike any potential jurors who indicated they opposed the
death penalty.

The jury remained deadlocked for more than eight hours—not over
whether Alvey was guilty, but whether he should die for his crime. We
later learned that eleven of the jurors favored death, but one had held
out.

Before final arguments, I had met with Judge Thomsen and Guttmacher and urged that Alvey be sentenced to life in prison. By the time
the jury finished deliberating, it was 12:15 in the morning and the
courtroom was nearly deserted. The jury returned a guilty verdict, but
with no sentencing recommendation.

I immediately asked "that Joseph Alvey be sentenced to life in prison
with a recommendation that he never be admitted to parole until he is
no longer a menace to society." Judge Thomsen quickly agreed, saying,
"The sentence must be life imprisonment in view of the fact that the
jury might have been more severe. I must recommend that he never be
released until the parole board is certain he will never be a danger to our
children or our children's children."[5]

The Alvey case was the only kidnapping and murder case our office
handled while I was US attorney, and I am glad of that. In hindsight, the

4. Manfred S. Guttmacher was born in 1898 to a family of rabbis. He and his brother,
Alan Frank Guttmacher, who later served as president of Planned Parenthood, graduated from
the Johns Hopkins University in Baltimore. Manfred Guttmacher was appointed chief medical
adviser to the Supreme Bench of Baltimore in 1930, and he served in that capacity until his
death in 1966. He was the author of at least five books regarding sex offenses, psychiatry and
the law, and the mind of the murderer. He testified at the 1964 trial of Jack Ruby, convicted of
killing Lee Harvey Oswald, whom the Warren Commission said assassinated President John F.
Kennedy. Associated Press, "Dr. Manfred Guttmacher Dies at 68; Psychiatrist at Trial of Jack
Ruby," *Washington Post*, November 9, 1966, B-10; "Manfred Guttmacher," Wikipedia, http://
en.wikipedia.org/wiki/Manfred_Guttmacher.

5. Jerry O'Leary Jr., "Alvey Guilty, Given Life in Boy Kidnapping," *Washington Star*, February 8, 1962.

decision not to execute Alvey was the right one. There can be no joy in trying a case involving such a brutal crime; there is only the satisfaction that, in the end, justice was done and someone who was a clear danger to society was put away for good.

Frozen Cash

Even before Robert Kennedy became attorney general of the United States, he had made a name for himself as a fighter against organized crime. He gained national visibility as chief counsel to the Senate Labor Rackets Committee in the late 1950s when he squared off with Jimmy Hoffa, president of the Teamsters union. When Bobby took over at Justice, he quickly established a special group to focus on organized crime. This move forced the previously reluctant J. Edgar Hoover to make organized crime a priority for the FBI. Convictions of gangsters suddenly were on the rise.

For most states, the Justice Department assigned a staff attorney to oversee organized crime prosecutions, but for Maryland, Bobby delegated that authority to me. Our organized crime team would meet regularly in the FBI office in our Baltimore federal courthouse, but the truth was we didn't have the kind of "Mafia warlords" in Maryland that were prevalent then in New Jersey, New York, and some other states. Most of our "organized crime" amounted to illegal gambling.

I was an activist chief of our organized crime efforts. In February 1962, I accompanied an IRS strike force of thirty-seven agents who conducted gambling raids on five houses in and around Annapolis. The most memorable target was a house that had a one-way mirror in the front so those inside could see who was approaching without being seen themselves. In the basement, agents discovered a hidden door behind shelves full of canned goods and kitchen utensils. Behind it they found an accounting room, gambling paraphernalia, and a large, chest-style food freezer. When they opened the top, they pulled out $8,000 in frozen cash.

That fall, Marion and I followed federal agents—some armed with axes and mauls—on another raid at a home in Dundalk. Inside, three phones were ringing off the hook, so for the next forty-five minutes Marion and I started answering them as one caller after another sought to place bets. At one point, one caller asked Marion to place a bet on a horse named Prosecutor.

In almost all of these cases, the first strategy for defense attorneys was to move to have evidence against their clients thrown out by claiming it had been illegally seized. As a result, Marion became the office expert on the Fourth Amendment, which prohibits unreasonable searches and seizures and requires any warrant to be sanctioned by a judge and based on probable cause. Once the evidence was determined to have been legally seized and admitted, most defendants pleaded guilty rather than face a likely conviction.[6]

Missiles in Cuba and the Army-Navy Game

In the midst of the broad array of cases we handled—chasing down gamblers, prosecuting former members of Congress, going after tax cheats, bank robbers, kidnappers, and forgers—came an unexpected and sobering interruption: the Cuban Missile Crisis.

In October 1962, the United States discovered that our global nemesis, the Soviet Union, had armed the island nation of Cuba—just ninety miles off the coast of Florida—with nuclear missiles. This led to a tense, thirteen-day international standoff during which many still believe the world came the closest it has ever come to nuclear war.

Sometime during that awful week I was instructed to prepare my office to relocate, if necessary. We went into the office safe and pulled out some instructions, untouched since the Eisenhower days, that said we should be prepared to move, if ordered to do so, to Hampstead High School in the northeastern corner of Carroll County. Not knowing what else to do, I dispatched Sachs and Civiletti to Carroll County to make arrangements.

The two drove up in Sachs's aging Chevy on what he recalls as a beautiful fall day. They presented their credentials to the principal of

6. In many of these cases, those who were arrested were charged with failing to buy a special fifty-dollar federal occupational tax stamp specifically for gamblers. This requirement presented gamblers with a Hobson's choice: if they purchased the stamp, it tipped off state authorities that they were running illegal gambling operations; if they did not, they could be prosecuted by federal authorities for failing to buy the stamp. In 1968, the Supreme Court of the United States decided in a Connecticut case that the 1951 law requiring the stamps was an unconstitutional infringement of the Fifth Amendment protection against self-incrimination.

Hampstead High, explained why they were there, and started asking about the availability of cots, drinking water, food supplies, and generators. The principal, Steve later reported, wanted no part of it and rerouted the two young assistant US attorneys to the firehouse in the nearby county seat of Westminster. There, the firefighters—"lazing in front of the engine"—were no more interested in Cuba or the plight of the US Attorney's Office than the principal had been. Fortunately, several days later President Kennedy announced he had reached a deal with Soviet Premier Nikita Khrushchev to remove the missiles from Cuba, and the crisis subsided.[7]

One subplot of all this was that we were required as part of our preparations to divide our staff into an A-list of those who would be relocated to Hampstead and a B-list of those who would have to remain behind at our Baltimore offices. Steve recalls that his secretary, Helen Brooks, a veteran in the office, was somehow placed on the B-list and never quite got over it. "I guess she thought she was going to be left to be incinerated at Ground Zero," Steve recalled.[8]

Our world in those days was always moving on multiple levels simultaneously. Usually we were in court, or before a grand jury, combing through files, or working with investigators. But sometimes on the weekends some of my assistants and their families came out to Oakington to swim, eat, and have fun on the lawn.

Toward the end of 1961, Sachs and I had been trying the tax evasion case against Grant Foster. When the jury returned the guilty verdict on a Saturday, however, I was not in the courtroom to hear it. Instead, I was aboard a special train accompanying the president and his large entourage to the annual Army-Navy game in Philadelphia, a trip organized by the president's friend, Red Fay.

I recall that trip clearly because Ginny had just broken her arm the day before, when she was thrown from her horse in a fox hunting accident. Ginny was a very good rider, but her horse apparently hit a big timber and she hit the frozen ground hard. But Ginny and I had a great time visiting with people on the train. Among the dignitaries in

7. Stephen H. Sachs, "What Did You Do During the Cuban Missile Crisis, Grandpa?," retitled "A Crisis in Cuba Meant Little to Carroll County," and published as a *Washington Post* op-ed, December 28, 2014.

8. Stephen H. Sachs, interview by the author, February 24, 2015.

the president's party were Vice President Johnson, Ohio Governor Mike DiSalle, and Admiral George W. Anderson Jr., chief of naval operations.

This was Kennedy's first Army-Navy game as president, and he officiated at the coin toss to start the game. Even though he had been a naval hero during World War II, he sat on the Army side during the first half before moving over to the Navy side for the second half. I can still remember him smoking a slim cigar and enjoying the party atmosphere. At some point during the day, the president autographed the cast on Ginny's broken arm.[9]

The Interpol Conference

In June 1963, shortly after the jury had returned guilty verdicts in the bribery case against former Congress members Johnson and Boykin, I received a congratulatory telephone call from President Kennedy. That brief conversation led to the president's dinner visit to Oakington on August 1 and to my appointment as the Justice Department representative to the annual meeting of Interpol, the international police organization, that September in Helsinki, Finland.[10]

As one of the few US attorneys designated as their district director for organized crime cases, it was easy enough for the administration to justify my appointment. Bobby coached me about how to plan a larger-scale trip culminating in Helsinki in order to bolster my foreign affairs credentials in advance of my expected run for the Senate in 1964. I had no background or training in foreign policy. Bobby instructed me to find someone to accompany me in case I got sick or something else unexpected happened, so I arranged for my good friend from Florida, Raymond Mason, to join me. Bobby also informed me that we would both have to pay our own expenses and airfare![11]

We landed in Europe August 7, about three weeks before the Interpol conference was to begin. First stop was Rome, where my friend

9. The Army-Navy game was played on December 2, 1961, at Philadelphia Stadium. Navy came from behind in the second half to win, 13–7, at the time the third consecutive victory it had achieved over Army.

10. Thomas T. Fenton, "President Is Cheered at Academy," *Baltimore Sun*, August 2, 1963, 38.

11. Bobby was worried that one of us might contract malaria or dysentery, but Raymond was the only one of us to get sick; he drank a milkshake in Cairo that did not agree with him.

Frank Gallagher—by then the legal counsel to the Catholic Archdiocese of Baltimore—had helped arrange an audience for us with Pope Paul VI at his summer residence, Castel Gandolfo.

From there, we embarked on a whirlwind trip through the Middle East, Africa, Scandinavia, and Eastern Europe, before meeting our wives in the lake district of northern Italy. We met King Hussein of Jordan and were wined and dined by US embassy personnel and local business executives everywhere we went. In the Middle East, we toured biblical sites, from the place where Jesus was born to where he was crucified. We visited Jerusalem, Jericho, and Bethlehem. We saw Roman ruins, forts built by Crusaders, the Church of the Holy Sepulcher, the Dead Sea, and the Garden of Gethsemane.

Everywhere I went, I spoke with judges, criminal justice officials, and lawyers, trying to understand the legal systems of each nation. Raymond, meanwhile, met with bankers, real estate investors, and others, always in search of opportunities for his expanding mortgage and insurance business back home.

We visited beautiful Beirut, the "Paris of the Middle East." Then it was off to Jordan and Egypt. This trip provided me with my first clear understanding of the profound Arab-Israeli conflict in the region. In Lebanon and at several other stops, we were met by representatives of the Bata Shoe Company, an international firm originally founded in Czechoslovakia but that had relocated the company headquarters to Harford County when World War II broke out in 1939.[12]

Next we flew to Nigeria, Ghana, Guinea, Sierra Leone, and Senegal, spending a couple of days at each stop. The Kennedy administration

12. Bata was founded in Zlín, Czechoslovakia, in 1894. Within ten years, it was producing twenty-two hundred pairs of shoes per day. The founders employed modern machinery and built housing, schools, and hospitals for the factory workers. After World War I, it expanded operations worldwide. The firm headquarters was relocated to a two-thousand-acre site on the Bush River in Maryland in 1939. My father, then in the Senate, helped Bata arrange for Czech citizens to immigrate to the United States to work in the factory despite opposition from labor unions, Bata competitors, and US government immigration restrictions. (As a way of returning the favor, the Bata family decided that while I was in Europe and the Middle East, they would do what they could to help me.) After the war, the company relocated to Canada and the five-story Bata factory in Belcamp was demolished in 2004. "Bata's Story Begins in 1894," Bata, http://www.bata.com/our-history/; Allan Vought, "'Bata Belcamp' Book Chronicles Rise, Fall of Footwear Manufacturing Center," *The Aegis*, http://www.baltimoresun.com/news/maryland/harford/abingdon/ph-ag-bata-history-book-0514-20140513-story.html#page=1.

was trying to foster the development of democracies in these countries, most of which had only recently won their independence from their colonial overseers.

From Africa, we flew to Finland for the Interpol conference. There we met the head of Scotland Yard and dined with the American ambassador, Carl Rowan, the nationally renowned journalist. It was interesting for me to see how those attending the Interpol conference passed information back and forth and tried to get police agencies from around the world to cooperate better.

The last leg of our official trip took us behind the Iron Curtain for visits to Moscow, Warsaw, and West Berlin. In Moscow, we dined at Spaso House, the residence of the American ambassador, where I posed for a photograph next to a picture of my grandfather, who had been the US ambassador there prior to World War II. Our visit was less than a year after the Cuban missile crisis, and the US relationship with the Soviet Union was still extremely tense. In Poland, I was impressed by how deep-seated the Poles' hatred of communism was and how hard they were working to rebuild their economy. This insight would help me in my Senate campaign the following year when questions arose about the United States' relationship with Poland.

West Berlin was then still a capitalist island in the midst of communist East Germany. We lunched with Chancellor Willy Brandt and, by coincidence, met a visiting American filmmaker, Walt Disney. This marked my first return to Germany since my army days right after World War II, and I was amazed at how much had been rebuilt. We visited the Berlin Wall, where we could peer over into dismal East Berlin and plainly see the contrast between the flourishing free society in the West and the drab, controlled society in the East.

The trip concluded in Bellagio, a magnificent resort town on Lake Como in northern Italy, where I attended an international penal conference. Our wives, Ginny and Minerva, met us there.

Going abroad was Bobby's idea, and since foreign embassies knew I was the attorney general's guy they rolled out the red carpet. That trip was an eye-opener, and it gave me a great deal of confidence.

A brochure produced for my Senate campaign the following year featured a series of pictures: me standing before the Berlin Wall; talking with Ambassador Rowan in Helsinki; meeting with His Holiness Pope Paul VI; and, finally, accompanying my "close friend," John F. Kennedy.

Part of the text read, "Tydings has crossed the Atlantic eight times, traveled extensively through free Europe, behind the Iron Curtain, and into the troubled lands of the Near East and Africa." That was all true, but much of the credit needed to go to Bobby Kennedy.

Farewell Lunch at the House of Welsh

After returning from my trip that fall, I began to develop plans in earnest to run for the US Senate.

On Wednesday evening, November 20, I was among seven hundred guests invited to attend the annual Judicial Reception at the White House.[13] I saw the president briefly after he left his private reception for Supreme Court justices and their wives. We spoke for a minute or so— just long enough for me to tell him that I planned to announce my resignation the following day to explore a Senate candidacy.

"You know, this is going to go great," he said with a mischievous grin. "You know, you just stay home and let your wife run the campaign." We both smiled.

After the Judicial Reception that night, there was a thirty-eighth birthday party for Bobby Kennedy at his Hickory Hill estate in Virginia, but neither the president nor his wife attended. They were packing for an important campaign swing through Texas.[14]

At eleven o'clock the next morning, I held a press conference to announce that I was resigning as US attorney, effective the following day, and that I was considering challenging the Republican J. Glenn Beall Sr. for the Senate in 1964. Although the Kennedy administration had publicly said it would stay neutral in any intra–Democratic Party primary fight, I figured many people knew I had the president's full backing and thought that would surely help me. My principal opponent for the nomination was likely to be two-term state comptroller Louis L. Goldstein of Calvert County, who, according to newspaper reports, was likely to announce his candidacy the following week.

To celebrate the end of my three years as US attorney, all of my assistants and I gathered on Friday for a luncheon at the House of Welsh, a favorite restaurant near our office. We had reserved a little room on the

13. Thurston Clarke, *JFK's Last 100 Days* (New York: Penguin Audio, 2013).
14. Ibid.

second floor, and there were probably eight or nine of us there. We also were celebrating the departure of Hardin Marion, who was resigning so he could manage my campaign. I was presented with a set of pens. Suddenly, Frank Udoff, the US marshal, came into the room.

"The president's been shot in Dallas," he grimly announced. I do not believe we knew at that point how serious President Kennedy's condition was, but Udoff came back a short time later and said simply, "President Kennedy is dead."

Only someone who lived through that awful day can fully understand how stunned we were. A wave of sadness blanketed us. There were a million questions and no answers. How could something like this happen? Naturally, the luncheon ended, and, almost in a trance, we returned to our office to see if we could find out more.

I was the only one in the office who actually knew the president, but all of us felt we were part of the Kennedy administration and were answering JFK's call to public service. My mind was a confused jumble of thoughts, images, and memories—and sudden worries about what Bobby must be going through and about the president's beautiful young wife and children. Who would do this? And why? And what did it mean for the future of the country?

I remember going up the elevator and running into Juanita Jackson Mitchell, the famous civil rights leader and wife of Clarence M. Mitchell Jr., the equally famous lawyer for the National Association for the Advancement of Colored People (NAACP). I do not know why she happened to be in the building, but we spoke briefly. We were both broken up by the news.

Upstairs, we listened to radio reports from Dallas. The FBI's office was on the same hall, and we tried to find out what they had learned. After a while, there was a knock on my door and in walked Chief Judge Roszel Thomsen. Judge Thomsen's chambers were on the floor above our offices, and I had never seen him—or any of the other federal judges—on our floor before. There was a rigid hierarchy in the courthouse, and the judges were indisputably at the top. We went to them; they never came to us.

But Judge Thomsen knew of my relationship with the president and his family. He came to deliver his condolences in person. Sachs, who later wrote about the incident, said he had walked out of my office that afternoon, only to be surprised to find Judge Thomsen standing alone in the hallway. The judge asked Steve if he thought it would be "all right" if he expressed his condolences to the US attorney.

"What Roszel Thomsen's unprecedented visit on that dreadful day demonstrated for me," Sachs wrote in a newspaper column that was published in commemoration of the fiftieth anniversary of JFK's assassination, "was the leveling effect of grief. It seemed to me then—and seems to me still—that his visit spoke the universal language of compassion, unmitigated by age, or station, or provenance. What I learned that day was that grief, and the imperative to comfort one another in moments of deep sorrow, knows no rank."[15]

I think Steve's description perfectly captured the feeling we all shared that terrible afternoon. The president's murder had changed everything.

15. Stephen H. Sachs, "Grief Knows No Rank," *Baltimore Sun*, November 21, 2013.

CHAPTER 11

Challenging the Democratic Machine

In shock, Hardin Marion and I retreated to the privacy of the offices at Tydings & Rosenberg to figure out when and how I should wage my campaign for the US Senate.

The Kennedy assassination had put everything on hold, including my run for the Senate. The assassination also forced Louis Goldstein to postpone his expected announcement about running for the Senate seat.

The nation was in mourning. It had lost a young, dynamic leader. No one was quite sure at the time whether Kennedy's assassin had acted alone or was part of a larger conspiracy. Lyndon Baines Johnson of Texas, a man far different from President Kennedy in appearance, experience, and upbringing, was suddenly our president. The Kennedy administration program was left unfinished, abruptly frozen in place. Kennedy's wife and children, his aides, his Cabinet secretaries, even his brother (whose antipathy toward Johnson was well known), all faced an unknowable future. The world had turned topsy-turvy.

I had lost someone I not only knew but greatly admired. The president was not some remote figure I had only read about in the newspapers. He was someone who had slept in my home, someone I had campaigned with side-by-side, who had invited my wife and me on boating excursions on the Potomac, to the Army-Navy game, and to events at the White House. He had eaten dinner at our table, seated between my wife and my mother. He and his wonderful family had become real friends. And he, of course, was my most important political benefactor, the one who made it possible for me to become US attorney and whose backing for my run for the Senate was already well known. His quiet support would have put any other candidate at an obvious disadvantage. Had he not been assassinated, I think I might have run unopposed for the Senate, notwithstanding the strong animosities I had created as a legislative reformer and federal prosecutor. The death of the president meant that the state organization now was free to draft a strong candidate it preferred—in all probability, the popular Goldstein—to enter the primary.

I knew I could not publicly launch a political campaign so soon following such a national tragedy, but I also knew the political clock was ticking and the Democratic primary in Maryland was coming up in May, barely six months away. At that early stage, I had neither the financial resources nor the political support to wage a successful campaign. What I did have were two important, influential friends, both of whom had supported President Kennedy and without whom I never would have succeeded: Jerry Hoffberger and Frank Gallagher. The president was assassinated around midday on a Friday. On Sunday morning, Hardin and I met with Jerry and Frank. Both said I should run, that the president would have wanted me to run, and that they would go all out to help.

Slowly, quietly, out of sight of the press, Hardin and I began to assemble a campaign team and to reach out to supporters around the state. I personally recruited our county campaign chairs, quality people like Lynn Clark and Dick Schifter in Montgomery County.[1] Although Hardin was a neophyte at running a statewide campaign, he handled the day-to-day campaign operations; Gallagher served as campaign treasurer, although his real job was political strategist; and Hoffberger oversaw fundraising and helped with advertising and media.

I would not have run in 1964 if Jerry Hoffberger had not said, "Joe, I'm behind you. You run and I'll worry about raising the money." Or, if Frank Gallagher hadn't said, "I'm with you. We'll walk the plank together." Without those two, I would not have run.

---

1. Richard Schifter has had a long and colorful career. He fled his native Austria after the Nazi annexation in 1938 and immigrated to the United States at age fifteen. He did intelligence work for the US Army during World War II and later graduated from Yale Law School and practiced law in Maryland. He has served in a number of capacities for the United Nations, including as US representative to the United Nations Commission on Human Rights and as deputy US representative to the United Nations Security Council with the rank of ambassador. In 1985, President Reagan appointed Schifter to be assistant secretary of state for human rights and humanitarian affairs. He has been an ardent supporter of the nation of Israel.

Against the Party Organization—Again

The biggest obstacle I faced was that the ruling Democratic Party organization in the state, which, from Governor Tawes on down, solidly backed Goldstein. I, of course, had been in this position before. Party leaders had fought with me when I was in the General Assembly; they vehemently opposed my appointment as US attorney, and they blamed me for embarrassing our party by prosecuting two Democratic members of Congress and the Democratic Speaker of the House of Delegates. They did not want me in the US Senate.

I have always believed that Goldstein did not really want to run for the US Senate. I certainly do not think he would have run if Kennedy had lived and was seen as backing me. Goldstein's real ambition was to be governor. It was widely expected that he would run for governor in 1966, when Governor Tawes's two terms were completed. But Tawes wanted Attorney General Tom Finan to succeed him and feared that Goldstein would defeat Finan in the 1966 gubernatorial primary. So the governor and his crowd pressured Goldstein to run for the US Senate in 1964 by promising him full party and labor support. This, they thought, would assure Finan a clear path for governor two years later.

This deal—what I labeled "a corrupt political bargain"—became the centerpiece of my campaign. I argued that voters should not give away a US Senate seat as a political chip in a state political power struggle over who should be elected governor in 1966. The week I formally announced my resignation as US attorney, Charlie Whiteford, the political reporter for the *Baltimore Sun*, wrote, "Mr. Tydings, a highly independent Democrat, can expect little help from machine politicians. So, he will be making the rounds, trying to find if his candidacy would draw support from civic groups and individuals who are willing to buck the dominant State organization headed by Governor Tawes." Whiteford added, "He has been a highly active prosecutor, to the chagrin of some Maryland politicians."[2]

Newspaper articles declared I had no chance of winning against the state party organization; it was just too strong. These stories actually made me realize that my campaign was about much more than

2. Charles Whiteford, "Tydings Set to Resign as U.S. Attorney," *Baltimore Sun*, November 18, 1963, 40.

just running for the Senate. I felt it just was not right that the organization could determine who could run for high office and block anyone it didn't want. I saw opportunity. Here, finally, was a chance to change the direction of our party, bring new and younger leadership to the fore, and follow in the direction that our fallen president had been leading us: civil rights reform, electoral reform, and progressive economic and political reform.

Times had changed, but the controlling Democratic leaders did not seem to realize it. It was largely a generational change. Kennedy was the youngest man ever elected president, and he had succeeded Dwight D. Eisenhower, who at seventy was the oldest president in history up to that time. After the 1960 election, young people flocked to Washington, excited about their potential to do good deeds through public service. We had been inspired by the Kennedys.

Throughout the early 1960s, Americans seemed to be shifting— where we lived, how we moved around, what kind of music we listened to, and what we thought about the traditional ways of doing things, from racial relations to sexual relations. There was a bolt of new energy coursing through the country. I was part of a generation of young leaders who felt we could harness that energy to improve everyone's lives and change our nation and the world for the better.

If the state organization wanted to fight me, good—that was a fight I was willing to take on.

I started calling our contacts around the state, trying to put in place a statewide network. I still knew people throughout Maryland from my days at the University of Maryland, law school, and the Young Democrats. I had friends and colleagues from the General Assembly and from my years as US attorney. And, of course, I had the goodwill of veteran politicians around the state who knew and admired my father.

Hardin pulled together a campaign made up primarily of volunteers. County headquarters were all self-supporting. Most of the money we raised was earmarked for television, radio, and print advertising. Almost every county had male and female co-chairs, but the real chairpersons were usually the women.

Gradually, we built a staff. We hired Jo-Ann Orlinsky from Baltimore to manage the campaign headquarters and help with city politics.[3] Joe

3. When Jo-Ann came for her first interview, she brought her husband, Wally, with her

McInerny appeared out of nowhere to work on the campaign, and he became my scheduler. We persuaded Edgar Feingold and volunteer Ruth Shaw to help with speeches and the press. Compensation was minuscule until after we won the primary.

On January 5, 1964, Goldstein, then fifty, formally entered the race, appearing at the Maryland State House with his wife, Hazel, and their three children to file formally as a candidate. Goldstein was in his second term as state comptroller (essentially the state tax collector and financial officer), but he had spent nineteen years representing Calvert County in the Maryland General Assembly, the last four as Senate president. Goldstein was smart and wily. He was good with money and became known for making shrewd land investments all over the state, particularly in southern Maryland and the Eastern Shore.[4]

I entered the race January 14 with a full-throated attack on the "old-guard machine" in the state. "No backroom lobbyist in an executive suite in Annapolis should have the power to dictate to the people of Maryland who shall run for United States Senator in 1964 and who shall run for governor in 1966," I said that night following a dinner in my honor in Aberdeen, about four miles from Oakington. "My candidacy gives the citizens of Maryland the opportunity to make a clear choice: a choice between 10 more years of the same old ways and the same old guard, or a new era with new ideas and a new voice responsive to the needs of all the people of our state," I said.[5]

because he wanted to make sure I was liberal enough. Walter S. Orlinsky was a piece of work! He was a brilliant idealist, the son of a biblical scholar from New York City who was the first Jew to be involved in the translation of the New Testament when the Revised Standard Version was produced. Wally rose to become president of the Baltimore City Council but was frustrated by playing second fiddle to Mayor William Donald Schaefer. Wally ultimately fell from grace after being convicted of taking a bribe. I guess I passed Wally's test because Jo-Ann came to work for us and stayed throughout my Senate career.

4. Goldstein's style was that of a "good ol' boy," an "aw, shucks," back-slapping, broadly grinning pol who never missed a chance to stand before a camera. When he campaigned, he handed out fake gold coins with his name on one side and his trademark slogan, "God bless you all real good," on the flip side. In one campaign years later, he was said to have climbed a telephone pole to shake hands with a lineman. He attended Washington College and University of Maryland Law School, enlisted after Pearl Harbor as a private in the US Marines, served on General Douglas MacArthur's War Crimes Commission investigating Japanese atrocities, and was discharged as a first lieutenant. He served fourteen years in the Maryland General Assembly, including a term as Senate president, and then as state comptroller for forty years. He died on July 6, 1998, at age eighty-five.

5. Stephen E. Nordlinger, "Tydings Says He Will Run for Senate," *Baltimore Sun*, January 15, 1964.

Our campaign theme was "Working for Maryland, Not the Machine."

I challenged Goldstein to debate me on domestic and foreign issues—a challenge he never accepted—and stated unequivocally my support for the major civil rights legislation then pending in the Congress, which was almost identical to the bill I had co-sponsored in the General Assembly. The long overdue legislation was a Kennedy legacy now being pushed by Johnson.

"Lip service is not enough," I said. "Our commitment must come from the heart as well as the mind."[6] Behind me was a red, white, and blue banner that showed an hourglass with the words, "Time for Tydings." We turned the hourglass symbol into a lapel pin that became as important to our campaign as Jack Kennedy's PT boat lapel pin was to his.

With Hoffberger's help, we began to do some polling. After the high-profile cases I had prosecuted as US attorney, I felt certain that people around the state would know who I was. They did not. Goldstein's name recognition was around 40 percent; mine was closer to 17 percent, and fully half of those who thought they knew me confused me with my father. I was pretty humbled by this revelation, and it showed how much work we had to do. While those numbers were disappointing, those who knew who I was seemed to like what I had done and were motivated to help.

What was funny, though, was how many times I would be out campaigning and people—particularly older people—would say, "Joe, the minute I walked in the room I recognized you—you're the spitting image of your father!" That was pretty amazing, since I had been adopted by Millard Tydings. There is no question I tried to emulate him in many ways.[7] We were both tall and the way we stood and spoke was similar, but other than that we really did not look that much alike.[8]

---

6. Quoted in ibid.

7. I was still regularly wearing my father's clothes, including one of his old overcoats that probably exhibited more wear than was acceptable for a candidate for the US Senate. Hardin and some of my other campaign aides thought it was time for a change, so they quietly asked Ginny to please lose that overcoat. And that is what happened—none of us ever saw it again.

8. Years later, when I was doing some work on law enforcement assistance in the Senate, I received a congratulatory letter from an elderly police officer who said, "The first time I voted for you was in 1926," and, clearly confused, he ended the note by asking, "Senator, there is some question: Are you your father or are you your father's son?"

Early on, it appeared that David Hume, who had made a surprisingly strong challenge to Tawes in the 1962 gubernatorial primary by attacking the governor's conservative record, might enter the Senate primary. I knew if Hume got into the race, it would hurt my chances because we both opposed the state organization and would be going after the same group of voters. Twice during this period I got grilled by activists in Montgomery County and in the progressive Mount Royal Democratic Club in Baltimore about whether I was liberal enough. I figured I would have the financial backing and organization necessary to run an effective race but that Hume would not. Hardin, Steve Sachs, and a strong western Maryland supporter named Victor Cushwa finally convinced Hume to give up the race and, instead, to chair my campaign.[9]

I remember telling Ginny that I might not win the Senate race, but if I did not, I would run two years later for governor because I knew the public was tired of the state organization controlling Maryland politics. My main goal was to clean up the political system in Maryland, and I was like a bulldog trying to pry loose the grip lobbyists and political bosses had on the system. I knew that issue was there, ripe for attack, and it would just be a matter of time before we would succeed. The more I campaigned, the more I realized this issue was striking a chord with voters.

It was unfair, I thought, for the organization to line up many of the unions behind Louis Goldstein because I had a stronger pro-union record. I had been one of the few, if not the only, rural legislator to vote against so-called right-to-work legislation. The party organization had also ingratiated itself with a number of prominent African Americans by putting them on the payroll, even though I had compiled a stronger civil rights record and had the backing of major civil rights leaders such as Clarence and Juanita Jackson Mitchell.

Civil Rights

Civil rights was a blistering issue in 1964. A century had passed since the Civil War had ended, but black Americans routinely suffered unspeakable indignities, abuse, even lynchings. Despite years of protest, support

9. Later in the campaign, Hume experienced some personal problems and I replaced him with Cushwa. Beginning in 1978, Vic served thirteen years in the Maryland Senate. He died in 1991.

from northern liberals, and modestly successful court challenges, African Americans had made only incremental gains toward equality across the South, including in Maryland. African Americans were still discriminated against in where they could eat, where they could sit in a bus, where or whether they could rent a hotel room for the night, where they could buy a house, and even whether they were allowed to vote in elections in their own hometown. For a decade, most of the southern states refused to desegregate their public schools, in blatant disregard of the Supreme Court ruling in 1954.

By 1964, the blister was about to break. There were sit-in demonstrations at luncheon counters, protests on college campuses, and boycotts of segregated establishments. "Freedom Riders" attempted to desegregate public buses traveling through the South. Efforts to register African American voters increased, as did the number of black students seeking admission to all-white universities.

Segregationists fought back just as hard to resist change, often with violence. Black demonstrators in the South were attacked with dogs, fire hoses, and police billy clubs. There were riots, church bombings, and murders. The Ku Klux Klan prospered.

Even in Maryland during that the primary campaign season that spring, police used dogs to attack protesters at a rally in Princess Anne—a tactic Goldstein and I both denounced.

"We must unleash freedom, not dogs," I said.[10]

By 1964, President Johnson was forcefully pushing the Senate to pass President Kennedy's civil rights bill, which would outlaw discrimination based on race, color, religion, and sex or national origin.[11] The long, southern-led filibuster against the bill that would follow began before my primary election with Goldstein and was not stopped until long after it was over.

The reaction in Maryland was mixed. The friction only intensified when Alabama Governor George Wallace, the best-known

10. "Goldstein Asks Wider Racial Law," *Washington Post and Times Herald*, March 4, 1964, E-1.

11. "We have talked long enough in this country about equal rights," Johnson said to Congress and the American people. "We have talked for one hundred years or more. It is time now to write the next chapter, and to write it in the books of law." President Lyndon B. Johnson, "Address before a Joint Session of the Congress," November 27, 1963, American Presidency Project, http://www.presidency.ucsb.edu/ws/?pid=25988.

segregationist politician in the nation, arrived in Maryland in early March to file as a candidate in the statewide presidential primary against President Johnson. Fear shot through the ranks of Maryland Democrats, who realized that a Wallace victory would give him control of the forty-eight Maryland delegates to the Democratic National Convention later that summer. Johnson had decided against entering state party primaries. I dispatched Gallagher, my campaign treasurer, to meet with a key Goldstein supporter, Senator Dan Brewster, to map out a coordinated response. They agreed our two camps would oppose Wallace by supporting a neutral Democratic surrogate for President Johnson—someone who was not a part of either campaign. But then Brewster unexpectedly broke his commitment and announced he was going to be President Johnson's surrogate on the Maryland ballot.

He soon discovered, however, that the civil rights issue was so divisive that when he campaigned as Wallace's opponent he was booed, cursed, and even spat upon. He attributed the reaction to "bias, and just plain hate."[12] As he realized the real danger of Wallace's candidacy, he ratcheted up his own rhetoric. "What Wallace represents is racism, bigotry and police state tactics," he said at one appearance in April.[13] A few days later he called Wallace "a professional liar, a bigot and an aspiring dictator."[14]

There has been a strong echo of these types of allegations ever since Donald Trump became a candidate for president in 2015 and won the presidency in 2016. He, too, has been called a liar, bigot, aspiring dictator, and worse. He and his Republican allies have, like Wallace and his racist backers, inflamed the rhetoric around race relations, immigration, and religious diversity.

What is dangerously different today, however, is that Trump and his coterie of defenders have real power, whereas Wallace never really had a chance at winning the presidency. Throughout his early months in office, Trump and his administration demonstrated to the country the

12. Jerry Doolittle, "Brewster Booed on Maryland Tour; Sees Sign of Wallace's Strength," *Washington Post*, April 15, 1964, B-1.

13. Donald L. Hymes, "Brewster Accuses Wallace of Lying," *Washington Post*, April 22, 1964, B-3.

14. Elsie Carper, "Sen. Brewster Calls Wallace 'Liar,' 'Bigot,'" *Washington Post*, May 7, 1964, B-1.

tragic consequences that can happen when a divisive racist and bully seizes power. It all makes me fear for the future of our country.

At one rally back in that 1964 presidential primary, Brewster refused to shake hands with Wallace, a snub that created animosity directed not only at him but also at Goldstein. That put me in the unique position of having strong support from African Americans because of my civil rights record but also the backing of conservative Democrats who supported Wallace.

Eight days before the primary, Wallace went to Cambridge, the epicenter of racial unrest in Maryland, and his presence incited a riot that had to be quelled by some four hundred National Guard troops, fifty state police, and the local eighteen-officer police force, armed with tear gas and rifles fixed with bayonets. By contrast, my campaign coordinator in conservative Somerset County, Alexander "Sandy" Jones, was seen as a civil rights leader throughout the Eastern Shore.

I was not immune to all of this, of course. When I appeared in East Baltimore just days before the primary, I was enthusiastically applauded when I spoke on my own behalf. But when I called for support for Brewster on behalf of the president, you could hear a pin drop. Stony silence.[15]

Goldstein claimed he favored civil rights legislation and asserted that he had voted "to repeal Jim Crowism in 1939," some twenty-five years earlier.[16] But the day after he filed as a candidate, the Maryland conference of the NAACP made public a telegram it had sent Goldstein questioning his civil rights credentials, pointedly demanding to know if he would support Johnson's civil rights legislation and asking why Calvert County, which he had represented in the General Assembly, had chosen not to enforce the new public accommodations law in Maryland. The telegram asked why hardly any black children were enrolled in the still segregated Calvert County public schools and why no black adults were employed by the Calvert County government, even though more than half the population of the county was African American.

Goldstein responded by saying he would support the civil rights legislation in Congress but added that he was the comptroller—not a

15. Arnold R. Isaacs, "Crowds Quiet on Brewster; Tydings Pleas for Senator Met by Silence," *Baltimore Sun*, May 15, 1964, 13.

16. Arnold R. Isaacs, "Tydings Meets with Goldstein," *Baltimore Sun*, April 15, 1964, 46.

legislator—when the Calvert County legislative delegation voted to exempt their county from the state public accommodations law. Later in the campaign, he said he would support a statewide public accommodations law in which no places were exempt.

"I'm not concerned whether people are Greek, Polish, Italian—I love everybody," Goldstein said the day he filed as a candidate. "I love Negroes, Methodists, Protestants, all people."[17]

His answers, however, did not satisfy young African American leaders, the NAACP, or me. I challenged the sincerity of his support because of his close ties to the Tawes administration, which had done little on civil rights.

Although the state NAACP normally did not endorse candidates, it decided to endorse me.

Making the Most of Television

Apart from the civil rights strife that affected all candidates for public office in 1964, by early March my campaign was really rolling. We were quietly building an entirely new, almost parallel state Democratic organization. In Baltimore, we relied on former Mayor Phil Goodman's organization, and in most of Baltimore County, Chris Kahl's organization was in charge.

Thanks to Hoffberger, our fundraising was keeping pace with Goldstein's. Jerry brought in the W. B. Doner advertising firm from Detroit, which also handled his National Brewing Company account. Doner's Al Salter moved from Detroit to Baltimore, and his major responsibility throughout 1964 was to plan and coordinate my campaign advertising. I spent hour after hour with Salter and the Doner people putting together campaign ads for television. We would sometimes spend half a day shooting a thirty-second ad.

The week after our first organization meeting, Hoffberger told me that I needed to improve my public speaking. He was right! He sent me to learn breathing exercises from an opera singer two days a week. This not only improved my public speaking but later proved invaluable when

17. John Maffre, "Goldstein, Bubbling Over with Love for All, Files as Democratic Candidate for Senate," *Washington Post*, January 7, 1964, B-1.

I gave closing arguments in front of juries. Before I would go onstage or in front of television cameras, I often would sit backstage and take long, deep breaths. It was a form of relaxation that would help me project my voice. Just as Kennedy had outperformed Nixon on the relatively new political medium of television in 1960, I, too, ended up doing a better job on television than Goldstein. After our ads started to appear, suddenly it seemed that everywhere I went people were waving at me and saying, "We're with you." Our poll numbers soon started to climb.

Teas for Tydings

Our most surprisingly successful strategy was one we adopted from the Kennedys—what we called Teas for Tydings. President Kennedy once mentioned to my mother that in the 1960 campaign his mother, sisters, and campaign workers helped swing the election in his favor by hosting a series of tea receptions mostly, but not exclusively, for women.[18] I was confident that dynamic women in my family—Ginny, my sister, and my still elegant and politically skilled mother—could do the same.[19]

To find out more about Teas for Kennedy, I sent Hardin to Washington to meet for the first time with Teddy Kennedy, who had just been elected to the Senate in 1962. Teddy graciously spent more than an hour discussing with Hardin the organization of the teas and political campaigns in general.

We held our first Tea for Tydings at Oakington on March 7, 1964, and more than three thousand attended. Guests were handed a cup of tea and a small white paper napkin printed with the words, "Tea for Tydings." These teas became major events, frequently held in hotel ballrooms, one in each county.

The teas would not have been successful without a huge turnout of volunteers, which became a hallmark of my campaign. Many of them were excited about a candidate who was finally giving them an opportunity to do political work apart from the party organization.

18. Baroness Stackelberg, "JFK Once Spoke about the Political Power of Teas," unidentified newspaper clipping, November 6, 1964, in possession of Senator Tydings.

19.   Jo-Ann Orlinsky had also participated in the Kennedy teas while she was a student at Mount Holyoke College in Massachusetts. She recalled how Rose Kennedy, the family matriarch, would call together all of the women serving as hostesses for a particular tea to encourage them to promote her son's candidacy, but she would also caution them, "Remember ladies, the thicker the mink, the sharper the elbows."

Modeling ourselves after the Kennedy campaign again, we set up an array of volunteer groups—Citizens for Tydings, Professors for Tydings, Teens for Tydings, Attorneys for Tydings, Young Citizens for Tydings, Athletes for Tydings, even Twins for Tydings. I recruited a young lawyer named Paul Sarbanes to serve as chair of Volunteers for Tydings. We used student volunteers rather than paid professionals whenever we could, often college students from the University of Maryland, Hood College, or Goucher College. For the November general election, we had some twelve hundred volunteer "block captains" in Baltimore city alone.

This worked because young people are idealistic. They are looking for candidates with high motivation, with integrity, men and women who are aware of the problems and are not averse to change. That was precisely what I thought our campaign was about. It was such a departure from the organization-run politics of the past because it was not dictated by political bosses and, more importantly, because the volunteers gave us the broadest possible political base.

In late October, just before the general election, an article in the *Baltimore Sun* said, "Never before in the history of state politics have there been so many still-wet-behind-the-ears but eager amateurs participating in a pre-election battle on behalf of a Maryland candidate for high office."[20]

Three Mistakes by Louis

I was also fortunate that Louis Goldstein sometimes shot himself in the foot while campaigning. Three unrelated incidents come to mind.

The first involved a full-page campaign ad we placed in the *Saturday Evening Post* on March 14, 1964. I think everyone thought we spent millions of dollars for an ad in a national magazine, but actually it was relatively inexpensive because it only appeared in the editions of the magazine distributed to people living in and around Maryland. Such regional advertising was a new approach for national publications in those days.

Goldstein, however, brought more attention to the ad than it might otherwise have received by having his campaign file a formal complaint

---

20. "Volunteers Help Tydings: Record Number of Amateurs Aid Senate Candidate," *Baltimore Sun*, October 23, 1964, 11.

with Baltimore State's Attorney William J. O'Donnell, asking him to investigate whether my campaign had violated the Maryland Corrupt Practices Act by failing to put the word "advertisement" at the bottom of the ad. The ad clearly stated that it was "By authority of Francis X. Gallagher, Treasurer, Joseph D. Tydings for U.S. Senate," and listed our campaign headquarters address, but it did not use the word "advertisement." O'Donnell was a loyal member of the state Democratic organization who clearly had been asked to try to embarrass our campaign. Newspaper headline writers did just what my opponents expected, blaring headlines that essentially said, "Tydings Accused of Violating Campaign Laws."

Up until that point, Goldstein had hardly acknowledged I was even his opponent.

Gallagher thoroughly researched similar political advertisements placed by other top Maryland elected officials. What this effort revealed was that they, too, had placed political ads without affixing the word "advertisement" at the bottom. I immediately requested that Gallagher and I be allowed to appear before the Baltimore city grand jury, despite my general belief that politicians usually do not help themselves by personally appearing before a grand jury. Bear in mind, I had been going before grand juries for almost three years as the US attorney, so I knew how they worked.

After the state's attorney described the charge against me, I told the grand jury that it was unclear whether the corrupt practices statute required the specific word "advertisement" to be attached to campaign ads. I then pulled out campaign ads the governor had run without using the word, as well as ads from other candidates in Maryland that also failed to say "advertisement." Then I revealed ads for Goldstein that also failed to use the word. The climax came when I said to the state's attorney, "You could have even done that yourself."

"Don't ever make an accusation like that against me, Mr. Tydings," I recall O'Donnell immediately shot back. That is when I proceeded to produce copies of his ads, which of course failed to include the word "advertisement."

Well, that finished that. The grand jury reported there had been "no violation of the law" but said the law should be amended to clarify whether the word "advertisement" was required or not. Goldstein gained nothing out of the incident other than to look vindictive. (I accused him of "character assassination."[21]) I, on the other hand, got more publicity than we had ever imagined possible when we placed that ad in the *Saturday Evening Post*.

The second incident involved communist-controlled Poland and "most favored nation" trade opportunities.

Goldstein's stumble came during the first month of the campaign when he agreed to be interviewed on a popular Washington radio station. In the interview, he appeared completely unprepared and uninformed on issues that were widely understood and discussed by many people who lived in and around Washington.

The interviewer asked Goldstein whether Poland, then under the heavy hand of the Soviet Union, should be granted "favored nation" trade status by the United States. Goldstein was not really prepared to discuss foreign affairs, but he must have figured that since the Poles were under communist control, he would oppose such change. What he did not understand was that the "favored nation" proposal was an attempt to lift the Polish people out from under their Soviet overseers, a fact I had learned when I toured Poland as part of my Interpol trip the previous year.

Goldstein's interview was so bad that we played a recording of it at political meetings and rallies to emphasize his lack of qualifications. His blunder also gave me an opportunity to excoriate him before the Polish Americans in the heavily Polish district controlled by longtime East Baltimore city council member Dominic "Mimi" DiPietro. To them, I suddenly was a hero.

Goldstein's third mistake came late in the campaign with a personal insult to me. In a widely covered political attack on me, Goldstein said at least he "knew who his father was." His comment was inexcusable, although I attribute it to end-of-campaign desperation. It was an insult to every adopted child in the state, and their parents resented it.

"A Body Blow to the Political Hierarchy"

The campaign I waged in that primary was different in many ways from the campaigns the Democratic organization had been running for decades. One change was that we sharply scaled back the amount of

21. John Maffre, "Phantom Reacts to Tydings Jab," *Washington Post*, March 28, 1964, B-1.

money given to Baltimore-area political organizations on the eve of an election, ostensibly to "get out the vote." I remember one East Baltimore pol, Clayton Dietrich, who was so unhappy about the amount of "walking around money" his club was getting that he taunted me at a private meeting by saying, "You're going to feel awful bad, Joe, when you wake up the next morning [after losing the election]." I responded by saying, "We Tydings know how to lose," and abruptly walked out.

The clash between the old and new way of doing politics often was revealed in more public settings. We brought in a veteran Italian American political operative named Joe Giordiano—better known by his professional name, "Joe the Barber"—to explain how elections really worked to some silk-stocking lawyers who were helping our campaign.

"If-a you look-a under the curtain," Joe the Barber told the lawyers, who were taking notes as if they were attending a lecture at Harvard, "and you see-a four feet, that is not a horse!"

With the primary fast approaching, both Goldstein and I were separately interviewed by the *Washington Post*. That was when I learned of a *Post* policy against making endorsements in primary elections. I personally appealed to *Post* publisher Katharine Graham, arguing that a candidate who was independent enough to challenge the entrenched statewide organization was worthy of an endorsement. To her credit, she reversed the decision. She asked her editorial board that if they were to endorse, who would they back? They said, "Joe Tydings." She told them to "Go ahead and endorse."

And that endorsement, plus one I received in the *Baltimore Sun*, really cemented our victory.

On primary election day, the vote was not even close. I received 279,564 votes to Goldstein's 155,086.[22] We totally swamped the Democratic Party machine—what one newspaper called "a body blow to the political hierarchy set up by Governor Tawes."[23] Goldstein carried seven counties, all of them rural and sparsely populated. I carried sixteen counties, plus Baltimore city, where I got 94,407 votes to Goldstein's 51,047. It was the only election Goldstein would ever lose.

22. Two other Democratic candidates, John J. Harbaugh of Glen Burnie and Morgan L. Amaimo of Baltimore, received 22,665 and 15,921 votes, respectively. *Maryland Manual*, 1965, 490, Maryland State Archives, Annapolis.

23. Charles Whiteford, "Brewster Beats Wallace; Alabamian Gets 42% of Vote; Tydings Is Winner," *Baltimore Sun*, May 20, 1964, 1.

Brewster managed to beat Wallace, 53 to 43 percent, but Wallace did much better than I and others had hoped, clearly demonstrating the divisive power of racial politics in Maryland.

In the 2016 election, Trump was a master of Wallace-style divisive politics, recruiting as his original political base neo-Nazis and white supremacist groups still scattered across our nation. Without this support, he would never have won the Republican nomination. Tragically, his presidential election has emboldened them. After the election, the Ku Klux Klan, for example, announced plans to hold a victory parade for Trump. In addition to public rallies of that type, incidents of racial harassment and xenophobia have surged.[24] As president, Trump continues to kowtow to these despicable groups with his constant and baseless criticism of President Obama's accomplishments.

In that 1964 primary, the Alabama governor took most of the rural areas, sweeping the conservative Eastern Shore, the three southern Maryland counties, as well as Howard, Carroll, and my home county of Harford. Wallace could now leave Maryland to campaign elsewhere, and I could move forward to the general election against the Republican incumbent, J. Glenn Beall Sr.

The National Democratic Convention of 1964

Although I had soundly beaten Goldstein and the party organization, Beall glibly dismissed my nearly two-to-one victory as "less a tribute to [my] leadership than an amplified howl of protest of the 'outs' against the 'ins.'"[25]

To some extent that was true, and I was darned proud of it. I saw my lopsided victory as a repudiation of the state party machine and all it stood for. I saw it as opening the door to a new generation of political leaders in Maryland. Newspaper writers in Maryland were already leapfrogging the general election as if my victory over Beall were a foregone conclusion, and they had begun speculating what effect my anticipated election would have on the gubernatorial race in 1966.

24. Jaweed Kaleem, "The Ku Klux Klan Says It Will Hold a Trump Victory Parade in North Carolina," *Los Angeles Times*, November 10, 2016; Alexis Okeowo, "Hate on the Rise after Trump's Election," *New Yorker*, November 17, 2016.

25. Washington Bureau of the Sun, "Maryland in Congress," *Baltimore Sun*, May 31, 1964.

Beall tried to temper our excitement, saying that while my victory in the primary had been impressive, I was "not necessarily the prophet who will lead the Democratic Party, united and in harmony, through the pearly gates."[26] In the short run, at least, he was right.

I was brimming with confidence and youthful exuberance. I felt as if the state Democratic Party was now our party, that due to our smashing victory we suddenly had an opportunity to take charge and could call some of the shots. I wanted to bring in new leadership, new faces, new vigor, a new purpose to the party, and I was in a hurry to do so. I intended to demonstrate all of that by taking some control of the party delegation to the Democratic National Convention, which was to be selected at a state party convention in late June.

The question was never whether the Maryland delegates to the convention would support the nomination of President Johnson, which was a given regardless of who was chosen. The question was who would be chosen as those Maryland delegates: the young newcomers who had backed me or the party regulars who had been around for years. I was eager to reward the new young leaders who had supported me. There were forty-six national delegate slots and another forty alternates, and I thought it was only right for our faction to control at least twelve of the delegate positions and half of the alternates.

My plan, however, turned out to be built on the weak foundation of bravado, overconfidence, and political naïveté. My father, had he been alive, would not have let that happen to me. During the primary, my campaign did not have the time, experience, or political savvy to nominate delegates to the state convention. The party machine had all the delegates to the state convention lined up, and they completely controlled selection of delegates to the national convention.

To chair the state convention, I backed Alfred L. Scanlan, a terrific lawyer from Montgomery County who was considered a reformer in the heated political fight over reapportionment of the General Assembly. But the party organization—the same organization I had just whipped in the primary—backed Delegate Marvin Mandel of Baltimore, with whom I had tangled in the legislature. I proclaimed—somewhat arrogantly, it seems in retrospect—that I did not want any "bloodletting" at

26. Ibid.

the convention, just our "fair share" of delegates. Instead, we got a thorough political spanking. Scanlan lost to Mandel, and we ended up with only four seats out of the ninety-six selected for the national convention.[27] Coming so soon after our big primary victory, it was a stinging defeat and a lasting lesson in the perils of overconfidence and hubris.

The convention, held in late August in Atlantic City, New Jersey, easily nominated Johnson for a full four-year term. Hubert H. Humphrey of Minnesota was picked as his running mate.

The most memorable moment of that convention—at least for me—came at the end when a sad and pencil-thin Robert Francis Kennedy took the stage to introduce a short memorial film about his brother, Jack. When it was over, the delegates applauded for twenty-two uninterrupted minutes. Bobby, quoting from Shakespeare's *Romeo and Juliet*, said of his brother, "When he shall die, take him and cut him out in little stars, and he shall make the face of heaven so fine that all the world will be in love with night and pay no worship to the garish sun."[28]

I had celebrated Jack Kennedy in my own small way about three weeks earlier, when I held a campaign pep rally on August 1 at Oakington to formally launch my general election campaign. I intentionally chose that date because it was one year to the day that President Kennedy had honored me and my family by dining at our home and encouraging me to run for the Senate.

27. The same day Scanlan was defeated by Mandel for chair of the Maryland State Democratic Convention, he won perhaps the most significant case of his legal career when the Supreme Court of the United States struck down a Maryland law that gave rural voters more power than urban voters to elect legislators. The "one-vote" high court ruling also outlawed the so-called "unit vote" system under which it was possible for legislative candidates to win districts in which they lost the popular vote. The decision in *Reynolds v. Sims* 377 U.S. 533 (1964) also applied to five companion cases from Colorado, New York, Virginia, and Delaware. Years later, Mandel, by then governor of Maryland, appointed Scanlan to the intermediate appellate court, the Court of Special Appeals, but he resigned ten months later, saying he was frustrated by the "semi-monastic" life of a judge. Scanlan, who lived in Potomac, died in 1993 at the age of seventy-three following a long illness. Norris P. West, "Alfred Scanlan, Lawyer and Former Appeals Judge," *Baltimore Sun*, April 27, 1993.

28. William Shakespeare, *Romeo and Juliet*, act 3, scene 2.

CHAPTER 12

A Break with the Past

In the Senate campaign that year, it was clear to me that change—generational change—was in the air. The Kennedys had ushered in a youthful revolution in American politics. When JFK took office at age forty-three, he was the youngest elected president in American history. His brother Bobby became attorney general at thirty-four. The president's press secretary, Pierre Salinger, was thirty-five; Kenny O'Donnell, one of his closest aides, was thirty-six.

I was just thirty-two when Kennedy was elected and only thirty-six by the 1964 campaign. By stark contrast, the graying J. Glenn Beall Sr. was seventy-one. One newspaper columnist said it was like "the urgent voice of the future" pitted against a "well-meaning . . . faintly fuddy-duddy echo from the past."[1]

Beall, I thought, was a decent man, but his time had passed. He seemed to have no clear vision for the future. In fact, he seemed a bit weary of it all. Ginny and I were out there campaigning every day, driving all across the state, accepting any and every invitation to speak. Beall did not even officially open his campaign headquarters until September 17, less than two months before the general election. When he traveled around Maryland, he often did so by private jet.

Midway through the campaign, the *Baltimore News-American* devoted a full page to side-by-side profiles of the candidates' wives, Ginny Tydings and Margaret Beall. To me, the profiles were a metaphor for the campaign itself: one side on the go, the other side more sedentary. Ginny was depicted as young, attractive, and active—a lover of the great outdoors, a rider and fox hunter, a woman who enjoyed tennis, swimming, and skiing. She was pictured astride a handsome gray thoroughbred hunter.

---

1. Bradford M. Jacobs, "Whose Hurrah?," political column for the *Baltimore Evening Sun*, October 27, 1964.

Margaret Beall, who by then had been married to Senator Beall for thirty-eight years, was described as spending her time quietly with her family, gardening, and cooking. She was pictured holding a cookbook she had helped write.[2]

On the campaign trail, I tried never to mention Senator Beall by name. I never attacked him. And when we met in a debate that fall, I was courteous, kind, and respectful. I did not want to say anything inflammatory. While I publicly disagreed with many of his positions (his opposition to federal aid to public schools and to the creation of Medicare and his support for the oil depletion allowance, which enriched already rich oil companies), I never attacked him personally. I just said we needed new ideas, thoughts, and leadership. That I was widely viewed as a protégé of Jack Kennedy was a powerful advantage. By the time I ran against Beall, our polls showed that my name was actually becoming better known than his.

As the political columnist Bradford Jacobs observed, "For Mr. Tydings, bullying his opponent would be just as disastrous as bullying Santa Claus."[3]

Beall was also saddled with the Republican candidate for president, Senator Barry Goldwater of Arizona. Goldwater was a far-right conservative challenging a Democratic incumbent who had inherited John F. Kennedy's progressive mantle. Beall was actually a moderate, who gave only a perfunctory endorsement to Goldwater and rarely mentioned Goldwater's name in public. But he could not separate himself from the nominee of his party, and that hurt his chances against me as well.

But beyond these advantages, I had pretty much burned my bridges with the state party organization, so I got little help from Governor Tawes or other Democratic leaders in Maryland. Marvin Mandel publicly complained that I was ignoring the wishes of the Democratic legislators from Baltimore city. Northwest Baltimore Democratic boss Jack Pollack, offended by my antimachine rhetoric, had supported Goldstein in the primary and now was backing Beall, quietly at first and then quite openly. Like Clayton Dietrich in the primary, old-style organization pols

2. Mildred Kahler Geare, "The Women behind the Candidates: Tydings, Beall Wives Play Dominant Role," *Baltimore News-American*, October, 8, 1964.

3. Jacobs, "Whose Hurrah?"

complained they could not get their hands on the usual pot of "walking-around money" that was customarily used to reward party soldiers.

By mid-October, a group of Democrats had sprung up that began to encourage voters to split their ticket between LBJ, the Democratic presidential candidate, and Beall, the Republican senatorial candidate. The chair of this group, Jerome M. Kennedy, a former aide to Baltimore mayor J. Harold Grady, viciously criticized me, calling me "a cold, arrogant, self-centered individual undeserving of Democratic support."[4] He attacked me for what he called my "tone."

"It is a tone of coldness, of remoteness, and of the type of self-centered haughtiness which leaves no door open for the suggestions and efforts of others," he complained. "It is a tone which is reflected in the candidate's constant efforts to ignore or downgrade the work being done for Maryland in the Senate by a member of his own political party, Senator Daniel B. Brewster. It is a tone which appears to be consciously designed to be as offensive as possible to certain Democratic members of the House of Representatives, the Governor, and numerous party colleagues now serving in the state legislature," he said, adding that Beall, by contrast, was the type of public servant who got along well with people "and thereby produced results."[5]

To me, such political criticism simply reflected the new reality in Maryland politics: the old-line Democratic bosses were no longer in control, and they were so unhappy about it that they preferred to have a Republican remain in the Senate rather than help that ungrateful upstart reformer, Joe Tydings.

As the columnist Brad Jacobs observed, "Mr. Tydings represents nothing short of a party revolution in the making. His nomination in May was achieved against the fiercest opposition Old Guard bosses could mount. The bitterness lingers on, each side acutely aware that in the Tydings arrival, Democratic independents have consolidated at last and that the Old Guard's back is to the wall."[6]

By then, we had such momentum it did not matter. We had so many volunteers that we had literally built a political party within a political

4. Quoted in Charles Whiteford, "Democrats Form for Beall; Fog Follows Tydings Train," *Baltimore Sun*, October, 18, 1964.

5. Ibid.

6. Jacobs, "Whose Hurrah?"

party. We intentionally kept our headquarters separate from the Democratic organization headquarters. We, of course, supported President Johnson and all of the Democratic congressional nominees, but we ran our own operation.

To top it off, we announced that Eunice Shriver, who was the late president's sister and the wife of Peace Corps director Sargent Shriver Jr., would co-chair our volunteer campaign organization, Citizens for Tydings.

I received the endorsement of a group of popular and well-known professional athletes from the Baltimore Colts football team, the Baltimore Orioles baseball team, and the Baltimore Bullets basketball team. Elmer Wingate helped me enlist players from the Colts, and newspapers carried a picture of me stretched out on the floor doing push-ups with Colts players Ordell Braase, Bobby Boyd, and Billy Ray Smith.

Wingate and Braase also joined me near Dundalk in Baltimore County on several early mornings to campaign at the gates of the Sparrows Point steel plant, which had thirty thousand workers. (After I won the general election but before I had taken office, I went back to the steel plant to thank workers for their support. One employee came up to me and angrily said, "I didn't vote for you. I would never vote for you. And what are you doing out here on taxpayer time when you should be working?" I almost rolled in the dirt laughing.)

By mid-October, we had run a four-page tabloid section titled "Fighting for Maryland's Future" in the Sunday *Sun*. The ad included pictures of me with President Johnson, with the pope, with the head of a Jewish organization, on a Frederick farm and in a Baltimore factory, and with Robert McNamara, the secretary of defense. On the back was a picture of Ginny, our three kids—Mary, Millard II, and Emlen—and me walking among the trees at Oakington.[7] There also was a picture of me with John F. Kennedy, of course.

"Integrity in public office and the courage to face every issue characterize Tydings' fight for a new era of leadership in Maryland," we proclaimed, and then, with a tip of the hat to my father, "Tydings, raised in a tradition of public service, offers a record of independence, courage and integrity to the people of Maryland."[8]

7. Mary was born in 1957, Millard in 1958, Emlen in 1960, and our fourth child, Eleanor, in 1967. Alexandra, my daughter with my second wife, was born in 1972.

8. "Fighting for Maryland's Future" tabloid section of the *Baltimore Sun*, Oct. 11, 1964, in possession of Senator Tydings.

As the election neared and Beall's defeat seemed inevitable, his campaign remarks became noticeably shrill. He accused me of "lying" about his votes and misrepresenting his record, but to little effect.

A week before the election, I began to win big newspaper endorsements. The *Baltimore Evening Sun*, for example, said of me, "He has political courage and he has the drive of a man who is eager to grapple with the serious questions of our times." As for Beall, it offered this backhanded compliment, saying he had been "in no way brilliant, [but] has been on the whole sound and commendable."[9]

On Election Day, I swept seventeen of the twenty-three counties in Maryland, plus Baltimore city. I pulled in 678,649 votes to Beall's 402,393. In Baltimore city alone, my margin of victory was 8-to-1 and I received more than 80 percent of the African American vote even though Beall had consistently said he supported civil rights legislation. "Senator Beall's fatal error was his endorsement of Barry Goldwater," the *Baltimore Afro-American* newspaper stated after the election.[10] In retrospect, I think I would have won that election with a clear majority even if there had not been a presidential race at the top of the ticket.

At 8:35 p.m. that night, not long after the polls had closed, I received a Western Union telegram from President Johnson, who was in Johnson City, Texas. It read, "The glad Tydings from Maryland tonight should be the able, intelligent Democratic candidate for Senate who has the best wishes of Lady Bird and myself on this election day."[11]

"My fondest hope," I told cheering supporters that night, "is that my election will be a signal for independent spirited young men and women of both parties to make politics of the Free State open politics, a politics of merit. I am hopeful that my election will serve as an invitation to these young men and women who aspire to public office to enter public life."[12]

There was immediate speculation about which of my campaign aides or other supporters would be next in line to run for governor, or for the General Assembly, or for other local, state, or federal offices.[13]

9. "Tydings for Senate," editorial, *Baltimore Evening Sun*, October 28, 1964.

10. "Why Beall Lost the Senate Race," *Baltimore Afro-American*, November 7, 1964.

11. President Johnson to Joseph Tydings, telegram, November 3, 1964, in possession of Senator Tydings.

12. Quoted in Donald Bremner, "Tydings Beats Beall; Democrats Take 6 of 8 House Seats," *Baltimore Sun*, November 4, 1964.

13. Despite our broad optimism in 1964, the 1966 gubernatorial election did not turn out as we had hoped. Four Democrats ran for the party nomination: the moderate attorney

"Vote Is Youth Serum to Maryland Politics," blared a headline in the Frederick newspaper. "Tydings Victory Paves Way for Crop of 'Bright Boys,'" read another in Baltimore.[14]

"The Tydings victory, a personal as well as party triumph, gave fresh encouragement to non-organization Maryland Democrats," one election postmortem stated.[15]

Among my "shiny brights" (as they were derisively called by the machine pols), Frank Gallagher was frequently mentioned as a potential candidate for governor.[16] Other young activists whose future political potential began to be mentioned as a result of my election included Ted Venetoulis of Baltimore County (then an administrative assistant to Representative Carlton Sickles), Julian L. "Jack" Lapides of Baltimore (who had run Young Citizens for Tydings), Jo Ann Orlinsky's husband, Wally (who had directed the Democrats' voter registration drive), Arthur Murphy (who had been an assistant US attorney when I ran that office), Vic Cushwa (my campaign chair), Paul Sarbanes (who oversaw the volunteers for the Johnson-Humphrey campaign), and Dick Schifter (who led our Montgomery County campaign). In their own way, all of them were reformers. Many of them were eventually elected in future races for public office—as were countless others who worked in and were inspired by our campaign.

My victory did not put an end to machine politics in Maryland, but

general, Thomas B. Finan, as heir apparent to Tawes; Carlton R. Sickles, the Maryland representative-at-large in Congress, the liberal in the field, and the candidate I hoped would win; Clarence W. Miles, a Baltimore attorney; and George P. Mahoney, the paving contractor and perennial candidate. Finan, Sickles, and Mahoney essentially split the vote three ways, with the small vote that Miles received probably detracting from Finan's total. Mahoney, a segregationist who inflamed the voting public with the slogan, "A man's home is his castle—protect it," won by fewer than 2,000 votes out of more than 430,000 votes cast. Opposition to Mahoney split the Democratic vote in the general election, clearing the way for the election of the Republican candidate and county executive of Baltimore County, Spiro T. Agnew. Two years after that, Agnew would resign to become Richard M. Nixon's vice president, and Marvin Mandel, by then Speaker of the House of Delegates, would be selected by the General Assembly to replace Agnew as governor. Martin Weil, "George P. Mahoney, 87, Dies," *Washington Post*, March 20, 1989.

14. "Vote Is Youth Serum to Maryland Politics," *Frederick (MD) Post*, November 5, 1964; Frank DeFilippo, "Tydings Victory Paves Way for Crop of 'Bright Boys,'" *Baltimore News-American*, November 4, 1964.

15. Bremner, "Tydings Beats Beall."

16. Donald Bremner, "Youth, Enthusiasm, Pep Mark Tydings Camp," *Baltimore Evening Sun*, May 22, 1964, B-30.

it put a big dent in it. Over the next several elections, most of the old machines—the Sasscer machine in Prince George's County, the Pollack machine in northwest Baltimore, James Pine's machine in Baltimore County, Irv Kovens's machine in Baltimore, and others—suffered defeats and gradually ran out of steam.

Many have told me over the years that my 1964 election changed the political culture in Maryland forever, that it was a demarcation line.[17] With the aid of hindsight, I now believe that is true.

Johnson, of course, defeated Goldwater that year in a historic landslide. And in New York State, my friend Robert F. Kennedy was elected to the US Senate.

Perhaps the most satisfying aspect of my victory, however, was that I had successfully redeemed the defeat of my father fourteen years earlier. When Millard Tydings was first elected to the Senate, he was thirty-six years old. When I was elected to the Senate, I too was thirty-six.

I had tried to follow in his footsteps. Now, I finally felt like I was doing so.

17. Tim Maloney, "Celebrating Maryland's New Frontiersman," *Washington Post*, September 19, 2004.

PART III

A Freshman Senator's Voice

Few will have the greatness to bend history itself;
but each of us can work to change a small portion of events,
and in the total,
of all those acts will be written the history of this generation.

—ROBERT F. KENNEDY

CHAPTER 13

Defending the Great Warren Court Decisions

I arrived in the US Senate on the national tidal wave that swept Democrats to extraordinary power in 1964, just one short but agonizing year after John F. Kennedy's assassination. President Lyndon Johnson won a full four-year term by a landslide over Republican Barry Goldwater, and Democrats captured greater than 2-to-1 majorities in both houses of the Eighty-Ninth Congress. Many of us in that incoming class were young, impatient, liberal reformers who had modeled ourselves after JFK.

In just my first two years, Congress enacted one of the most important pieces of civil rights legislation in US history: the Voting Rights Act of 1965. It also enacted laws that created Medicare and Medicaid, expanded federal support for higher education, and reformed immigration law. It put in place new air pollution control standards, measures to preserve historic places, and national support for the arts and humanities. It also passed the Freedom of Information Act, which in the decades since has made government more transparent to the public. The Eighty-Ninth Congress has been called—justifiably, I believe—"arguably the most productive in American history."[1]

In those two pre-Nixon congresses—the Eighty-Ninth and Ninetieth—we also beat back a series of efforts by conservatives to pass constitutional amendments or legislation that would have overturned or undermined many of the great decisions by the Supreme Court under Chief Justice Earl Warren, including those requiring public schools to desegregate, protecting the rights of criminal defendants, outlawing

---

1. Karen Tumulty, "LBJ's Presidency Gets Another Look as Civil Rights Law Marks Its 50th Anniversary," *Washington Post*, April 9, 2014.

organized prayer in schools, and requiring that population be used as the standard for apportioning representation in all state legislatures. These monumental decisions were constantly under attack during my years in the Senate, and I was constantly in the fight to defend them.[2]

I came in ranked one-hundredth in Senate seniority and was, quite literally, a backbencher. Senate desks were arranged, as always, in a semicircle four rows deep facing the rostrum. Because there were so many Democrats that term, four seats were placed in a fifth row behind all the other Democratic desks. That's where I sat. To my left was the freshman senator from New York, Robert F. Kennedy, and to my right, Fred Harris, formerly the Speaker of the House in Oklahoma. To Bobby's left was another freshman, Walter Mondale, the former attorney general of Minnesota and future vice president of the United States. Our seats were so far back that Bobby's mother once told him that she had better seats at *Hello, Dolly!*

Ginny and my mother, who had visited the Senate many times during my father's twenty-four years there, attended my swearing-in on January 5, 1965.

Hardin Marion, now my administrative assistant, had begun working in our new Washington office not long after my election. Our first tasks were to assemble a staff, assign responsibilities, and develop operational procedures for the office. We divided the duties into three areas: administrative, legislative, and public relations.

Hardin oversaw everything, but particularly the administrative work: how we would handle constituent problems, office visitors ranging from schoolchildren to political leaders, volunteers, political issues, staff meetings, hiring, and other employment issues. Jo-Ann Orlinsky came with us to serve as manager of our Baltimore office and deal with

2. Earl Warren was appointed to the Supreme Court of the United States by President Eisenhower in 1953, a year after Warren had helped Eisenhower win the presidency. Warren had served in the district attorney's office in Alameda County, California, then as state attorney general, and as the thirtieth governor of California. He ran for vice president with Thomas E. Dewey in 1948, but the ticket lost to President Truman. When Chief Justice Fred M. Vinson died unexpectedly in September 1953, Eisenhower appointed Warren as his replacement. The following year, after the justices handed down their controversial *Brown v. Board of Education* school desegregation ruling, billboards that read "Impeach Earl Warren" sprang up all across the South. In 1963, President Johnson persuaded Warren to head the commission to investigate the assassination of President Kennedy. Warren retired from the court in 1969 and died in 1974.

volunteers, constituent services, and Maryland political issues. We needed to hire other office staff, and the pressure to put a team in place quickly was intense.

Vice President Humphrey gave me one bit of sound advice. He told me that the two most important appointments I was likely to make were my chief of staff and my primary front office receptionist, and he said I should make those two appointments myself. I had already picked Hardin to serve as chief of staff, and I decided to hire a Montgomery County campaign volunteer named Lynne Astrich (later Lynne Cashman) as our primary receptionist.

In those days, many senators had no staff specifically designated as legislative assistants, who were typically charged with keeping track of committee activity and legislation on the Senate floor, researching speeches, and drafting amendments to offer on pending bills. This is amazing when compared with the huge staffs in congressional offices today. I decided to stretch the allowance we received for Senate staff to hire two legislative assistants, each to serve for no more than two years so I could keep fresh ideas coming my way. I later teamed with Senator Thomas Kuchel, a moderate from California and the Republican whip, to amend the Congressional Reorganization Act to provide funds so every senator could have at least one designated legislative assistant.

My first legislative assistant was a young lawyer named Alan Wurtzel, hired on the recommendation of Dick Schifter, a supporter and powerful figure in Montgomery County Democratic politics. I initially wanted to hire Paul Sarbanes, who had worked on my campaign, but Paul ran for the Maryland House of Delegates instead. Alan's job was to attend hearings, monitor political developments, follow legislation, and wherever possible advance the legislative issues I sponsored or cared about.[3] Ruth Shaw and Edgar Feingold joined us in Washington to handle press, just as they had done in the campaign.

I was fortunate in my staff selections over the years. Their ability was great, their morale high, their camaraderie strong, their devotion

3. Alan Wurtzel had no political experience, but he was a Yale Law School graduate and had clerked for the progressive David L. Bazelon, a judge of the US Court of Appeals for the District of Columbia. He knew Steve Sachs from their days together at Yale and discovered during his initial interview with Hardin that he and Hardin had been in the same homeroom together at Thomas Jefferson High School in Richmond in 1951, though neither remembered the other. Wurtzel's assistant was Tom Curtis. Mary Zalar and Martha Robinson served as secretaries and legislative researchers.

to our common enterprise of trying to make a positive difference for our country intense. Even now, nearly a half century later, our staff alumni still meet each year on my birthday (May 4) for a reunion, and, in 2015, we celebrated together the fiftieth anniversary of the 1964 election that had brought us all together.

Despite my low seniority, my committee assignments fit my interests and background. The most important assignment was to the Judiciary Committee and the associated Constitutional Amendments Subcommittee. Within a matter of months, I maneuvered my way into chairing a moribund Judiciary subcommittee that dealt with the federal courts, a rare coup for a freshman and the prelude to major changes I would introduce and see adopted to strengthen the federal judiciary. This role gave me a level of stature that was extraordinary for a first-year senator, but I will say more about this work later.

I also was assigned to the Aeronautics and Space Sciences Committee and to the Committee on the District of Columbia. By the middle of that first year, I had traded the Space Committee for a seat on the Public Works Committee, where I wanted to work with Maine Senator Edmund Muskie on his Air and Water Pollution Subcommittee. This change allowed me to focus on environmental issues and pursue my interest in protecting the Chesapeake Bay. I attended nearly every hearing and went on almost every trip Muskie made. I co-sponsored just about every environmental bill of his and introduced a substantial number of environmental bills myself.

Serving on the District of Columbia Committee was a task many senators avoided, but I saw it as my responsibility to help the many Maryland constituents who worked there.

In those early days, I sent a flurry of memos to staff, seeking to bring in student government leaders from around the state, to set up weekly luncheons with political movers from around Maryland, to get letters answered promptly and casework expedited, to respond immediately to any calls from other senators, and to churn out press statements on an almost daily basis. I was surely guilty of micromanaging, sending, for example, one memo that told our receptionists exactly how I wanted them to answer the telephone ("This is Senator Tydings's office, how may we help you?").[4]

4. The pace of a newly elected senator was necessarily frenetic. During just my first

A US senator is constantly in high demand. During 1965 alone, I spoke to scores of groups all over the state and around the country.[5] I kept up that pace for six years.

That first month, I went to LBJ's inauguration with my two best friends in the Senate, Bobby and Teddy Kennedy. I remember being on the platform where US senators stood; President Johnson was giving his inaugural address, and I was thinking that President Kennedy should have been the one there being inaugurated, and the tears started streaming down my face.

But that was all just the political backdrop to the issues of national significance being considered in the Congress. In my first few months, I found myself absorbed by matters as disparate as the drive to assure the voting rights of African Americans, the need for national immigration reform, a proposed rail transit system for the District of Columbia, national protection of Assateague Island, the need for stricter gun control, home rule for the District of Columbia, family planning services, the festering war in far-off Vietnam, and establishing the US magistrates within the federal court system.

My upbringing, my experiences in the General Assembly and as US attorney, and my political connections to the Kennedys had all led me to this position, and I could not get enough of it. This, I thought to myself, was my true calling. Because of my father's influence, I arrived with an instinctive understanding of how the Senate worked and a ready-made introduction to the southern Democratic bulls who had served with him, including Richard Russell of Georgia, Sam Ervin of North

month in office, I met with Senator Mondale and Secretary of State Dean Rusk; attended a reception with NBC foreign correspondents and a Capitol Hill event with Ginny for the Red Cross; met with representatives of the Lions Club of Kitzmiller, a tiny town in far western Maryland; attended a pre-inaugural dinner; spoke to Young Democrats at the Mayflower Hotel; dined at the swanky Sulgrave Club; was briefed on space issues; attended the inauguration of Johnson and Humphrey; sipped cocktails at the embassy of Ghana; and had a photo taken with a Girl Scout troop on the Capitol steps.

5. Examples: the Baltimore Junior Association of Commerce, George Washington University Young Democrats, North Carolina Federation of Women's Clubs, Harford Junior College, the opening of the 1965 Aberdeen Little League season, the Edgewood Methodist Youth Fellowship, American Law Student Association, the Order of the Sons of Italy in America, Prince George's Chamber of Commerce, Delaware Highway Day in Wilmington, the New Frontier Democratic Women's Club, Scout-o-Rama at Timonium Fairgrounds (where I did a photo op doing push-ups), the Hagerstown Retailers Bureau, diners at Benny's Kitchen in Westminster, students at Frostburg State College, the Garrett County Young Democrats in Accident, and the volunteer fire department in Lexington Park.

Carolina, or James Eastland of Mississippi. These men, who wielded profound power over nearly every major issue considered by the Senate, were willing to work with me because my name was Tydings. At the request of other senators, I often accepted requests to speak to civic or political organizations in their states—such as in Arkansas for Senator J. William Fulbright, in South Carolina for Senator Ernest "Fritz" Hollings, and in New York for Robert Kennedy. I collected a lot of IOUs doing that. I was perfectly comfortable in the US Senate and realized that, as part of a huge Democratic majority, I had a rare opportunity.

Rotten Boroughs

My first major legislative fight, however, was not over some proposal I wanted to pass but over one we had to stop. And that work turned out to be one of the two or three most important accomplishments of my entire Senate career.

In June 1964, about five months before I was elected, the Supreme Court of the United States broke with long tradition and ruled that state legislatures had to be apportioned by population rather than by counties or other geographic districts.[6] This was a catastrophic blow to rural interests in most state legislatures, including that of Maryland, where for decades rural jurisdictions held sway despite having only a fraction of the population.[7] It also hurt business and industry interests, which typically had found it easier to influence legislatures controlled by rural representatives. These groups generally supported lower taxes, less government spending, less government regulation, and antiunion measures. But with the "one-man, one-vote" ruling, the Supreme Court sought to ensure that residents of cities and other populous areas were fairly represented, which meant it would then be more likely their legitimate needs could be met.

6. Reynolds v. Sims, 377 U.S. 533 (1964). This decision reversed an earlier 1946 decision, *Colegrove v. Green*, which concluded that only state legislatures had the power to decide on apportionment.

7. As early as 1928, the Baltimore writer H. L. Mencken complained that gross overrepresentation of rural interests in the Maryland legislature had created what he called "barnyard government," in which lawmakers were "more concerned with the salaries of county surveyors or the permissible size of rockfish than with slum housing or mass transit." Senator Joseph D. Tydings, "The Last Chance for the States," *Harper's*, March 1966, reprinted in 112 Cong. Rec. (daily ed. March 9, 1966).

"Legislators represent people, not trees or acres," Chief Justice Earl Warren famously declared in his majority opinion. "Legislators are elected by voters, not farms or cities or economic interests."[8]

Years later, just prior to his retirement, the chief justice would call the "one-man, one-vote" decisions the most important of his tenure— more important than *Brown v. Board of Education* or the many other history-making decisions handed down from the high court.[9]

The concept of rural areas dominating legislative bodies was nothing new. When this tactic was used in Ireland and Great Britain in the eighteenth and nineteenth centuries, parliamentary areas with small or even no real electorates were derided as "rotten boroughs." The practice spread in the United States following the Civil War, when cities swelled with the sudden influx of farmers, immigrants, and those moving from small towns. Rural residents, fearing their political power would be lost, froze the method of apportionment that assured them of overrepresentation in their state legislatures, often by embedding the practice in state constitutions.

There were plenty of examples of the problem.[10] In the Connecticut General Assembly, for instance, one House district had 191 people, while another had 81,000. The city of Los Angeles, with its 6 million residents, had one member in the California Senate, the same as one rural county with 14,000 residents. In Idaho, the smallest Senate district had 951 people and the largest had 93,400, or 97 times more than the smallest.

After the Supreme Court ruling, it became clear that the concept of rural domination of state legislatures in America was not going to go away without a fight. The US House of Representatives approved a constitutional amendment that would have denied federal courts jurisdiction to consider the apportionment of either house of a state legislature. In southern states in particular, rural overrepresentation increased the

8. *Reynolds v. Sims*, 377 U.S. 533 (1964).

9. J. Douglas Smith, *On Democracy's Doorstep: The Inside Story of How the Supreme Court brought "One Person, One Vote" to the United States* (New York: Hill and Wang, 2014), 3. The "one-man, one-vote" rulings were in *Baker v. Carr*, 369 U.S. 186 (1962); *Reynolds v. Sims*, 377 U.S. 533 (1964); and *Wesberry v. Sanders*, 376 U.S. 1 (1964).

10. The most rotten British example was Old Sarum, the English borough with no inhabitants and two representatives in Parliament until the Reform Act of 1832. Tydings, "Last Chance for the States."

likelihood that white supremacists opposed to integration, civil rights, or voting rights would be elected.[11] This first attempt at a constitutional amendment, however, failed in the Senate, where opposition was led by Democrats Paul Douglas of Illinois and William Proxmire of Wisconsin.

By the time I arrived there, Senator Everett Dirksen of Illinois, the Republican minority leader, was forcefully pushing a new constitutional amendment to permit one house of a bicameral state legislature to be apportioned on the basis of factors other than population. Dirksen and other opponents of the court ruling were quick to note that under the Constitution only one house of the US Congress was apportioned by population and that the other, the Senate, was apportioned by geography—two senators for each state. The Dirksen amendment would let states do something similar.

His resolution was referred to the Constitutional Amendments Subcommittee, chaired by Birch Bayh, a young Democrat from Indiana who had been elected two years before me. Among the subcommittee members were Roman Hruska, a Republican and outspoken conservative from rural Nebraska, and me. Hruska supported the Dirksen resolution. Bayh, at least at first, was more in the middle. I, on the other hand, strongly backed the high court decision. As a result, I became the "go-to guy" on the Judiciary Committee for Douglas, Proxmire, and other liberals in the Senate who opposed the Dirksen amendment.

The Senate had a tradition in which any senator could come to the floor between noon and 1:00 p.m.—what was called the "morning hour"—to make political statements for the record, provide extended remarks on some topic, or say something that might please their constituents. Every day, it seemed, Dirksen would show up in the well of the Senate with some article or speech or local editorial in his hand and talk about the importance of his proposed constitutional amendment to overturn the "one-man, one-vote" ruling.

I was only a lowly freshman, but I felt like I could not let his remarks go unanswered. So I started showing up for the morning hour, too, and after Dirksen would make his point, I would get up and answer him. Gradually, I became seen as a leader of and voice for the opposition to the Dirksen amendment. By March, only my third month in the Senate, I

11. Smith, *On Democracy's Doorstep*, 5.

was testifying before the Judiciary Committee against Dirksen's amendment.

Until this controversy could be resolved in the Congress, however, state legislatures across the country—including the Maryland General Assembly—had no choice but to try to find a way to abide by the Supreme Courts ruling.[12] Frankly, I was so busy campaigning for the Senate in 1964 that I had paid little attention to the "one-man, one-vote" controversy raging in Annapolis.

In late spring 1965, while challenges to the apportionment plan in Maryland were still moving through the courts, I gave my maiden speech on the Senate floor on the "one-man, one-vote" issue. My speech traced the "rotten borough" system in England, the history of gerrymandering, and the problems with Dirksen's proposed amendment. We must have printed and circulated thousands of copies of that speech. We sent them to the mayor of every major city in the country and urged our allies to distribute it to smaller municipalities in their states. In July, the National League of Cities voted 429–116 to oppose the amendment. Our speech became the standard set of talking points for Douglas, Proxmire, the Kennedy brothers, Philip Hart of Michigan, Joseph S. Clark of Pennsylvania, Clifford Case of New Jersey, my Maryland colleague Danny Brewster, and others who helped fight Dirksen's amendment.[13]

The Dirksen amendment would "weaken, not strengthen, our federal system," I said. "The fundamental illness, the overriding malady, of our state governments lies in their malapportionment."[14] The result, I emphasized, was that state governments failed to meet the needs of their urbanized areas.

12. For decades, every county in Maryland had a state senator, regardless of population. A rural county on the Eastern Shore or in western Maryland had the same representation in the state Senate as heavily populated suburban Montgomery, Prince George's, or Baltimore Counties. This oversized rural representation translated into oversized rural power, with rural legislators controlling many of the committees and other leadership positions in the General Assembly. It was a level of authority that none of them wanted to give up, and that was true in other state legislatures around the country as well.

13. I felt some trepidation making that first speech. After all, I was standing in the same chamber where my father had distinguished himself for four terms. After the speech was over, I remember going home and celebrating my son Millard's seventh birthday. Shirley Elder, "Sen. Tydings Takes Issue with a Minor Institution," *Washington Daily News*, June 3, 1965, 20.

14. Elder, "Sen. Tydings Takes Issue with a Minor Institution."

Dirksen's amendment finally came up for a vote on August 4, 1965. Supported by southern and rural senators, the vote was 57 to 39 in favor, but still seven votes short of the two-thirds required for passage of a constitutional amendment.[15]

Dirksen did not give up. After the defeat, he held up Senate work for a month until the Judiciary Committee agreed to reconsider the amendment the following spring. Backed by the US Chamber of Commerce and the National Association of Manufacturers, Dirksen worked behind the scenes through the fall, even engaging a public relations firm, to create national support for his amendment.

Contrary to the arguments made by states' rights advocates such as Dirksen or Senator J. Strom Thurmond of South Carolina, I firmly believed the Supreme Court decision would strengthen, not weaken, state governments and would do more to rebuild the withering federal system than any other event. It was easy for me to cite examples of how in state after state proposals to address legitimate urban concerns, such as raising the minimum wage, providing free polio vaccinations or mental health services, or increasing unemployment compensation, were easily defeated by legislative majorities that represented sometimes half as many people as those who had voted for such measures. Most states were simply out of touch with their constituents because of the way their legislatures were apportioned.

To prevent Dirksen from getting the two-thirds vote he needed for his amendment, Proxmire, Douglas, and I organized a filibuster in the spring of 1966. In April, the Senate rejected Dirksen's proposal once again, this time on a 55-to-38 vote, nine votes shy of the required two-thirds.

Filibusters

The tactics we employed to thwart Dirksen's amendment made us experts in filibusters. In those days, you really had to pose a threat that somebody would stand on the floor and talk forever, if necessary, to delay the business of the Senate until the other side gave in. Filibusters

15. David E. Kyvig, "Everett Dirksen's Constitutional Crusades," *Journal of the Illinois State Historical Society* 95, no. 1 (2002): 78, http://www.jstor.org/stable/40193488.

were such marathons that presiding officers often brought in cots so the weary could remain close to the Senate floor. Filibustering senators would take shifts, tag-teaming so their opponents could not get the floor. It has become much easier to conduct a filibuster today because of the way Senate rules have been changed or interpreted, but in my day you really had to stand there and talk if you wanted to hold the floor.[16]

In one of the most embarrassing episodes of my Senate career, I was part of a team organized by Senator Fred Harris of Oklahoma in 1967 to filibuster against a welfare reform bill being pushed by Senators Russell Long of Louisiana and Robert Byrd of West Virginia. The bill was aimed, in part, at stopping what Long and Byrd said was an intentional practice by unwed welfare mothers of having more children for the purpose of increasing the size of their welfare checks. Long derisively referred to such women as "broodmares." Our side, which included Bobby Kennedy, saw the effort as undermining the welfare program and particularly offensive to African Americans.

My job was to be on the floor in case any other senator asked for a unanimous consent agreement to move to immediate consideration of the welfare bill. If that happened, I was to object immediately and launch our side into a filibuster. That particular morning the Senate convened early, and Robert Burt, a relatively new legislative assistant who had replaced Wurtzel, was to help me keep an eye on the floor until my aide John McEvoy arrived. But when McEvoy got there, he found Burt chatting with someone in the Senate cloakroom and me opening mail at my desk on the Senate floor, both of us oblivious to what was going on around me.

By the time McEvoy rushed to my side, he could hear a worrisome exchange between Byrd and Ohio Senator Frank Lausche, who was then presiding. "Senator, I think they're passing the bill," McEvoy urgently said. "No, no, it is just preliminary morning business," I replied, but as I spoke the gavel came down and the bill was passed. Neither Burt nor I had been paying attention. I was mortified. When Bobby Kennedy found out what happened, he was furious with me. Whether I had been

16. In 1975, for example, the Senate reduced the number of votes required for cloture—that is, to end a filibuster—from two-thirds to three-fifths, or sixty votes. Filibuster and Cloture, US Senate History, http://www.senate.gov/artandhistory/history/common/briefing/Filibuster_Cloture.htm.

too trusting of my Senate colleagues, too naïve, or simply too distracted, it was a terrible, embarrassing mistake.

The Call for a Constitutional Convention

After Dirksen's amendment failed for the third time, he shifted to a new strategy: he would try to get every state legislature to call for a constitutional convention to address the apportionment issue. Privately, Dirksen told confidants that if it seemed likely such a convention would be called, he expected Congress would opt to avoid the uncertainties of a constitutional convention and, instead, would propose an apportionment amendment for the states to ratify.[17]

In March 1967, a *New York Times* front-page story caught Congress off guard when it reported that thirty-two states had followed Dirksen's lead by requesting a constitutional convention to address the apportionment issue. It appeared that only two more states were needed.

I challenged the validity of these state petitions on several grounds, arguing that most were void because they sprang from malapportioned legislatures that were already under court order to redistrict.[18] It was a race against time. If a convention could be held off, the courts would have time to reapportion enough state legislatures so that a convention would never happen and the Dirksen amendment would never be ratified.

Proxmire and Douglas were relying on me to work with the League of Women Voters to keep tabs on what states were doing. One afternoon, the league called me to warn that the Alaska state Senate was about to become the fatal last state to call for a convention by passing a bill already passed by the Alaska House. The league provided me with the name and number of the majority leader of the Alaska Senate, and I called him to tell him what was at stake. The majority leader said that until my call, he had thought the bill was innocuous. He agreed to kill it, and he was as good as his word.

That alone may have been the end of the Dirksen amendment, although the risk of opening the Constitution to changes that could go

17. Kyvig, "Everett Dirksen's Constitutional Crusades," 79.

18. On closer inspection, it also became apparent that some states had proposed a convention for the purpose of adopting a resolution different from Dirksen's. In addition, at least two states had not even bothered to forward their resolutions to Congress.

far beyond the narrow issue of apportionment began to dawn on leaders in Congress and around the country. Conservatives like the North Carolina Senator and constitutional scholar Sam Ervin worried that convention participants could dismantle the Bill of Rights or do other grave damage to the document that guided our nation. Support for such a convention began to erode, a retreat that picked up speed when a number of newly reapportioned state legislatures rescinded their original calls for a convention. The threat had passed.

Despite the setbacks, Dirksen stubbornly pushed to overturn the "one-man, one-vote" ruling right up until his death from lung cancer two years later.

Protecting Other Warren Court Decisions

"One-man, one-vote" was not the only issue springing from the decisions of the Warren court that we had to fight to protect in those days.

Dirksen and the southern senators all pushed for an amendment to the Bill of Rights that would have reversed Supreme Court rulings prohibiting organized prayer or required Bible readings in public schools.[19] They were trying to legitimize longtime practices that the court said violated the constitutional separation of church and state. Dirksen, who often quoted from the Bible or otherwise demonstrated his Christian faith in public statements, strongly opposed those decisions and assumed many Americans did as well.[20]

I supported Senator Bayh, who offered a "sense of the Congress" resolution that would have allowed voluntary prayer or silent meditation in schools. But Bayh's resolution was defeated, 52–33.

Unable to pry his stronger constitutional amendment out of Bayh's subcommittee, Dirksen boldly substituted it for the language in a minor bill already on the floor proclaiming National UNICEF Day. We then debated the proposed amendment for the next three days. I and other opponents, including Sam Ervin, the conservative constitutional expert, said that officially sanctioned prayer in school or required readings from the Bible or other religious texts would threaten the religious freedom of

---

19. *Engel v. Vitale*, 370 US 421 (1962); *Abington School District v. Schempp*, 374 U.S. 203 (1963).

20. Kyvig, "Everett Dirksen's Constitutional Crusades," 75.

any religious group that found itself in the minority. Dirksen's supporters, however, said the Supreme Court ruling was an unwarranted step
toward atheism.

In the end, Dirksen's school prayer amendment failed much the way
his "one-man, one-vote" amendments had failed—with a majority vote
but short of the two-thirds required for constitutional amendments.[21]

Meanwhile, segregationists such as Strom Thurmond, Sam Ervin,
James Eastland of Mississippi, John McClellan of Arkansas, and other
southerners tried without success to repeal or otherwise undermine
other Supreme Court decisions that provided protections for criminal
defendants.

The southerners particularly disliked the high court's *Miranda* ruling, which required that those arrested be told that they have a right to
remain silent and to be represented by legal counsel. They also opposed
an earlier but related ruling that required publicly funded legal counsel
for all indigent criminal defendants.[22]

When Thurgood Marshall was nominated by President Johnson to
become the first African American on the Supreme Court, Thurmond
and the other southerners on the Judiciary Committee relentlessly grilled
him about the *Miranda* decision in particular, hoping he would answer
in a way that showed he had already made up his mind on an issue that
might one day come before the court. They wanted to prove that Marshall was only too willing to become another "activist" on the Warren
court. But Marshall was too sharp for them and carefully deflected their
insistent questions.

Many of these fights played out in 1967 and 1968, and Attorney
General Ramsey Clark depended on me to stay on top of them. My role
was to keep him informed, to speak out, and to do everything I could to
keep the high court decisions from being reversed, and we were successful.

Even though we sometimes were diametrically opposed on specific
topics, Everett Dirksen was an easy man to like. Almost every Thurs-
day afternoon around five o'clock, he would hold court in his office and

21. The September 21, 1966, vote on the school prayer amendment was 49–37.

22. *Miranda v. Arizona*, 384 US 436 (1966); *Gideon v. Wainwright*, 372 US 335 (1963).

serve drinks to anyone who joined him. Frequently, it was a group of us young Democrats from the Judiciary Committee—Teddy Kennedy, Birch Bayh, myself. Dirksen was an interesting man, a good speaker, and an entertaining conversationalist. He would often have you in stitches. We talked at length about the issues of the day.

When Dirksen was on the Senate floor, whether he was arguing for or against something, he always seemed to bring up George Washington and the heroes of the American Revolution and say that they surely would have been on his side.

I regret to say that Everett Dirksen and I were on opposite sides during many of the big battles in the Senate over the Warren court decisions, especially on school prayer and "one-man, one-vote." Yet, I thought of him as a master legislator, skillful adversary, determined advocate, and warm friend.

Dirksen supported a bond issue in 1962 that saved the United Nations from bankruptcy, and he backed the Nuclear Test Ban Treaty (1963), the Civil Rights Act (1964), the Voting Rights Act (1965), and the Fair Housing Act (1968). In each of those instances, he was initially skeptical and under partisan pressure to oppose. But he ultimately stood above his party, took a historical perspective, and moved our nation forward.

How well the nation would be served if we could have as the Republican leader of the Senate today a person of Everett Dirksen's caliber, leadership, and integrity.

CHAPTER 14

"A Voteless People Is a Hopeless People"

Before my first year in Congress was at an end, it was obvious that the US Senate had fundamentally changed, especially on the politically explosive issue of civil rights. The southern conservatives who had run the Senate for decades were gradually losing their power. In their place, a new generation of young, progressive, reform-minded senators was rising.[1]

"About 20 first-term and second-term Democrats, most of them youthful by Senate standards, were drawn together by mutual interests and a liberal political philosophy," the *New York Times* noted late in 1965. "They constituted a major voting bloc on some issues."[2]

The shift on civil rights had actually started much earlier, in 1948, when Minneapolis Mayor Hubert Humphrey gave a speech at the Democratic National Convention in Philadelphia urging adoption of the first civil rights plank in the party platform. It was time, he said, to "get out of the shadow of states' rights and walk forthrightly into the bright

1. The phrase used as the title of this chapter is attributed to S. W. (Samuel) Boynton, an early civil rights activist in Selma, Alabama. Gary May, *Bending toward Justice: The Voting Rights Act and the Transformation of American Democracy* (New York: Basic Books, 2013), 13.

2. JFK's youngest brother, Teddy, had been elected to the Senate in 1962 at the age of thirty-one. Also elected that year were Birch Bayh, thirty-seven, of Indiana, and George McGovern, thirty-eight, of South Dakota. I was elected two years later, at thirty-six, as was Bobby Kennedy, age thirty-nine. The House of Representatives underwent a similar transformation. The year I won, voters sent other young progressives to the House: John Tunney, thirty, of California, who was the son of heavyweight champ Gene Tunney; John Culver, thirty-two, of Iowa; and W. R. Anderson, forty-three, of Tennessee. Anderson, the former skipper of the first American nuclear-powered submarine, the USS *Nautilus*, turned out to be far more liberal than his conservative constituents expected. "Young men, many still in their 30s and early 40s, are taking over much of the work of the staid old United States Senate. One of these days, they may become its masters." Quoted in Robert C. Albright, "A Young Crew Usurping Senate," *Washington Post*, August 1, 1965, E-1. "Session Marked by Shift in Power," *New York Times*, October 25, 1965, 41.

sunshine of human rights."[3] When that effort succeeded, the entire Mississippi delegation and most of the Alabama delegation walked out of the convention and formed their own states' rights party, known as the Dixiecrats, and nominated their own candidate for president, South Carolina Senator Strom Thurmond, who at the time was a Democrat.

It took another dozen years before John F. Kennedy pressed for stronger civil rights protections for African Americans during his 1960 campaign for president. This was politically risky in that era of segregation because Kennedy needed to carry the conservative and historically Democratic states of the so-called "solid South."

A pivotal point came that October, when Senator Kennedy and his brother Bobby rejected the advice of senior Democratic Party leaders and decided to intervene on behalf of the Reverend Martin Luther King Jr. The civil rights leader had been arrested in Georgia, and there were serious concerns about his safety—worries that a mob could try to break into the jail and lynch him. Senator Kennedy directed Bobby to telephone the Georgia judge and plead with him to release King, which the judge finally agreed to do. JFK also called King's wife, Coretta Scott King, to express his support for her husband and his leadership for civil rights.[4]

African Americans had been skeptical of Kennedy when the 1960 campaign began, but when word of his support for King began to circulate, their support shifted strongly in his favor. Although African Americans were still denied the right to vote in most southern states in 1960, in the end as much as 70 percent of the black vote nationwide went to Kennedy—enough to tip the outcome in his favor in at least eleven states, including four southern states: South Carolina, Texas, North Carolina, and Maryland.[5]

Once Kennedy was elected and his brother installed as attorney general, the federal government began to step up intervention on civil rights issues, slowly at first, but with increasing urgency.

3. Hubert H. Humphrey's civil rights speech to the 1948 Democratic National Convention, Minnesota Historical Society, St. Paul, www2.mnhs.org.

4. The civil rights effort of the Kennedy campaign in 1960 was headed by the candidate's brother-in-law, Sargent Shriver, and Harris Wofford, who years later would become a US senator representing Pennsylvania.

5. The other seven states were Illinois, New Jersey, Michigan, Delaware, Missouri, Pennsylvania, and Nevada. Theodore H. White, *The Making of the President, 1960* (New York: Atheneum, 1961), 354.

In 1961, Byron R. "Whizzer" White, the deputy attorney general, was put in charge of protecting black "Freedom Riders," who were trying to desegregate interstate buses by riding them into the segregated South.[6] A year later, James Meredith, a black college student, attempted to enroll in the all-white University of Mississippi. The ensuing confrontation over Meredith's enrollment forced President Kennedy to nationalize the Mississippi National Guard and to send five hundred US marshals and federal troops in to quell a riot on the Ole Miss campus. In that riot two men were killed, hundreds more injured, cars burned, and university property damaged. When Meredith was finally admitted on October 1, 1962, he was personally escorted into the school by John Doar, an assistant attorney general in the Kennedy administration.[7]

The Mississippi drama was repeated in 1963 in neighboring Alabama, where Governor George Wallace literally stood in the doorway to block the enrollment of two black students, Vivian Malone and James A. Hood, at the all-white University of Alabama. President Kennedy again had to nationalize the National Guard before Wallace would stand aside. This time, it was Nicholas Katzenbach, deputy attorney general, who accompanied the two students as they entered the university to enroll.[8]

Putting Civil Rights to the Test

In 1963, Kennedy introduced legislation that would open hotels, restaurants, and other "public accommodations" to anyone, regardless of race or gender. Against the predictable wall of southern opposition, the legislation finally died in a Senate filibuster. Then Kennedy was killed.

Suddenly, Lyndon Johnson, a southerner who had long sided with the segregationists in Congress, was president.

6. The Freedom Riders were greeted by mobs of white men wielding baseball bats and iron pipes. At least one bus was firebombed. Kennedy administration representative John Seigenthaler was among those beaten. Many Freedom Riders were arrested and sent to local jails. In Mississippi, they were sent to the state penitentiary. In Alabama, White had to negotiate for their protection with Governor John Patterson, who had supported Kennedy in the election but was nonetheless a segregationist who had ordered black students at one Alabama college expelled after they participated in a sit-in demonstration.

7. By then, both the Mississippi governor and lieutenant governor had been held in contempt of court by federal judges.

8. Katzenbach succeeded White, who by then had been named to the US Supreme Court by President Kennedy.

But Johnson changed direction and resurrected Kennedy's civil rights legislation. "No memorial oration or eulogy could more eloquently honor" him, Johnson said in his first nationally televised speech after Kennedy's assassination. "We have talked long enough in this country about equal rights. We have talked for one hundred years or more. It is time now to write the next chapter, and to write it in the books of law."[9]

Many, including the southern senators who had been his allies, found Johnson's shift on civil rights unexpected. Yet, from the time he was a young man in an impoverished corner of Texas, Johnson had quietly demonstrated concern for Hispanics, African Americans, and the poor. "Throughout his life," wrote his biographer, Robert Caro, "there had been hints that he possessed a true, deep compassion for the downtrodden, and particularly for poor people of color, along with a true, deep desire to raise them up."[10]

Work on the civil rights bill began anew in 1964, while I was still running for election to the Senate. Through brilliant legislative maneuvers, Johnson forced the bill to the Senate floor on March 30, but that only ignited a nonstop, fifty-seven-day southern filibuster.

At the time, senators from the South chaired ten of the sixteen standing Senate committees—powerful committees such as Armed Services, Banking and Currency, Finance, Foreign Relations, Judiciary, and Labor and Public Welfare. These southerners, whose average age was seventy, were elected and reelected every six years until their accumulated seniority assured them de facto control of the Senate. They were able to block virtually every attempt to pass civil rights legislation—even going so far as to defeat a bill that would finally have outlawed at the federal level the heinous practice of lynching.[11]

But with Johnson in the White House, and with the images on nightly television news reports or newspaper front pages of black

9. President Lyndon B. Johnson's Address to a Joint Session of Congress, November 27, 1963, Center for Legislative Archives, National Archives, http://www.archives.gov/legislative/features/civil-rights-1964/lbj-address.html.

10. Robert A. Caro, *The Passage of Power: The Years of Lyndon Johnson* (New York: Vintage Books, 2013), 9.

11. One exception was the Civil Rights Act of 1957, pushed by then–Senator Lyndon Johnson as a means of making himself more acceptable to northerners as a candidate for the presidency in 1960. It was the first civil rights bill to be enacted since Reconstruction. It set up the Civil Rights Division within the Department of Justice and the Civil Rights Commission to investigate national voting practices. It also empowered the attorney general to punish anyone who interfered with or prohibited any citizen from exercising the franchise to vote. May, *Bending toward Justice*, 49.

Americans in the South being blasted with high-powered fire hoses, viciously attacked by police dogs, and targeted for beatings, bombings, and murder, and with sympathy for the martyred president still running high, Johnson ultimately broke the Senate filibuster, and the Civil Rights Act of 1964 became law.[12] It had taken Kennedy's courage to introduce it and Johnson's legislative skill to enact it.

That fight knocked some of the wind out of the southern opposition.[13]

"If You Can't Vote, Then You're Not Free"

The Civil Rights Act of 1964 outlawed racial discrimination in restaurants and hotels, but it failed to stop the pervasive practice throughout the South—and in a few other states—of denying black Americans the most fundamental right in a democracy: the right to vote. This was accomplished through poll taxes that poor African Americans could not afford to pay, or impossible-to-pass literacy tests, or trick questions that no one could answer, such as the one posed to would-be black voters in one Alabama county to name every judge in the state. A single mistake rendered the applicant ineligible.

While mostly it was black citizens who were subjected to these kinds of tests, voter registrars could use their power against would-be white voters as well. The poll tax disenfranchised voters who were poor regardless of race. Southern registrars often prevented African Americans from registering by severely limiting election office hours.

If all of that was still not enough, African Americans with the temerity to try to register to vote faced the loss of their jobs, intimidation, beatings, or even death.

These strategies worked. There were counties throughout the South with majority black populations but with virtually no registered black

12. The 71–29 Senate vote on June 10, 1964, marked the first time cloture (a motion to end debate) had been invoked on a civil rights bill and only the second time since 1927 it had been invoked on any issue. On June 19, a substitute Senate bill offered by Senator Humphrey passed, the House quickly agreed to it, and Johnson signed it into law on July 2, 1964.

13. The old guard of the Senate was beginning to fade. Some in the southern bloc seemed sapped of their energy by illness and old age. Richard Russell of Georgia, the erudite leader of the southern obstructionists, was sixty-eight and missed most of the 1965 session following surgery. Harry Flood Byrd of Virginia, the seventy-eight-year-old chair of the Finance Committee, suffered from a debilitating knee ailment, although he remained mentally sharp. Olin D. Johnston, sixty-nine, of South Carolina, chair of the Post Office and Civil Service Committee, died suddenly, in April 1965.

voters. The issue came to a head in early 1965 in Selma, Alabama, where civil rights workers had been unsuccessfully pressing local officials to allow black residents to register.[14]

"If you can't vote, then you're not free," Hosea Williams, a civil rights activist who was part of King's inner circle, told one youth rally. "And if you ain't free, children, then you're a slave."[15]

King and others hoped a confrontation over voter registration in Selma might prompt Johnson to introduce legislation to guarantee African Americans their voting rights.

To draw attention to the issue, civil rights activists launched a march on March 7, 1965, that was to take them fifty-seven miles, from Selma to the state capital, Montgomery. Instead, as they left Selma they were met by the Alabama state police as they crossed the Edmund Pettus Bridge (named after a Confederate general). The marchers were attacked with tear gas and billy clubs. Many were severely injured, including Williams and another King aide, John Lewis.[16] News and TV coverage of the incident, which became known as Bloody Sunday, inflamed the nation, and soon thousands of protesters poured into Selma to join a renewed march to Montgomery. Within a week, President Johnson announced that he was sending voting rights legislation to Congress.

Johnson's voting rights legislation got quick bipartisan support and sixty-four co-sponsors in the Senate. This figure represents a level of constructive cooperation tragically impossible in the polarized Congress of today, where a faction of conservative Tea Party Republicans regularly denounce and kill any attempts at compromise between the two parties.

I immediately joined the voting rights fight. When my father was in the Senate, he frequently voted with the southern bloc on civil rights issues and, in many respects, was a "southern Senator" himself. But on the issues of civil and human rights, the stronger influence on me was my mother, who was originally from Wisconsin.

14. In Dallas County, which surrounds Selma, 57 percent of the population in 1963 was African American, but only 1 percent of black residents were registered. In some rural Alabama counties, the percentage of black residents was even higher and none was registered. May, *Bending toward Justice*, 7.

15. Williams quoted in May, *Bending toward Justice*, 56.

16. After years as one of the most prominent civil rights leaders in the nation, Lewis was elected to the US House of Representatives in 1987, representing the northern portions of Atlanta, Georgia. As of this writing, he is the dean of the Georgia congressional delegation and still a revered figure in civil rights circles.

I can recall an incident during a severe snowstorm when Dad was still in the Senate and I was a student at McDonogh. Mother arranged for a Senate attendant to drive her to pick me up at McDonogh. When we stopped in Edgewood to get something to eat, the diner refused to serve our driver, who was African American. Mother was infuriated; she castigated the diner's owner, and we immediately headed home without eating.

My mother's views of tolerance, empathy, and compassion have always stuck with me, which is probably why I never hesitated to step out in front on civil rights issues from the time I was in law school through my years in the General Assembly, the Senate, and up until today.

The first challenge for the voting rights bill was to get it past the chair of the Senate Judiciary Committee: James O. Eastland of Mississippi. While I generally got along well with Senator Eastland, there was no doubt about his racial views, or those of his constituents. In the Mississippi county where he lived, only 161 of more than 13,500 black residents were registered.[17] Of the voting rights bill he said, "I am opposed to every word and every line in it."[18]

But with the votes of our group of young senators—some of us half the age of our Senate elders—we managed to push the legislation out of the Judiciary Committee on a 12–4 vote, albeit "without recommendation." When it reached the Senate floor, Senator Phil Hart of Michigan became the lead whip for the bill, assisted by Senators Teddy Kennedy, Birch Bayh, and myself. We were responsible for rounding up and counting votes. The principal floor leader—the ultimate nose-counter, with whom we regularly met—was not a Democrat but rather a man from the "party of Lincoln," the Senate minority leader, Everett Dirksen of Illinois.

Teddy, however, immediately caused a rift in our coalition by proposing an amendment that would prohibit poll taxes in all state elections.[19] Poll taxes had already been outlawed in all federal elections by ratification

17. May, *Bending toward Justice*, 7, 150.

18. Eastland quoted in ibid.

19. Teddy had only recently returned to the Senate after suffering serious injuries in a plane crash in Massachusetts. He supported himself on the Senate floor with the aid of a silver-headed cane. Bayh had also been on that small plane but had not been injured as seriously as Kennedy.

of the Twenty-Fourth Amendment in January 1964, but the statute did not cover state elections. Dirksen and many other voting rights supporters, including Johnson's point man, Vice President Humphrey, despised poll taxes and emphatically agreed with Teddy's position, but they feared his amendment would render the bill unconstitutional. They therefore opposed it.

Southerners tried to kill or weaken the legislation, proposing more than seventy amendments. This time, however, all of them were easily defeated.[20] After twenty-five days of debate, the Senate again voted for cloture (that is, to end debate), 70–30. The bill passed, 77–19, but without Teddy's amendment.[21]

When the bill reached the House, however, not only was the amendment banning poll taxes restored, but also added were stronger legal protections for civil rights workers, voter registrars, and others who try to help African Americans exercise their right to vote; the new protections included potential fines and jail time for violators. The amended bill was overwhelmingly approved, 333–85, and returned to the Senate. There it stalled as the divided proponents of the bill debated whether the poll tax ban would give courts the opportunity to nullify the entire effort. Dirksen argued that it was a question of risk versus sureness.

Johnson, fearful he could lose the bill entirely, summoned King to the White House and convinced him to support the bill without the ban on the odious poll tax in exchange for a letter from Attorney General Katzenbach pledging to sue immediately the four states that still levied such a tax. That ended the stalemate. The final vote was 328–74 in the House and 79–18 in the Senate. Johnson signed the Voting Rights Act on August 6, 1965.[22]

20. Senator Sam Ervin of North Carolina, frustrated by the sudden impotence of southerners on civil rights issues, complained, "The way things are, I don't think I could get a denunciation of the Crucifixion in the bill." Quoted in May, Bending toward Justice, 160.

21. The nineteen included seventeen senators from the South plus Republicans Strom Thurmond of South Carolina and John Tower of Texas.

22. One by one throughout 1966, federal courts in Texas, Alabama, Virginia, and Mississippi declared poll taxes in each of those states to be unconstitutional. In March 1966, the Supreme Court of the United States, in the case of Harper v. Virginia Board of Elections, also reversed an earlier decision and prohibited poll taxes in state elections as a violation of the Equal Protection Clause of the Fourteenth Amendment.

Voting Rights Results

I think the Voting Rights Act of 1965 was the most important federal civil rights legislation because it goes to the essence of a democracy: the ability of every citizen to have a say in who runs our government and sets government policy. The Voting Rights Act not only opened the door to African American voters but also to African American office holders, although that second change was slower in coming. It is not a stretch to trace the 2008 election of Barack Obama as the first African American president to the passage of the Voting Rights Act of 1965.

The law prohibited any act that interfered with or denied a citizen's right to vote because of color or race. It eliminated voting tests or the "character tests" some states employed in which someone of "good standing" in the community was required to vouch for a would-be voter before he or she could be registered.

An amendment pushed by Bobby Kennedy outlawed English-language proficiency requirements, making it possible for as many as three hundred thousand Puerto Ricans, many of them living in New York, to vote.

Senator Hiram L. Fong, a Republican from Hawaii, and I also added an amendment that authorized poll watchers to be on hand at polling places to observe voting activities firsthand. A year later, we had to write to Katzenbach and urge him to instruct poll watchers in an Alabama primary of their right to protect against misleading advice being given to voters.

One of the most important provisions gave special treatment to seven southern states and portions of four others where less than 50 percent of eligible voters were registered in 1964. Before those states were allowed to implement any new voting practices in the years to come, they were required to first obtain "preclearance" from the US attorney general or the US District Court in Washington.[23] This was designed to make sure that states with a history of discrimination did not implement new discriminatory practices. Before a state could be removed from federal supervision, it had to demonstrate that it had not used any test or other device to interfere with voting in the previous five years.

23. The affected areas were Alabama, Alaska, Georgia, Louisiana, Mississippi, South Carolina, and Virginia, plus specific political subdivisions in Arizona, Hawaii, Idaho, and North Carolina. US Department of Justice, Civil Rights Division, http://www.justice.gov/crt/about-section-5-voting-rights-act.

As soon as the law was enacted, federal voter registrars were dispatched to Selma and eight other locations in Alabama, Mississippi, and Louisiana, where they began signing up thousands of black voters. On March 7, 1966—the one-year anniversary of the Bloody Sunday march in Selma—the US Supreme Court ruled in a South Carolina case that the Voting Rights Act was constitutional.

The Voting Rights Act finally succeeded where other laws, court decisions, and even constitutional amendments over the previous century had failed. In the first four years after passage of the legislation, the percentage of the nonwhite population that was registered to vote increased from 19 to 52 percent in Alabama, 32 to 59 percent in Georgia, 37 to 51 percent in South Carolina, 38 to 56 percent in Virginia, and a staggering increase from 7 to 60 percent in Mississippi.

There were almost no black elected office holders in the South in 1965, but by 1969 there were more than 260, and of course that number has multiplied since then. Racist white residents of the South did what they could to frustrate black office seekers by redrawing congressional district lines, creating at-large districts where white voters would dominate, and using similar tricks.

Johnson, who understood politics better than most, predicted that support for civil rights would cost the Democrats votes in the South for at least a generation, and he was right. Many southern Democrats became Republicans. Nixon, elected in 1968, quietly developed the "Southern Strategy," which capitalized on the white voter backlash against civil rights.[24]

In the years since passage of the Voting Rights Act, the preclearance requirement has been attacked by those who say it was intended to be "temporary" and is no longer necessary. But over the years, the law was reauthorized and extended four times, each time with a Republican in the White House.[25]

In 2013, however, the conservative-leaning Supreme Court under Chief Justice John Roberts finally weakened the preclearance provision by ruling that the formula used to determine which jurisdictions are

24. Nixon also used opposition to the war in Vietnam as the basis to claim that Democrats were soft on national defense and the military. Republicans continue to pursue both of these strategies to this day.

25. Those presidents were Nixon in 1970, Ford in 1975, Reagan in 1982, and George W. Bush in 2006.

subject to the requirement is unconstitutional. The result is that juris-dictions identified as covered by the law no longer have to seek preclear-ance for new voting changes unless they are covered by a separate court order under a different section of the Voting Rights Act, thus making it easier once again to deny minorities the right to vote.[26]

It is tragic to have to say that strong efforts continue today to disen-franchise minority or poor voters—efforts led by the Tea Party extrem-ists who control the Republican Party in Congress and in many state legislatures. Republicans have tried to curtail voting by black and His-panic Americans, students, the elderly, and others by requiring voters to produce identification cards under the ruse of preventing voter fraud, which most studies have shown to be almost nonexistent. They also have undermined efforts to expand the electorate by attacking laws that permit early voting or voting by former felons, the majority of whom are minorities.

To further institutionalize this undemocratic attempt to suppress voting, the Trump administration has tapped a former Kansas Secretary of State Kris Kobach, known for his efforts to disenfranchise voters, to head an "Election Integrity Commission" to investigate a voter fraud problem that does not exist. Clearly, the intent is to use this bogus "study" to justify further efforts by Republicans to stifle voting among African Americans, Hispanics, the elderly, and others who would be likely to vote Democratic.[27]

None of that, however, has been able to hold back the tide of African Americans' involvement in the political process that was brought on by the Voting Rights Act in 1965. The opportunity for African American voters and African American office holders was forever changed.

Thurgood Marshall

President Johnson punctuated the national shift on civil rights in June 1967 by nominating Thurgood Marshall to become the first

---

26. US Department of Justice, Civil Rights Division, http://www.justice.gov/crt/about-section-5-voting-rights-act.

27. "Academics who have studied the issue for decades say that voter fraud—particularly of the type that strict voter-identification laws championed by Kobach and others are intended to combat—is rare and that voter-ID requirements are a burdensome solution to an almost nonexistent problem." Christopher Ingraham, "Trump's Election Panel Seeks All Voter-Roll Data," *Washington Post*, June 30, 2017.

African American to serve on the Supreme Court of the United States.

Marshall was a Maryland lawyer who had led NAACP efforts to overturn racial discrimination laws and who regularly risked his own life—often having to move from one safe house to another—to defend innocent African American defendants throughout the South. It was Marshall who had successfully argued the landmark *Brown v. Board of Education* school desegregation case before the Supreme Court, the decision southern segregationists hated above all others.[28]

Johnson faced two problems, however: first, there was no vacancy on the Supreme Court for his nominee to fill; second, the senior members of the Senate Judiciary Committee—Eastland (who was chair) of Mississippi, John McClellan of Arkansas, Sam Ervin of North Carolina, and Strom Thurmond of South Carolina—were all southern segregationists intent on keeping Marshall off the high court.

Here's how Johnson cleverly opened a seat on the court for Marshall. First, he encouraged Attorney General Katzenbach to resign, with the intention of replacing him with his deputy, Ramsey Clark. Clark was the son of an old family friend, Tom C. Clark, who had been appointed by President Truman to the Supreme Court in 1949.[29] Because the son's appointment would create a potential conflict of interest with the father's role on the court, Johnson persuaded the elder Clark to resign.[30]

The southern senators, all clever lawyers in their own right, relentlessly attacked Marshall as a "judicial activist" who surely favored the *Miranda* ruling that protected criminal defendants, as well as other controversial Warren court decisions. Marshall's attackers claimed he would willingly stray from the letter of the Constitution to meet his own goals. They stretched out committee hearings for weeks and then held off a floor vote for several more weeks. It was my job to sit in those confirmation hearings to defend him and protect him from the unfair questioning unleashed by the southerners. Along with Hart, Ted Kennedy,

28. In 1961, Marshall was appointed to the US Court of Appeals for the Second Circuit by President Kennedy. Four years later, President Johnson appointed him as US solicitor general; he was the first African American to hold that post.

29. In a move that would be impossible for any Supreme Court nominee today, Clark refused to testify at his Senate confirmation hearing.

30. A grateful Johnson rewarded Justice Clark and his wife with an exotic around-the-world "goodwill trip," ostensibly sponsored by the State Department. Wil Haygood, *Showdown: Thurgood Marshall and the Supreme Court Nomination That Changed America* (New York: Knopf, 2015), 15.

and Bayh, I then helped round up votes for the nominee, just as we had done for the Voting Rights Act. Dirksen again joined our fight. Hart and I concentrated on senators from the western and northern parts of the country, such as Charles Percy, the newly elected Republican from Illinois; Warren Magnuson of Washington; and William Proxmire of Wisconsin. Vice President Humphrey, who had been battling the Dixiecrats for nearly two decades, also helped lock down the votes for Marshall.

Our task was complicated by almost daily news reports of riots in urban slums and attacks on African Americans in the South as anger in both places turned to violence. The first was a reaction to changes in race laws that were too slow in coming; the second was backlash against the fact that there were changes at all.

In the end, Marshall's opponents simply did not have the votes. His appointment was approved by the Judiciary Committee, 11–5, with all five dissenting votes coming from southerners. The full Senate approved the nomination, 69–11, on August 30. The vote deceptively appeared to be lopsided because President Johnson had convinced twenty segregationist senators, who lacked the votes to filibuster the nomination, simply to refrain from voting.[31] Marshall went on to serve on the high court for twenty-four years.

Fair Housing

Passage of the Voting Rights Act and the appointment of Thurgood Marshall, of course, were hardly the end of efforts to assure the civil rights of African Americans and other minorities during my years in the Senate or, for that matter, in the decades since. African Americans were still discriminated against in housing—restricted from where they could buy or rent a home simply because of the color of their skin.

When the fair housing bill arrived on the Senate floor, I again became one of the floor leaders fighting for passage. Co-sponsored by Mondale and Senator Edward Brooke of Massachusetts, the bill would make it illegal to refuse to sell or rent a dwelling to any person because of his or her race, religion, or national origin.

That seemed fair to me, but you almost cannot imagine how contentious and vicious the fight over this issue was. Because of my support for this legislation, I received telephoned threats to my family and was

---

31. Haygood, *Showdown*, 331.

forced to make my home telephone number unlisted. That was scary.

For decades, housing authorities, local governments, lending institutions, and real estate agents had quietly but intentionally steered home buyers and renters away from certain parts of cities and towns based on their race. The inescapable result was a segregated pattern of living, with white people living in one part of town—usually the more affluent part—and black people in another. This situation was reinforced by the subtle and not-so-subtle decisions of political and business leaders to invest in the white communities and not in African American communities. Even the federal government mapped where to steer investments through a now discredited practice known as "redlining." Without investments in infrastructure or other government services, businesses avoided black communities. As poverty increased, so did crime. Whole communities spiraled into despair.

This time it was Ervin of North Carolina who launched the southern filibuster designed to kill the fair housing bill. Despite a letter from President Johnson endorsing the legislation and lobbying from Clarence Mitchell of the NAACP and major labor unions, the filibuster appeared to be succeeding: our side failed three times to cut off debate.

Those of us backing the bill—myself, Mondale, newly elected Howard Baker of Tennessee, Joe Clark of Pennsylvania, and others—convened in the ornate Senate Caucus Room to figure out what to do. Opposition was so rock solid, we saw no way to get the votes we needed. The growing consensus in the increasingly somber room was that it was time to move on to some other issue; this one was not winnable.

Just then, Teddy Kennedy arrived at the meeting late. When Mondale told him of our conclusion, Teddy exclaimed, "That's unacceptable." After all the work we had put into this legislation, he said, we could not go back to King or other supporters and tell them we could not produce a housing bill. We had to keep going, he implored.

Roused by Kennedy's pep talk, our group suddenly came alive and determined to find a way. I suggested that Baker, who was Dirksen's son-in-law, be dispatched to see what it would take to get him to support the bill—just as Dirksen had done on other civil rights issues.

Dirksen agreed to join our side, but we still did not have enough votes.[32]

32. "I do not want to worsen . . . the restive condition in the United States," Dirksen said, and then he referred to the war in Vietnam: "There are young men of all colors and creeds and

A fourth vote to cut off debate was scheduled for March 4, and we knew if we failed again, that would be it. Three days before that vote, a presidential commission established to look for the root causes of riots that had ravaged black neighborhoods in Los Angeles, Newark, Detroit, Chicago, and elsewhere in 1967 concluded, "Our nation is moving toward two societies, one black, one white—separate and unequal." It recommended breaking up the all-white and all-black development patterns and abandoning the high-density public housing in favor of smaller units on scattered sites, and it concluded that government had to do more to provide employment opportunities for African Americans.[33]

Whether it was due to the impact of that report or the intense lobbying on the bill is hard to say, but on March 4, the Senate voted 65–32 to end the filibuster, thus assuring Senate passage of the bill. The final vote for cloture was cast by E. L. "Bob" Bartlett, an illustrious and pioneering senator from Alaska. Bartlett's vote was a surprise because he, like other westerners from oil and mining states, had been party to a corrupt bargain with the southern segregationists: the southerners would protect the western oil and mining interests if the westerners helped defeat civil rights legislation. By then, however, Bartlett was critically ill with heart disease, and his switched vote may have simply been a final act of conscience. He died nine months later.[34]

The final hurdle for the bill was the House of Representatives, where it was almost immediately bottled up in the Rules Committee, essentially a hospice for progressive legislation that was sent there to die. But on April 4, King was assassinated in Memphis.

"Last night, for the second time in five years, a giant among us was cut down by a lunatic's bullet," I said in a statement issued the following day. "In a few years of his life, Dr. King achieved far more through

origins who are this night fighting 12,000 miles or more away from home. They will return. They will have families. . . . Unless there is fair housing . . . I do not know what the measure of their un-appreciation would be for the ingratitude of their fellow citizens." Dirksen quoted in Jean Eberhart Dubofsky, "Fair Housing: A Legislative History and a Perspective," *Washburn Law Journal* (Washburn University, Topeka), 8 (1969): 156–57.

33. "Report of the National Advisory Commission on Civil Disorders: Summary of Report" (1968), Homeland Security Digital Library, accessed May 29, 2017, https://www.hsdl.org/?abstract&did=35837. The commission, appointed by President Johnson, was headed by Ohio Governor Otto Kerner and is thus often referred to as the Kerner Commission.

34. Bartlett was posthumously honored with a statue in the Capitol as the "Architect of Alaska Statehood."

nonviolence than all his black apostles could dream of or hate's white apostles could stop."[35] I canceled my schedule and headed to Atlanta with Bobby Kennedy and Fritz Hollings, the Democratic senator from South Carolina, to be at King's funeral.

There were riots in more than one hundred American cities, including Baltimore and Washington. Five days later, with National Guard troops that had been called up in response to the DC riots still stationed in the basement of the Capitol, the House approved the Senate version of the fair housing bill without change. President Johnson signed it into law at the White House on April 11, 1968.[36]

The Sad Aftermath

Despite the landmark progress made with Civil Rights Act of 1964, the Voting Rights Act of 1965, the Fair Housing Act of 1968, and the major programs of Johnson's Great Society initiative, change in the lives of African Americans was much too slow in coming. Frustration with economic conditions and the lack of opportunity, coupled with the assassination of Dr. King and the increasingly violent protests over the war in Vietnam, had pushed the nation to the brink.

"I am really frightened," I admitted in a speech to the Chicago Anti-Defamation League at the end of April. "Last summer's violence and the events of the past month may be a prelude to a holocaust ahead. The specter of racial war is before us. Negroes see the threats of 'shoot to kill or maim or cripple' as declarations of war. And whites see fires, looting, and street mobs as open warfare which threatens them."[37]

35. Senator Joseph Tydings, statement on the death of Reverend Martin Luther King Jr., April 5, 1968, on file in the Joseph D. Tydings Collection, Hornbake Library, University of Maryland, College Park.

36. In the spring of 1968, I appeared before the Housing and Urban Affairs Subcommittee of the Senate Banking and Currency Committee to urge reform of the federal public housing programs. I talked about how cheaply and inadequately built the housing was and how it was then shamefully allowed to deteriorate. (Conditions are not much better today.) It was so bad, tenants viewed public housing as the end of the line. These projects thus became sites of failure and a breeding ground for crime and despair. The tenants felt no stake in the projects and no responsibility, only resentment. Mondale and I also introduced legislation that would have allowed public housing tenants to purchase their units and would have earmarked funds for rehabilitation and modernization, guaranteed tenants' rights in tenant councils, and provided funds so public housing authorities could provide social services.

37. Senator Joseph D. Tydings, speech to the Chicago Anti-Defamation League, April 28, 1968, Tydings Collection, Hornbake Library.

As I reread my words a half century later, I cannot help but realize that despite enormous advances in racial relations since the 1960s, the interactions between the races in too many American cities are still so raw that they often explode with horrible consequences, as was the case after twenty-five-year-old Freddie Gray died while in custody of police in Baltimore in 2015. Whether it is the shooting of young black men by white police officers, the attack by a white gunman on innocent black churchgoers, or the embittered or retaliatory attacks on white Americans—on citizens and police officers alike—by outraged black Americans who suffer from discrimination and feel they have nothing to lose, we have to acknowledge that we have not made nearly as much progress in this area as we would like to think.

The cause of the riots back in the 1960s was obvious to me: "Poverty—rising expectations, unsatisfied expectations, corrupted from hope into hopelessness. The problem is poverty and we haven't touched it."[38] The same could be said today.

In the years I was in the Congress, we adopted a massive War on Poverty program. We provided important help to inner-city African American youth by financing summer job programs. I also supported funding for what was known as the Model Cities Program, a new federal program of jobs, welfare system reform, education upgrades in poor urban areas, and an investment of billions of dollars each year to clean up the slums. But none of those programs exists today—they died thanks largely to successive Republican administrations that never saw our cities as a priority and that refused to continue to support the taxes necessary to pay for such programs.

We are rich enough. We are no poorer now than we were in the 1960s or 1970s. We suffer from a lack of will.

Bobby

After JFK's death, my hopes for the future of our country rested with my friend, Bobby Kennedy. On March 16, 1968, with fellow Democrat Lyndon Johnson still in the White House, Bobby announced he was going to run for president. Fifteen days later, LBJ stunned the nation by announcing that he was not going to seek reelection.

38. Ibid.

"In my judgment, the man best able to lead America out of bewilderment and cynicism into a new era of hope and fulfillment is Robert F. Kennedy," I said, becoming the first US senator to endorse Bobby other than his brother, Teddy. "He offers experience, initiative, and idealism to meet the foreign and domestic crises we face."[39] I hit the road to campaign for him in Maryland and nationwide almost immediately.

Bobby's motivation was compassion. He was one of the most idealistic young men in the country, yet he had the knowledge, the experience, and the pragmatism to realize what could be accomplished and what could not. He had grown, learned, and surrounded himself with talented people. He knew when to compromise, how to compromise, the need for compromise, and when not to compromise. He had an extraordinary combination of talents. To have one man with that kind of judgment and courage was highly unusual.

Bobby ran a great campaign, one of growing confidence. Thousands turned out for his rallies, drawn by his genuine empathy for the downtrodden. After enduring years of shock and depression following his brother's death, Bobby had finally found his voice and it was beginning to resonate around the country.

Everyone knows the sad ending of this story, how in the minutes after winning the crucially important California primary in June, Bobby—like JFK and Dr. King before him—was gunned down by an assassin. It was almost too much for me to bear. It was almost too much for the country to bear.

In the two and a half weeks leading up to the California primary, I campaigned for Bobby in a number of states, from California to Wisconsin to Indiana. The week before the California vote, Bobby and I crossed paths—for the last time, as it turned out—in the airport in Omaha, Nebraska. We went for a quick bite together, and I asked him if there was anything specific he wanted me to say, or anyone in particular he wanted me to meet as I traveled through the small towns of rural Nebraska. He said, "Joe, here is what I want you to do. Look around and see how Native Americans are treated and then, when you come back to Washington, try to do something about it."

39. Senator Joseph Tydings, statement endorsing the candidacy of Robert Kennedy for president, April 2, 1968, on file in the Tydings Collection, Hornbake Library.

At the time, I thought that was an extraordinary response from someone running for president. I still feel that way. When I got back to Washington, I did what I could every chance I got to help Native Americans, including supporting programs to send assistance into reservations to help alleviate poverty and create job opportunities.

I returned to Havre de Grace several days after our airport meeting in Omaha to vote for Bobby in the Maryland primary. The night I got home, Bobby was assassinated. To say I was devastated is insufficient to describe how I felt. How could anything be worse? It was like all hope had been extinguished, like idealism had died along with Bobby.

For the third time in my short political life, assassins had changed the course of our history, not to mention the lives of people I knew and cared for. As my legislative aide, John McEvoy, said later, "Bobby Kennedy was much more than a political figure, much more than a Kennedy. The man was a volcano of passion."[40]

When Bobby died, it seemed like the end. We continued to put one foot in front of another, but it was never the same after that.

Here is the public statement I gave after Bobby was killed:

> Justice Holmes once said, "As life is action and passion, it is required of a man that he should share the passion and action of his time, at peril of being judged not to have lived." Robert Kennedy lived the action and passion of our time. He died in action. He spent his life, he gave his life in highest service to his country and to his fellow man. To those ignored he gave attention; to those in despair, he gave hope; to those in need, he gave help. To citizens blind to the fate of their fellow man, he presented the discomforting specter of the other America. He gave himself. Bob Kennedy, my friend, is dead. But the challenge of a newer world he pursued so selflessly remains. Let us be equal to that challenge. In the long roll of history it will be marked for Bob Kennedy, as it was for his brother, John: "There was a Man!" We will not soon forget these men, or their compassion.
>
> As Pericles said centuries ago, "Heroes have the whole earth for their tomb; in lands far from their own—where the

40. John McEvoy, interview by the author, October 13, 2015, Alexandria, VA.

column with its epitaph declares it—there is enshrined in every breast a record unwritten with no tablet to preserve it, that of the heart." God have mercy upon the soul of Robert Kennedy. God have mercy upon his family. God have mercy upon us all.[41]

Enough time has passed by now to allow us to speculate on what might have happened if Bobby had lived. I am certain he would have become the Democratic Party nominee. Rioters might not have marred the Democratic convention in Chicago late that summer. And I believe that he would have easily beaten Nixon and then ended the Vietnam War.

But, once again, because of an assassin's bullet, we will never know.

41. Senator Joseph Tydings, press release issued June 6, 1968, after the assassination of Senator Robert Kennedy, on file in the Tydings Collection, Hornbake Library.

CHAPTER 15

Fairness in Federal Court

If Senator Olin Johnston had not died when he did, my Senate career might have turned out much differently.

At the beginning of the Eighty-Ninth Congress, Johnston was ninth in Senate seniority.[1] In addition to chairing the Post Office and Civil Service Committee, the South Carolinian was second-ranking Democrat on both the Judiciary Committee and the Agriculture and Forestry Committee.

Among his lesser assignments was chairing an obscure Judiciary subcommittee with a boring name: the Senate Subcommittee on Improvements in Judicial Machinery. As far as my staff could tell, it rarely, if ever, met. Even though few freshmen ever chaired Senate subcommittees, my legislative aide, Alan Wurtzel, saw an opportunity.

Because of my father's long service in the Senate, I had a leg up on many other newcomers. My father had taught me a reverence for the Senate and how the place worked. Soon after my election, I began paying my respects and seeking guidance from the likes of Senator Richard Russell of Georgia and others. I knew they would be important to my future. They understood I was a liberal and not likely to side with them on some issues, but because Dad was fondly remembered, I had what my aide John McEvoy called the "halo effect." They had liked Millard Tydings, so they helped me.

As soon as I was appointed to the Judiciary Committee, I paid my respects to the chair, James Eastland of Mississippi, and his two senior aides. He had a huge office with a fully stocked bar. "Mr. Chairman," I said, "I just want to tell you what a great opportunity it is to serve under you."

"What are you drinking, Joe? We have bourbon, Scotch, whatever you want. What are you having?"

---

1. Johnston had been a state legislator, two-term governor of South Carolina, and four-term member of the US Senate, first elected in 1944.

"Well, Senator," I said, "I don't really drink much."

"Joe, I'm drinking bourbon," he persisted. "What are you drinking?"

"I'm drinking whatever you are drinking, Mr. Chairman," I replied, and we each had a big glass of bourbon.

At this early juncture, Eastland and I had not yet fought over voting rights or other contentious civil rights legislation, although our respective positions were no secret. I was on good terms with him because I had agreed to chair the formal hearings on new federal judges, a responsibility no other more senior Judiciary Committee members wanted.

Under committee rules, when a president nominated a federal judge, courtesy required the senators of the president's party to send the committee chair (in this case, Eastland) a white slip indicating approval. Once the slip was received, the approval was automatic and the hearing merely a formality to extol the virtues of the new judge. If the white slips were not delivered, the nomination was dead. Appointments to the federal bench were the most important patronage jobs senators had to fill, followed by US attorney and federal marshal. At Eastland's request, I sat for hours chairing the hearings for more than forty new judges.

This, in fact, was how I learned the intricacies of judicial appointments. That year, when new judicial seats were created for both the US District Court for Maryland and the US Court of Appeals for the Fourth Circuit in Richmond, I cut a deal with Senator Danny Brewster that, in the end, allowed me to name nominees for both seats and also to name the next US attorney for Maryland. Although Danny was the senior senator, he agreed to fill only one district court seat.

Danny had become unnerved by the 1964 Democratic primary, when he was booed by voters and I had won big. After that, he pretty much followed my lead. I suggested that we get President Johnson to elevate Harrison Winter to fill the new Fourth Circuit seat. Veteran Senator Sam Ervin had recommended his own North Carolina nominee, and the president sent down both names the same day. I, however, was in position to put Winter's name forward for confirmation as chief judge of the Fourth Circuit first before Ervin could push his own nominee. Elevating Winter created a second vacancy at the district court level in Maryland. For that seat, I recommended Frank Kaufman, and Brewster recommended Alexander Harvey for the newly created district court seat. At the same time, I persuaded Governor Agnew to appoint Tom Kenney, my successor as US attorney, to the Maryland Circuit Court. That created a vacancy at US attorney, which I filled—after Danny, once again, stepped aside—by recommending my former assistant, Steve Sachs.

In Congress today, every judicial nomination is unfortunately contested on ideological grounds, and the mere scheduling of hearings stretches out for months and frequently for years. Sometimes a vote on a nominee is never taken. Current Senate rules are horrific. They allow an individual senator to secretly block a nominee. In one particularly despicable act in 2016, the Republican-led Senate headed by Mitch McConnell of Kentucky defeated President Obama's nominee to replace the late Justice Antonin Scalia on the Supreme Court, Merrick Garland, by simply—and quite publicly—refusing even to hold hearings on the Garland nomination for almost the entire final year of Obama's presidency. Sadly, McConnell's deceitful trick worked: it denied President Obama his constitutional right to have the Senate consider his nominee for the high court. In February 2017, the new Republican president, Donald Trump, nominated federal appellate judge Neil M. Gorsuch, a conservative, to fill the vacant seat. The Republican majority in the Senate then confirmed the appointment on April 7, 2017, but only after invoking what was called the "nuclear option"—a rules change that allowed them to halt a Democratic filibuster of the Gorsuch nomination with a simple majority vote rather than the previously required supermajority of sixty votes.

I had been in the Senate roughly three months when Olin Johnston died on April 18, 1965. Next in line to succeed him as chair of the Judicial Machinery subcommittee was John McClellan of Arkansas, followed by Phil Hart of Michigan and Sam Ervin of North Carolina. I spoke with Senator Eastland about the chairmanship, and he said if the others in line for the post waived their seniority rights to the job, I could have it.

I went to each senator, and each agreed to waive seniority. By May of my freshman year in the Senate, I became a subcommittee chair and, with that position, I had the opportunity to build a subcommittee staff.

Over the next five and a half years, that subcommittee enacted more than twenty-five pieces of legislation that helped modernize and transform the federal judiciary. We reformed the jury selection process by abolishing the old "blue-ribbon" jury system, we abolished the discredited US commissioner system, and we set up an important system of federal magistrates. We also created the Federal Judicial Center, the education and research agency of the federal courts; authorized federal appellate courts to employ court executives; and created the multidistrict litigation system, which allowed related litigation filed in several different courts to be consolidated into a single court. We also pushed through other smaller bills that improved the day-to-day performance of federal courts.[2]

I was a judicial reform advocate. I had been a US attorney, headed the Junior Bar of Maryland, and worked with great federal judges. The subcommittee filled a void that neither the Congress nor the courts even realized existed, that is, there did not seem to be any person or body whose sole or primary responsibility was to address problems faced by the federal courts.[3] I think it is fair to say that no other senator had ever spent the time and effort I did in strengthening the judicial system. In effect, I became the lobbyist for the federal judicial system.

When we started, constituencies such as judges and lawyers, which would eventually benefit from the work of the subcommittee, did not even know this obscure panel existed. By the time we were through, we were speaking regularly to state and local bar associations and judicial conferences all over the country and working closely on judicial issues with both Chief Justice Earl Warren and his successor, Warren Burger.

The success of the subcommittee during the next three years was spearheaded by a brilliant young lawyer we recruited as staff director. William T. "Tom" Finley Jr. had clerked for Associate Justice William J. Brennan of the Supreme Court.[4] I was fortunate to have one of the

2. The Federal Judicial Center, authorized by law in 1967, was a recommendation from the Judicial Conference of the United States and has become the research arm for the federal judiciary. It helps federal judges devise solutions for internal problems. Court executives, authorized in the lame duck session of 1970, have had the effect of freeing up the chief judge of each circuit by taking over from the judge the day-to-day tasks of running an appellate court.

3. M. Albert Figinski and Lee M. Miller, "Judicial Reform and the Tydings Legacy," *Judicature* 55, no. 2 (1971): 77.

4. Tom was a graduate of Harvard College and Harvard Law School and also studied international law at Trinity College of Cambridge University in England. He served as chief counsel to the Subcommittee on Improvements in Judicial Machinery from 1965 to 1967, then as a deputy attorney general in the Justice Department, and then as a lawyer in private practice. Sadly, Tom died much too early in life, at age fifty-six, in May 1992.

smartest staffs on Capitol Hill, but no staffer was brighter than Tom Finley.

Jury Selection

Jury selection reform had been part of the original Voting Rights Act of 1965, but it was so controversial that that part of the bill never got out of the Judiciary Committee. Of all the big issues my subcommittee dealt with, this one probably had the broadest impact because it cleared the way for African Americans to serve on federal juries. It represented another important civil rights victory.

Up until that time, there really was no federal jury selection process. The standard way federal juries were selected in many states was that the federal judge and the clerk of the court would identify several leading citizens—so-called "citizens of rectitude"—who would be asked to identify other prominent citizens to be jurors. They, in turn, would be asked to identify others until a sufficient pool of potential jurors had been selected. The result, however, was that these so-called "blue-ribbon juries" were inevitably all male, generally well-to-do, and, in the South, all white. A poor African American on trial in a southern federal court had no chance of being tried by someone of the same race or station in life.

When jury selection came up again in 1967 as a part of the fair housing bill, it was split into separate legislation. I asked Senator Eastland to let my subcommittee handle it because I knew what to do with it.

The ranking Republican on the subcommittee was Roman Hruska. He was a crusty conservative from Omaha, Nebraska, but had supported the Civil Rights Act of 1964, and I was sure I could work with him. I said, "Senator Hruska, this is the problem. Let's have hearings. Let's see what we should do," and he said, "All right, I'll work with you." Our cooperative work set the tone for the next five years of judicial reform in our subcommittee.

Our bill was based on two principles: that federal jurors must be selected from broad-based lists of names and that jurors may be disqualified only on an objective basis.[5] By the time we were done, the bill

5. Figinski and Miller, "Judicial Reform and the Tydings Legacy," 76.

had cleared both the committee and the full Senate without a dissenting vote. That was how closely Democrats and Republicans worked together in those days—a far cry from today, when the concept of compromise is seen as a sign of weakness.[6]

Magistrates

The first major issue my subcommittee investigated was the century-old system of federal court commissioners. Commissioners were attached to federal courts but ranked lower than the clerks of the court. They dealt with minor infractions of federal law, issued arrest and search warrants, determined bail, and held preliminary hearings. Most citizens who had contact with the federal criminal justice system dealt with commissioners more often than judges.

Most commissioners, however, were drastically underpaid; they operated under a fee system that may have been unconstitutional; and, across the country, almost a third of them were not even lawyers. Because the legal jurisdiction of commissioners was limited, they could do little to relieve the workload of judges. In some cases, federal charges were downgraded from felonies to misdemeanors just so they could be handled by commissioners.[7]

I came to the Senate knowledgeable about the need to replace the system with a professional system of qualified judges. Commissioners were paid a fee that depended on the volume of business they transacted. I knew that fee system had to go. Commissioners received a fee only if they issued a warrant, so they had a personal financial stake in any proceeding before them requesting a warrant. That was clearly wrong. The whole system was an anachronism—and probably unconstitutional.

6. The Jury Service and Selection Act, signed into law March 27, 1968, declared as follows: "It is the policy of the United States that all litigants in Federal courts entitled to trial by jury shall have the right to grand and petit juries selected at random from a fair cross section of the community in the district or division wherein the court convenes. It is further the policy of the United States that all citizens shall have the opportunity to be considered for service on grand and petit juries in the district courts of the United States, and shall have an obligation to serve as jurors when summoned for that purpose." Public Law 90–274, sec. 1861.

7. Maryland, in contrast with many states, was fortunate to have some outstanding lawyers who served as US commissioners. Judges Frank Volkart and Sam Melay worked with me while I was US attorney and educated me on the dangerous inefficiencies of the system.

I also knew this would be a sensitive issue with federal judges, who were protective of their own authority, so I turned to my old mentor from my US attorney days, Chief Judge Roszel Thomsen of the US District Court in Maryland. I asked him to help set up and then chair a committee composed of the best federal judges in the country to develop a proposal to modernize the commissioner system.

In October 1965, we held our first hearing on what I called "the forgotten men of the federal judicial system." In sweeping recommendations, Judge Thomsen's committee said we should replace the commissioner system with a magistrate system, require the magistrates to be lawyers, substantially broaden their legal jurisdiction beyond that of the commissioners, raise their pay, and eliminate the fee system. The judges were nervous about losing some of their power, so we let each district court decide what their magistrates could and could not do in the civil area.

By the time the bill was enacted on October 3, 1968, after three years of work, it had been endorsed by the Judicial Conference of the United States, the American Bar Association, the National Association of Commissioners, constitutional scholars, and local bar associations. I had forty bipartisan co-sponsors and even grudging praise from the in-house constitutional expert, Senator Sam Ervin of North Carolina, who had initially opposed the bill.[8]

Without the US magistrate system, the whole federal district court system today would be dysfunctional and could not operate effectively. The workload would be too much. Federal judges are now able to transfer both procedural and time-consuming judicial responsibilities to a magistrate, such as discovery and damage hearings that often take many hours, to relieve the burden on the judges.

Unfit Judges

One of my few regrets from our work on federal judicial issues was our failure to pass legislation that would have provided an effective way to

8. President Johnson signed the bill on October 17, 1968, saying one effect of the Federal Magistrates Act "will [be to] enable judges to spend more time on priority matters—and [it] should relieve their congested dockets. There should be speedier justice, then, for all." President Lyndon B. Johnson, remarks upon signing bills relating to the United States Magistrates and to Judges in the District of Columbia Courts, October 17, 1968, online text compiled by Gerhard Peters and John T. Woolley for *The American Presidency Project*, http://www.presidency.ucsb. edu/ws/index.php?pid=29185.

penalize or remove unfit judges. A judge who is corrupt, lazy or incompetent, mentally or physically incapacitated, an alcoholic, or otherwise unfit to serve is really almost impervious to rebuke, let alone removal. Impeachment was not a practical option. There was simply no way to censure, reprimand, or remove a bad judge.

In February 1966, I announced my intention to address this issue. I emphasized that the federal bench was characterized by judges of remarkable integrity and ability but that they needed proper tools to police their own house fairly and efficiently.

California had put in place a law to deal with this problem in 1960, and I thought it might be a good model. At the time, the only way to remove federal judges was to have the House of Representatives impeach them and then try them in the Senate. In the history of the United States, only eight judges had been impeached and only four convicted.

We held hearings all over the country and in February 1968 introduced judicial reform legislation. Among other provisions, the bill would have created a commission on judicial disabilities and tenure with the power to investigate complaints of misconduct or physical or mental disability of any federal judge, to recommend the removal of a judge, and to effect the involuntary retirement of physically or mentally incapacitated judges who do not retire voluntarily. The commission would be composed entirely of judges and could launch an investigation based on a complaint from a citizen.

The proposal also contained a conflict of interest section that required every judge to disclose all financial or nonjudicial business interests. Moreover, it would make judges' participation in any matter in which they had any financial interest grounds for removal.

As you might expect, many federal judges did not appreciate what they probably saw as congressional meddling in their livelihood. It was such a hot topic that, in June 1969, Chief Justice Warren asked me to address the Judicial Conference to explain the need for the bill.

I really campaigned for this bill, speaking to judicial conferences, bar associations, judges, and others across the country.[9] We won support from the American Bar Association, and later the Nixon Justice Department attested to the constitutionality of the bill and pledged to support

9. In one speech in Hot Springs, Virginia, I also challenged the Supreme Court to impose financial disclosure regulations on itself.

it.[10] But federal judges and the influential Sam Ervin were against it, and we just couldn't get it through. Since then, most individual federal circuits have instituted their own rules to address the issue, but I believe a common national process, such as the one used in California, is needed.

Unqualified Judges

Our investigation into unfit judges made me particularly sensitive to the importance of appointing only the most qualified judges to begin with. I believed this so strongly that I found myself going against the grain three separate times in my Senate career—once against the Kennedy family that had been so good to me and twice against President Nixon.

Toward the end of my first year in the Senate, I was faced with one of the most wrenching personal, professional, and political decisions of my career. Former Ambassador Joseph P. Kennedy, the powerful patriarch of the Kennedy family, asked President Johnson to nominate to the federal bench in Massachusetts a family retainer named Francis X. Morrissey. Morrissey was clearly unqualified, and I was not the only one who knew it. When Robert Kennedy had been attorney general, he had refused to let President Kennedy even consider the appointment of Morrissey.

Morrissey was a "go-fer" for Joe Kennedy. He had done advance work in Massachusetts for Jack Kennedy's Senate campaigns, but his principal allegiance was to the old man.[11] In 1958, Morrissey was appointed by the governor of Massachusetts to be a judge on the Boston municipal court. When LBJ nominated Morrissey, Teddy Kennedy became his Senate sponsor.

As soon as the Judiciary Committee hearings began in October, it became obvious the nomination was in trouble. The question was fully focused on Morrissey's qualifications or, in his case, the lack thereof.

To become a lawyer, Morrissey had traveled to Georgia, where he "earned" his degree in a three-month cram course at a fly-by-night "law school" that had one dean, one professor, and no law library. In

10. Figinski and Miller, "Judicial Reform and the Tydings Legacy," 79.

11. Morrissey regularly kept the elder Kennedy informed about Massachusetts political matters and the activities of the ambassador's three sons. He was sometimes asked by the family patriarch to handle the most personal and sensitive tasks. When Jack and Jackie's son, Patrick, was born prematurely and died in 1963, the family turned to Morrissey to arrange the funeral. He chose a white gown and a small white casket and was the only person other than family members at the funeral mass besides Cardinals Richard Cushing and Francis Spellman. Thurston Clarke, *JFK's Last 100 Days* (New York: Penguin Audio, 2013).

exchange for their degrees, graduates had to promise they would stay on to practice law in Georgia, but Morrissey skipped out and returned to Massachusetts almost immediately, where he was admitted to practice law and later became a state judge.

Bernard Segal, a spokesperson for (and later president of) the American Bar Association, said of Morrissey, "From the standpoint of legal training, legal experience and legal ability, we have not had any case where these factors were so lacking—and I say so to my deep regret." Charles Wyzanski, the chief federal district court judge in Massachusetts, put his finger on the real problem, saying that "the only discernible ground for the nomination of Judge Morrissey is his service to the Kennedy family." Dirksen and other Republicans on the committee pounced on the nomination. The *New York Times* weighed in with an editorial that called Teddy's defense of Morrissey a "tiresome display of familial arrogance and personal effrontery."[12]

I had a real challenge. Here I was, a leader on judicial reform, and I'm asked by my closest friends and supporters to approve a candidate I knew was incompetent.

I met privately with Teddy to tell him I was going to have to oppose the nomination. It was not a happy conversation. His father was leaning on him, and he wanted to please the old man. Teddy had invited me to join him on a special trip to assess the war in Vietnam, so he encouraged me to depart early, to say I was just joining some other members of Congress who had already left for Southeast Asia. What he really wanted me to do was to "take a walk" and let the vote happen without me. I declined.

I took a statement of my position to the Senate press gallery myself. It hit like a bombshell. For me to do this, for someone considered as close to being a Kennedy as anyone in the Senate not named Kennedy, it was almost unthinkable. Once it was known that even I could not support the nomination, it became clear the nominee was unfit. Teddy had no choice but to withdraw it. The Kennedy family always put a high value on loyalty, and my relationship with Teddy Kennedy was never the same again.[13]

---

12. Quotations from John Lofton, "Teddy Kennedy, Last Man on Earth Qualified to Question Ethics, Integrity of Judicial Nominees," *The American View*, accessed 2015, Theamericanview.com.

13. A year after the Morrissey incident, I was part of a congressional delegation that went to Switzerland to attend an international conference on refugees. There was a huge

Teddy was two years younger than I, and we initially were close. The summer before the Morrissey nomination, Teddy and his lovely wife, Joan, took Ginny and me for a weekend at the family compound in Hyannis Port. When I first met Teddy, he was one of the finest-looking men I'd ever seen. He had a great build and had been a great athlete. He could have been a star in Hollywood. On top of that, he had a world-class sense of humor and a great ability to meet people. He could turn a boring party into a lively one. He had that capacity. But in his younger years, Teddy was also reckless. After Bobby's death, he became so distraught that he did not come back to the Senate for weeks. He suffered deeply from losing both of his brothers, but the loss of Bobby became almost too much for him to bear.

For a time, the Morrissey incident severely strained my relationship with Bobby as well. The day after the nomination was withdrawn I was walking across the back of the Senate chamber near the cloakroom doors when I saw Bobby approaching from the other direction. I started to say something, but just as I did Bobby gave me a pretty hard shoulder into the chest, knocked me back toward the wall, and just kept on walking. It could have been an accident, but I don't think so. We never spoke of it.

Bobby and I later fully reconciled and worked together on almost every important issue while we were in the Senate together. I remained his close friend and one of his most ardent supporters when he ran for president in 1968.

Haynsworth

By the beginning of the Ninety-First Congress, the final two years of my Senate term, Richard Nixon was president and everything had changed, including the mood of the country. It had been transformed from liberal and optimistic to conservative and scared.

Our huge Democratic majorities had been trimmed in both houses. Nixon had initiated a cynical campaign designed primarily to capture white voters disaffected by advances in civil rights, the hippie counterculture, protests over the escalating war in Vietnam, and riots and turmoil in the cities.

reception the opening night of the conference, but I was the only one in the American delegation who was not invited. I cannot prove it, but I am sure that snub was quietly arranged by Teddy.

The backlash in the South really began in 1963, when President Kennedy introduced his civil rights legislation. By the summer of 1964, the same year President Johnson and I were elected, some southern "Dixiecrats" had boycotted the Democratic convention in Atlantic City. And even though the Republican presidential candidate, Barry Goldwater, was buried by the LBJ landslide that fall, the conservative from Arizona had captured five southern states that had been solidly Democratic for decades. As Johnson had predicted when he signed the Civil Rights Act of 1964 into law, it was the beginning of a Republican takeover of the Deep South that has continued to this day.

Nixon was a cunning politician. He recognized that black citizens who were newly registering to vote in the South were flocking to the Democratic Party. To counter that, he began to build his "Southern Strategy" to attract white Democrats to the Republican cause, often using code words such as "law and order," rather than directly criticizing civil rights protests, or "states' rights," to counter the resistance to federal intervention, federal court mandates, or forced busing to public schools. Nixon sided with segregationist politicians, led by Senator Strom Thurmond of South Carolina, and even put several Thurmond followers on the federal bench.[14]

Against this backdrop, it was not surprising when Nixon in 1969 nominated a southern conservative and Thurmond favorite from South Carolina, Clement F. Haynsworth Jr., to replace Associate Justice Abe Fortas on the Supreme Court. Johnson had put his old friend Fortas on the high court in 1965, and Fortas was in line to become chief justice when Earl Warren decided to step down. But Fortas, considered too liberal by the conservatives, who by 1968 were exercising more control of Congress, was forced to resign over conflict of interest charges first revealed in a *Life* magazine article, thus opening a vacancy on the high court.

I not only knew Haynsworth but was socially close to him and had planned to support him. He was an old-school southern gentleman. When I was US attorney, Haynsworth was chief judge of the US Court of Appeals for the Fourth Circuit, which included the District of Maryland. Because of my work as US attorney and later as a champion of

14. Gary May, *Bending toward Justice: The Voting Rights Act and the Transformation of American Democracy* (New York: Basic Books, 2013), 203–4.

the judiciary in the Senate, I was often invited to speak at Fourth Circuit conferences, so I knew him both professionally and socially.

When his nomination reached the Senate, however, questions arose about his court decisions, which appeared to be consistently antiunion. Both the AFL-CIO and the NAACP lined up against him, as did other civil rights groups and some moderate northern Republicans.

I was under huge pressure from organized labor in Maryland to vote against him, but the Maryland Bar Association supported him. These were lawyers who knew Haynsworth through the Fourth Circuit, and many also were my friends.

My view changed when I learned that Haynsworth had not disqualified himself from cases in which he appeared to have a personal financial interest. The cases involved textile mills in South Carolina granting franchises to a fast-growing vending machine company in which the judge had invested. Haynsworth could have recused himself, but he did not.

Somewhat reluctantly, I joined the Senate majority that rejected the Haynsworth nomination on November 21, 1969, on a 55–45 vote. That marked the first time a Supreme Court nominee had been rejected since Herbert Hoover nominated Judge John J. Parker of North Carolina, also the chief judge of the Fourth Circuit, in 1930.

But the fight over Haynsworth, coming on the heels of the nasty fight over Fortas, opened a new front in the war over Supreme Court nominees between liberals and conservatives in the Senate and the White House. And the situation was about to get worse.

Carswell

Again, Nixon looked to the South for a judicial nominee. On January 19, 1970, two months after Haynsworth had been rejected, the president nominated G. Harrold Carswell of Florida. Carswell had been a US attorney and then a federal judge. Nixon had elevated him to the US Court of Appeals for the Fifth Circuit a mere eight months before nominating him to the Supreme Court.

Carswell had the regular two days of hearings before the Judiciary Committee and was set to receive formal approval the following week. There was some talk about how he had belonged to a country club in

Florida that would not allow African Americans to join, although in those days there was no other kind of country club south of the Mason-Dixon line, including in Maryland.

Then, just as we were all about to go home for the weekend on the Friday prior to the week the committee was to vote on Carswell, a young Department of Justice lawyer came to our office to see Al Figinski, who had replaced Tom Finley as chief counsel to my Subcommittee on Judicial Improvements. He told Figinski a story about run-ins with Carswell during days that this young lawyer had helped register black voters in Florida during the presidential campaign in 1964. The young man said he had assisted volunteer attorneys with voter registration in Florida but that Carswell—then the federal district judge—would pull those attorneys into a private room and verbally excoriate them for their activities. None of this had been raised when Nixon appointed Judge Carswell to the Fifth Circuit appellate court.

Carswell's deplorable conduct, mind you, happened in 1964—the same year that three civil rights workers who were attempting to register black voters in Mississippi were abducted and murdered.[15] Registering black voters in the South was a difficult and extremely dangerous job in those days, and the federal courts were often the only place to which civil rights workers could turn for protection. Carswell's court was not such a place.

When Figinski told me what he had learned, we quizzed the young Justice Department lawyer and asked if he would be willing to testify before the Judiciary Committee about what he had heard. He said he could not, that he had a wife and family, and that he was sure it would cost him his job in what, by then, was the Nixon administration Justice Department. We asked if he knew any top lawyers who might have witnessed Carswell's actions and would be willing to testify. He said he did and gave us their names. I contacted them personally over the weekend to see if the story checked out. If it did, I planned to ask Judiciary Committee chair Eastland if he could postpone a committee vote on confirmation and give me two more days of hearings. That is when my close relationship with Eastland really proved beneficial.

15. James Earl Chaney of Mississippi and Andrew Goodman and Michael Schwerner of New York City were abducted and shot on June 21–22, 1964, in Philadelphia, Mississippi.

For two days we made the calls, and the story was corroborated. I informed Eastland that I had heard some bad reports about Carswell, and he gave me three days to produce our witnesses. We had also noticed that Carswell's nomination had not been endorsed by a single one of his fellow judges on the Fifth Circuit, which we thought was telling.[16]

One witness was John Lowenthal, a law professor at Rutgers University who had volunteered to help register black voters in northern Florida in 1964. He recounted a story of how after seven voter registrars were arrested and jailed, allegedly for trespassing, Judge Carswell put one obstacle after another in his way as he attempted to get the registrars freed before they were harmed in jail. The judge required filing fees that had been ruled illegal elsewhere, required a special form to be used to file routine petitions with the court, and had marshals eject from his courtroom the lawyers representing the registrars. He then tried, convicted, and jailed the registrars, who by then had no legal representation.

"He expressed dislike at northern lawyers such as myself appearing in Florida, because we were not members of the Florida bar," Lowenthal testified.[17]

Norman Knopf, another witness who had helped Lowenthal in that 1964 campaign, recalled, "Judge Carswell made clear, when he found out that [Lowenthal] was a northern volunteer . . . that he did not approve of any of this voter registration going on and he was especially critical of Mr. Lowenthal. In fact, he lectured him for a long time in a high voice that made me start thinking I was glad I filed a bond for protection in case I got thrown in jail. I really thought we were all going to be held in contempt of court. It was a very long, strict lecture about northern lawyers coming down and not [being] members of the Florida Bar and meddling down here and arousing the local people. . . . He, in effect, didn't want any part of this, and he made it quite clear that he was going to deny all relief that we requested."[18]

---

16. When I questioned Louis H. Pollak, dean of the Yale Law School, about Carswell's qualifications, Pollak testified that based on his research, Carswell was the least qualified of some forty Supreme Court nominees dating back to 1902. Transcript of the Hearings before the Committee on the Judiciary, US Senate, 91st Cong., 2nd sess., p. 245, on nomination of George Harrold Carswell, of Florida, to be Associate Justice of the Supreme Court of the United States, January 27, 28, 29 and February 2, 3, 1970, Library of Congress.

17. Ibid., 141.

18. Ibid., 177.

Perhaps the most damning charge against Judge Carswell came from his own lips when he ran (unsuccessfully) for the state legislature in his home state of Georgia in 1948. "I believe," the then twenty-eight-year-old candidate said in a statement that was rediscovered and entered into the Judiciary Committee record, "that segregation of the races is proper and the only and correct way of life in our state. I have always so believed and I shall always so act."[19] Carswell later tried to repudiate that statement, but the nomination had been fatally damaged.

Carswell's detractors also complained that he had been a "mediocre" judge, but Hruska, the Nebraska Republican who was among his strongest defenders, famously said, "Even if he were mediocre, there are a lot of mediocre judges and people and lawyers. They are entitled to a little representation, aren't they, and a little chance? We can't have all Brandeises, Frankfurters, and Cardozos."[20]

But it was Carswell's 1948 statement, coupled with the testimony about his behavior toward those trying to register African American voters in 1964, as well as his involvement in establishing a Tallahassee country club that excluded African American golfers, that spelled the end of his candidacy.[21]

Clarence Mitchell, the famous African American civil rights lawyer from Baltimore who represented the NAACP and the Leadership Conference on Civil Rights, summed up the opposition in his testimony before the Judiciary Committee: "The stark fact now is this: An advocate of racial segregation has been named by the Nixon administration to serve on the U.S. Supreme Court. Now that this fact is known, those

19. Carswell also stated, "I shall be the last to submit to any attempt on the part of anyone to break down and to weaken this firmly established policy of our people. . . . I yield to no man as a fellow candidate or as a fellow citizen in the firm vigorous belief in the principles of white supremacy and I shall always be so governed." Carswell hearings transcript, 22, 23.

20. His mention of the three Jewish justices in his statement prompted accusations of anti-Semitism. The Wikipedia entry on Hruska notes, "Hruska is best remembered in American political history for an anti-Semitic 1970 speech he made to the Senate urging them to confirm the nomination of G. Harrold Carswell to the Supreme Court." Roman Hruska entry, Wikipedia, https://en.wikipedia.org/wiki/Roman_Hruska.

21. In addition to the various law professors and scholars publicly opposing the Carswell nomination was the feminist writer Betty Friedan, president of the National Organization for Women and author of *The Feminine Mystique*. She castigated Carswell for a 1969 appellate ruling in which he allowed industries such as Martin Marietta Corporation to deny women—but not men—employment because they had preschool-age children at home. That, she said, was in violation of the Civil Rights Act (1964), which forbids job discrimination on the basis of sex as well as race.

who vote for the approval of this nomination will be voting to place a segregationist on the U.S. Supreme Court."[22]

Mitchell said Carswell's nomination was an intentional attempt by Nixon to put someone on the court who would delay public school desegregation in particular and civil rights progress generally.

"We urge our citizens to rely upon the law, but we appoint prejudiced law officers as enforcers," Mitchell observed. "We breathe a sigh of relief when Negroes go into the courts instead of into the streets, but we then confront them with judges who have decided to deny them relief even before they enter the courthouse door."[23]

On April 8, 1970, after this second bruising confirmation battle, I was part of the Senate majority that rejected the Carswell nomination, 51–45. Nixon claimed Democrats had an antisouthern bias.

The silver lining from all of this, of course, is that we kept two unqualified judges off the Supreme Court. Nixon eventually nominated a third candidate, Judge Harry Blackmun, of Minnesota, who was unanimously approved by the Senate. Blackmun became a fine jurist, best known for his landmark *Roe v. Wade* decision upholding the abortion rights of women.

22. Carswell hearings transcript, 271.
23. Ibid., 276.

CHAPTER 16

Congress and the City of Washington

I knew that serving on the District of Columbia Committee would not help me politically in Maryland, but I felt it my responsibility because the committee had great power over the interests of the many Marylanders who worked in DC.

"The people who live in the District of Columbia are entitled to have a voice in their own affairs," I said in a speech in fall 1965. "They have a right to say who shall make their laws, how their taxes shall be spent, what steps they will take to deal with the problems in their midst."[1]

In the days before home rule, serious crime was a problem in Washington, much of it related to drug abuse. City courts were a mess. No transit existed except for a disjointed bus system. There were plans to ram an interstate highway right through the middle of the city, possibly under the National Mall. There were public health problems, soot and grimy air pollution from the always burning Kenilworth dump, and unscrupulous lenders who preyed on the most destitute residents of the city.

Complicating these problems was our system of local governance. Washingtonians had no say in who ran their city, no ability to vote leaders into—or out of—office, and no representation in Congress, the body that under article I, section 8, of the Constitution was granted full authority over the capital.

When I arrived in the Senate, the city was run by three commissioners appointed by the president and confirmed by the Senate.[2] As a can-

---

1. Senator Joseph D. Tydings, speech in support of home rule for the District of Columbia, delivered at the annual conference of the Greater Washington chapter of Americans for Democratic Action, Washington, DC, September 18, 1965, in the Joseph D. Tydings Collection, Hornbake Library, University of Maryland, College Park.

2. One of the commissioners had to be chosen from the US Army Corps of Engineers.

didate in 1964, I had called for home rule for DC, but it was not until 1967 that President Johnson was able to convince Congress to approve even a limited form of home rule.[3] His legislation replaced the three commissioners with a nine-member city council and a mayor-commissioner, Walter E. Washington. Even then, the council members and the mayor were all appointed by the president, and, as before, their decisions on budgets, taxes, legislation, or virtually any other matter were subject to approval and second-guessing by the Congress.[4]

Over the years, this congressional oversight has too often proved to be partisan and unduly influenced by campaign contributions to committee members.[5]

I was put on the DC Committee almost as soon as I was elected. It was customary for senators and representatives from neighboring Maryland and Virginia to be tapped for the Senate and House DC Committees because we had a parochial interest in what happened in Washington and because members of Congress from elsewhere usually did not.

Robert Kennedy was the rare exception—a senator who volunteered to serve on the DC Committee. Bobby put his heart into the work. He saw it as an opportunity to really learn about the root causes of urban problems.

The committee chair was Alan Bible, a conservative Democrat from Nevada.[6] He and I worked well together, and he often empowered me to

3. The idea of granting home rule to the District of Columbia was stalemated for years by the House DC Committee, which was chaired for twenty-four years by Representative John L. McMillan of South Carolina. His committee always seemed more interested in helping local businesses than the black residential majority, which often accused McMillan of racism. McMillan, the longest serving congressional representative in South Carolina history, was defeated in 1972 and died in 1979.

4. On Christmas Eve 1973, Congress approved a home rule charter for the District of Columbia that provided for the direct election of a mayor and city council, although Congress retained both authority to review all legislation before it could become law as well as final budget authority. The president was empowered to appoint judges for DC, which still lacked voting rights in Congress. The charter also contained a number of specific restrictions, including a prohibition on the imposition of a commuter tax for those who work in DC but live elsewhere.

5. When Republicans took over both houses of Congress and the White House in 2017, Republican members of Congress with right-wing agendas immediately began to micro-manage city government operations, opposing efforts in Washington to make abortions available to women who wanted one or city efforts to control the sale and spread of firearms.

6. In addition to Bible, Kennedy, and me, the members of the Senate DC Committee at the beginning of the Eighty-Ninth Congress were Democrats Wayne Morse of Oregon and Thomas J. McIntyre of New Hampshire and Republicans Winston L. Prouty of Vermont and Peter H. Dominick of Colorado. The House District Committee, of course, was much larger: in 1965, there were seventeen Democrats and eight Republicans on it. The committee was chaired by a

get DC legislation through. I remained on the District of Columbia Committee my entire six years in the Senate and became chair by default the final two.

Gun Control, Crime, and the Courts

I thought that reducing crime in the city should be a high priority. I rode in police patrol cars at night and worked closely with the city police commissioner, as I also did in Baltimore.

Beginning in just my third month in the Senate, I began pushing for stronger gun control laws for DC. I introduced legislation to require all pistols in DC to be registered and to make it illegal for minors, felons, addicts, or persons with mental illness to possess a pistol. I said the registration fee could not exceed one dollar but that there had to be a five-day waiting period between the purchase and the possession of a pistol.

This all sounds pretty similar to the bitter fights we see in Congress and the courts today—half a century later—over almost precisely the same call for strong, commonsense measures to prevent gun violence. Sadly, my efforts in 1965 met with the same fate as gun control proposals do today—defeat, in large part because of fear-mongering from the National Rifle Association and the misguided, confused opposition of hunters. So I attacked the crime problem in a number of ways.

In May 1966, I was invited to speak to about forty judges and leaders of the local bar at the annual Judicial Conference in DC. I initially planned to update the audience on what was going on in Congress, including the work of my Subcommittee on Improvements to Judicial Machinery. But that was before Bill Greenhalgh met with me.

I had asked Bill, a law professor at Georgetown University, to draft a speech for me for the event. I knew Bill well. He had been one of my principal political backers in Montgomery County, helping to raise money and organize the county on my behalf. He was an expert in judicial reform and highly knowledgeable about the court system in DC.

What a speech he drafted for me! It simply ripped apart the existing city court system. It detailed the huge backlog of cases in the court and the slow docket, how defense lawyers often went shopping

South Carolina conservative, John L. McMillan, and ten of the other Democratic representatives on the committee were also southerners. Representative (and later Senator) Charles McC. Mathias Jr. of Maryland was also one of the Republicans on that committee.

for sympathetic judges, and how despite thousands of felony charges each year, only a fraction resulted in indictments and a much smaller number in actual convictions. I used almost everything he suggested, because he was right!

That speech seemed to shock everyone in attendance. The *Washington Post* and other newspapers, which had been reporting about the festering problems in the city courts for years, used that speech to turn court reform into a high-priority topic, as did reform-minded judges and lawyers.

Judge Harold Greene, then chief judge of what was known as the DC Court of General Sessions, began working with me to devise a major reform of the court system. I respected Judge Greene.[7] Rather than him lobbying me, I would be the one calling him for advice.[8] We also worked with Judge Gerhard A. Gesell of the US District Court for DC. Gesell chaired a special committee set up by the other judges to look into this issue.

The fundamental problem was that the court system for DC—both criminal and civil—operated like little more than a police court. The civil jurisdiction of the District of Columbia courts was limited to cases not exceeding $10,000, and the only criminal cases it could handle were misdemeanors, not felonies. Everything else—felonies and civil cases exceeding $10,000—was referred to the already overloaded federal district court for DC. Moreover, the city court system was disorganized, and city court judges, by comparison with those who served on state or federal courts, were poorly qualified and inadequately compensated.

The court reform legislation merged three local trial courts (general sessions, juvenile, and tax) into a unified local court system, the Superior Court of the District of Columbia. It added new judges, increased

7. President Jimmy Carter believed in court reform but could not overcome the patronage preferences of the US Senate in order to appoint reformers to the bench. The only courts for which he could appoint judges were the US District Court for the District of Columbia and the US Court of Appeals. In all other US district courts, the US senator from the state where the court is located controlled the nomination. President Carter created a nominating commission to recommend judicial nominees for these two courts and appointed me to chair this commission. The first recommendation we made was for him to appoint Judge Harold Greene, which he did. Greene replaced Judge John J. Sirica of Watergate fame when Sirica retired in 1978. Judge Greene later earned his own national reputation by presiding over the multiyear government antitrust suit that dismembered the AT&T monopoly.

8. Tom Schoenberg, "Home Court Advantage," *Legal Times*, December 20, 1999, 12, 15.

judicial salaries and benefits, established nomination and removal procedures, and set fifteen-year judicial terms.[9] It permitted the city courts to hear civil cases at any level and any criminal cases arising under the DC code. It also established a DC Court of Appeals.[10]

By the time we put this plan into legislative form in 1969, Nixon had become president and I was chair of the District of Columbia Committee in the Senate.[11] The number of homicides in Washington by then had soared so high the city was called the "crime capital" of the country.[12] The Nixon administration slowed passage of the plan for two more years. While the administration may have been interested in court reform, it was more interested in being seen as tough on crime, so the court reform proposal was folded into Nixon's broader, more controversial DC crime bill. That was a mixed blessing.

To have the president as a sponsor made it much more likely that court reform would pass than if it had been stand-alone legislation. But to get it through was something of a quid pro quo as I found myself lobbying for—and identified with—two of the most controversial anti-crime measures in the revised bill: "no-knock warrants" and "pretrial detention."

No-knock warrants were particularly significant in dangerous arrest cases. The idea behind them was to give police authority to enter a place without first knocking or otherwise announcing themselves, if they had reason to believe a crime was being committed or that evidence might be destroyed.[13] That was particularly significant in suspected drug cases. If police simply announced their presence and said, "Let us in," people inside would have a chance to flush drugs down the toilet or otherwise

9. By upgrading judicial salaries, city courts began to attract better-qualified lawyers who were willing to become judges—lawyers who never would have considered such a post before the reform went through.

10. Write-up on DC Court Reform Act, February 1, 1971, under the Court Reform and Criminal Procedure Act of 1970, *Judicature* 54, no. 7 (February 1971): 304.

11. Alan Bible had moved to another committee, Wayne Morse had been defeated, and Bobby Kennedy had been assassinated, so I, at age forty-one, became the youngest chair of a standing Senate committee.

12. In just three years, from 1966 to 1969, the number of homicides in the city had doubled, from 144 to 289. Schoenberg, "Home Court Advantage," 12.

13. Some drug dealers in those days kept records on what was known as "flash paper," which they could instantly incinerate if they thought police were approaching.

destroy evidence. Worse, they could answer the police knock with a bullet through the door.

The Supreme Court had already outlined no-knock entry procedures that were legal, so I just took Nixon's crime bill legislation and rewrote it, incorporating what the high court had already stated. Nixon was trying to look tough on crime, and he did not really care about the proscribed practices and protections outlined by the Supreme Court. I thought then, and think now, that as long as there are reasonable safeguards over when such authority can be used, no-knock warrants make sense both for apprehending criminals and for protecting evidence and the safety of police.

The other sensitive topic was pretrial detention. It essentially said that if a judge believes that a person charged with a crime is likely to commit another crime or be a threat to the community if released prior to trial, then the judge may deny release. I believe judges must have that authority.

For me, the whole point was to get the court reform measures passed. To do that, I had to take Nixon's whole DC crime bill, fix it, and get it enacted. And that's what I did.

Both issues—no-knock warrants and pretrial detention—were easily susceptible to political demagoguery from the left wing. I took a political beating for supporting these changes from those who accused me of stripping away the legal rights of individuals. Opponents even picketed me. In retrospect, these reforms have helped.

Treating Drug Addiction

In addition to long overdue court reform and the expansion of police powers, the DC crime bill also revolutionized the approach to drug abuse that the federal government would take. My office again was squarely in the middle of that change.

As happens with any change of administrations, a lot of Democrats began losing their jobs after Nixon and the Republicans returned to power in 1969. I got a call one day from Sargent Shriver, who said he had a young man on his staff who was about to lose his job and wondered if we might be interested in hiring him. John McEvoy, whom I had installed as staff director for the District of Columbia Committee, interviewed the young man.[14] McEvoy thought he was bright and would fit in with our staff, so I hired him. His name was Al From.[15]

Right out of graduate school at Northwestern University, From had gone to work for the War on Poverty programs Shriver developed. At the time we hired him, we were starting to hold hearings on crime problems in DC and were looking for ways to reduce prison recidivism. This was hardly a new issue for me. Since my first year in the Senate, I had been making speeches about the need to provide job training for prison inmates so they would have a chance to survive once they were eventually released.

People convicted of felonies in the District of Columbia were usually sent to a DC prison then located in suburban Lorton, Virginia, where they received little if anything in the way of job training. Frequently, there were multiple generations of a family—grandfathers, fathers, and sons—all jailed at the same time at Lorton. We sent From down to the prison to see if some sort of job training for inmates might be a solution.

From came back and said to me, "Forget all of that. It's drugs. Drugs are the issue in the District of Columbia. That's where the crime comes from. People either have to commit a crime to get it or have to commit a crime to sell it. And if you do something with the drug culture, you'll do something with the crime issue."

So that became our approach—do something about the drug problem. That's when we first met Dr. Robert L. DuPont and learned about methadone.

Methadone was a medication that could be given to heroin addicts to reduce withdrawal symptoms without causing the "high" associated with drug addiction. It was a treatment being recommended by Bob DuPont, the psychiatrist who was then director of community services

14. As soon as I took over as chair of the Senate District of Columbia Committee, I was under pressure from a lot of constituents to name them, or one of their protégés, as staff director. McEvoy was already on my staff and I liked his work, so on my first day as chair I made him committee staff director, and that eliminated all the competition.

15. In later years, From variously worked as the executive director of the House Democratic Caucus, as a deputy adviser to President Carter, and as a chief subcommittee staffer to Maine Senator Edmund Muskie. But From really made his name in 1985, when he founded the Democratic Leadership Council (DLC) and served as chief executive of the council until 2009. During that period, From played a prominent role in the 1992 election of Bill Clinton as president, and many of the ideas developed by the DLC have become part of the core agenda of the Democratic Party.

for the DC Department of Corrections with oversight of parole and half-way houses.[16] With DuPont educating me and my staff and testifying at our hearings, methadone treatment soon got the attention of Nixon's people and was incorporated into the DC crime bill as mandatory treatment for certain addicts.

We were the first to publicize and popularize this approach, which was soon used nationwide.

The Metro Subway System

The year I got to the Senate, I joined Senator Bible, chair of the District of Columbia Committee, to co-sponsor a program to build a twenty-five-mile subway system in Washington—a system that is five times that big today. I have long believed in the wisdom of promoting balanced transportation systems, with transit fully complementing highways. Major cities throughout the world had such systems, but not Washington.

Our proposal was crafted to create a Washington Metro compact—an agreement between the states of Virginia and Maryland, the District of Columbia, and the federal government—to build the subway system. The federal government initially provided about 60 percent of the cost of constructing the expanded 103-mile system, with the other three jurisdictions contributing the rest in rough proportion to how many stations and miles of track they were to receive.[17] In 1966, Bible asked me to take over the effort to get the Metro bill passed, and I became floor leader for the bill. Bible relied on me and I delivered.

While important to our region, the plan at this point was not that controversial. All four Maryland and Virginia senators supported it.[18] In August 1966, the Senate unanimously passed the bill to create the Washington Metropolitan Area Transit Authority (WMATA) and build

16. Bob DuPont went on to become director of the National Institute on Drug Abuse and, in 1973 under Nixon, the second White House drug czar. Biography of Robert L. DuPont, from Institute for Behavior and Health, http://www.ibhinc.org/biorld.html.

17. "Mass Transit: Information on the Federal Role in Funding the Washington Metropolitan Area Transit Authority," US General Accountability Office, GAO-05–358T, February 18, 2005, https://www.gpo.gov/fdsys/pkg/GAOREPORTS-GAO-05–358T/html/GAOREPORTS-GAO-05–358T.htm.

18. The four were Harry Flood Byrd Jr. and A. Willis Robertson of Virginia, and Daniel Brewster and I from Maryland.

the rail system and, eventually, to take over operation of what were then four privately owned and dysfunctional bus companies. President Johnson signed the bill into law in November, and WMATA opened for business in February 1967. It still runs the transit system today, although it has been massively underfunded.

We later encountered opposition from the so-called "highway user lobby," which viewed transit systems as competition and wanted a bigger piece of the pie for highway interests. Their champion was Representative William H. Natcher of Kentucky, who had a well-deserved reputation as a voice for the highway lobby.

Natcher chaired the Subcommittee on Appropriations for the District of Columbia of the House Appropriations Committee. In Congress, money can be "authorized," but that means nothing until it is also "appropriated." Natcher, in the pocket of manufacturers of steel, concrete, and heavy machinery (such as the influential heavy machinery firm Barber Greene), refused to permit the appropriation of the federal share of Metro construction costs unless we acceded to highway user lobby demands.

What the highway lobby wanted was for Virginia, DC, and Maryland officials to allow construction of Interstate 95 south from Maryland through the city, under the Mall, and over the proposed new Three Sisters Bridge across the Potomac, where it would connect with Interstate 66 in Arlington County, Virginia. The District of Columbia, which was already legally controlled by Congress, had to give in to some of Natcher's demands for highway construction within the city before he would let Congress release any of the Metro funds destined for the District of Columbia.

I opposed Natcher's interstate highway plans. I thought tunneling under the Mall and building the Three Sisters Bridge would be a financial and environmental disaster and would desecrate the heart of the city, as had been done by superhighway construction through downtown San Francisco.

This was not the first time I had opposed plans to ram a big interstate highway through a major city. When I served on the Public Works Committee, I quietly helped a young Baltimore social worker named Barbara Mikulski and several community organizations stop construction of a portion of I-95 that would have bisected—and decimated—the Fells

Point and Canton neighborhoods of East Baltimore. That fight, which saved the Little Poland and Little Italy sections of the city, was how she got her start in politics.[19]

The impasse with Natcher over the Metro funds dragged on for years and was not finally resolved until 1973, two years after I had left the Senate. Natcher's plan finally died when Maryland Governor Marvin Mandel and his transportation secretary, Harry R. Hughes, dropped plans to extend I-95 from the Capital Beltway to the District of Columbia line. That explains why to this day, when East Coast travelers on I-95 approach Washington, they must drive halfway around the Capital Beltway in order to get back on the north-south portions of I-95.[20]

By the time Natcher finally got out of the way and construction on the Metro transit system began, inflation brought on by the Vietnam War had driven up the cost of construction about three times what it would have been had it been built when originally planned in 1968–69.

In recent years the Metro system has experienced serious maintenance and safety problems, but it is hard to look at the overall effect of the system on the Washington region and not agree that it has been hugely successful.[21] Many of the current problems could have been addressed if Congress had only provided the financial resources necessary to run a dependable, efficient transit system. Once again, the mindless Republican Tea Party mantra of "no new taxes" stands in the way—an attitude of "let someone else pay for it sometime in the future."

Rail construction began in 1969, and Metro ran trains for the first time in 1976. By the end of 2014, 118 miles of track had been built to service ninety-one stations and the system was carrying more than 204 million train passengers a year, plus another 134 million bus riders.[22]

19. Barbara Mikulski, of course, went on to be elected a member of the Baltimore City Council, and she was a five-term member of the US House of Representatives and a five-term member of the US Senate. She was the first woman to chair the Senate Appropriations Committee, and by the time of her retirement in 2017 she had served longer in the US Congress than any other woman.

20. Without I-95 running through the city, there was no need to tunnel under the National Mall. Ultimately, plans for the Three Sisters Bridge across the Potomac were also abandoned.

21. Over the years, the rail system has been continuously expanded from the original 25 miles to 127 miles in 2002. Milestones in Metro History, Washington Metropolitan Area Transit Authority, http://www.wmata.com/about_metro/.

22. Metro Facts, Washington Metropolitan Area Transit Authority, http://www.wmata.com/about_metro/.

Without Metro, all of those riders would likely be driving cars, whose emissions damage our air and help overheat our planet, on roads that are already clogged with traffic.

It is hard to imagine the Washington metropolitan area without Metrorail and Metrobus. Not only has it connected this far-flung community as never before, it has also become the focus for billions of dollars in office, retail, and residential development, with still more planned for the years to come.

The Washington Metro system has been a landmark achievement, and I am proud that I was there to help create it.

An Endless Set of Challenges

I dealt with the full breadth of issues facing the city of Washington while I chaired the District of Columbia Committee. Beyond crime, court reform, and transit was a seemingly endless set of challenges: how to recruit and properly compensate police, firefighters, and teachers; how to identify and treat the mentally ill, many of whom were homeless; how to prevent the spread of syphilis or other diseases; how to mediate disputes between tenants and their landlords; what to do about uninsured motorists; and how to educate young couples about family planning. At one time or another, I was involved all of these issues.

One city problem was the lack of public parking. "Parking is so bad in the District of Columbia," I joked during my Senate years, "that to find a parking space you have to buy a car that is already parked."

I wanted a system with inexpensive off-street parking, like they had then in Baltimore. But the House District Committee was controlled by business interests in the city who were buying up lots, holding them, and then developing them as office buildings. Smart developers might buy a lot for $25,000 to $50,000 in 1945 or 1946, hold it for eighteen or twenty years, then develop it into an office complex that might be valued at $10 million to $30 million. They would make millions on each lot, and they did not want the DC Committee to interfere. I could usually get my proposed parking changes through the Senate, but they were always stopped in the House. The most I could do to get legislation passed was to require newly constructed buildings to provide sufficient parking for tenants.

I was more successful in fending off attempts by business interests to rescind or alter a restriction on the permissible height of buildings in the District of Columbia that had been in place for more than a century. The Height of Buildings Act of 1910 limits commercial buildings to 130 feet in height and residential buildings to 90 feet.[23] The height limit is constantly under attack, even today. We protected it when I was in the Senate, and I am glad to say—and a bit surprised—that Congress has held firm on this issue.

Consumer Fraud

Bobby Kennedy helped me to get the District of Columbia Committee focused on another important issue: consumer fraud.

I chaired a series of hearings that lasted a year, and Bobby was particularly effective at exposing the improper practices of unscrupulous lenders. His appearance alone at a hearing was enough to attract the press, and together we exposed the fraudulent practices that were being perpetrated on the poorest DC residents. Press attention was one thing that such lenders did not want.

We pushed through legislation that provided important consumer protections for DC residents and became model legislation for other parts of the country. One act regulated finance charges on retail sales, limited interest rates, and prohibited disguised forms of interest. Another protected consumers from making hasty decisions or falling for high-pressure sales techniques by giving them the right to cancel home improvement contracts within three days of signing. A third law protected home owners from foreclosure without first being given a day in court.

Bobby and I were both concerned about protecting those who needed protection the most, and the DC Committee gave us an opportunity and a forum in which to do that.

In those early years, when we had such a strong Democratic majority and everything seemed possible, Bobby and I used the District of Columbia Committee to push our progressive agenda. By the time I became chair, times were changing, and I was fortunate to have a politically astute staff

23. After the twelve-story Cairo Hotel was constructed on Q Street in 1894, Congress enacted the Height of Buildings Act in 1910, worried in part that tall buildings would obscure or detract from the Capitol and other monuments.

director in John McEvoy, who kept me focused on issues, such as crime and drug abuse, that made the most sense to my Maryland constituents.

I am proud of the work we did on the DC Committee and think the city of Washington is better off because of it. But I would be the first to admit that when election time rolled around in 1970, not many of my Maryland constituents outside of Montgomery and Prince George's Counties appreciated what I had done or the time I had spent doing it.

PART IV

The Hardest Fights

I would rather be ashes than dust!
I would rather that my spark should burn out
in a brilliant blaze than it should be stifled by dry-rot.
I would rather be a superb meteor, every atom
of me in magnificent glow, than a sleepy and permanent planet.
The function of man is to live, not to exist.
I shall not waste my days trying to prolong them.
I shall use my time.

—JACK LONDON'S CREDO

CHAPTER 17

Vietnam and the Political Costs of War

If John F. Kennedy had not been assassinated, he unquestionably would have gotten us quickly out of Vietnam following his reelection in 1964.

JFK had made up his mind: we were coming out. Mike Mansfield, the Senate majority leader, was strongly behind him, and the young president had high enough approval ratings that he could have pulled it off without much backlash. He had already announced in October 1963 plans to withdraw 1,000 of the 16,732 personnel then in Vietnam by the end of the year and had endorsed recommendations to withdraw the bulk of American personnel by the end of 1965.[1]

But Kennedy did not live and the United States became mired in a war in Southeast Asia that dragged on until 1975, a dozen years after he was slain and two decades after President Eisenhower first sent a batch of US military advisers to a Southeast Asian country few Americans had ever heard of.

By the time the Vietnam War ended, more than fifty-eight thousand Americans had been killed, Lyndon Johnson's dream of a Great Society was gone, his presidency was in ruins, the American economy had been wrecked, and political reputations on both the right and the left—including my own—had been forever damaged.

Hundreds of thousands of South Vietnamese, North Vietnamese, Cambodian, and Laotian soldiers and civilians had also been killed, their villages burned, and their major cities reduced to rubble, all raising the sad, retrospective question: for what? Returning US soldiers were shamefully shunned by Americans who were against the war, creating a strain

---

1. Robert A. Caro *The Passage of Power: The Years of Lyndon Johnson* (New York: Vintage Books 2013), 402–3, 534–35.

on our national psyche that is still palpable today. And, in the end, of course, we lost the war at a horrendous fiscal and societal cost.

Like most Americans, I started out supporting LBJ and our efforts in Vietnam. Call it patriotism, or just faith that our leaders knew what they were doing. The stated justification was that communists from North Vietnam were trying to take over democratic South Vietnam, and if they were not stopped there, communism would spread to neighboring countries. This, in turn, would create a global threat to the United States and other Western democracies. It was called the "domino theory," and our advisers—and later our troops—were sent to Vietnam to halt communist aggression before the next domino could be tipped.

But, like many Americans, the more I learned about Vietnam and the longer the war dragged on, the more I grew to oppose it.

Seeing Vietnam with My Own Eyes

US involvement in Vietnam was already escalating by the time I arrived in the Senate in 1965. JFK had increased the number of military personnel in South Vietnam to sixteen thousand, up from the nine hundred advisers Eisenhower had sent.[2] Reports of a 1964 naval engagement involving US warships in the Gulf of Tonkin prompted Congress—in an election year—to enact a resolution that gave President Johnson broad powers to use military force in Vietnam without a formal declaration of war. This move gave LBJ the opportunity to be seen as militarily tough and determined to stop the spread of communism.

In Washington in those days, there was still a powerful anticommunist hangover that could be traced to the vicious crusade waged against communists (real or imagined) by Wisconsin Senator Joseph McCarthy in the 1950s. McCarthy had helped defeat my father and had even intimidated President Eisenhower, among others. American political leaders who lived through those days, including John Kennedy and Lyndon Johnson, did not want to be seen as complicit in communist expansion.

By 1965, Johnson had begun deploying regular US combat troops to Vietnam. Public support for the deployment was high, and General

2. Eisenhower had turned down a French request to send in troops to bail out the French garrison at Dien Bien Phu, besieged by Viet Minh freedom fighters supported by communist China. The French presence in Indochina ended soon after their defeat at Dien Bien Phu in 1954.

William Westmoreland, the American commander in Vietnam, predicted victory by the end of 1967. The new young Democratic senator elected from Maryland believed him.

In early fall 1965, I was eager to see the situation with my own eyes, so I accepted an invitation from Senator Ted Kennedy to accompany him and two of his closest friends on the Hill, Representatives John Tunney of California and John Culver of Iowa, to Vietnam. Teddy and I were on the special subcommittee on refugees under the Judiciary Committee, and the main focus of our tour was how refugees were being treated. Unfortunately, this trip began immediately after Teddy and I had our falling out over the Morrissey nomination to the federal bench. Teddy was so angry with me, he was barely speaking.

We landed at Tan Son Nhut airfield in Saigon after a tense twenty-nine-hour flight. Over the next few days, we were taken to Pleiku in the central highlands, to Da Nang in the far north near the border with North Vietnam, to Qui Nhon, which was the site of the largest single concentration of refugees, and to An Khe, where the 1st Cavalry Division was headquartered.[3] By then, more than 720,000 Vietnamese were already homeless.

US troop levels were approaching 150,000, and huge artillery pieces were being shipped in. Each of us tried to meet with as many troops from our own state as possible. I took down the names and home phone numbers of the Marylanders I met and relayed them home to Ginny, who called their families to advise them that I had met with them and they were well.

Some troops asked about the antiwar protests that were already beginning to make headlines back home, but both Teddy and I assured them that the overwhelming majority of Americans backed President Johnson's policies and that the news media had made the protests seem more important than they really were.[4]

The biggest headlines we got came after Viet Cong on the ground fired on our fleet of seven helicopters as we flew into a US Army Special Forces camp in the Mekong Delta about one hundred miles southwest

3. Ernest B. Ferguson, "Tydings Arrives in Viet Capital," *Baltimore Sun*, October 24, 1965, 2.

4. Ernest B. Ferguson, "Wounded GI Asks about Protests," *Baltimore Sun*, October 26, 1965, C26.

of Saigon on October 26. No one was hit or hurt, and, quite frankly, I never realized they were shooting at us. "There are a lot of guys out on the firing line. Don't over-dramatize this," Teddy told reporters.[5]

From Vietnam, we flew to Thailand, where Teddy was joined by his wife, Joan, and soon returned home. Tunney, Culver, and I flew on to India, Lebanon, Jordan, and Israel to study the terrible refugee problems in those countries. When I got home, I toured high schools and colleges around Maryland to report on the trip. One thing that worried me while I was in Vietnam was that it seemed like none of the Americans on the ground could speak Vietnamese, and the scenes of Vietnamese children waving tiny American flags at places we visited were clearly staged.

An important lesson from this trip, which I learned from Bobby Kennedy after I returned, was that when US senators travel abroad, they should never let the State Department or the military dictate where to visit, what to see, or to whom they should speak. Listen to their suggestions, but decide that yourself. Talk to academics or others knowledgeable about the areas you are going to visit and set your own agenda. It was a lesson I followed for every overseas trip I took after that first visit to Vietnam. Unfortunately, not many members of Congress followed this advice.

"There is a feeling of optimism in South Vietnam, in Laos, and Thailand and as far away as India," I reported upon my return in November, saying there was so much fear throughout Asia of what was then called "Red China" that the US presence was actually welcomed by noncommunist nations. I said that US troop morale was "extraordinarily high" but that "the boys were puzzled by the anti-war demonstrations in the United States." I cautiously predicted that the war might last another five years—much longer than the administration had suggested.[6]

Speaking to students at Salisbury State College, I went even further, saying the visit made me abandon previous reservations about the war: "I was, I must confess, not entirely 100 percent in favor of our policies in Vietnam early this year. Although I remained silent, I had very strong reservations." But the trip, I said, convinced me "our position in South Vietnam is correct."[7]

5. "Edward Kennedy's Copter Escort under Fire," *New York Times*, October 27, 1965, 3.

6. Tydings quoted in Washington Bureau of the Sun, "GI's Praised by Tydings," *Baltimore Sun*, November 11, 1965, C5.

7. Tydings quoted in Douglas D. Connah Jr., "Tydings Viet View Changes," *Baltimore Sun*, November 19, 1965, A11.

Doubts

Despite these public pronouncements and a genuine desire to support the president, I was privately having troubling doubts and so were many of my Senate colleagues. We were sending more and more troops to Vietnam and pouring billions of dollars into this war, but our long-term strategy was unclear and the South Vietnamese did not seem to be doing their share. It was rapidly becoming our war, not theirs. There was a growing feeling within the Senate that we had remained too quiet in the face of this continuing escalation.

The most outspoken war critic in the Senate was Wayne Morse of Oregon. Majority Leader Mansfield also opposed LBJ's policy of all-out involvement in Vietnam, but in March 1966 he tabled without debate an amendment by Morse that would have rescinded the Gulf of Tonkin resolution. That would have implicitly repudiated the president's Vietnam policies. It was becoming clear, however, that the war was beginning to divide the Senate, just as it was beginning to divide the country.[8]

About sixteen of us began meeting in the offices of Senator J. William Fulbright of Arkansas, then chair of the Foreign Relations Committee, in search of a resolution that would show our support for President Johnson but somehow stop the escalation. Johnson was going to run for reelection in two years, and none of us wanted to undermine him.[9]

I tried to push us in a different direction, suggesting the United States should do more to help Vietnam and other Asian countries develop economically, to remove the conditions that give rise to discontent and armed rebellion. It was the same argument, quite frankly, I had been making about poverty at home as the root cause of unrest and riots in American cities.

In a long speech about Vietnam at Washington University in St. Louis in spring 1966, I said, "In the long run, the future of freedom in Asia will surely be determined by the number of babies born healthy, not the number of bullets expended; the number of schools constructed,

8. Senator Richard Russell of Georgia, chair of the Armed Services Committee, threatened to put in an alternate amendment to reaffirm the Gulf of Tonkin resolution.

9. Similar concerns about the war were being raised in the House of Representatives, where seventy-five members—including Maryland Representatives George Fallon, Samuel Friedel, Edward Garmatz, and Carlton Sickles—banded together to say they would support a new $4.8 billion Vietnam military authorization bill, but not "unrestrained or indiscriminate enlargement of the military effort." Joseph R. L. Sterne, "Policy Rider for Vietnam Bill Opposed," *Baltimore Sun*, March 1, 1966, A1.

not the number of bridges destroyed; and by the achievement of decent housing, sanitation and nutrition, not the stockpiling of bombs." I argued that the United States must be willing to provide massive economic development to struggling nations "to avert an endless succession of Vietnams."[10]

I recalled the late Indian Prime Minister Jawaharlal Nehru's sage observation that a nation cannot have democracy on an empty stomach.

In a passage that was eerily echoed when the United States invaded Iraq a half century later, I told the Washington University audience that the enormous task in Vietnam was "nothing less than an attempt to build a nation; and nations are not built quickly or easily. Our goal is a South Vietnamese government which is independent, able to protect its people, responsive to their needs and desires, and capable of providing them with at least the necessities of life."[11]

Bombing and Defections

By 1967, however, Johnson and his generals had sharply increased the intensity of bombing in both South and North Vietnam, and the more the war expanded, the more the president's supporters defected. In April, three hundred thousand Americans demonstrated against the war in Central Park in New York City.

The belief in the Senate was that peace talks would be impossible as long as we continued our bombing raids on Hanoi, the Haiphong harbor, and other targets in North Vietnam. Bobby Kennedy was becoming more and more publicly critical of the war, and his opposition gave me confidence in my own judgment about the war. By late summer, Senate support for LBJ had dwindled to a thin majority.

In August, I finally broke with the president over the war.

"I believe our growing commitment of military forces to Vietnam is a mistake, which no degree of retrospective or rationalization can justify," I said in a speech to the National Student Association meeting,

---

10. Senator Joseph D. Tydings, "Vietnam and the Balance of Power in Asia," speech delivered at Washington University, St. Louis, Missouri, May 5, 1966, Joseph D. Tydings Collection, Hornbake Library, University of Maryland, College Park.

11. Ibid.

held at the University of Maryland.[12] Naturally, the president was not pleased that a fellow Democrat would abandon him on such a high-profile issue.

I told the student leaders that I had concluded that the United States was supporting a Vietnamese government "which is either unknown, uncared for, or despised by many of the people it rules." Another major concern was that the cost of the war was disrupting the US economy and diverting funds that otherwise could have been used for "urgent domestic priorities." This was the classic "guns or butter" argument anew.[13]

Public opposition to the war was escalating as quickly as the war itself. On October 21, more than one hundred thousand war opponents marched on the Pentagon, a rainbow collection of radicals, liberals, black nationalists, hippies, professors, women's groups, and war veterans. Dr. Benjamin Spock, the most famous pediatrician of the era and a strident antiwar activist, called LBJ "the enemy." The writer Norman Mailer and a pair of United Press International (UPI) reporters were among those arrested. One week later, Father Philip Berrigan, a Josephite priest and World War II veteran, led a group that became known as the Baltimore Four to a draft board office in Baltimore, where they drenched the draft records with blood and then waited to be arrested.

Tet and the Democratic Party Debacle in Chicago

Through it all, the White House and US military leaders insisted that their strategies in Vietnam were working and that victory was in sight. But young American men were being killed in shocking numbers, and people back home began demanding an end to the carnage.

It is important to remember that in those days the "all-volunteer army" of today did not exist. Almost any young man without a college or medical deferment—or without political ties, like the future president George W. Bush—could be drafted and sent off to war in the jungles of

12. Senator Joseph D. Tydings, "Vietnam," speech delivered at the National Student Association meeting, University of Maryland, College Park, August 26, 1967, Tydings Collection, Hornbake Library.

13. Tydings quoted in John S. Carroll, "Tydings Talk Is Attack on Viet Policies," *Baltimore Sun*, August 27, 1967, 24.

Southeast Asia. That captured the undivided attention of parents, other military-age men, and the public in general in a way that US deployments of volunteer soldiers to Afghanistan and Iraq following the 9/11 terrorist attacks never have.[14]

Suddenly, in January and February 1968, the North Vietnamese and their Viet Cong allies launched coordinated attacks in more than one hundred towns and cities throughout Vietnam in what became known as the Tet Offensive. The attacks surprised the American public, revealed the vulnerability of South Vietnam, and rendered suspect the Johnson administration claims that victory in Vietnam was within reach.

By March, the Senate—led by Fulbright, Mansfield, Bobby Kennedy, and myself, among others—was in full revolt against the war. As usual, Bobby was one of the most articulate among the critics, saying it was "immoral and intolerable to continue the way we are" in Vietnam. He said the president was making "a major mistake to escalate" the war "without the support and understanding of the Senate and the American people." He demanded to know, "Are we like the God of the Old Testament that we can decide, in Washington, D.C., what cities, what towns, what hamlets in Vietnam are going to be destroyed?"[15]

What happened next was a cascade of history-altering events.

On March 16, Bobby announced he was going to challenge Lyndon Johnson for the presidency.[16]

Two weeks later, on March 31, Johnson stunned the nation by announcing that he would not seek reelection.[17]

14. In February 1968, I called for a complete revision of the military draft system, specifically taking exception to the denial of educational deferments for junior college students pursuing occupational courses of study. I proposed abolition of the existing draft system and that it be replaced with a lottery.

15. Robert F. Kennedy quoted in John W. Finney, "Criticism of War Widens in Senate on Build-Up Issue," New York Times, March 8, 1968, 1.

16. There was a narrow alley between the Senate office buildings that you could see if you looked down from the windows of our fourth-floor offices. For weeks leading up to Bobby's announcement, my staff and I frequently caught a glimpse of him pacing back and forth alone, his hands clasped behind his back, clearly deep in thought. I am sure he was searching his soul and weighing the personal and political ramifications of launching a bid for the presidency against the incumbent president of his own party.

17. Toward the end of his televised speech about the war, Johnson said, "With America's sons in the fields far away, with America's future under challenge right here at home, with our hopes and the world's hopes for peace in the balance every day, I do not believe that I should devote an hour or a day of my time to any personal partisan causes or to any duties other than

Four days after that, Dr. Martin Luther King Jr. was assassinated in Memphis, and riots broke out in cities across the country.

Then, exactly two months after that, Bobby was assassinated in Los Angeles.

That year, 1968, may have been one of the worst years in our history. It certainly was the worst I have lived through.

The country was coming unglued. All the explosive issues— Vietnam, civil rights, women's rights, black power, the lack of jobs in American cities, and more—were colliding. In reaction to such enormous change, a new, mean-spirited, conservative backlash was building. Complicating it all was the sudden vacuum of leadership—Bobby was gone, King was gone, and Johnson was on his way out.

Against this backdrop, the Democratic National Convention convened in Chicago that August, and the streets quickly exploded in violent confrontations between antiwar demonstrators and the billy club–wielding Chicago police force. The divisive fights on the floor of the convention were not much better; at one point a shouting match erupted between Connecticut Senator Abraham Ribicoff and Chicago Mayor Richard Daley. It was all televised on the nightly news, which only added to the stress and unrest in the nation.

I tried to get the Platform Committee for the convention to adopt a strong position against the war, calling for an immediate cessation of bombing of North Vietnam, complete withdrawal of US troops, the release of all noncommunist political prisoners detained by the Saigon government, and the formation of a coalition government that represented all the people of South Vietnam.[18] "The new Democratic President should bring American involvement in Vietnam to a prompt end, without regard to past mistakes and old administrations, and this platform should spell that out," I said.[19]

I recalled Bobby Kennedy's opposition to the war. "He thought it was

the awesome duties of this office—the Presidency of your country. Accordingly, I shall not seek, and I will not accept, the nomination of my party for another term as your President," Lyndon B. Johnson, "The President's Address to the Nation Announcing Steps to Limit the War in Vietnam and Reporting His Decision Not to Seek Reelection," March 31, 1968, online text compiled by Gerhard Peters and John T. Woolley for *The American Presidency Project*, http://www.presidency.ucsb.edu/ws/?pid=28772.

18. "Anti-War Plank Urged by Tydings," *Baltimore Sun*, August 19, 1968, C18.

19. Quoted in Richard Homan, "Tydings to Propose Strong Anti-War Plank," *Washington Post, Times Herald*, August 18, 1968, A14.

unacceptable. I think it is unacceptable. I hope the Democratic National Convention will say so," I told the committee.[20]

But, like the country, the party was split. The party hierarchy wanted Hubert Humphrey to be the nominee, and since he was Johnson's vice president, they felt they could not saddle him with an antiwar plank in the party platform. Rank-and-file delegates, however, could see that Vietnam was killing the Democrats' chances in November.[21]

I always thought Humphrey was a fine man and a courageous, thoughtful senator. But I could see no way he could be elected in November given his connection with the Johnson administration and his continuing support of the war. A few who had supported Bobby suggested his brother, Teddy, should run. Eugene McCarthy, the senator from Minnesota, had been the first prominent Democrat to challenge Johnson in 1968 and was a favorite antiwar candidate, but I had no confidence in his abilities to be president. I threw my support behind—and seconded the nomination of—Senator George McGovern of South Dakota, a decorated World War II aviator who strongly opposed the war. But Humphrey won the nomination.

I did what I could for Humphrey, applauding him, for example, when he promised in the closing days of the election to terminate bombing of North Vietnam and reduce the US troop presence in South Vietnam.

As that election approached, Johnson thought he had persuaded the South Vietnamese to reach a truce with the North—a peace settlement that the always political Johnson figured would give Humphrey the extra push he needed to win a close election. But, as was later publicly revealed, Johnson had discovered just before the election that Nixon, the Republican candidate, was secretly and illegally sabotaging the negotiations. Working through Anna Chennault, his liaison to the South Vietnam government, Nixon had persuaded the South Vietnamese to

20. Tydings quoted in Associated Press, "Tydings Urges Action on Vietnam, Gun Law," *Washington Post*, August 12, 1968, A8.

21. Pierre Salinger, who had been JFK's press secretary, helped draft the antiwar plank. "If Robert Kennedy were alive today," he said, "he'd be here speaking for the minority plank." But Representative Wayne Hays of Ohio got pro-administration cheers when he linked those supporting the antiwar plank with the unshaven, long-haired hippies and "Yippies" who were demonstrating in the streets of Chicago. "They would like to substitute beards for brains. They want pot instead of patriotism, sideburns instead of solutions," he said. Salinger and Hays quoted in Ernest B. Ferguson, "Democrats Defeat Dove Viet Plank," *Baltimore Sun*, August 29, 1968, A1.

back away from the peace talks. Chennault essentially told them that if they waited until after the election, they could get a better deal with the North Vietnamese, who had pledged to end the war once the United States agreed to halt the bombing. As a result, the South Vietnamese refused to meet or negotiate.

Johnson privately accused Nixon of treason. The Logan Act, signed by President John Adams in 1797, prohibits private citizens from intruding into official government negotiations with a foreign nation.[22] According to a 1973 memo by Walt W. Rostow, a former Johnson national security adviser, Johnson had gathered evidence of what some have called Nixon's "dirtiest trick" by having the FBI monitor communications to the South Vietnamese embassy in Washington. LBJ complained about Nixon's attempt to sabotage the peace talks to Dirksen, the Republican leader in the Senate, and then to Nixon himself. The president and his advisers, however, decided that, for the good of the country, they would not make the transgression public.[23]

Humphrey narrowly lost the election, the war continued for four more years, and the United States unnecessarily invested billions of dollars more and thousands of young men's lives.[24] George Wallace, the racist former governor of Alabama, ran as a third-party candidate and campaigned against the school desegregation ruling of the Supreme Court. As a result, he swept the Deep South, peeling away a part of the Democratic coalition that had been in place since Roosevelt's New Deal; some of those votes might otherwise have gone to Humphrey. Playing on public fears—just as the modern crop of Republicans and Tea Party extremists, including President Donald Trump, have done with regard to Muslims, immigration, and terrorism—Nixon's campaign capitalized on the riots that had swept through American cities by pledging

22. Accusations of a potentially similar violation of the Logan Act were raised in 2017 concerning allegedly illegal contacts with Russian officials by members of Donald Trump's presidential campaign in 2016 and 2017. Amid concerns by the US intelligence community that Russia interfered in the 2016 presidential election, the allegations against the Trump campaign were deemed so serious that the US Justice Department brought in former FBI Director Robert S. Mueller III to investigate. This investigation has already lead to prosecution of several Trump-affiliated aides.

23. Walt W. Rostow, "Memorandum for the Record," May 14, 1973, Lyndon Baines Johnson Presidential Library, Austin, TX.

24. My Senate colleague, Danny Brewster, was also defeated in that 1968 election, by Republican Charles McC. Mathias Jr., suddenly making me the senior senator from Maryland.

to restore law and order. He also demonized the antiwar activists and public officials who sided with them as being soft on defense and soft on communism. Given the mood of the country, and the failure to reach a peace agreement, it worked.

The Paris Peace Accords were not signed until January 1973, more than four years after the 1968 election.

"The United States Has Lost the War"

I had no way of knowing what Nixon had done. By the time the election was over, all I knew was that, despite promises from the generals, promises from President Johnson, and now promises from President Nixon that the end of the war was in sight, it dragged on.

At a commencement speech before an audience of two thousand at Goucher College in Baltimore in June 1969, my frustration peaked. "There is no avoiding the harsh fact that the United States has lost the war," I said. Our experience in Vietnam, I added, "overturns shibboleths and long-cherished myths we have lived with for two decades." The first myth, I said, was that of American omnipotence; the second was that American capitalism and democratic principles work everywhere; and the third was that all foreign conflicts will have clear winners and losers.[25]

While I still think these observations were indisputably true, saying them aloud hurt me politically. The *Aegis* in Bel Air, a powerful voice in my home county of Harford and a consistent supporter for years, all but disowned me. Some political columnists suggested I was saying such things to position myself for my reelection campaign the following year, but I knew almost immediately that my words would come back to haunt me. Within days, a letter to the editor appeared in the *Baltimore Sun* accusing me of being quiet about the escalation of the war when Johnson was president but changing my tune once Nixon was in the White House.

"Now, because we have a Republican President, out he comes with this foolish statement," the Frederick County resident wrote. "Senator Tydings is one of the group of liberals in Washington who might receive

---

25. Tydings quoted in Alvin P. Sanoff, "Vietnam War Lost Tydings Says," *Baltimore Sun*, June 16, 1969, A-1.

a rude awakening one of these days. Senators McGovern, Hart, Kennedy, Muskie and others should remember what happened to the old standby from Oregon, the former Senator Morse. He is gone with the wind."[26]

By October 1969, huge antiwar demonstrations were being planned all over the country and overseas as well. I joined a bipartisan group of seventeen senators and forty-seven members of the House who endorsed the demonstrations and called for an end to the war.[27] More than two million Americans joined the protests in cities across the country. McGovern spoke at the Boston rally, joined by Mayor Kevin White, Richard Cardinal Cushing, and Governor Francis W. Sargent. Faculties at Harvard and MIT voted for a quick American withdrawal. The mayors of New York City and Cleveland joined the protests. Public schools in New York and Duluth, Minnesota, released students so they could take part in moratorium activities. At Oxford University in England, a young American Rhodes Scholar named Bill Clinton organized a demonstration.[28]

The following month, the March on Washington became one of the largest antiwar demonstrations of the Vietnam era. Nixon, who had said he would not be moved by the protests, reported that he had watched sports on TV rather than news accounts of the demonstrations, which unfolded within shouting distance of the White House.

By 1970, the year I had to run for reelection, the war had gotten even worse, if that was possible. Nixon had begun to withdraw some troops, but he also expanded the war with incursions into the neighboring countries of Laos and Cambodia. The Ohio National Guard opened fire on antiwar demonstrators at Kent State University, killing four young people and wounding nine others, sending the antiwar faction throughout the country into a frenzy. Frustrated that nothing they did or said seemed to have any effect, war protesters became more confrontational. One group arrived at my Senate office, camped out on the reception room floor, and refused to leave. Another, larger group occupied my new campaign office in Baltimore.

26. The letter, printed under the headline "Tydings and the War," was signed by J. Tyson Lee of Frederick. *Baltimore Sun*, June 24, 1969, A12. Morse had been defeated for reelection by a Republican, Bob Packwood, in 1968.

27. Nathan Miller, "Lawmakers Endorse Viet Protest," *Baltimore Sun*, October 10, 1969, A1.

28. Like George W. Bush, Bill Clinton also used his connections to avoid being drafted.

Then in May, in reaction to the US invasion of Cambodia, thousands of students at the University of Maryland rioted on the College Park campus. I am convinced that the intensity of violence was caused, at least in part, by anarchists who had no connection to the university but who came to the Maryland campus expressly to stir up the students. Protesters threw bricks, rocks, and bottles and were met by police using tear gas, riot batons, and dogs. Demonstrators set fires on campus, vandalized the main university administration building and the Reserve Officer Training Corps (ROTC) offices, and blocked traffic on busy US Route 1, the major highway that runs through the campus.

I felt that someone in leadership had to speak to the young students and tell them we were doing our best to bring the war to an end. But I began to get blamed for what was happening on the largest college campus in the state.

My new Maryland colleague in the Senate, Mac Mathias, also opposed the war, but he had the political acumen to keep silent about his position. By contrast, my public opposition was so well known that I became a lightning rod for veterans' groups and others who thought I was unpatriotic, or who were disgusted by the demonstrators, or who drew a direct connection between a high-profile war critic like me and the violent riots on college campuses. That's when my approval rating began to drop precipitously. And that's when my old nemesis, George P. Mahoney, decided to jump into the 1970 Democratic primary against me.

I tried to control the political damage, telling a student audience at the Johns Hopkins University in August that the University of Maryland riots were "inexcusable." And I warned the students, who were mostly against the war, that continued campus riots would threaten the reelection chances of many opponents of the Vietnam War.[29]

I did not need to mention that one of those whose reelection was already being threatened was Senator Joseph D. Tydings of Maryland.

---

29. "Unrest Threat Cited by Tydings," *Baltimore Sun*, August 29, 1970, B5.

CHAPTER 18

The Environment and Overpopulation

In my youth, the Chesapeake Bay was a cornucopia.

I was only a second grader when my family moved to Oakington in 1935, but I still vividly recall watching the Susquehanna Flats off the mile-long waterfront our farm had along the bay. In winter the area turned white from the huge flocks of migrating swans. Canvasback ducks soared and twirled and dived into the grass-filled waters, while huge flocks of redhead and blackhead ducks crisscrossed the gray winter sky.

In steamy summers, the other boys on the farm and I would set trot lines and easily pull in five, six, sometimes even seven dozen blue crabs a day, which we then could sell for maybe thirty cents a dozen at Joe Good's grocery store in Havre de Grace. Or we would push through the tea leaf on the shoreline to find an even more profitable delicacy—soft-shell crabs, or "peelers," which were just getting ready to molt their hard outer shell. Fishing was bountiful, too—pike, perch, and bass. The seaweed and wild celery that grew so plentifully throughout the Upper Bay provided food and shelter for all kinds of marine life. The water was clean, sparkling, beautiful.

Our natural world seemed healthy back then.

When I returned from Germany in 1947, I began to notice changes. The number of ducks began to decline, as did our ability to catch crabs and rockfish. When I moved into the Maryland House of Delegates in 1955, I began what has become a lifelong passion for me: trying to find better ways to protect our environment and natural resources.

I am sad to report, however, that despite hundreds, perhaps thousands, of new laws and regulations at the federal, state, and local levels, and the expenditure of millions of taxpayer dollars; despite the determined work of our smartest scientists and university researchers;

despite the good intentions of many public officials, environmental groups, enlightened business leaders, teachers, parents, and others; and despite my own best efforts, we are steadily losing this fight. We have clearly made some progress in recent years, but the long-term trend in the Chesapeake and the tributaries to it is one of decline.

It may be unpopular to say so, but the reason for this decline is that there are more people living on the shoreline than it can support, and more people on earth than our planet can support.

This is particularly true in Africa, Asia, and parts of Latin America. Even if the United States and every other developed nation were to provide generous aid programs to the less developed parts of the world, it would not be enough. Our planet simply cannot keep up with the population expansion.

In those blissful days of my youth at Oakington, the world population was a little more than 2 billion. By 1960, when John Kennedy was elected, it had increased to 3 billion. When I left the Senate just a decade later, it had reached 3.3 billion—a level that brushed up against what some scientists said would no longer be sustainable. Since then, the global population has more than doubled, to 7 billion.

One of the scariest effects of this surge in population is that we are rapidly running out of fresh, potable water. Over half of the global population lives in countries where water tables are falling and wells are drying up, due in large part to global warming and overuse. At the same time, the planet is adding tens of millions more mouths to feed each year. According to the World Health Organization, each year more than one million children die, directly or indirectly, either from lack of water to survive or from diseases they got from drinking polluted water while trying to survive.

The United States is no longer immune to this water crisis. We now know, for example, that the huge Ogallala Aquifer, which lies beneath portions of eight states throughout the Great Plains, is being depleted by our demands for agricultural irrigation. Here and elsewhere in the world, water is becoming more precious and expensive than oil.

In rural areas of many developing countries, increasing numbers and concentrations of poor people are being forced to destroy their own natural resource base in the search for food, water, fuel, or fodder. In a desperate quest for money, they slaughter elephants for their ivory, or tigers for their skins, or rhinoceroses for their tusks, thus driving more species toward extinction. They chop down forests faster than they can grow. They deplete water supplies and overgraze rangeland. They are compelled to farm marginal lands at unsustainable levels. If you can't picture this, just think of Haiti.

In just fifty years, we have lost more than half of our rainforests. Besides the uniqueness of the rainforest ecosystem, those forests affect climate by absorbing carbon dioxide and storing enormous amounts of water. We are also dependent on rainforests for species of plants that are used for medicine, food, and biotechnology.

The final troubling global trend is the transformation of previously habitable lands into deserts. This is becoming a serious problem in China, which was already finding it difficult to feed the 1.4 billion people of that country. In some parts of the world, herds of sheep and goats devour the plants that otherwise could stave off desertification. The loss of areas where grain historically was grown is a major reason Africa has failed to match overall population growth with food production.

Fisheries around the globe are also being depleted, the result of overfishing and pollution. As hundreds of thousands of suburbanites now crowd the shoreline of our beloved Chesapeake Bay, it, too, is slowly dying, unable to produce the crabs, oysters, and fish that once made it the most abundant and productive estuary in the world.

Connecting the Dots

In my days as a young state legislator, I worked on environmental issues such as placing restrictions on the catching of rockfish or deciding how much drinking water the city of Baltimore should be allowed to withdraw from the Susquehanna River and from where.

It was not until I reached the Senate, however, that I began to connect the dots—discovering the linkages between population, natural resource depletion, and environmental degradation.

The principal influence on me was General William H. Draper Jr., a World War II veteran and friend of General Eisenhower. Draper was a brilliant entrepreneur and business leader who in 1965 started a nongovernmental organization called the Population Crisis Committee.

That group, later supported by Ambassador Angier Biddle Duke and his brilliant wife, Robin, helped persuade the US Agency for International Development to establish the Office of Population and later helped the United Nations create the Fund for Population.[1] General Draper and John D. Rockefeller Jr. also were responsible for helping to save and rebuild the World Family Planning Organization, a part of the World Health Organization.

Another influence on me was Senator Ernest Gruening of Alaska.[2] He was the leading Senate Democrat on the issue of family planning and population control, but the principal leaders on this issue at the time were Republicans, such as Senators Kenneth Keating of New York and Robert Taft of Ohio—a level of bipartisanship on family planning issues you certainly would never see today.[3]

In 1965, the District of Columbia Committee began a series of hearings on the rate of illegitimate births in DC. It was clear to me that many such mothers were ignorant of basic family planning and contraception, which was directly linked to their living in poverty. I had become intrigued by a series of articles in the *New York Times* by a Harvard professor named Daniel Patrick Moynihan describing the link between unwed mothers, their lack of information about family planning, the absence of fathers in the home or others who could provide child care, and the resulting poverty of the family. I was so impressed, in fact, that

1. Draper, who had a distinguished career in the military, as a diplomat, and in private business, was the US delegate to the United Nations Population Commission from 1969 until 1971. He was renowned for his work ethic. Despite health problems and ignoring the advice of his doctors, he worked relentlessly right up until his death at age eighty in 1974. When he died at Walter Reed Army Medical Center, he is said to have been found in bed with a telephone still clutched in one hand.

2. Gruening became the first US senator from Alaska after it gained statehood, and he was primarily known as the first senator to make public his opposition to the war in Vietnam. He and Wayne Morse of Oregon were the only two senators to vote against the original Gulf of Tonkin resolution in 1964, which authorized the president to use military force in Vietnam without a declaration of war. Gruening was a Harvard-trained medical doctor, a longtime journalist, and then governor of the Alaska Territory for fourteen years prior to statehood.

3. When I was in ROTC in college, one of my professors talked about the potentially serious impact of the global population explosion. His lecture impressed me. Then, when I became US attorney, I got to know Manfred Guttmacher, whose brother Alan was then the national head of Planned Parenthood. By the time I arrived in the Senate, I was ripe to be recruited on these issues.

I took the entire Baltimore City Council to Cambridge, Massachusetts, with me to discuss these issues with Moynihan.[4]

"In our society, there is no effective solution to the crime and delinquency problem which does not include prevention of the births of unwanted children," I said, and I pushed for broader dissemination of family planning information to anyone who asked for it.[5]

Pretty soon I began testifying before a Senate subcommittee urging creation of an Office of Population Problems within the Department of Health, Education, and Welfare.

"I do not advocate, and this bill does not provide for, making birth control information available to persons who by reason of religious conviction, or otherwise, do not choose to practice family planning," I testified. "But available medical information on human fertility should not be denied the poor, the uneducated, or the illiterate family that wishes to limit its growth."[6]

At the same time, I began working more on the water pollution problems affecting the Chesapeake and other coastal areas, as well as the serious air pollution problems that had made difficult the simple act of breathing in urban areas, including the District of Columbia.

I intentionally moved onto the Public Works Committee because it dealt with environmental issues. Members included Gruening, my friends Birch Bayh of Indiana and Thomas Eagleton of Missouri, and Edmund Muskie of Maine. Muskie, who chaired a subcommittee on environmental issues, was one of the first environmentalists to be elected to the Senate and was an even greater influence on me than Gruening.

4. Moynihan was a sociologist and director of the Harvard-MIT Center for Urban Studies. Although a Democrat, he went on to work as a counselor to President Nixon, who later appointed him to serve as ambassador to India. President Ford then appointed him ambassador to the United Nations. He also worked in both the Kennedy and Johnson administrations. In 1976, New Yorkers elected him to the US Senate, where he served four terms until his retirement in 2000. He died in 2003.

5. Tydings quoted in Associated Press, "Many D.C. Unwed Mothers Hazy about Birds and Bees," *Lancaster (PA) Intelligence Journal*, June 24, 1965.

6. Senator Joseph D. Tydings, testimony before the Subcommittee on Foreign Aid Expenditures of the Senate Committee on Government Operations in support of legislation that would create a new Office of Population Problems within the Department of Health, Education and Welfare, June 23, 1965, copy in the Joseph D. Tydings Collection, Hornbake Library, University of Maryland, College Park.

Following Muskie's lead, I supported and introduced measures over the next several years to control harmful aquatic plants, to study the availability of water resources in the Delaware-Maryland-Virginia peninsula, and to make a national estuarine pollution study a key part of the Clean Water Act of 1966. Recognizing that the "edge" area where water meets land is usually the key to the health of rivers and bays, I pushed for legislation to do a national shoreline study in 1968 and supported the creation of the National Coastal Zone Management Program.

To address air pollution issues, our committee held hearings in 1967 in Los Angeles, Seattle, Denver, St. Louis, and elsewhere—and I attended them all. One of the biggest local problems we faced in my own locale was the air pollution spewing from the Kenilworth dump, a landfill in northeast Washington adjacent to Prince George's County where municipal waste was burned almost around the clock. You could see the pollution in the air and, worse, depending on which way the wind was blowing, you could smell it.

Gladys Noon Spellman, a member of what was then called the Prince George's County Board of Commissioners and later the representative of that district in Congress, was my ally and the star witness at our hearings. "Senator," she testified, "I don't know how bad to tell you the problem is, but I tell my children to take their breaths in small gulps."[7]

By 1968, I had finally stopped the burning at the landfill, and the Kenilworth dump had closed by 1970. The land, which is on a tributary to the Anacostia River, has since been reclaimed and is now a small national park.

Federal Involvement in Family Planning

The Johnson administration, as part of the War on Poverty, began requiring the federal government in 1965 to provide subsidies to help lower-income families obtain access to birth control.

7. Representative Gladys Noon Spellman's testimony at a hearing on air pollution issues was recounted by John McEvoy in an interview by the author on October 13, 2015, in Alexandria, Virginia, October 13, 2015. McEvoy was Tydings's principal staff director when he chaired the DC Committee.

It was obvious to me that any effective campaign to eliminate poverty had to include programs that made family planning information and contraceptive devices available to all who desired them, particularly the poorest of our citizens. It is imperative that we give all our citizens the right to plan the size of their families—a right the affluent have long enjoyed.

To expand this effort, in 1967 I introduced a bill for national family planning services and research, but the legislation stalled. Then my staunchest ally, Senator Gruening, was defeated for reelection in 1968, and I became the Senate leader on family planning issues by default.

Although I was worried about the population problem in the United States, I was even more concerned about the huge increases in developing countries, a population boom that could be traced to the public health revolution that had spread around the globe in the decades following World War I. Before that, rural farming families in third world countries often produced huge families to compensate for the low infant survival rate. Once people in those countries learned not to drink contaminated water or began to eliminate pools of standing water where mosquitoes bred, they began to avoid epidemics such as cholera or malaria. Family survival rates increased geometrically, and with that the number of mouths to feed. It did not take long before these families sank into poverty and began abandoning young children they could not afford to feed. This, in turn, has contributed to the growth of horrible slums in India, parts of Asia and Africa, Brazil, Central America, and elsewhere.

With the help of Senator Fulbright, who chaired the Foreign Relations Committee, I was able to tack onto the foreign aid appropriation bill an amendment requiring that a percentage of US foreign aid had to be spent on voluntary family planning projects. I am distressed to say that, to our ultimate detriment, the newly installed Trump administration immediately began trying to halt funding for similar programs around the world. Such actions are so shortsighted.

I remained deeply involved in the campaign for population control even after I left the Senate in 1971. General Draper, in fact, asked me to head the Population Crisis Committee, but I faced the cost of school tuition for my four young children and felt I could not afford to do so. Instead, I negotiated a payment to my law firm in exchange for about a quarter of my time to help raise money for the cause.

We recruited Senator Taft and Generals William Westmoreland and Maxwell Taylor of the US Army to the Population Crisis Commission board. The generals immediately understood the threat that burgeoning population growth was having on global stability. We also helped organize the first international worldwide family planning conference, held in Bucharest, Romania, in August 1974. That conference helped leaders of countries in the developing world begin to see why it was in their interest to slow their population growth so they could afford to educate young people and provide them with job opportunities.

The United Nations effort became hugely successful after the United States agreed to match every dollar contributed by other countries. It was successful until the conservative Republican Ronald Reagan became president in 1981 and halted all US contributions, essentially killing the world population program.

The Population Bomb and Born to Starve

The population issue received an unexpected boost in 1968 with the publication of a hugely influential book called *The Population Bomb*, written by Paul Ehrlich, a Stanford University professor. A short summary of Ehrlich's thesis was that humans faced certain and almost imminent mass starvation due to overpopulation. Clearly that has not happened, at least not on the global scale he predicted, but the book and the dire forecasts it contained became a national sensation. People everywhere—including in Congress and the White House—suddenly began talking seriously about the population problem.[8]

Two years later, I followed up with my own book on the topic, *Born to Starve*. While it never had the broad impact of *The Population Bomb*, *Born to Starve* recommended that the United States launch a comprehensive attack on the population problem, both at home and abroad. It called for expansion of family planning services and clinics and support for groups such as Planned Parenthood that provide family planning information to those who want it. It recommended that the country support more research on contraception and develop a better birth control pill. It said Congress should create a joint standing committee on

---

8. Paul R. Ehrlich, *The Population Bomb* (New York: Ballantine Books, 1968).

population issues, that a Cabinet-level department dealing with population and the environment be established, and that the president should have a special assistant focused on the topic. I thought the threat of overpopulation was that important.[9]

Even more controversially, the book made the case that, regardless of one's personal view of the morality of abortions, the legal restrictions on abortions should be repealed because they had created an illegal abortion racket that was dangerous to women. Of course, the restrictions that are being placed on abortions in many states today—states, I must point out, that are almost uniformly controlled by Republicans— are just as draconian and threatening to women.[10]

I find this strange because in the days I was in the Senate, Republicans were as supportive of the expansion of family planning services as Democrats—Richard Nixon among them.[11] My counterpart in the House of Representatives on family planning matters, in fact, was none other than George H. W. Bush, later the forty-first president. We worked so closely together on the issue that I later honored him with a luncheon reception at Oakington.

Like so many things in the Congress, it took several years before the National Family Planning Services Act was realized. By the time it was

9. Joseph D. Tydings, *Born to Starve* (New York: William Morrow 1970). The foreword to the book was written by Professor Ehrlich.

10. "Since 2011, more than 280 laws have been passed across 31 states to limit or restrict access to abortion. Some target women seeking the procedure, making the process more onerous (multiple clinic visits), more time-consuming (mandatory waiting periods), more costly (the procedure is not covered by federal Medicaid programs and in some states cannot be covered by private insurance plans that participate in Obamacare) and more shaming (forced ultrasounds, brochures on adoption, and mandatory counseling services replete with false information and scare tactics that operate under the assumption that a woman cannot be trusted to make an informed decision on her own). But the real game-changer came when the anti-choice movement realized that instead of targeting women—which was kind of bad for PR and maybe flew in the face of the Constitution—they could target providers . . . under the auspices of 'protecting women's health. . . . States can't overturn *Roe v. Wade*, but they can regulate health care." Alex Morris, "The War on Planned Parenthood: Inside the Republican Stealth Campaign to Dismantle Women's Reproductive Rights," *Rolling Stone*, April 21, 2016, 60.

11. Despite his many faults, Richard Nixon was actually a moderate and successful president on domestic issues. I supported him, for example, when he established the Council on Environmental Quality in 1969 and created the US Environmental Protection Agency in 1970. These two entities have helped protect our air, water, and land for nearly half a century, and without them I am afraid our environment would resemble that of China.

finally signed into law by President Nixon at a special ceremony the day after Christmas in 1970, I, too, had lost my seat in the Senate and was not even invited to the signing ceremony, though I was the author and still in office.

Opposition to family planning efforts soon started with religious zealots but has since been totally subsumed by the Republican Party. The GOP has become nothing short of an extremist group with regard to family planning. Typical of the party approach was the Republicans' recent—and totally unjustified—attack on federal funding for Planned Parenthood.

I not only have supported and raised money for Planned Parenthood for decades but was honored in 1970 to receive the annual Margaret Sanger Award from the organization in recognition of the work I had done in the Senate on behalf of family planning.[12] After all these years, I am still proud to be the author of the legislation that provides federal funding for family planning. Current arguments over abortion and Planned Parenthood are, in some ways, about the family planning legislation my allies and I pushed through the Congress a half century ago.

The Chesapeake Bay

Throughout my life, I have tried to keep tabs on the health of the Chesapeake, in part, by monitoring the annual harvest of crabs and oysters. Those numbers go up and down year to year, but the general trend has been down. The biggest crab haul in Maryland was back in 1993, some 57 million pounds. By 2000, it had dropped to its lowest level ever, 21.7 million pounds. By 2015, the catch had rebounded to 31 million pounds,

12. The Margaret Sanger Award citation reads as follows: "Senator Joseph D. Tydings guided Congress toward recognizing family planning as a basic human right of all Americans. He introduced 15 different bills concerned with the provision of family planning services and the exploration of population issues. In 1966, when he first introduced legislation to provide voluntary family planning services to American women, such services were virtually nonexistent. The following year, he led the way as Congress included family planning services in the maternal and child health provisions of the Social Security Act amendments and in the Economic Opportunity Act amendments. He also worked for the inclusion of family planning provisions in foreign aid legislation." PPFA Margaret Sanger Award Winners, 1970, Planned Parenthood, https://www.plannedparenthood.org/about-us/newsroom/ppfa-margaret-sanger-award-winners#Tydings.

but I am not optimistic that crabbing will ever again be like it was.

The decline of oysters in the bay is even more frightening because it threatens one of the most productive estuaries on earth. Oysters are critically important to the bay because they serve as natural filters for the water. But disease, pollution, and overharvesting have decimated oyster numbers. From an all-time high harvest of 3.24 million bushels in 1937, the catch fell to an all-time low of only 27,000 bushels in 2003. It, too, has rebounded slightly, to 380,000 bushels in 2014, but that is only about 12 percent of the all-time high.[13]

It is sad what has happened to the bay. Part of the problem stems from our inability, or unwillingness, to protect it from nutrients that are robbing the water of life-supporting oxygen. We have done a pretty good job cleaning up sewage disposal systems and other so-called "point sources" of pollution. Where we have failed is in the harder-to-regulate "nonpoint sources" of pollution, such as the massive runoff of nutrient-rich fertilizer from farm fields and the stormwater runoff from shopping centers and massive suburban development along the shoreline. In many of the rural counties in the state, heavy political contributions from the real estate industry have given it tacit control over local environmental regulations.

I attribute our failing in this area, at least in part, to the political power wielded by industrial agricultural operations—Big Chicken in Maryland, Delaware, and the Eastern Shore of Virginia, and Big Pork, which operates the feedlots in North Carolina and other states. Using richly compensated lobbyists in Annapolis, Dover, Richmond, and Raleigh, these industries have all but purchased the regulations they want. The Chesapeake Bay and other waterways have suffered as a result.

If we want even the environmental regulations that are currently on the books to be enforced, then as a society we need to insist that our state legislatures provide the funding necessary—at a minimum—to hire a sufficient number of environmental inspectors to monitor what is happening, quite literally, in the field. Instead, the Trump administration has already begun a massive rollback of environmental regulations, including gutting the critically important Chesapeake Bay protection

13. Crab and oyster harvest statistics provided by the Fisheries Service of the Maryland Department of Natural Resources, http://dnr2.maryland.gov/fisheries/Pages/default.aspx.

program, opening national parks to mining and other damaging industries, and eliminating a science advisory panel at the Environmental Protection Agency. Worse, Trump has withdrawn the United States from participation in a 2015 global compact to reduce the causes of climate change. These are unforgivable attacks on the environmental protections that make our air safe to breathe, our water safe to drink, our land safe from toxic poisons. It undermines the global attempt to keep our planet from dangerously overheating, which is already causing floods, forest fires, hurricanes, tornadoes, and other increasingly frequent incidents of extreme weather.

Trump has been aided and abetted in these attacks by the billions of dollars spent by Charles G. and David H. Koch, the fabulously rich, right-wing oil industry barons who head Koch Industries and back a variety of conservative and libertarian causes. Among other activities, the Koch brothers have fought to keep pollution protections off the books in every state and county in the nation by donating millions of dollars to Tea Party and other extremist candidates. Republican members of Congress and state legislatures blindly follow the Koch brothers' lead, fearful that if they do not the Koch brothers will finance a political opponent or run political ads against them.

Our children, grandchildren, and great-grandchildren will pay a tragic, tragic price for the greedy, shortsighted, and insane policies being promoted by the Trump administration and the Koch brothers.

The other way to protect the environment for future generations is to preserve the most beautiful and pristine areas we have left. In my first year in office, I helped Danny Brewster pass legislation to establish Assateague Island National Reserve, an action that permanently cost us votes in Worcester County. The thirty-three-mile-long Assateague Island had been in imminent danger of being forever changed by planned large-scale residential and commercial development, and the moneyed interests did not like our intrusion into their local affairs. Representative Rogers C. B. Morton, a Maryland Republican, supported us on the Assateague proposal, something it is difficult to imagine antienvironment Republicans doing today.

I also supported the creation of Tuckahoe State Park on the Eastern Shore of Maryland, and it was my bill that included the Youghiogheny River, which runs north through far western Maryland toward

Pittsburgh, under the new Wild Rivers Act. I successfully stopped the construction of power lines that would have marred the vistas of the historic Antietam National Battlefield west of Frederick; I warned of the dangers of pesticides, such as DDT; and I supported efforts to create a model of the Chesapeake Bay so that scientists could study the effects of currents and salinity.[14] I spoke at the first Earth Day celebration in Maryland at my alma mater, the University of Maryland. (By contrast, Trump and his Interior Department have reduced the size of two federally protected national monuments in Utah—Bears Ears and Grand Staircase-Escalante—despite opposition from local Native Americans, preservationists, and environmentalists.)

When plans were unveiled to build a nuclear power plant at Calvert Cliffs in southern Maryland, I organized and chaired nearly two weeks of public hearings about the potential environmental effects. I must admit, however, I went into those hearings opposed to building the plant and came away from them educated on the issues and a lifelong advocate for nuclear power.

Prayer Breakfast

Beginning in my days in the Senate, I have been invited about once every four or five years to speak at the National Prayer Breakfast. Over the past two decades, I have often given the same message about the damage we are collectively doing to our fragile environment.[15]

I often open my talk by quoting from the Book of Isaiah in the Bible, which says, in part, "The earth mourneth and fadeth away, the world languisheth and fadeth away, the haughty people of the earth do languish. The earth also is defiled under the inhabitants thereof; because they have transgressed the laws, changed the ordinance, broken the everlasting covenant."[16]

---

14. The model, built on Kent Island, did not open until 1978, and it operated for only three years before high operating costs and technical problems forced closure. It covered a surface eight acres in size, was sculpted by hand in cement, and was a 1:1,000 scale analog of the actual bay.

15. When Albert Gore Jr., of Tennessee, was a freshman senator, he heard my speech at one of the prayer breakfasts and was so taken by the environmental message that he asked me for a copy. He later told me it influenced his own thinking on environmental issues.

16. The whole passage I usually offer is as follows: "Behold, the Lord maketh the earth empty, and maketh it waste, and turneth it upside down, and scattereth abroad the inhabitants

Then, before reviewing the depressing global statistics about population growth, deforestation, water shortages, the expansion of deserts, and the depletion of natural resources, I read the poignant letter the Suquamish Chief Seattle sent to President Millard Fillmore in 1852 in response to a request by the US government that the tribe sell land in what is now Washington State to accommodate the western migration of US citizens:

> The President in Washington sends word that he wishes to buy our land. But how can you buy or sell the sky? The land? The idea is strange to us. If we do not own the freshness of the air and the sparkle of the water, how can you buy them?
>
> Every part of this earth is sacred to my people. Every shining pine needle, every sandy shore, every mist in the dark woods, every meadow, every humming insect. All are holy in the memory and experience of my people.
>
> We know the sap which courses through the trees as we know the blood that courses through our veins. We are part of the earth and it is part of us. The perfumed flowers are our sisters. The bear, the deer, the great eagle, these are our brothers. The rocky crests, the juices in the meadow, the body heat of the pony, and man, all belong to the same family.
>
> The shining water that moves in the streams and rivers is not just water, but the blood of our ancestors. If we sell you our land, you must remember that it is sacred. Each ghostly reflection in the clear waters of the lakes tells of events and memories in the life of my people. The water's murmur is the voice of my father's father.
>
> The rivers are our brothers. They quench our thirst. They carry our canoes and feed our children. So you must give to the rivers the kindness you would give any brother.

thereof. . . . The earth mourneth and fadeth away, the world languisheth and fadeth away, the haughty people of the earth do languish. The earth also is defiled under the inhabitants thereof; because they have transgressed the laws, changed the ordinance, broken the everlasting covenant. Therefore hath the curse devoured the earth, and they that dwell therein are desolate: therefore the inhabitants of the earth are burned, and few men left. . . . The earth is utterly broken down, the earth is clean dissolved, the earth is moved exceedingly." Isaiah 24:1, 4–6, 19 (KJV).

If we sell you our land, remember that the air is precious to us, that the air shares its spirit with all the life it supports. The wind that gave our grandfather his first breath also receives his last sigh. The wind also gives our children the spirit of life. So if we sell you our land, you must keep it apart and sacred, as a place where man can go to taste the wind that is sweetened by the meadow flowers.

Will you teach your children what we have taught our children? That the earth is our mother? What befalls the earth befalls all the sons of the earth.

This we know: the earth does not belong to man, man belongs to the earth. All things are connected like the blood that unites us all. Man did not weave the web of life, he is merely a strand in it. Whatever he does to the web, he does to himself.

One thing we know: our god is also your god. The earth is precious to him and to harm the earth is to heap contempt on its creator.

We love this earth as a newborn loves its mother's heartbeat. So, if we sell you our land, love it as we have loved it. Care for it as we have cared for it. Hold in your mind the memory of the land as it is when you receive it. Preserve the land for all children and love it, as God loves us all.

CHAPTER 19

Gun Control

On a sweltering Sunday morning the day after Bobby Kennedy was laid to rest next to his brother at Arlington National Cemetery, my staff and I met in our otherwise empty Senate offices to talk about what I should say later that morning on the NBC news program *Meet the Press* and how could I use the opportunity to honor Bobby's memory.

All of us were emotionally destroyed. Heartbroken. Almost physically sick. It was as if all hope was gone. Part of the feeling was anger—anger that the world could be so cruel, so heartless, so savage.

Although distraught, I had agreed to a request from Bobby's staff to take his place on *Meet the Press*. Because he had been assassinated with a handgun, we thought the issue of gun violence would come up. I thought I really had to take advantage of this opportunity to do something meaningful in his memory. I knew gun control was a nearly impossible issue but that this was probably the best opportunity I would ever have to lay it out before the American people. I thought that one way to pay proper tribute to Bobby was to find some way to convince voters to do something to curtail gun violence.

I began dictating to my staff elements of the gun control legislation I intended to introduce as soon as the Senate reconvened. I wanted every gun in the country to be registered and local police departments to issue licenses before people were allowed to keep or purchase guns. Licenses would help keep guns out of the hands of felons, drug addicts, alcoholics, the mentally ill, or others who could pose a danger to society. I wanted to make it clear that sports enthusiasts who wanted guns for hunting or target shooting, or families who wanted guns for home protection, would have access to them. But the evidence was overwhelming: we had to get control of the gun violence in our country—violence that had taken the lives of President Kennedy, Dr. Martin Luther King Jr., and now Senator Robert F. Kennedy, not to mention the lives of thousands of ordinary citizens.

I certainly knew that my proposal would be unpopular with hunters in rural Maryland, including blue-collar union members who otherwise should have been supporting me. But I did not want to squander the opportunity to add meaning to Bobby's tragic death.

On the air that morning, I tried to be measured in my comments, telling the moderator, Lawrence Spivak, that "we need a responsible, sane gun policy in this country."[1] But when asked specifically what I thought about confiscation of firearms, particularly pistols, I could not hold back. I said the legislation I intended to propose would let local police refuse to issue a gun license if an applicant had a criminal record.

"I think that is a minimum step, a responsible step, and if you couldn't meet those requirements, then I think the government should pay you just compensation and you should turn [the gun] in," I said. "A person who is an alcoholic, who has a record of conviction involved in riots or a felony, they shouldn't be permitted to own a gun. The gun should be turned in and confiscated."[2]

I had co-sponsored and supported gun-control laws ever since I arrived in the Senate, so the National Rifle Association (NRA) was not particularly friendly toward me even before my *Meet the Press* interview. But those legislative proposals really got their attention, and I would later pay the price.[3]

---

1. Senator Joseph D. Tydings, transcript of televised interview on the NBC television show *Meet the Press*, vol. 12, no. 23, June 9, 1968, 1.

2. Ibid., 5.

3. The National Rifle Association (NRA) was an old institution, first chartered in New York State in 1871. It was organized in part to improve the poor marksmanship that Union soldiers had displayed in the Civil War. The founders of the group were Colonel William C. Church, editor of the *Army and Navy Journal*, and General George Wingate, and the first NRA president was former Union General Ambrose Burnside. The NRA formed the Legislative Affairs Division after the National Firearms Act of 1934 became the first federal gun-control law. Karl Frederick, the NRA president, testified in 1934, "I have never believed in the general practice of carrying weapons. I seldom carry one. . . . I do not believe in the general promiscuous toting of guns. I think it should be sharply restricted and only under licenses." Quoted in "National Rifle Association," Wikipedia, https://en.wikipedia.org/wiki/National_Rifle_Association. For decades, the NRA focused on sports enthusiasts, hunters, and target shooters. But that changed in the mid-1970s, when a group of gun-rights activists took control of the organization and established a lobbying arm, the NRA Institute for Legislative Action. The organization became an increasingly potent force both in Congress and in state legislatures around the country. Lily Rothman, "The Original Reason the NRA Was Founded," *Time*, November 17, 2015, http://time.com/4106381/nra-1871-history/; "A Brief History of the NRA," National Rifle Association, https://home.nra.org/about-the-nra/.

Mail-Order Rifles

I first became focused on the need for gun control after President Kennedy was assassinated. The rifle Lee Harvey Oswald used had been ordered through the mail under an assumed name from an ad he had seen in the NRA magazine, the *American Rifleman*, no questions asked. The gun was delivered to a Dallas post office box without violating any laws. In my second month in the Senate, I issued a long statement on firearms control, saying I intended "to exert every effort to obtain adequate and effective gun control laws."[4]

At the 1965 national meeting of the American Bar Association during my first year in the Senate, I agreed to publicly debate Harold Glassen, the NRA president, about the need for Congress to pass a bill I had co-sponsored that would stop the mail-order sale of rifles and shotguns. No other more senior senator was willing to do so. I argued the statistics, saying that in 1965 alone, guns had been used in 5,600 murders, 34,700 aggravated assaults, and the vast majority of 68,400 armed robberies. Of all law enforcement officers murdered that year, 96 percent were killed with firearms.

"The startling fact is that it is easier in nearly every state in the Union to buy a gun than to register to vote, get a driver's license, or even [obtain] a prescription cold remedy," I said.[5]

I realized then, as I do now, how difficult it would be to pass gun-control legislation. Not even a half century of increasingly frequent mass shootings in this country has sparked a movement that can overcome the well-funded opposition of the NRA. Not even the horror of the massacre of twenty six-and seven-year-olds and six adult educators at Sandy Hook Elementary School in Newtown, Connecticut, in 2012 could pry loose the ferocious grip the NRA has on Congress. Our inability, or unwillingness, to address our culture of gun violence is an international embarrassment.

4. Senator Joseph D. Tydings, statement on firearms control, February 25, 1965, Joseph D. Tydings Collection, Hornbake Library, University of Maryland, College Park.

5. Senator Joseph D. Tydings, in debate with Harold Glassen, president of the National Rifle Association, National Press Club, June 29, 1967. "Who Can Reasonably Oppose Firearms Control?" statement by Senator Joseph D. Tydings, National Press Club, Washington, DC, June 29, 1967, Tydings Collection, Hornbake Library.

I proposed in 1965 what I thought would be an acceptable, commonsense amendment to the National Firearms Act to prohibit unrestricted shipment of long guns through the US mail.

"It does not in any manner infringe upon the rights of hunters, sportsmen, gun collectors, or the average citizen who wants to protect his home or business," I said, adding, "We know that President John F. Kennedy was shot and killed with a mail order gun. Had there been effective control on the sale of firearms, this great man might be living today. . . . The need for firearms control is unquestionable."[6] At this time the issue was bipartisan. The NRA did not gain complete control of the Republican Party until Nixon was president.

Because I was on the Senate District of Columbia Committee, I next proposed that all pistols in the district be registered and that felons, addicts, and persons with mental illnesses be prohibited from having them. By summer, I was applauding a Prince George's County ordinance that required a five-day waiting period before a gun could be purchased. I engaged in a series of gun-control debates around the country with NRA representatives. I had supported gun-control measures introduced in the Senate by Thomas Dodd of Connecticut.

But nothing happened. The proposed ban on mail-order sales died, and the Senate just moved on to other issues.

After race riots broke out in more than 150 American cities in 1967, the controversy over guns was suddenly back in the news. But while some saw the riots as a reason to enact tougher laws to control guns, others saw the riots as a reason for more Americans to be armed. We see the same phenomenon today: every time there is a mass shooting somewhere, gun sales soar. By some measurements, there are almost as many guns as people in the United States. What research conclusively shows is that where there are more guns, there are more incidents of homicide, of suicide, and of children or others being killed in gun accidents. States with stricter gun-control laws have fewer deaths from gun-related violence.[7]

I debated the gun issue on TV and wrote newspaper and magazine articles on the topic. In a *Baltimore Magazine* article in April 1968, I

6. Tydings statement on firearms control, February 25, 1965.

7. Max Ehrenfreund, "Shooting in Oregon: 11 Essential Facts about Guns and Mass Shootings in America," *Washington Post*, October 1, 2015.

noted that polling done by the Gallup organization showed that three-quarters of all American citizens wanted mail-order gun sales prohibited, that 85 percent wanted all handguns registered, and that 73 percent wanted rifles and shotguns registered. Using the best comparative statistics I could find, I noted that there had been 4,954 gun murders in the United States in 1962, compared with 29 in Great Britain, 9 in Belgium, 6 in Denmark, 5 in Sweden, and none in the Netherlands.[8]

Still, nothing would move Congress to act. This was the result of intense NRA lobbying, as well as opposition from rural southern and western legislators—including Senator James Eastland, the Judiciary Committee chair—who simply opposed the concept of gun control, especially federal gun control. They generally supported the right of Americans to own almost any kind or number of guns they wanted. The NRA public relations campaign had effectively convinced US hunters that gun control was really the first step in a campaign to completely disarm law-abiding citizens and to impose unfair restrictions on legitimate gun use. They said criminals, meanwhile, would still get guns regardless of any law.

The NRA public relations team and lobbyists latched onto a position that gun-control laws would violate the Second Amendment to the Constitution, which states, "A well-regulated militia being necessary to the security of a free state, the right of the people to keep and bear arms shall not be infringed."

The Second Amendment was adopted by the first US Congress in the Bill of Rights as a direct result of the British attempt in 1775 to seize the firearms that the Massachusetts militia had stored in Lexington. (In that era, most members of the militia could not have afforded to buy their own firearms.) I found this Second Amendment argument the least valid of all, but in recent years the conservative majority on the Supreme Court under Chief Justice John Roberts has overturned two hundred years of prior Supreme Court rulings by declaring local gun-control laws to be in violation of the Second Amendment, thus opening the floodgates to gun violence in America.[9]

---

8. "The Gun Bill: Should It Pass?" "Yes" and "no" companion pieces by Senator Joseph D. Tydings and Baltimore outdoor writer G. Howard Gillelan, respectively, in *Baltimore Magazine*, April 1968.

9. In a 2010 case, *McDonald v. Chicago*, the Supreme Court overturned the gun-registration law in Chicago by concluding that the right of an individual to "keep and bear arms" was protected by the Second Amendment and that right supersedes state laws. In a 2008 case, *District of Columbia v. Heller*, the high court reached the same conclusion with regard to federal

The National Gun Crime Prevention Act of 1968

"Our gun laws are about as flimsy as those of any nation in the world," I bitterly observed after Bobby was assassinated in June 1968. "We tolerate a level of gun crime in this country which is unthinkable in any civilized nation in the Western World. . . . How much longer will we tolerate this carnage? I intend to move in Congress for much stronger federal gun laws to keep guns from maniacs, criminals and juveniles. I am confident the American people will support such an effort."[10]

Or so it seemed. When I introduced a national gun crime prevention bill on June 12, 1968, eighteen senators—including Majority Leader Mike Mansfield from rural Montana and some Republicans—signed on as co-sponsors. Within a week, I had received more than ten thousand letters, telegrams, and telephone calls from all over the country demanding, by a 20-to-1 margin, a strong federal gun-control law. I also received petitions with fourteen thousand signatures in favor of such a law. In speeches, I noted that Bobby Kennedy had been the only presidential candidate in 1968 to support stronger gun control.

"For history will also record, with tragic irony, that on June 5, 1968, a madman with a cheap pistol cut down that candidate for President of the United States and took his life," I said.[11]

I hoped that this latest tragedy would awaken Congress and finally persuade it to act. But I felt I needed President Johnson's backing to get it through, even though by then Johnson was a lame duck. There had been rumors that he might introduce a gun bill of his own, and I wanted to make sure that whatever the president proposed was at least as strong as my bill.

Johnson had always been cautious about me because I was so closely identified with the Kennedys, and he had become seriously unhappy with me after I came out publicly against the Vietnam War. I knew, nevertheless, I had to have the president's backing. I reluctantly agreed to

enclaves, such as the District of Columbia, and overturned the DC ban on handguns. Both rulings were made on 5-to-4 votes. But in 2015, the Supreme Court allowed a ban on assault rifles in a Chicago suburb (*Friedman v. Highland Park*) by refusing to hear an appeal of a lower court ruling supporting the ban. Whether that will prompt other communities to enact similar bans remains to be seen.

10. Senator Joseph D. Tydings, statement regarding the assassination attempt on Robert F. Kennedy (released before it was known that Senator Kennedy had died), June 5, 1968, Tydings Collection, Hornbake Library.

11. Senator Joseph D. Tydings, speech on gun-control issues delivered during a conference at the University of Maryland, June 18, 1968, Tydings Collection, Hornbake Library.

have my secretary call the White House to see if she could schedule a meeting for me with the president, but I told my staff I would be surprised if I could get in to see him within two months.

My secretary put in the call and suddenly she said to me, "The president's on the line."

"What?" I asked incredulously. "The president's on the line?"

"Yes," she replied. "The president's on the line!"

"Mr. President," I blurted into the phone as if I had fully expected him to take my call. I then went on for probably three or four minutes about what a great job he was doing leading the country, how I admired his courage and moral leadership, and how respected he was throughout America. Finally, I got to the point and said, "Mr. President, I really need your help on this gun-control matter."

"Gun control? Gun control?" Johnson almost shouted into the phone. "Who am I talking to? Who the hell am I talking to?"

"Mr. President," I said, "it is Joe Tydings, the junior senator from Maryland."

"Joe, Jesus Christ, I've got five important telephone calls on here waiting to talk to me. Write me a letter, will you?" And he hung up.

Somehow, my secretary's request for a meeting had been inadvertently switched directly into the Oval Office and Johnson had blindly taken the call. When he picked up, he had no idea who he was talking to! In the end, though, it was effective because the president dispatched Attorney General Ramsey Clark to testify in support of my bill. Not long after that, the president introduced his own gun-control legislation, which pretty much copied mine.[12]

In June 1968, President Johnson sent me a letter expressing his support for licensing and regulation of all guns. "I want to tell you how much I value your efforts and leadership in this field as we strive to bring sane, sensible and long-overdue gun controls to the American people,"

12. The legislation would have eliminated mail-order gun sales across state lines, prohibited over-the-counter sale of handguns to nonresidents of the state in which the sale is made, prohibited the sale of rifles and shotguns to anyone under eighteen, and prohibited the sale of handguns to anyone under twenty-one. It also would have required federal licensing of all dealers, importers, and manufacturers of firearms, but—importantly—did not seek to require registration of firearms or licensing of firearm owners. The legislation also would have prohibited importation of military surplus handguns, would have regulated importation of all firearms, and would have placed stringent controls on devices such as hand grenades, antitank guns, bazookas, mortars, and similar military weapons.

he wrote.[13] The president's bill was endorsed by Clark, by state and local police, and by FBI Director J. Edgar Hoover. It appeared to have strong public backing. But even with all of that support, the NRA lobbying was so strong that Congress produced little more than a half-measure.

We had trouble, in fact, even getting a bill reported out of the Judiciary Committee. I kept calling for a vote and the committee chair, Eastland, kept saying, "Joe, I don't think we're going to vote today."

Steadily, our co-sponsors withdrew their support. In the end, we got the tiniest of victories: rifles and shotguns were added to a previously enacted ban on the mail-order sale of handguns across state lines. I tried one last time to amend the bill on the Senate floor to reinstate registration and licensing, but by then even Majority Leader Mansfield had abandoned the effort.

Bobby Kennedy's death was not avenged. In future years, assassins attempted to kill two presidents (Gerald Ford and Ronald Reagan) and one candidate for president, George C. Wallace; Representative Gabrielle Giffords of Arizona, as she met with constituents in her home state; and Representative Steve Scalise of Louisiana as he and other Republicans practiced for a charity baseball game.

And the carnage in our communities continues unabated.[14] Names such as Newtown, Connecticut; Columbine, Colorado; the Navy Yard in

---

13. President Lyndon B. Johnson to Senator Joseph D. Tydings, June 24, 1968, in possession of Senator Tydings.

14. There has been considerable private research on gun violence and mass shootings, yet there are many variables for each study, including the countries and the periods of time studied, how the term "mass shooting" is defined, and many other details, including the point of view or political persuasion of the researchers. Adam Lankford, an associate professor at the University of Alabama in the Department of Criminal Justice, studied mass shootings around the world from 1966 to 2012. Among his conclusions:

- Countries with higher rates of gun ownership recorded more mass shootings per capita.
- The United States ranks first in gun ownership per capita, with roughly 270 million firearms, or 89 firearms per 100 residents, according to the Small Arms Survey 2011, a Geneva-based research project that collects information on small arms. Yemen ranks second; Switzerland, where every citizen is obligated to serve in the national militia, is third.
- The United States represents less than 5 percent of the 7.3 billion global population but accounted for 31 percent of global mass shootings during the period from 1966 to 2012, more than any other country.
- Researchers counted 23 mass shootings in 13 European nations in addition to Russia from 2000 to 2014, with 203 deaths. During that time, the United States had 133 such shootings and 487 deaths.

Joe Palazzolo and Alexis Flynn, "Researchers Cite Link between Gun Ownership, Attacks but Say Comparisons Difficult," *Wall Street Journal*, October 3, 2015.

Washington, DC, and the Emanuel African Methodist Episcopal Church in Charleston, South Carolina, have all become shorthand for senseless mass slaughter with firearms purchased with no reasonable checks or restrictions.

Public polling continues to show that the majority of Americans strongly support background checks for private and gun show sales, preventing those with mental illnesses from purchasing guns, a federal database to track gun sales, a ban on semiautomatic weapons, and more.[15] Yet Congress remains frozen by the power of the NRA.

Few have so eloquently captured the deep anguish caused by this shameful aspect of American culture as President Obama did after yet another mass murder of innocents at Umpqua Community College in Oregon in October 2015.

"Somehow this has become routine," he said, his weary sadness obvious. "The reporting is routine. My response here at this podium ends up being routine. The conversation in the aftermath of it. We've become numb to this."[16]

Just a month later, fourteen were killed and twenty-one injured in a terrorist shooting at a social services office facility in San Bernardino, California. The assault rifles they used in the attack had been legally purchased by a friend. Some Republican candidates in the 2016 presidential race responded with the insane assertion that such attacks might be prevented if only more Americans were armed! Betsy DeVos, the woman President Trump nominated for secretary of education, even defended the idea of allowing guns in public schools with this bizarre rationale: "I would imagine that there's probably [the need for] a gun in the school to protect from potential grizzlies."[17] To me, it is all just unbelievable.

With every passing year, the problem only seems to get worse. In June 2016, the allegedly homophobic son of an Afghan immigrant claimed

15. Ehrenfreund, "Shooting in Oregon."

16. Gun control, President Obama said, has to be a large part of the solution. "The United States of America is the one advanced nation on Earth in which we do not have sufficient common-sense gun-safety laws—even in the face of repeated mass killings," he said. Quoted in Jesse Singal, "We Can't Predict Who Will Commit a Mass Shooting; Gun Control Is the Only Way Out," *New York Magazine*, October 2, 2015, http://nymag.com/scienceofus/2015/10/gun-control-is-the-only-way-out.html#.

17. Quoted in Alastair Jamieson, "Betsy DeVos Cites Grizzly Bears during Guns-in-Schools Debate," NBC News, January 18, 2017, http://www.nbcnews.com/news/us-news/betsy-devos-schools-might-need-guns-due-potential-grizzlies-n708261.

to be a follower of the Islamic State and then entered a gay nightclub in Orlando, Florida, armed with an assault rifle and handgun. He killed forty-nine people and injured fifty-three more. He had apparently bought the weapons legally just two days before the massacre even though he had previously been on an FBI terror watch list. In October 2017 yet another assailant grimly claimed a new US record for mass shooting deaths by killing fifty-eight people and injuring another 546 at a Las Vegas music festival.

The idea that the United States is the only country in the world where any citizen, even one with a criminal record or who is a clear danger to society, can buy one of these military-style automatic assault weapons is insanity and endangers the life of every citizen.

Here is how bad it has gotten: there have been so many incidents of serious gun violence in this country that, following the San Bernardino shooting, the *Washington Post* felt compelled to write a half-page-long article sorting out the statistical differences between "regular shootings, mass shootings, mass killings, and massacres."[18]

As this senseless (and, to some extent, preventable) carnage has continued unabated, the *Post* has published an updated roundup of mass shootings, complete with an interactive online graphic: "The death tolls change, the places change: Nine in a church, 26 in an elementary school, 49 in a nightclub, five in an airport. The faces in the memorial photos change every time. But the weapons are the common denominator," the *Post* reported on June 6, 2017. "Mass killings in the United States are most often carried out with guns, usually handguns, most of them obtained legally."[19]

NRA Opposition

I had always hoped that I could defend myself against the NRA attacks because I was such an avid hunter. I had spent a good portion of my formative years with my father and his friends hunting ducks and geese on

18. Christopher Ingraham, "What Makes a Shooting a 'Mass Shooting'?," *Washington Post*, December 4, 2015, A11.

19. Bonnie Berkowitz, Lazaro Gamio, Denise Lu, Kevin Uhrmacher, and Todd Lindeman, "The Math of Mass Shootings," *Washington Post*, June 6, 2017, https://www.washingtonpost.com/graphics/national/mass-shootings-in-america/?hpid=hp_no-name_graphic-story-a%3Ahomepage%2Fstory.

our farm and all over Chesapeake Bay country. The day I introduced the gun-control legislation in 1968, I told my Senate colleagues, "My love for hunting and shooting is second to none in this Chamber. . . . I love to shoot. I learned to shoot at my father's knee. My son is learning to shoot at my knee."[20]

Anybody who knew me, or who did the slightest bit of research, would have known I was not about to push for legislation that would take guns out of the hands of hunters. The NRA must have known that, but that was not what they told hunters. In the end, their deliberately deceitful campaign against me succeeded.

No organization seems to have more fear of the proverbial camel's nose pushing under the tent than the NRA. They oppose anything that has even the whiff of gun regulation. They have even persuaded their allies in Congress to enact legislation that forbids the federal government from collecting data to study gun violence. They don't want the public to know what is really happening.

I truly do not believe the NRA cares about public safety. They are funded by the entities that make and sell guns and gun accessories and are supported by the hardware and other stores that sell guns and bullets. The goal of the NRA is to increase the profits for those businesses, the public be damned.[21]

Tragically, the Republican Party appears now to be in lockstep with the NRA, although it was not always that way. President George H. W. Bush became so incensed at the extreme NRA positions that he renounced his lifelong NRA membership. But NRA influence has grown so strong since then that when his son, George W. Bush, ran for president in 2000, the NRA publicly bragged that if he won, they would have "an office in the White House."[22]

20. 114 Cong. Rec. (daily ed. June 12, 1968) (statement of Senator Tydings).

21. According to an Associated Press report in 2013, the bulk of NRA funding comes from contributions, grants, royalty income, and advertising, much of it originating from gun industry sources. Since 2005, the AP reported, the gun industry and corporate allies have given between $20 million and $52.6 million to the NRA, plus the NRA made another $20.9 million from selling advertising to companies marketing products in NRA publications. "Today's NRA is a virtual subsidiary of the gun industry," Josh Sugarmann, executive director of the Violence Policy Center, told the AP. "While the NRA portrays itself as protecting the 'freedom' of individual gun owners, it's actually working to protect the freedom of the gun industry to manufacture and sell virtually any weapon or accessory." Walter Hickey, "How the Gun Industry Funnels Tens of Millions of Dollars to the NRA," Associated Press, *Business Insider*, January 16, 2013, http://www.businessinsider.com/gun-industry-funds-nra-2013–1.

22. Julian Borger, "Gun Lobby Claims It Would 'Work Out of President Bush's Office,'"

In fact, the national Republican Party platform now reads like it was drafted by the NRA. It opposes federal licensing, national gun registration, and lawsuits against gun manufacturers. It supports—by name— the two Supreme Court rulings that overturned gun regulations in Chicago and Washington, DC.[23]

The responses of Republican presidential candidates to one of the mass shootings that occurred during the campaign for the 2016 election ranged from blaming the victims for not attacking the shooter to former Florida Governor Jeb Bush's insensitive reply, "Stuff happens."[24] Several candidates deflected questions about gun control by saying the real problem was mental illness, yet it was Republicans in the Senate who had blocked efforts by the Obama administration in 2013 to increase funding for mental health programs and other initiatives designed to identify and help people who are potentially dangerous.

By the time I ran for reelection in 1970, the NRA had—no pun intended—turned its sights on me. It launched an ad campaign that twisted my genuine effort to enact a responsible gun-control law into something unrecognizable. It intentionally confused hunters—even friends I had hunted with all my life—into believing I was trying to take away their guns and somehow prohibit hunting.

I still believe we need comprehensive gun control—now more than ever. But the successful attack the NRA launched on me has intimidated those who would otherwise champion commonsense gun control to this very day. It is painful for me to admit that.

Guardian, May 4, 2000, https://www.theguardian.com/world/2000/may/05/uselections2000.usa.

23. The cases are *District of Columbia v. Heller* and *McDonald v. Chicago*. See "Republican Party on Gun Control, Party Platform," compiled from the Republican platform adopted at the GOP National Convention, August 12, 2000, at On the Issues, http://www.ontheissues.org/Celeb/Republican_Party_Gun_Control.htm.

24. Candace Smith, "Jeb Bush Says 'Stuff Happens' in Response to Gun Violence," ABC News, October 2, 2015, http://abcnews.go.com/US/jeb-bush-stuff-response-gun-violence/story?id=34209380.

CHAPTER 20

One Progressive Position Too Many

In early 1970, the year I ran for reelection, *Washingtonian* magazine published a long feature story about me with a provocative but worrisome headline: "Will the Gun Lobby Get Joe Tydings?"

The subtitle to that headline was a bit more hopeful: "In This Year of Spiro Agnew, Can a Kennedyite Liberal, Unloved by the Party Pros, Hated by the Gun Lobby, with Only Good Looks, a Famous Name, Guts, and $2,581,520, Win Reelection to the United States Senate and Grow Up to Be Vice President? . . . Why Not?"[1]

It was a clever title that pretty much said it all.

The gun lobby was undoubtedly after me. So were Agnew and the Nixon administration, which didn't like my stand on Vietnam or my opposition to the two judges it nominated to the Supreme Court. And it was true that the hierarchy in the Maryland Democratic Party had never liked me because I had always operated pretty much as an independent as a state legislator, federal prosecutor, and US senator.

Yet, it also was true that I had a famous last name, particularly in Maryland, and that I still carried the aura of the Kennedys, even though both Jack and Bobby were gone by then. I had a substantial campaign war chest, had built a reputation for "never ducking the tough ones," and my name had been mentioned as a potential candidate for vice president one day.[2]

The Republican candidate I feared the most, Representative Rogers

---

1. Ernest B. Ferguson, "Will the Gun Lobby Get Joe Tydings?," *Washingtonian Magazine*, February 1970.

2. Tydings's 1970 campaign slogan was "Joe Never Ducks the Tough Ones." It was later referenced in many news stories, e.g., in John W. Finney, "Administration Aiming Its Big Guns at Tydings," *New York Times*, October 23, 1970, http://www.nytimes.com/1970/10/23/archives/administration-aiming-its-big-guns-at-tydings.html; and "Is 1970 Another Tydings to Beall Year?," *Hagerstown Morning Herald*, October 30, 1970, 2.

Morton from the Eastern Shore, had announced that he was not going to challenge me, so I was fairly confident I would win reelection. I had compiled a strong record—particularly strong for a freshman senator. And early that year, it was not even clear who was going to oppose me.

Campaigning

I beat the bushes hard. I set up a huge number of interviews with newspapers, television and radio stations, editorial boards, and magazine writers—everything from the *New Yorker* to the *Diamondback*, the student newspaper at the University of Maryland. UPI reporters asked me about population issues; a Maryland radio reporter interviewed me about Vietnam; a writer for the *New Republic* asked about the gun lobby.

I hit the Baltimore- and Washington-area markets hardest but also took a statewide tour that allowed me to visit with local officials and news organizations in the smaller towns on the Eastern Shore and in southern and western Maryland. I spent a lot of my time mending fences with local Democrats who disagreed with me on Vietnam, or gun control, or civil rights, or some other issue.

I carved out time to attend and be seen at special events—the University of Maryland homecoming football game, the Baltimore Orioles' appearance in the World Series that fall, the White House Correspondents' Association dinner at the Sheraton Park Hotel, and the Goshen Hunt point-to-point race in Montgomery County. I emphasized conservation issues on a fifty-mile hike with Goodloe Byron, a Democrat then running for the congressional seat representing western Maryland.[3]

We began a new series of Teas for Tydings, the receptions that had been so helpful during my 1964 campaign. I held private meetings with my longtime supporters, Frank Gallagher, Irv Blum, Dick Schifter, and others to make sure we were hitting our fundraising targets.[4] And I made a number of appearances before chapters of the Young Democrats, trying to enlist their young members in my cause. At a meeting at

3. Byron would be elected and serve in the House of Representatives until his death from a heart attack while jogging on the C&O Canal tow path in October 1978. He was succeeded by his widow, Beverly Byron.

4. Irv Blum was a business and civic leader in Baltimore, brother-in-law to Jerry Hoffberger, and one of my closest political advisers and fundraisers.

Oakington, I helped organize a group of young labor leaders to support my reelection.

Speaking before Young Democrats at Towson State College (now Towson University), I focused on how discrimination was hurting women economically and urged ratification of the pending Equal Rights Amendment to the Constitution. To make my case, I quoted famous people through the ages who had impugned women: Aristotle, Saint Thomas Aquinas, Samuel Johnson, and the sitting Vice President of the United States Spiro Agnew.

"'Three things have been difficult to tame—the ocean, fools, and women,'" I quoted Agnew as saying. "'We may soon be able to tame the ocean; fools and women will take a little longer.'"[5]

The Tough Issues

As much as I enjoyed campaigning, tough issues in Washington demanded my attention. Nixon had started the year by nominating Carswell for the Supreme Court, and that fight lasted until April.

After Nixon ordered the invasion of Cambodia, student protests at the University of Maryland—and at other campuses across the country—exploded.[6] I worried the war was turning off an entire generation of young people because it appeared that no one in power was listening to them. After all, I was with them—I wanted to end the war, too.

In retrospect, my political mistake may have been that I was too public about my opposition to the war. When no one else would debate the conservative pundit William F. Buckley on TV about the war, I did. At an early antiwar rally in Baltimore, Jo-Ann Orlinsky and others on my staff urged me to speak out, to make sure the young people knew I was listening to them. I can still remember the boos raining down on me from the hard-hat workers at a nearby construction site, who must have thought I was being unpatriotic.

5. Senator Joseph D. Tydings, speech on equal rights for women at a meeting of Young Democrats at Towson State College, April 6, 1970, Joseph D. Tydings Collection, Hornbake Library, University of Maryland, College Park.

6. Between 1970 and 1972, there were at least three major anti-Vietnam demonstrations at College Park that became so violent that Governor Mandel had to declare a state of emergency on campus and send in the National Guard to restore and maintain order. But the May 1970 protest was the most violent.

As a candidate for reelection, my stance on Vietnam once again rubbed against the grain. People thought I had fired up all those young people and had somehow instigated the campus riots.

My approval rating dropped like a stone. Mahoney sniffed the political winds, decided I was vulnerable, and once again jumped into the September Democratic senatorial primary—the sixty-eight-year-old Baltimore County paving contractor's ninth race for statewide political office.

By midsummer, the gun lobby was really coming after me. Pending in the Senate once again was my legislation to regulate the purchase of firearms, including a prohibition against selling guns to convicted felons, narcotics addicts, alcoholics, the mentally ill, and juveniles. I had managed to get bipartisan support for it the previous year and thought I might have a long-shot chance at finally passing it this time.

First came the bumper stickers, financed and distributed by the gun lobby. This was still an era before political advertising was dominated by television, and bumper stickers had an impact.

One bright orange bumper sticker, mailed to one hundred thousand Marylanders and aimed specifically at hunters, read, "If Tydings Wins, You Lose." The slogan was paired with a picture of a pipe-smoking hunter, his son, and a dog on a lakeshore, with a big X superimposed over the picture. The message was clear: if Tydings is reelected, you will never be able to shoot or hunt again.[7]

Another NRA-financed bumper sticker read, "Gun Registration Means Confiscation." Still another warned, "Don't Be a Bearer of Ill Tydings."

The first gun-inspired bumper sticker actually showed up in 1969, shortly after I wrote an article arguing for gun registration that appeared in the March 1969 edition of *Playboy* magazine. The gun lobby pegged me with a bumper sticker that read, "Playboy Joe Has Got to Go."

I fought back. I reminded voters I had been a lifelong hunter. I pointed out that gun-lobby money was pouring in from outside for the purpose of changing Maryland votes. I accused the NRA of using the "Big Lie" technique in an effort to purge me from the Senate. I blamed the gun lobby for flooding the state with "slick publicity, half truths,

7. Richard M. Cohen, "Gun Lobby Takes Aim at Tydings," *Washington Post*, June 21, 1970, D-1.

and deliberate lies in order to create the impression that my proposals are an effort to abolish hunting as a sport."[8]

"I want to send this word back to the gun lobby," I said. "I am prepared to make my re-nomination and re-election a referendum on whether the people of Maryland want their man in Congress to stand up for law enforcement against the special interests."[9]

Life Magazine

By August 1970, my internal polling was showing me to be ahead of Mahoney despite the backlash over Vietnam and the lies being spread by the gun lobby. I felt fairly confident.

But I also had known for months that trouble was brewing. An old family friend had warned me the previous Christmas Eve that the Nixon administration intended to smear me in the fall campaign, somehow using my business connections with the Charter Company. Charter was the company built over the previous two decades by a longtime Florida friend and business associate, Raymond Mason. Through Raymond, in 1957 I became a stockholder in and director of the Insurance Company of the South, which later became a Charter subsidiary. Raymond had bought the Insurance Company of the South out of bankruptcy. The company provided fire, extended coverage, and homeowners' insurance policies on new houses with mortgages from savings and loan associations or banks. I was an expert in federal S&Ls, and I knew these investments were as solid as you could have. We were successful from the day we opened the doors. And it was a sound investment for me. A decade or more later, Insurance Company of the South was merged into the Charter Company. Beginning in 1965, I became one of eleven directors of Charter, but as soon as I received that political warning at Christmastime in 1969, I resigned as a director.

---

8. "Some of my friends have told me to trim my sails on the gun issue, to play it down," I admitted. "Well, the safety of my fellow citizens is too important. I am not going to duck or run. I am willing to stake my career of public service on the belief that Marylanders are fair and respect the truth; that Marylanders want independence and courage from their United States Senator and not subservience, fence straddling, and issue ducking. . . . I cannot and will not duck this fight." Senator Joseph D. Tydings, statement on gun-crime legislation, June 26, 1970, 3, Tydings Collection, Hornbake Library.

9. Tydings, statement on gun-crime legislation, June 26, 1970, 3.

By summer, my staff and I had gotten wind that *Life* magazine was about to write a big story about me, the subject of which was totally unknown. When you are a public official—not to mention a candidate for reelection—and learn that an influential national magazine is about to write about you, and you have no idea what the story will be about, it makes you nervous.

I asked Vernon Eney, a distinguished lawyer whom I had admired for years and who headed the Baltimore firm of Venable, Baetjer and Howard, to convene a small group that included Hardin Marion, my former Senate chief of staff; Steve Sachs, my former assistant in the US Attorney's Office; and John McEvoy, my senior Senate aide, to try to figure out what the *Life* story was going to be about.

By this time, my marriage to Ginny was failing and I had fallen in love with a beautiful California woman, whom I would later marry and who would become the mother of my fifth child (and fourth daughter), Alexandra. Okay, okay: what the public would have seen is that a married US senator with four young children was having an affair. Obviously, such a story would be politically damaging. The Eney group could not help but wonder, at first, if that was the story the Nixon administration had planted with *Life*.

Then, in late June, I got a visit from William Lambert, the senior investigative reporter for *Life*, and I discovered that the story was, in fact, about my friendship with Raymond Mason and my relationship to the Charter Company. To my surprise, Lambert began asking me about a meeting that Mason and I had had nearly six years earlier with Paul Bridston, a mid-level bureaucrat in the US Agency for International Development at the State Department who worked on loan guarantees for overseas housing programs. I could barely remember Bridston or the meeting, which had taken place after I had been elected but before I was sworn in. Lambert, however, insisted the meeting had taken place during my first year as a US senator and implied that it showed that I had used my position to benefit Charter and, indirectly, myself.

The gist of the *Life* story was that I had used my prestige as a senator to convince Bridston and USAID to approve about $7 million in federal loan guarantees that Charter had been seeking for housing projects it controlled in Central America. I denied any such thing had taken place and—as far as I could remember—that Charter had even been discussed at the meeting. Mason had known Bridston and the meeting had been his idea. I thought of it as a strictly social affair. We never mentioned Charter. Afterward, I never gave it a second thought.

It was later revealed that the loan guarantees in question had been approved by USAID *before* Mason and I ever met with Bridston. At the time Lambert began questioning me, however, I had no reason to know that or anything else about the loan guarantees because I had never discussed the issue.

After Lambert left, my secretary found my appointment book from 1964, which contained a handwritten entry by me that placed the meeting on December 1, less than a month after I had been elected and about a month before I was sworn in. By the time Lambert returned to my office a second time in early August, Bridston's secretary had also confirmed the December 1964 date. I told this to Lambert, but he refused to believe me! He was determined to stick with his original story that this meeting had happened after I was already in the Senate. He insinuated that I had doctored the old appointment book with a new entry. He demanded that I allow the appointment book to be subjected to an "ink freshness test" to determine when the December 1, 1964, annotation was written.

I was appalled and infuriated that he would question my truthfulness, but I agreed to the test because I had nothing to hide. But it seemed clear to me he was determined to nail me. I let *Life* choose the expert who would review the entry (my understanding was that *Life* was so skeptical of my answer that it was willing to spend up to $1,000 on this test). On August 17, 1970, the results came back stating unequivocally that the entry had been made in 1964, not in 1970.

Still, *Life* persisted. As publication of the story appeared imminent, we demanded that the magazine editors give us an advance copy so we could prepare a response. They refused. I brought Raymond to Washington, and we talked with him and his legal counsel to get their take on what *Life* might be investigating. Finally, less than a week before the magazine was to hit newsstands on August 24, *Life* provided me with a basic copy of the story.

I again tried to dissuade *Life* from running it, even offering to fly to New York to meet with the editors, but they again refused. Feeling the need to get out in front of this, we decided to call a preemptive news conference on Friday, August 21, which, in turn, prompted *Life* to release prepublication copies of the thirty-five-hundred-word piece. When that happened, all hell broke loose.

Almost immediately I spoke with Senator Fulbright, told him the story was untrue, and with my blessing he demanded a State Department investigation to determine the validity of the allegations. Throughout the fall campaign, he repeatedly badgered State Department officials to issue their report quickly, prior to the election, even if it was only an interim report. He even wrote a letter to that effect to Secretary of State William P. Rogers but never received the courtesy of a reply.

Finally, eleven days *after* the election was over, the results of the State Department investigation were released, and, as I had predicted, it completely exonerated me. But, of course, by then it was too late. As we were later to learn, the report had been completed well before the election, but the Nixon administration intentionally sat on it until the voting was over.

The *Life* story pointedly stated that the magazine was not accusing me of doing anything illegal. Rather, it claimed that my actions "form a pattern of conduct not in keeping with the strict standards he so eloquently urged upon his fellow Senators."[10] I had publicly called for members of Congress to voluntarily disclose their financial assets, believing that the public deserved such transparency. To set an example, I had voluntarily disclosed my own financial assets, including my relationship with Charter.

It was no secret that the Nixon administration was after me, and it had plenty of reasons. Most recently, in a speech on the Senate floor, I had called out by name Nixon economic adviser Peter M. Flanigan over a favorable administration decision that delivered a $6.5 million windfall to a shipping company he formerly headed. My intervention forced the administration to cancel the waiver that would have produced the windfall.[11]

10. William Lambert, "What the Senator Didn't Disclose: Joseph Tydings Hasn't Met the Standards He Has Set," *Life*, August 28, 1970, 28.

11. Flanigan, a New York investment banker, served as national volunteer director for Nixon's 1960 campaign against John F. Kennedy. After Nixon won in 1968, Flanigan became an assistant to Nixon on business issues and, in 1972, became assistant to the president for international economic affairs. In 1975, he returned to the investment banking firm Dillon, Read, as managing director. The 1970 controversy had to do with a coastal shipping waiver that the Treasury Department granted and then abruptly canceled for a tanker named the

I was certain that someone in the Nixon White House had planted the *Life* magazine story, and I said so publicly. This was the smear about which I had been warned.

It was small comfort that just four days after the *Life* story was published, WETA, the public television station in Washington, became the first—but not the last—news organization to tie the *Life* story to Charles W. Colson, a young White House adviser to President Nixon who, over the coming years, would develop a well-deserved reputation for dirty political tricks. This was his first trick, the one that really put him on the map. On at least one occasion, Colson had taken Bridston to New York to meet with Lambert, and it became increasingly clear Lambert had been coached and directed by Colson all along. At the time, though, the president's press secretary, Ronald L. Ziegler, predictably denied White House involvement in the *Life* story.[12]

But I knew better. It was all just as I had feared.

In response to the story, I explained that in December 1964, the month of the meeting with Bridston, I was not yet a US senator, nor was I a stockholder, officer, or director of Charter, although I was then a stockholder in what later became a Charter subsidiary. "In no way, shape or form, directly or indirectly, have I ever used my office as a United States Senator to advance the interest of the Charter Company or of any other company in which I have a personal stake," I said.[13]

Even before it was confirmed elsewhere, I accused Lambert, the *Life* reporter, of working with the Nixon administration to develop the story. Republicans owed Lambert a favor. He was the reporter who had written the Pulitzer Prize–winning 1968 exposé that had brought down Abe Fortas, the Supreme Court justice who was a close associate of Lyndon Johnson and other Democrats. Lambert denied that the magazine and the administration had worked together on the story, but subsequent investigations and his own belated admissions proved that he had.

SS *Sansinena*, which would have saved Flanigan's former company, the Barracuda Tanker Corporation, about $6.5 million. Naomi S. Rovner, "Senators to Probe Ship Waiver," *Baltimore Sun*, March 20, 1970, A-9; Douglas Martin, "Peter M. Flanigan, Banker and Nixon Aide, Dies at 90," *New York Times*, August 1, 2013, A-22.

12. Ben A. Franklin, "Tydings Links *Life* Article to White House Sources," *New York Times*, August 25, 1970, 28.

13. Quoted in John Hanrahan, "Federal Loan in Contention," *Washington Post*, August 20, 1970, A1.

For now, the damage had been done. Every major newspaper in the region ran long, front-page stories with banner headlines that trumpeted the *Life* magazine allegations. Typical was the *Baltimore Sun* headline, "*Life* Says Tydings Used Senate Prestige Financially," or the one in the *New York Times*, "*Life* Article Questions the Ethics of Senator Tydings."[14]

"The political impact of the *Life* article was, by all accounts, likely to have a stunning effect in this state," the *New York Times* said, in what, to me, was a gross understatement.[15] Here was a malicious, damaging article, intentionally appearing just three weeks before the primary, clearly designed to take me down. I had been considered a "white hat"— a reformer who championed transparency for public officials, and suddenly I found myself tarnished as if they had caught me with my hand in the till. But I had done nothing wrong, and I bitterly resented the accusations. I was not guilty as charged!

The *Life* magazine incident immediately brought back to me the sickening, helpless feelings I felt when another Republican, Senator Joseph McCarthy, smeared my father at the end of his 1950 reelection campaign. That dirty trick ultimately helped end my father's magnificent Senate career.

Once such allegations are made, you are permanently stained. The dirty tricksters in politics, those intent on character assassination, know that. It really doesn't matter what you say, or what proof you produce, or who comes to your defense. Once an allegation of impropriety is leveled against someone, the stigma remains forever, the questions always just beneath the surface. You never, ever recover. Oh, time passes and memories fade, but you never quite get your good name back. You have been wounded and will always bear the scar.

Anti-Tydings candidates—like Mahoney or Walter G. Finch, a minor candidate in the primary that year—piled on. Stories started appearing with headlines like, "Beleaguered Senator: Joseph Davies Tydings," or "A Senator under Fire."

Colson, of course, would become infamous a few years later for his involvement in a series of White House dirty tricks during Nixon's 1972 reelection campaign. Those activities were exposed as part of the

14. Louis P. Peddicord, "*Life* Says Tydings Used Senate Prestige Financially," *Baltimore Sun*, August 21, 1970, C-20; Ben A. Franklin, "*Life* Article Questions the Ethics of Senator Tydings," *New York Times*, August 21, 1970, 16.

15. Franklin, "*Life* Article Questions the Ethics of Senator Tydings," 16.

investigation into the Watergate scandal, and for his involvement he was ultimately fined and sent to prison. But the *Life* magazine article about me was the trick that first burnished his reputation as a political operative who would stoop to almost any level. The week after my defeat, the president signaled Colson's rising stature by inviting him to his home in Key Biscayne, Florida.[16]

The Federal Reserve Board Meeting and the *Washington Post*

The day the initial story broke, the *Washington Post* ran two pieces: a main story about the *Life* magazine allegations and a sidebar that focused on the federal housing loan guaranty approved by Bridston that I had been accused of influencing. Deep in that second piece, the *Post* quoted unnamed sources as saying that just six months earlier, in February 1970, I had personally appeared in the audience of a Federal Reserve Board meeting, ostensibly because the board was discussing a banking issue related to Charter.[17]

The problem was that I was not at the Federal Reserve Board that day, or any other day. I had never visited the Federal Reserve. I was not even sure where their offices were located. Now I was being tarred with a second false allegation, one that made it seem as if I had been running around Washington on behalf of Charter.

I called the *Post* and told them I had not been where they reported I was, that I had instead been at the Capitol filming a campaign commercial at the time the meeting occurred, but the overly ambitious reporter refused to believe me. I called the *Post* continually over the next few days, spoke to each of the reporters on the story, and told them I had never set foot in the Federal Reserve building, but they simply refused to believe me. The newspaper merely ran the allegation a second time, this time paired with my denial. The following day, Dr. Arthur F. Burns, who chaired the Federal Reserve Board, released a statement that said I

16. Within a year of my defeat, Colson had gained such notoriety that he was featured in a front-page *Wall Street Journal* story headlined, "Nixon Hatchet Man," and detailing some of the dirty tricks for which he was already becoming known. John Pierson, "Nixon Hatchet Man: Call It What You Will, Chuck Colson Handles the President's Dirty Work," *Wall Street Journal*, October 15, 1971, 1.

17. Ronald Kessler, "Florida Firm's Role Queried," *Washington Post*, August 21, 1970, A1.

was not at the February meeting, but that only resulted in at least two additional *Post* stories—a third and a fourth—perpetuating the falsehood by quoting people claiming either I had or had not been there. It later became known that Florida Senator George Smathers had been at the Federal Reserve meeting in question, and maybe someone confused him with me. Burns himself admitted he had not been at the meeting and that the Federal Reserve did not keep attendance records, but Burns said he had spoken to others who were there and none of them saw me. That is because I was not there!

"The damage to me from this false story is, of course, irreparable," I said. "Millions of people have now heard it and the truth may never overtake it. Even more regrettable, however, is the damage the story does to my family and to the political movement I have tried to represent in Maryland."[18] I asked the *Post* to print a front-page correction, but, of course, the newspaper did not do that.

I felt we had gotten control of the *Life* story to the extent possible, but we could not contend with the damage the Federal Reserve story was doing to me in suburban Washington, particularly in Montgomery County. The refusal of the *Post* to adequately check out the story and the refusal of *Post* reporters to believe me was at least as damaging, if not more so, than the *Life* story.

On Monday, the day *Life* hit the newsstands, I called another news conference at my campaign headquarters in Baltimore and read aloud every word of a thirty-page statement my staff and I had prepared over the weekend to refute, item by item, the *Life* allegations. It took me sixty-five minutes to read it all. I said I owed such a response to the people of Maryland, to my Senate staff and campaign supporters, to the Senate itself, and, finally, to myself and my family.

"The *Life* charges will hurt. They will hurt not because I am in fact guilty of any impropriety—I am absolutely not. But they will hurt because they will sully the Tydings name and the Tydings honor," I said.[19]

I talked about my fifteen-year friendship and business relationship with Mason, how we had met at a national conference on savings and loan associations in the mid-1950s, not long after I had helped organize

18. Ronald Kessler and John Hanrahan, "Burns Letter Says Tydings Wasn't Seen at Key Hearing: Post Story Criticized," *Washington Post*, August 22, 1970, A1.

19. Senator Joseph D. Tydings, statement in response to *Life* magazine article, August 24, 1970, Tydings Collection, Hornbake Library, and in possession of Senator Tydings.

the First Harford Federal Savings and Loan Association in Aberdeen. I described every detail of my financial involvement with Mason's companies over the years. I said I had examined my relationship with Charter at the time I was elected to the Senate and concluded there would be no conflict of interest because Charter did not operate in Maryland and no activities of the company would cause me to deal with the federal government or any state government or regulatory agencies in regard to it. I conceded, however, that I could understand how our meeting with Bridston could be misconstrued and, in hindsight, said I regretted that I went along.

But I repeatedly insisted, "At no time and in no case did I ever lend the prestige of my office as a United States Senator to any business activity. At no time did my activities interfere with my Senate duties. At no time did I ever permit my office to be used in any fashion to advance Charter's interests with any private investor. At no time did I ever intervene with any government agency—state or federal—on behalf of Charter."

The Fallout

I tried to regain my footing. I hit the campaign trail in Maryland and willingly answered any questions about the *Life* allegations. I had nothing to hide. I picked up a union endorsement. I voted in favor of an amendment pushed by George McGovern of South Dakota and Mark Hatfield, an Oregon Republican, to end the war in Vietnam and bring our troops home. I criticized the Nixon administration for not putting enough money into narcotics treatment programs. I tried to get somewhat back to normal.

Attacks from the gun lobby accelerated. A gun group based in Michigan placed full-page ads in outdoor magazines around the country targeting for defeat 309 members of Congress (out of 535!) solely on the issue of guns. They were so rabid they even went after Senator Paul Fannin, a right-wing conservative Republican from Arizona, because he had voted for a 1968 anticrime bill that contained a ban on the mail-order sale of pistols. But I had the honor of being singled out as their primary target, even though on the stump I would brag about owning five shotguns and being a lifelong hunter.[20]

20. Arlen J. Large, "The Gun Lobby Works to Defeat Lawmakers Who Support Controls," *Wall Street Journal*, September 11, 1970, 1.

I had enormous support within the black community. When the *Baltimore Afro-American* newspaper endorsed me, it said *Life* had besmirched my "moral character by insinuation" and had ignored my "distinguished record on issues—on racism in the U.S., on civil rights, on welfare, on labor legislation, on Social Security, on Vietnam, on U.S. foreign responsibility." The editorial said it was telling that *Life* began the article about me by stating that none of my activities had shown any illegality.[21]

By primary election day, most of my forty-two-point lead had evaporated. I beat Mahoney by 64,000 votes, but my 238,000-vote total was about 41,000 less than I had rolled up against Goldstein in 1964. Some 48 percent of voters in the Democratic primary had voted for Mahoney and two other opponents.[22]

J. Glenn Beall Jr., a freshman House member and son and namesake of the man I had defeated in the 1964 general election, won the GOP nomination. He and others in Maryland political circles looked at my disappointingly close race with Mahoney and read into it the same conclusion: I was vulnerable.

Absent other factors, Beall should have been beatable. He was a freshman representative with almost no record of accomplishment other than support for Nixon and the Republican agenda.

Like his father, Beall had been a respected state legislator. He had served in the navy in World War II, graduated from Yale, and been elected to the Maryland House of Delegates. But in Congress, he had done very little, while, by contrast, I thought I had built an impressive record of achievement in the Senate.

But that election functioned like Newton's third law of physics: for almost every high-profile issue I championed, I had created an equally potent opposition.

- Vietnam was killing me with veterans' groups and blue-collar Marylanders, who considered my position unpatriotic.
- In rural areas, the NRA and allied groups were vilifying me as someone determined to stop all hunting and to take away everyone's guns. Anti-Tydings mailers were sent to fifty-one

21. "The Tydings Affair," *Baltimore Afro-American*, September 5, 1970, 5.

22. Mahoney got about 37 percent of the vote. The rest went to candidates Walter G. Finch and Charles D. White.

thousand Marylanders who held hunting licenses, and anti-Tydings bumper stickers appeared everywhere. One gun group, called Citizens against Tydings, spent more than $60,000 to defeat me, and much of that sum they raised out of state.

- Those who still favored the segregationist past, of course, hated my support for African Americans and civil rights. My support for voting rights, fair housing, and Thurgood Marshall was widely resented, especially among rural white voters. By extension, I was indirectly blamed for the riots, fires, and looting that had swept through American cities.

- Marylanders who opposed for religious reasons the idea of the federal government providing family planning services to anyone, much less information about how to obtain abortions, found my sponsorship of such legislation yet another reason to oppose my reelection.

Even longtime supporters took issue with some of my positions.

- Conservative lawyers in Maryland objected to my opposition to the Supreme Court nominations of Haynsworth and Carswell.

- A number of liberal Marylanders who otherwise would have been behind me misconstrued my support for the DC crime bill, which legalized pretrial detention and "no-knock" warrants. They thought those measures weakened the Bill of Rights, jeopardized the rights of African Americans and other minorities, and betrayed the reformist philosophy that had been the basis of their support for me in 1964.

- I had never had a close relationship with the dominant Democratic Party organization in the state, and, in fact, I had run against the Democratic machine in 1964. Consequently, many in the party hierarchy took this as an opportunity to get back at me. Now, thanks to my support for the Supreme Court "one-man, one-vote" ruling, local Democratic Party office holders, particularly in rural areas that had lost representation in the General Assembly as a result, had a new reason to sit on their hands when I needed their backing.

I broadly defended myself by saying, "My record reflects my belief that a U.S. Senator must be his own man and never duck the tough issues, even if that means bucking his own political party." Beall's voting record, I said, was more partisan than those of all but eleven members of the entire US House of Representatives.[23]

Part of my problem was that I had become overconfident after receiving consistently high polling numbers throughout my years in the Senate—numbers that seemed to show me comfortably ahead in a run for a second term and possibly toward a spot on some future presidential ticket. That was before the *Life* magazine article, before the Federal Reserve Board allegations, and before the White House really turned up the heat.

Two weeks before the election, Vice President Agnew savagely unloaded on me, labeling me a "radical liberal" before a cheering crowd at a Republican fundraising dinner in Baltimore. I had worked closely with Agnew on the appointment of judges and the convening of a state constitutional convention when he was governor. When he ran against Mahoney in 1966, I refused to back Mahoney and many of my followers did likewise. Agnew was appropriately appreciative. This is the same Spiro Agnew who, in the spring of 1968, was liberal enough to agree to manage the Maryland presidential campaign of Republican candidate Nelson Rockefeller. But all of that, of course, was before he became Nixon's running mate.

Again, I flashed back to memories of my father, who had withstood an attempt by President Franklin D. Roosevelt to purge him from the Senate in 1938, after my father had led the opposition to FDR's proposal to pack the Supreme Court. I called Agnew's intervention "the White House Purge, 1970 Edition."

"It should come as no surprise to Marylanders that the administration will make every effort to purge an independent U.S. senator and

23. Quoted in Thomas B. Edsall, "Beall Is a 'Do-Nothing Rubber Stamp': Tydings," *Baltimore Evening Sun*, September 23, 1970.

replace him with a rubber stamp," I replied to the Agnew attack.[24] The *Baltimore Sun* seemed to agree, endorsing my reelection by saying I had "maintained a praiseworthy degree of independence" and adding that "it is simply absurd to call him 'ultra' or a 'radical.'"[25]

What I did not know then, or find out until after the election was over, was that the White House had secretly funneled at least $180,000 into Beall's campaign, which enabled it to buy the support of Democratic political organizations in Baltimore and to flood the airwaves with attack ads against me in the final two weeks before the election.[26]

The Long Trip to the Belvedere

By Election Day, I was plenty worried. It had started to rain and continued to rain all day, weather that certainly was not going to help my turnout, particularly in Baltimore. I still thought I was going to squeak through, though I knew it would be close. At Oakington the night before, I warned my son and daughters that I might not win and told them how I expected them to handle themselves should I lose.

By evening, the signs were not encouraging. When I arrived at the crowded election night party at a townhouse on Mount Vernon Square in Baltimore, the mood was nervous and tense. This was a party for our closest friends and supporters; the main election night party for the campaign workers and others was several blocks away at the Belvedere Hotel.

Not long after the polls closed, Tommy D'Alesandro, the Baltimore mayor, arrived at the party after checking the latest numbers at election headquarters in the Baltimore Armory. We knew from early returns that my numbers in lightly populated rural parts of the state were bad, as we expected, but we hoped to make that up in Baltimore. But Tommy's face was grim. Standing face to face in the crowded, noisy room, he told me the city numbers were lower than what we needed to win. The turnout

---

24. Quoted in Lawrence Meyer, "Agnew Turns Fire on Tydings as a 'Radical Liberal,'" *Washington Post*, October 21, 1970, 16.

25. "Senator Tydings for Re-election," *Baltimore Sun*, October 25, 1970, PE4.

26. The money came from what became known as the Townhouse Fund, a $3 million slush fund set up by the Nixon White House to funnel money into Republican campaigns around the country. Herbert W. Kalmbach, Nixon's personal lawyer, was the chief fundraiser. Bill Peterson, "Bush Says He Reported 1970 'Townhouse' Donation," *Washington Post*, February 8, 1980.

just was not there that day. Maybe it was the rain, or maybe I had simply embraced one progressive position too many. Whatever the cause, I suddenly knew I was going to lose my seat in the US Senate. I spent that awful night, and the next few years, trying to pinpoint precisely why I lost the Senate election of November 3, 1970. It was a terrible night. A great loss.

I lost by 24,538 votes out of 956,400 ballots cast, which means if only 12,270 more votes had gone my way, I would have won.[27]

As I walked to the Belvedere that night to deliver my concession speech, I thought about my reputation as someone "who never ducked the tough ones" and could not help but wonder if I should have shown more restraint. In the end, I lost that election myself. I took on too many issues and thought I was stronger than I was. If my father had been alive, I am sure he would have advised me to be careful about taking on too many issues at one time.

In various interviews since then, I have confidently explained that I would have won had it not been for the gun issue, or I just as confidently pinned my loss on Vietnam and the riots at the University of Maryland. There is no doubt the smear by *Life* magazine hurt me, as did the repetition of the untrue allegations about me appearing at the Federal Reserve Board meeting, as did the vicious attacks by Agnew.

In a 1973 interview reflecting on why I lost in 1970, I said that if I could do it over again, I would not do it the same way. "It's not that I'd basically change, but I'd surely, well, I guess the word I want is 'temper.' I'd surely temper my position," I admitted. "I wouldn't stop standing for what I have believed in, but I'd be less out front all the time. I was 36 when I went to the Senate and I was fired up. I was . . . perhaps I was too strongly convinced of the rightness of the things I favored. I took on too many issues at one time. I think I'd be more considered now about what I supported, and how."[28]

The other major mistake I made was not fully internalizing the fact

27. I beat Beall in Baltimore city by a two-to-one margin, 128,392 to 66,552, but because of the rain and the resulting low turnout, I did not receive nearly as many votes as Hubert Humphrey had received in the city two years earlier in the 1968 presidential race against Richard Nixon and George Wallace. In that election, Humphrey received 178,450 votes in Baltimore to Nixon's 80,146 and Wallace's 31,288. While my percentage in Baltimore was higher than Humphrey's, 65 to 62 percent, his vote total was much higher. Had I had Humphrey's turnout in Baltimore, I would have won.

28. Quoted in John Adam Moreau, "Defeat, Time Temper Ex-Senator Tydings's Outlook," *Baltimore Sun*, May 20, 1973, A-32.

that times had changed. John and Bobby Kennedy were dead and little remained of Camelot. Martin Luther King Jr. was dead; the civil rights movement had lost his voice and the momentum it had provided. Vietnam dragged on with no end in sight, splintering the country. LBJ's War on Poverty and his dream of a Great Society had been replaced by the conniving Richard Nixon and his band of Republican operatives. Americans had become frightened by riots that had burned and leveled entire blocks within their own cities, and parents watched with trepidation the rise of a new generation of young people who, in the folk singer Bob Dylan's perceptive line, were "beyond your command."[29]

The country had changed, but I had not sufficiently readjusted my approach and outlook. Maybe I was hopelessly optimistic. Maybe I was insulated in a bubble of my own making. My critics said I was too aloof, or too arrogant, or too distant from the travails of everyday citizens. Maybe.

After the Election

A week and a half *after* my defeat, the State Department released a report detailing the investigation it had undertaken into the *Life* magazine allegations, and it completely cleared me of any wrongdoing. It totally vindicated me, just as I said it would. Among other findings, the investigation showed that the housing loan guarantees I had allegedly influenced had actually been approved *before* Mason and I ever met with Paul Bridston.

Think about this for a second: the Nixon administration helped concoct a bogus charge that contributed to my defeat and then after it was too late to reverse the damage, it issued a report that essentially said, "Oh, never mind." I was outraged, but not surprised.

The State Department simply sat on those findings until November 14, 1970. Senator Fulbright angrily accused the administration of "stalling" and launched his own counterinvestigation of why that had happened. By then, though, everyone knew: it was too late.

29. "Come mothers and fathers throughout the land, and don't criticize what you can't understand. Your sons and your daughters are beyond your command; your old road is rapidly agin'. Please get out of the new one if you can't lend your hand, for the times they are a-changin'." Third verse to "The Times They Are A-Changin'," by Bob Dylan, copyright 1963, 1964 by Warner Bros., Inc.; renewed 1991, 1992 by Special Rider Music.

As more information about the 1970 election came to light over the next few years, Colson's direct involvement in the *Life* magazine article became indisputable. It was Colson who had given Lambert the information that Mason and I had met with Bridston in 1964. Without that, "I would have had a feeble story . . . I'm not sure I would have printed it," Lambert admitted in a 1971 article.[30]

That same article also reported that the State Department had completed the investigation by September 18, seven weeks *before* the election, but did not release the report on it until November 14.[31]

As I conceded in my 1973 reminiscence about the election, "If I wanted to, I could replay this all the rest of my life."[32] And, in some ways, maybe I have.

30. Quoted in Martin Schram, "Tydings Loss: Nixon Aide Tied; New Evidence Links Presidential Aide to the *Life* Article That Criticized the Senator," *Long Island Newsday*, February 15, 1971.

31. In a 1973 book aptly titled *The Politics of Lying*, Colson was again linked to the *Life* magazine article and identified as the brains behind the campaign of political sabotage the Nixon administration directed against Democratic presidential candidates in 1972. Frederick B. Hill, "Colson Linked to 1970 Article, Campaign Tactics Used against Tydings," *Baltimore Sun*, May 9, 1973.

32. Quoted in Moreau, "Defeat, Time Temper Ex-Senator Tydings's Outlook," A-32.

CHAPTER 21

Citizen Public Service

Politics are almost as exciting as war, and quite as dangerous. In war you can only be killed once, but in politics many times.
—SIR WINSTON CHURCHILL, 1920

In the mornings just after the election, I did not want to get out of bed. When I did, I spent the days roaming the farm at Oakington. I did not want to go back to Washington, particularly Capitol Hill.

When I returned to serve out the term, my first priority was to get everyone on my staff another job. I owed it to them. But nothing was the same. People looked at me differently, and, of course, they talked to me differently. It was depressing, very depressing.[1]

Over my career, I had modeled myself in many ways after the examples set by my father, Millard Tydings, and my maternal grandfather, Joe Davies. Both men committed much of their lives to public service, but both were also successful lawyers in private practice. My grandfather in particular was a spectacularly successful trial and corporate lawyer.

Early in my own career, my father cautioned me that when you run for public office, you can sometimes get out in front of issues that prove to be unpopular, and, before you know it, you are suddenly out of a job. He said that such a circumstance is when it is good to have a law practice to support your family.[2]

---

1. On December 29, 1970, seventeen of my colleagues spent nearly two hours on the floor of the Senate giving me a farewell tribute I shall remember for the rest of my life. Walter Mondale, John McClellan, Ralph Yarborough of Texas, J. William Fulbright, Edward Brooke of Massachusetts, and others spoke. Perhaps the highest compliment came from Sam Ervin, the North Carolina conservative with whom I had done battle on many an issue. "Joe Tydings is a hard fighter and no one in the Senate can testify to that more than I," Ervin said. "He has a quality that I regret to say is in short supply, and that is courage. He is a gentleman and a worthy opponent. I deeply regret to see him depart." "Tributes to the Honorable Joseph D. Tydings of Maryland in the United States Senate, upon the Occasion of His Retirement from the Senate," 91st Cong., 2nd sess., S. Doc. No. 91–126 (January 3, 1971).

2. When I served in the Maryland House of Delegates, annual compensation was about $1,800, and more than a third of the legislators were lawyers.

I found myself in just that situation in 1971.

As I gradually got over my reelection loss, I returned to the practice of law but decided against rejoining Tydings & Rosenberg, the old family firm in Baltimore. Instead, I joined Joe Danzansky's successful Washington law firm as a named partner.[3] Joe had been a big supporter of mine, and his firm represented the Giant Food supermarket company and a great many prominent Washington development and building firms. I was asked to represent many of these major firms that were parties in a class-action antitrust case brought against the gypsum industry in San Francisco. It was not long before my law practice began to take off. I was fortunate in becoming lead counsel in a number of major class-action cases, which resulted in verdicts and settlements for our clients and the classes that were represented.

• • •

In the years since I left elective office, I have been fortunate to be able to balance my career as a lawyer by accepting a variety of requests to provide volunteer public services.

I was elected a trustee for the McDonogh School in Baltimore, where I had graduated from high school in 1945. When I left the Senate, the Vietnam War was still raging and that controversy made it almost impossible to recruit young male students to a military school. The idea of opening the school to female students had come up in the past, but the decision had always been postponed. After I joined the board, however, we made the decision to begin enrolling female students, starting in 1975— arguably the best decision the McDonogh Board of Trustees ever made. McDonogh was already a very good school, but the influx of top-notch female students has helped raise the overall level of academic excellence and national standing.

I was also recruited by General Bill Draper, one of the most prominent global leaders in the efforts to slow global population growth, to become an unpaid senior financial consultant to the United Nations Fund for Population Activities, continuing the global family planning and population efforts we had worked on together when I was in the Senate.

In 1974, Governor Marvin Mandel appointed me to the seventeen-member board of regents of my alma mater, the University of Maryland. Thus began my first of three terms on that board, each coming in a different decade and each appointment by a different Maryland governor.

---

3. This became the firm of Danzansky, Dickey, Tydings, Guint, and Gordon.

The board was responsible for directing the affairs of all University of Maryland activities until 1989, when the legislature expanded and changed the responsibilities of the university to include all of the publicly funded universities and colleges in the state, except for Morgan State University and St. Mary's College of Maryland.[4]

With a flourishing law practice and a great deal of overseas work on population issues, I really was not thinking about returning to politics.

The 1976 Senate Campaign

As the 1976 election approached, Paul Sarbanes, the young attorney who had run Volunteers for Tydings in my 1964 Senate campaign and who had first been elected to Congress in 1970, decided to run against Glenn Beall for the Senate seat I had once held. I told Paul that I had no plans to run for reelection again and that I was happy to support him. I was content practicing law.

But my new wife really wanted me to run for the Senate. Although I was reluctant at first, she finally persuaded me to join the race.

I had loved my time in the Senate and, if I may say so, thought I had been a pretty effective senator. I was now older, wiser, and sure I would do an even better job a second time. I also felt I had been robbed of reelection in 1970 through a combination of Nixon-Colson dirty tricks, tainted money, and miserable Election Day weather. A part of me wanted another crack at it.

Before I could get into the race, however, I had the awkward task of going to Sarbanes to tell him I had changed my mind and was now going to compete against him in the May 18 Democratic primary. Paul was gracious, but by that time he already had a several-month head start on me putting together a campaign apparatus and raising money.[5]

---

4. The regents oversee academic, administrative, and financial operations; formulate policies; and appoint the chancellor as well as the presidents of the twelve separate academic institutions in the University System of Maryland. The name was changed from the University of Maryland System to the University System of Maryland to allow more political flexibility for newly named members of the board of regents.

5. Paul had made something of a name for himself as a member of the House committee that voted to impeach President Nixon as a result of the Watergate scandals. Those hearings had gavel-to-gavel televised coverage and then were replayed nightly on the evening news. Little-known members of Congress like Sarbanes suddenly gained strong national name recognition.

I also soon discovered that organized labor was backing Sarbanes, as were other groups and individuals who had supported me in 1964 and 1970. Supporters who had helped raise funds for my two previous Senate races had migrated to the Sarbanes camp. I ended up putting $100,000 of my own money into the campaign, which was a tremendous amount for me, and we produced some great ads. I still think that if I could have raised more money to wage a strong media campaign all the way to Election Day, the outcome might have been closer. As it was, I worked as hard as I could but ended up finishing a distant second in the seven-candidate primary.[6]

Sarbanes went on to beat Glenn Beall in the November general election.[7] He remained in the Senate until he retired in 2007.[8]

The Death Penalty and Walter Correll

In 1976, I worked in the presidential campaign of Governor Jimmy Carter of Georgia, who of course went on to be elected president. During that time, I met and worked closely with a courageous Alabama lawyer named Morris Dees, who founded the Southern Poverty Law Center. This law center has become the national bastion of legal protection for the rights, the property, and the lives of poor and underprivileged minorities, including women, who have been the target of bigotry, discrimination, and violence by terrorist groups such as the Ku Klux Klan and others. Dees's work has made him the target of assassination attempts, including bombings of his offices, by the terrorist groups he has been fighting.

During the late 1980s and early 1990s, I was often in Montgomery, Alabama, on business and had the opportunity to spend time with Dees. From him I learned how critically important it is in capital murder cases to find competent trial lawyers who are willing to represent poor or minority defendants, especially in the South. Through my work

6. Sarbanes received 302,983 votes, or 55 percent, to my 191,875, or 35 percent. At his victory rally in Baltimore that night, I pledged to support him in the fall campaign, saying, "He's too good to lose." Barry C. Rascovar, "Sarbanes Defeats Tydings," *Baltimore Sun*, May 19, 1976, A-1.

7. Sarbanes received 772,101 votes to Beall's 530,439.

8. Paul's son, Representative John Sarbanes, is an able young Democratic leader and considered one of the brightest lights in Congress.

with Dees, I became convinced that the central reason a vast number of defendants in death penalty cases are executed—even when they are innocent—is because they are poor, often uneducated, and cannot afford and thus are rarely represented by a competent lawyer.

As a result of Dees's influence, I became involved with the American Bar Association Death Penalty Project, which identified trial lawyers to do pro bono work on behalf of impoverished death row inmates. I was asked by several lawyers whom I respected, and who were already providing pro bono services in death penalty cases, to undertake the postconviction case of Walter M. Correll Jr., a poor young man with some developmental disability. He was from Roanoke, Virginia, and had been sentenced to death for murder in a prosecution that these lawyers believed had been unjust.

It was a difficult challenge. I had to reverse all the decisions made in Correll's first trial. His initial appeals had been exhausted all away to the Supreme Court of the United States.[9] I spent the next seven years investigating and providing pro bono legal defense in an effort to overturn Correll's unjust conviction and death sentence.

The basic facts of the case were as follows. In August 1985, Correll, who had an IQ of 68 and had lived in a series of foster homes, was recruited by two older men to stand on the side of a road for the purpose of luring a homosexual man who was known to drive that stretch of highway in search of other men. When the driver stopped, they planned to rob him. But the driver, who was from a wealthy, politically connected family, was stuffed into the trunk of his maroon Buick, driven to a wooded area, robbed, and then stabbed to death. When the two older men were later arrested, they blamed the murder on Correll.

As I became immersed in the case, I discovered that the older men were the real killers and that Walter had refused to participate. But at the time they were arrested, the older men, who were represented by paid legal counsel, successfully pinned the crime on Correll.

When Correll was later arrested, he was held in solitary custody for three days and denied a lawyer. During that time he gave two confessions. Then, contrary to regulations and state law that required a judge's prior approval, he was taken to Appomattox for a polygraph test

9. Only two justices voted to hear his case: Thurgood Marshall and William J. Brennan Jr.

and then to the Franklin County jail, where he was persuaded to sign a third confession. At trial, the judge cited the vile nature of the crime and sentenced him to death. The two older men received prison sentences. I later interviewed a prison inmate who said the two men bragged in prison about pinning the murder on Correll.

Stories about the case appeared in the local newspapers. One person who read them and who thought there was something wrong with the case was Lynn Florence, a special agent investigator for the Defense Department. He contacted me and volunteered to help in his spare time. We worked together weekends and holidays for seven years investigating and litigating the Correll case, starting with the original trial and following every step of the case. In exchange for his volunteer assistance, I paid his expenses.

Tragically, the facts we found showed that Correll's court-appointed lawyer had done a terrible job. He did not want the case, did no serious research, and provided his semiliterate client with an ineffective and miserable defense. The lawyer advised Correll to waive a jury trial and instead let the judge decide the case, which was a mistake.

Because the original postconviction case had already gone to the Supreme Court on appeal, my only legal option was to use the great writ of habeas corpus, which allows federal courts to intervene to determine if the basis for the detention of a prisoner by the state is valid. To be successful in such a case requires extraordinary diligence and investigative research. You must find a federal court that is willing to hear and review the complicated facts of the case and overturn multiple previous rulings by federal and state courts.

My one chance was to prove that Correll had been denied his constitutional rights to be represented by an attorney under the famous *Miranda* decision of the Warren court and then prove that the defendant was actually innocent.[10] The first two of Correll's confessions had already been ruled inadmissible because he had requested a lawyer but none was supplied. We argued that the third confession was tainted by the first two and also should have been ruled as inadmissible.

---

10. *Miranda v. Arizona*, 384 U.S. 436 (1966). Also cited in the case was a related Supreme Court ruling, *Edwards v. Arizona*, 451 U.S. 477 (1981).

Postconviction death penalty appeals that have already been affirmed by the Supreme Court are extremely difficult to win because you must challenge multiple court rulings. You have to go back through all of the original transcripts and evidence to determine if the defendant's trial lawyer produced all the witnesses and evidence that should have been produced or whether the conviction or sentence might be unconstitutional for some other reason. On weekends or during vacations, Florence and I would drive the four hours from Washington to southwestern Virginia to find and interview witnesses, or I would drive down to the state prison about three times a year to talk to Correll and gather more facts while he was awaiting his fate on death row. I was trying to boost him up so that if we won a new trial, he would be a good witness. During his years there, Correll learned to read and write and became a changed young man.

Our appeals to Virginia courts were unsuccessful, so our last resort was the federal court system. Finally, Judge James C. Turk of the US District Court for the Western District of Virginia recognized the validity of our case and ordered a new trial. "This court cannot imagine a more deliberate and egregious violation of (the right to counsel) than exists in this case," Judge Turk wrote.[11]

But the state appealed that ruling and on August 24, 1995, a three-judge panel of the Fourth US Circuit Court of Appeals reversed the district court and ordered Correll's execution. By then, much of the Fourth Circuit Court, including our entire panel, was packed with conservatives appointed through the political influence and power of the archconservative senator from South Carolina, Strom Thurmond.

My final hope was to persuade the Republican governor of Virginia, George Allen, to grant clemency, but he refused even to meet with me. As Correll's execution became imminent, I telephoned Governor Allen's office and stayed on the line almost all day, begging his staff to get the governor to listen to me and spare Correll's life. But Allen was not known for political courage. He refused to talk with me.

On January 5, 1996, a Virginia prison official administered a lethal injection to thirty-four-year-old Walter Correll. His death was a tragic blow.

11. *Correll v. Thompson*, 872 F.Supp. 282, US District Court, Western District of Virginia, Roanoke Division, Civ. A. No. 91–131-R, August 24, 1994. Thompson was the warden at the Mecklenburg correctional facility where Correll was held.

Three weeks before his execution, Correll handwrote a half-page last will and testament. In it he said, "I would like each and every person who worked on my case to know how grateful I am to them. I pray I will be going to heaven and, if so, I will do my best to watch over each of you. None of you have a reason to feel you have failed, because you couldn't make the courts do the right thing."[12]

A few years later, I also received a warm thank-you letter from Lynn Florence and a beautiful painting he had done. In the letter he wrote, "Throughout the long and sometimes grueling hours spent in the appeals, you did not flag in your energies, leadership, empathy and generosity. Few know of your efforts in defense of those without a voice in the affairs of men." Then he added, "You gave Walter something they couldn't take away. You erased the bars of his isolation. For the first time, he had a sense of entitlement and belonging and a place in the warmth and light at the campfires of his fellow men."[13]

It was one of the most heartwarming tributes of my life, yet I will never be able to shake the memory of poor Walter Correll, who was framed and unfairly executed. His case became so notorious in legal circles that it became the subject of a play written and put on by a major law school in Canada.

Ever since I tried the Alvey kidnapping and murder case when I was US attorney, I have been concerned about whether the death penalty in this country is fair and just, and I have concluded without a doubt that it is not. There is no question that poor and uneducated people, particularly minorities in the South, are arrested and convicted in too many cases when they are innocent. They probably would have been acquitted had they been able to afford a competent attorney to defend them. As a general rule, in the United States the wealthy do not get executed.

I and others have tried to get Virginia to abolish capital punishment, but to no avail. When in 2013 Governor Martin O'Malley made Maryland the latest state to abolish the death penalty—based on recommendations from a commission headed by Ben Civiletti, the former US attorney general who had started out as my assistant—I joined those

12. Last Will and Testament of Walter M. Correll Jr., December 14, 1995, copy in possession of Senator Tydings.

13. Lynn A. Florence, Arlington, Virginia, to Senator Joseph D. Tydings, April 2, 2001, in possession of Senator Tydings.

who testified in support of the measure, and I am glad that it passed.

As of 2017, thirty-one states allow convicted criminals to be executed; nineteen do not. The map of states with or without the death penalty closely resembles the political map of the nation, with most of the so-called "red states" that tend to vote Republican supporting the death penalty and most of the so-called "blue states" that tend to vote Democratic prohibiting it. As I write this, nearly three thousand inmates are on death row around the country.[14]

The University of Maryland Board of Regents

Not long after my reelection defeat in 1970, I turned my attention to one of the loves of my life: the University of Maryland.

One important contribution I made during my first term as a regent was in persuading the board to create the University of Maryland Foundation, which would become a vehicle to raise money for the university that could then be spent on university projects without first having to obtain line-item approval by the state legislature.

But perhaps my most important early contribution was to block an effort by the chair of the board of regents and the director of university athletics to join other Atlantic Coast Conference (ACC) schools in their decision to stonewall the requirement to implement Title IX, the 1972 federal law that prohibited discrimination on the basis of sex in any federally funded education program or activity, including intercollegiate sports. Working with Regents Peter O'Malley and Mary Broadwater, we took the lead in persuading a majority of the board members to reverse the prior position of the athletic department—to tell them to stop stonewalling and, instead, to support fully the implementation of

14. A peer-reviewed nationwide study of death penalty cases released in 2014 concluded—conservatively—that at least 1 of every 25 people sentenced to die in the United States since 1973 is or was innocent. The report concluded that it "is all but certain" that several of the 1,320 defendants executed since 1977 were innocent. That is a horrible, shameful record that should be unacceptable to all Americans. Samuel R. Gross, University of Michigan Law School, Ann Arbor; Barbara O'Brien, Michigan State University College of Law, East Lansing; Chen Hu, American College of Radiology Clinical Research Center, Philadelphia; and Edward H. Kennedy, Department of Biostatistics and Epidemiology, University of Pennsylvania School of Medicine, Philadelphia, "Rate of False Conviction of Criminal Defendants Who Are Sentenced to Death," *Proceedings of the National Academy of Sciences* 111, no. 20 (May 20, 2014).

Title IX. Then we called a special meeting and told the chair that he had two options: he could join the rest of the regents and fully support Title IX, or, if he did not agree, we would replace him with O'Malley as chair of the board of regents. We were prepared to act but fortunately did not have to.

Because of this shift, the University of Maryland became the only athletic department in the ACC that embraced Title IX. As a result, we built women's athletics at the university into the strongest athletic program in the Atlantic Coast Conference for many years and, in many sports (basketball, lacrosse, field hockey, etc.), among the strongest in the country.

One other achievement, which I worked on with Edward V. Hurley, a fellow regent, in 1977, was to push the university to divest itself of $1.5 million in holdings in companies that dealt with South Africa. This was done to protest apartheid—a system of strict segregation rules—then in place in South Africa.

The Birth of the University of Maryland Medical System

In 1982, two years after I was appointed to a second term on the University of Maryland Board of Regents by Governor Harry R. Hughes (whom I had known since we served together on the House Judiciary Committee of the General Assembly back in 1955), O'Malley resigned to serve in a similar capacity at Mount St. Mary's College in Emmitsburg. I agreed to take over as chair of the regents, but only if O'Malley agreed to stay on the board.

In my years as chair, perhaps the biggest accomplishment was the decision to ask the legislature to separate the University of Maryland Hospital in Baltimore from the University of Maryland and have it converted into an independent, 501(c)(3) nonprofit institution with a separate board of directors. The hospital is used to train medical school students and residents.

University Hospital was then part of and under the complete control of the university and the dean of the medical school. Doctors, who taught at the School of Medicine each year, negotiated a contract with the hospital for all hospital medical services. Unfortunately, the dean, supported by the president of the university, allowed the University

Hospital to be vastly overcharged for the services of the doctors, which generated huge operating deficits for the hospital.

I do not believe the board of regents would ever have challenged both the president of the university and the dean of the School of Medicine on this issue were it not for the work of two outstanding legislators: Senator Frank Kelly of Baltimore County and Delegate Robert Neall of Anne Arundel County. It was their objections to how the hospital was being run that motivated the vice-chair of the regents, Allen L. Schwait, and me to investigate how a number of great public university hospitals, including the Johns Hopkins Hospital, were organized and managed.[15] As a result, we persuaded the regents to ask the legislature to remove the hospital from their oversight and control and create the present University of Maryland Medical System.

In the early 1980s, the hospital had total revenues of $200 million to $300 million a year and was running up an annual deficit of more than $20 million. Today, the independent University of Maryland Medical System that was created in 1984 has brought into the system an additional ten hospitals around the state, some of which were facing their own difficult financial problems. Annual operating revenues are now about $3.5 billion a year. It has become a national referral center for trauma, cancer care, cardiac care, and other serious medical conditions, and it boasts one of the most successful kidney transplant programs in the world.

By turning the hospital into a nonprofit organization, the medical center was freed from the cumbersome personnel and procurement requirements of the state and of the chronic need to go hat-in-hand to the General Assembly each year to cover operating deficits. It was a bold idea, but one that has proved to be extraordinarily successful.

In 2008, Governor Martin O'Malley appointed me to the University of Maryland Medical System Board of Directors, where I still actively serve.

15. Allen Schwait grew up in Philadelphia, graduated from the University of Pennsylvania with a degree in economics, and earned a law degree from the University of Maryland School of Law. In 1997, he was appointed to the Baltimore City Circuit Court, and he retired in 2007.

A Change of Chancellors

In 2000, Governor Parris Glendening became the third Maryland governor to appoint me to the University of Maryland Board of Regents. That was a presidential election year, and Governor Glendening was a strong backer of Vice President Al Gore's candidacy. Many believed he would be rewarded with a Cabinet post once Gore was elected. But Gore, of course, lost the closest presidential election in American history to his Republican opponent, George W. Bush.[16]

Before becoming governor, Glendening had taught government and politics at the University of Maryland for twenty-seven years. With a Cabinet position no longer in the cards and his own final term as governor coming to an end in January 2003, word quickly spread that Glendening—soon to be in need of a job—was interested in becoming the next chancellor of the University System of Maryland.

The incumbent chancellor was a physicist named Daniel N. Langenberg. Three months after I had rejoined the board in the fall of 2000, the regents all received an email from Lance Billingsley, a close Glendening ally who had become the chair of the board, advising us that he had resigned from the board to accept a newly created position as a university vice president handling lobbying, public relations, and fundraising—a full-time position offered to him by Langenberg at a salary of $185,000 a year. This transaction between Billingsley and Langenberg took place shortly after the regents had met and, at Billingsley's suggestion, approved a major financial bonus for Langenberg.

Many of the regents, including myself, were shocked and appalled. The action creating the new post was unlawful because it had not been created and approved by the board of regents. We promptly convened an executive session of the board to consider what to do, including making the decision as to whether Langenberg was fit to continue as chancellor. This was all before the 2000 presidential election had been decided, and Governor Glendening passed word to some of the regents that we should act in the best interests of the university and that he would be governed by whatever we decided.

16. Although Gore won the popular vote with a half-million vote plurality, the Supreme Court finally decided the election by awarding Bush the electoral votes from Florida, which enabled the Republican to claim victory.

After Chancellor Langenberg appeared before the board and failed to justify his actions, we told him he would have to announce his resignation by the end of the year, effective in February 2001. The chancellor insisted he had done nothing wrong, but the board was adamant that he had to leave. The board then hired a national firm to assist in the search for Langenberg's successor, who would take office by June 2001.

Billingsley was succeeded as chair by Nathan A. Chapman Jr., a Baltimore investment banker who also was close to Glendening. Chapman was able to keep the board from selecting a new chancellor throughout 2001 and into the spring of 2002.[17]

During 2001, there were public and private indications that Glendening wanted to be named chancellor. After he publicly admitted his interest in the post, the search firm we had hired resigned. In late 2002, there were five vacancies on the board of regents, and Glendening decided to fill all five with his political allies from Prince George's County—packing the board that would pick the next chancellor.

Three of us on the board of regents—Admiral Charles Larson, Cliff Kendall, and myself—felt that if we allowed a politically dominated board of regents to make the governor who had appointed them the chancellor, it would be a devastating blow to the academic standing of the University System of Maryland and would forever taint the entire system of higher education in Maryland. With the support of prominent alumni and contributors, I organized and helped lead the fight to stop Glendening's appointment as chancellor.

In August 2002, the board of regents settled the issue by selecting a great candidate, William E. "Brit" Kirwan, to be the third chancellor of the University System of Maryland. Kirwan had served on the faculty at College Park for thirty-four years and had been the twenty-sixth president of the University of Maryland before becoming president of Ohio

17. In August 2004, Chapman was convicted in the US District Court for Maryland on twenty-three counts of fraud and filing false tax returns. It was quite a fall from grace for someone who had once been prominent in Maryland political and business circles. Chapman was one of the first black stockbrokers at the Baltimore investment firm of Alex, Brown & Sons, Inc., and had launched his own brokerage business in the 1980s, which he took public in 1998. He was convicted of defrauding both the Maryland state employee pension system and his shareholders. Michael Dresser, "Chapman Guilty of Defrauding Pension System and Investors; Banker Convicted on 23 Counts but Is Cleared of Seven Others," *Baltimore Sun*, August 13, 2004, A-1.

State University. His decision to return to Maryland was sealed with a call from Representative Steny Hoyer of Maryland.

The Horse Protection Act

One issue I will never relinquish until it is no longer necessary is the effort to protect the beautiful Tennessee Walking Horses from the vicious and cruel practice of soring.[18]

Because of my lifelong love affair with horses and ponies—from my childhood with Percherons at Oakington, or riding at McDonogh, or serving in the Horse Platoon, 6th Constabulary Regiment, as part of the army of occupation after World War II, or fox hunting in Maryland—it was not by coincidence that horse lovers from the South came to me for help in ending the soring practices that crippled Tennessee Walking Horses, all for the sole purpose of winning trophies.

I introduced a horse protection bill in 1968, then again in 1969, and finally got it passed in 1970, but with penalties watered down from felonies to misdemeanors. Lobbying and campaign contributions to key senators from Kentucky and Tennessee in the years since then have made further progress impossible.

In 2000, I accepted the pro bono position as general counsel to Friends of Sound Horses, a group that works to protect Tennessee Walking Horses and other "gaited" horses from soring and other cruel practices. Once again, I'm working to try to strengthen the Horse Protection Act.

Over the decades since I left the US Senate, I have been able to work on these and other important causes. There are many ways citizens can contribute to the public good and provide a public service. I feel that in my own small way I have done so throughout my life.

18. Some unscrupulous trainers or owners have resorted to hurting or, in some cases, all but crippling a horse's front feet until they are so sore that when they touch the ground, they abruptly lift them. This is done to display the desired gait. This can be done through the use of chains, tacks, chemical salves, or creams. It is a horrible, unforgivable thing to do to a horse. Although illegal, it is a practice still sometimes used.

Epilogue

The energy, the faith, the devotion which we bring to this endeavor
will light our country and all who serve it—
and the glow from that fire can truly light the world.
And so, my fellow Americans,
Ask not what your country can do for you—
Ask what you can do for your country.
My fellow citizens of the world:
Ask not what America will do for you,
but what together we can do for the freedom of man.
Finally, whether you are citizens of America or citizens of the world,
ask of us the same high standards of strength and sacrifice which
    we ask of you.

—PRESIDENT JOHN F. KENNEDY, INAUGURAL ADDRESS,
    JANUARY 20, 1961

An Open Letter to My Grandchildren (and Their Generation)

Dear Ben, Sam, Jill, Jay, Maggie, Will, Ruby, Emma and Faeve,

The night I was elected to the US Senate more than a half century ago I told cheering supporters, "My fondest hope is that my election will be a signal for independent spirited young men and women of both parties to make politics of the Free State open politics, a politics of merit. I am hopeful that my election will serve as an invitation to these young men and women who aspire to public office to enter public life."[1]

My fondest hope *today* is that this book will awaken and encourage some of you—my nine grandchildren, as well as others in your

---

1. Quoted in Donald Bremner, "Tydings Beats Beall; Democrats Take 6 of 8 House Seats," *Baltimore Sun*, November 4, 1964.

generation—to devote a portion of your lives to public service and help this wonderful country overcome the severe problems it currently faces. I do not really care if you do this work as a Democrat, as a Republican, or as an independent as long as you get involved and work diligently on the challenges facing our nation.

I am proud of my elective public service and hope it represents what can be achieved when individuals are interested in working on behalf of the American people and are willing to stand up for what they believe is right. There is nothing our country needs more urgently now than for a new generation of young people—those who have recently graduated or are graduating now from high schools or colleges across our nation—to realize that you have a vital stake in how our government is run and that you can individually make a difference.

Throughout my career, I have been known as a progressive or liberal, but what I am calling for in this letter to you is actually the argument of a *conservative* intent on protecting the freedoms, the free exchange, the traditional institutions, and the fundamental fabric of our democracy.

Perhaps the most significant achievement of President John F. Kennedy's political career was his ability to inspire an entire generation of young people to commit their lives—or a major portion of their lives— to public service. In response, many of the sharpest young minds in the country flocked to Washington with the clear intent of making sure the American government was working for the benefit of the American people.

Today our nation needs a new influx of bright young people equally committed to public service and determined to address and resolve the serious problems currently threatening our democracy and our nation. We need them in the White House, in the Congress, in state legislatures, and in federal, state, county, city, and town governmental bodies.

The critical issues facing our nation are many, but it seems to me the most serious are these: (1) the debilitating and corrupting influence of money in politics; (2) the resulting paralysis within our Congress, in particular, but in our political processes in general; and (3) the lengthening list of serious national and global problems—climate change, immigration reform, the need for effective gun control, and the failure to provide financial support for infrastructure construction and maintenance, to name just four—that demand smart, innovative, and immediate attention, yet languish endlessly for lack of leadership and consensus. We must try to conserve and enhance the assets our generation inherited.

Money in politics—the untold amounts of special interest dollars—is the major reason our system of democracy no longer works as it should. Hundreds of millions of dollars are spent annually on lobbying and contributions, both reported and unreported. This business-as-usual corruption robs everyday citizens of fair, honest, and impartial representation. It tilts the system in favor of those with money, and against everyone else.

The citizen who wants to become involved in the political process by giving a favored candidate a donation of $5—or even $100 or $1,000—has no voice or influence when matched against billionaires, national and international corporations, large labor unions, and other donors who can and do spend millions of dollars—often with no transparency—on single candidates or campaigns or issues. Members of Congress who want to be able to compete in a reelection battle now feel they must spend as much as a third to half of their time raising money—time they should be spending working for the people who elected them.

Much of this money is funneled into Congress through political action committees (PACs) run by various special interests. During the 2014 election cycle, for instance, the average amount of PAC money received by each member of Congress was $680,000. The average amount for members of just one committee, the House Energy and Commerce Committee, was $857,000. This money has become so much a part of the congressional fabric that, as far as I can determine, only one or, at most, two members of the entire House of Representatives refused to accept any PAC contributions during the 2014 election cycle. To take such a commendable, principled stand meant they must rely on individual contributions to finance their campaigns and were undoubtedly at a financial disadvantage against challengers who readily accepted PAC contributions.

The average American cannot compete with that. When special interests can give as much money to politicians as they wish—whether they are pharmaceutical companies, oil or other natural resource interests, abortion opponents, or business leaders who oppose government regulation—the politicians naturally do what they have essentially been paid to do. The quid pro quo is so obvious we have become numb to it. The results seep into our laws and regulations. It directly affects what laws are passed or which nominees are considered and, just as importantly, which ones fail even to get a hearing. This problem must be fixed.[2]

In the years I served in the Senate, Congress worked as it was created to work. There were serious disagreements, of course, and not everything I or others supported was enacted. But that is as it should be. Congress debated and voted on hugely controversial issues: the Voting Rights Act of 1965 and the Fair Housing Act of 1968; the Vietnam War; the "one-man, one-vote" and school prayer Supreme Court rulings; gun control; Supreme Court nominations; and measures to establish the EPA, to reform the federal court system, and to address air pollution, poverty, and joblessness. Today, genuine debate is stifled by one-party dominance.

It is a shame that public service in this country has been denigrated and vilified ever since President Ronald Reagan—in his first inaugural address—proclaimed, "Government is not the solution to our problem; government is the problem."[3]

To me, that attitude is tragically shortsighted and dangerous. In a civilized society, we voluntarily band together to form a government to establish the rules we all live by and to raise collectively the money

---

2. This is hardly a new problem, but it is one that has been exacerbated by two danger-ous and broadly condemned Supreme Court decisions, one in 1976 captioned *Buckley v. Valeo*, and the other egregious decision in 2010, *Citizens United v. Federal Election Commission*. The *Buckley* ruling, which challenged campaign finance restrictions imposed following the fundraising abuses of the Nixon administration, essentially said that any and all forms of regulating election spending are unconstitutional. The *Citizens United* case then flung open the doors to unlimited political giving. First, it ruled that a 2002 federal law restricting certain types of political advertising as an evasion of campaign donation limits was unconstitutional because such advertising was protected by the First Amendment right to free speech. The high court then went further, concluding that Congress had little power to regulate any form of independent spending. This ruling has empowered rich individuals, corporations, and unions to spend limitless amounts of money on elections. Justice Ruth Bader Ginsburg, who dissented in the case, called it the most tragic decision in her twenty-two years on the court. President Obama, in a rare public condemnation of a Supreme Court ruling, said during his 2010 State of the Union address, just a week after the decision was handed down and with the Supreme Court justices sitting immediately in front of him, "With all due deference to separation of powers, last week the Supreme Court reversed a century of law that, I believe, will open the floodgates for special interests, including foreign corporations, to spend without limit in our elections." Barack Obama, "Address before a Joint Session of the Congress on the State of the Union," January 27, 2010, online text compiled by Gerhard Peters and John T. Woolley for *The American Presidency Project*, http://www.presidency.ucsb.edu/ws/?pid=87433.

3. Ronald Reagan, "Inaugural Address," January 20, 1981, online text compiled by Gerhard Peters and John T. Woolley for *The American Presidency Project*, http://www.presidency.ucsb.edu/ws/?pid=43130.

needed to protect us from danger or to share in countless other societal costs, ranging from public education to highway construction to protection from disease. Government is not the problem; government, properly run, is the means for assuring our collective happiness and well-being.

When an intrinsically honorable profession is repeatedly slandered and dishonored, as many Republicans and particularly the Club for Growth and Tea Party–type radicals have done for the past thirty-five years, they fulfill their own prophecy of dysfunctional government. Voters who support antigovernment politicians essentially get the government they deserve. But we all, of course, suffer the consequences.

Compounding the conservatives' drumbeat distrust of government is the thoughtless mantra of the extreme right wing: "no new taxes." This is a doubly selfish pledge: selfish of the politicians who mindlessly repeat it solely as an argument for their own election and selfish of those who vote for such politicians because in doing so they fail to honor their obligation as citizens to consider when and by how much they may need to contribute toward the common good. When outdated bridges collapse, or the drinking water in Flint, Michigan, is poisoned by lead, or the Zika virus threatens public health, or Wall Street hedge funds swindle billions of dollars because there are not enough regulators to keep watch on them, the "no new taxes" crowd blames government for the failure, not themselves.

When I was in the Senate, we worked collaboratively across the aisle. Representative George H. W. Bush, a Texas Republican, was my partner in most of the family planning measures we brought before the Congress. Minority Leader Everett Dirksen of Illinois helped Democrats pass the major civil rights legislation of the 1960s. We were often personal friends, regardless of party affiliation. We did not always agree, of course. We did not always win. But we worked together, talked together, and tried to find a middle ground—and we learned to compromise.

In the political world of today, "compromise" has become a dirty word. Collaborating with someone from the opposite party becomes a negative "talking point" for a senator's or representative's political opponents to use. The interest of everyday Americans is shoved aside in the interest of incumbents raising the millions of dollars necessary to position themselves for reelection.

One reason Congress acts this way is that centrists and moderates—those who historically staked out the middle ground in Congress and worked on compromise solutions—have all but disappeared from both parties. They have been driven from the Congress by big money—the special interest campaigns that have "bought" the representation they want. This problem has only been exacerbated by politically driven, computer-generated redistricting plans that let the Congress members choose their voters, rather than the other way around.[4] As Tom Hofeller, the Republican National Committee redistricting director, confessed to the National Conference of State Legislatures, "in the politics of redistricting, politicians get to choose the voters."[5]

These are serious problems that demand the devoted attention of smart people—like you, my grandchildren, and like so many others in your young generation—who have the best interests of American democracy at heart.

If, by reading this book, you—or any other reader—becomes inspired to enter public service, then this book has been a success.

With my love and confidence for the future,

Joseph D. Tydings
Harford County, Maryland
June 14, 2016

P.S. Here are the full names of my grandchildren and their parents: Benjamin Tydings Smith, son of J. T. Smith and Mary Tydings; Sam Tydings Gollob, Jill Campbell Gollob, and Jay Davies Gollob, children of David Andrew Gollob and Eleanor Tydings Gollob; Margaret Campbell Tydings and William Davies Tydings, children of Millard E. Tydings II and Susan Howe Tydings; and Ruby Tydings Luzzatto, Emma Tydings Luzzatto, and Faeve Tydings Luzzatto, children of Ben and Alexandra Tydings Luzzatto.

---

4. In every congressional race from 1964 to 2012, at least 85 percent of incumbents nationwide retained their seats, according to the Center for Responsive Politics and data compiled by Bloomberg. Michael B. Mariois, "California's Redistricting Shake-Up Shakes Out Politicians," *Bloomberg Businessweek*, March 22, 2013.

5. Quoted in Joanne Dann, "Redistricting Works against Moderates," *Washington Post*, December 16, 2001.

Selected Bibliography

Caro, Robert A. *The Passage of Power: The Years of Lyndon Johnson.* New York: Vintage Books, 2013.

Clarke, Thurston. *JFK's Last 100 Days.* New York: Penguin Audio, 2013.

Congressional Quarterly. "Boykin, Johnson Convicted." *CQ Almanac* 1963, 19th ed., 1964, 1106–7. http://library.cqpress.com/cqalmanac/cqa163–1315443

Ditzen, Eleanor Davies Tydings. *My Golden Spoon.* Lanham, MD: Madison Books, 1997.

Dubofsky, Jean Eberhart. "Fair Housing: A Legislative History and a Perspective." *Washburn Law Journal* (Washburn University, Topeka) 8 (1969).

Ehrlich, Paul R. *The Population Bomb.* New York: Ballantine Books, 1968.

Figinski, M. Albert, and Lee M. Miller. "Judicial Reform and the Tydings Legacy." *Judicature* 55, no. 2 (1971).

Haygood, Wil. *Showdown: Thurgood Marshall and the Supreme Court Nomination That Changed America.* New York: Knopf, 2015.

Hughes, Harry Roe, with John W. Frece. *My Unexpected Journey: The Autobiography of Governor Harry Roe Hughes.* Charleston, SC: History Press, 2006.

Jacobs, Bradford. *Thimbleriggers.* Baltimore: Johns Hopkins University Press, 1968.

Keith, Caroline H. *"For Hell and a Brown Mule": The Biography of Senator Millard E. Tydings.* Lanham, MD: Madison Books, 1991.

Kyvig, David E. "Everett Dirksen's Constitutional Crusades." *Journal of the Illinois State Historical Society* 95, no. 1 (2002): 68–85. http://www.jstor.org/stable/40193488

Lambert, William. "What the Senator Didn't Disclose." *Life*, August 28, 1970.

May, Gary. *Bending toward Justice: The Voting Rights Act and the Transformation of American Democracy.* New York: Basic Books, 2013.

Polk, Ryan. "Good Tydings—Career Notes and Time Line: Senator Joseph Tydings." Archives of Maryland Online, accessed May 16, 2014. msa.maryland.gov/megafile/msa/speccol/sc3500/sc3520/002100/ . . . /tydings_1st.doc

Rubin, Nancy. *American Empress: The Life and Times of Marjorie Merriweather Post.* New York: Villard Books, 1995.

Smith, J. Douglas. *On Democracy's Doorstep: The Inside Story of How the Supreme Court Brought "One Person, One Vote" to the United States.* New York: Hill and Wang, 2014.

Tydings, Joseph D. *Born to Starve.* New York: William Morrow, 1970.

———. *Final Report.* Washington, DC: US Senate, January 1971.

———. Transcript of interview by Doug Washburn, June 30, 2013. Harford Living Treasures Oral History Project, Harford County Public Library, Belcamp, MD.

White, Theodore H. *The Making of the President, 1960.* New York: Atheneum, 1961.

Index

Page numbers in *italics* indicate photographs.

Trump, Donald J.: environmental deregulation, 287–289; family planning, 283; gun control, 300; Mar-a-Lago, 20–22, *110*, *132*; relations with Russia, 87, 273; relations with immigrants and African Americans, 174, 182, 274; voter suppression, 220–21; Supreme Court nominee, 232;

Tunney, John, 210, 265–66; Gene Tunney, 210

Turk, James C., 330. *See* Correll, Walter M., Jr.

Tydings, Eleanor Davies, (mother of Joseph D. Tydings), 2–4, 10, 16, 18, 22, 27–28, 30–31, 39, 47, 78, 80, *109*, *110*, *114*, *115*, *117*, 177, 196, influences regarding civil rights, 54, 216; marriage to Millard Tydings, 13; 56–60; marriage to Tom Cheesborough, 11, 13, 56; *My Golden Spoon*, 11–12; purchase of Oakington, 2, 12–13; Senate candidacy, 59–60

Tydings, Emlen (daughter of Joseph D. Tydings), *121*, *130*, 188

Tydings, Emlen (grandmother of Joseph D. Tydings), 12–13

Tydings, Mary (daughter of Joseph D. Tydings; husband, Smith, J.T.), 41, *121*, *130*, 188, 344

Tydings, Millard E., (adoptive father of Joseph D. Tydings), 1–2, 6, 8–9, 15, 17–18, 24–29, 31, 39–40, 47, 49–50, 73, 161, 183, 188, 191, 199, 301–02, 324; adoption, 25, 171, 180; Armed Services

Committee, chairman, 33–36, *115*; composite photograph in 1950 Senate campaign; *117*; "favorite son" candidate in 1940 Maryland presidential primary, *114*; "halo effect," 230; helped found University of Maryland, 25, 35, *108*; illness ends 1956 comeback, 76, 95; marriage to Eleanor Davies Cheesborough, 11–13, *110*; McCarthy investigation and Butler campaign retaliation, 26–29, 39, 57–60, *116*, 313; Philippine independence, 25, *116*, *120*; relationship with Roosevelt, 26, 80, 319–320; Speaker of the Maryland House of Delegates, 35; World War I hero, 10, *108*. *See* Oakington. *See also* Tydings, Eleanor Davies

Tydings, Millard, II (son of Joseph D. Tydings; Tydings, Susan Howe), *121*, *130*, *131*, 188, 203, 230, 324, 344

Tydings, Virginia Reynolds Campbell (wife of Joseph D. Tydings), 2–3, 18, 74, 79, *119*, *121*, 162, 166, 196, 199, 240, 265, 309, and Campbell, Captain Frederick MacGregor, 56; with horses, 16, 159–160; marriage, 50, 56–58; twin sister (Mary Campbell), 56, 91, 178; US Senate campaign, 1964, 171–72, 177, 185, 188;

Udoff, Frank, 164

unions, 6, 49, 57–58, 101, 138, 157, 161, 200, 223, 242, 293, 316, 341, 342; right-to-work, 52, 61, 88, 172